PRISONERS AFTER WAR

A VOLUME IN THE SERIES
VETERANS

EDITED BY
BRIAN MATTHEW JORDAN AND J. ROSS DANCY

PRISONERS AFTER WAR

VETERANS IN THE AGE OF MASS INCARCERATION

JASON A. HIGGINS

University of Massachusetts Press

Amherst and Boston

This book is freely available in an open access edition thanks to TOME (Toward an Open Mono-
graph Ecosystem)—a collaboration of the Association of American Universities, the Association of
University Presses, and the Association of Research Libraries—and the generous support of Virginia
Tech. Learn more at the TOME website, available at: openmonographs.org.

ISBN 978-1-62534-753-4 (paper); 754-1 (hardcover)

Designed by Sally Nichols
Set in Garamond Premier Pro
Printed and bound by Books International, Inc.

Cover design by Sally Nichols
Cover art by Paul Crudgington/EyeEm, *Shadow of a Man Behind Bars*, stock.adobe.com.

Library of Congress Cataloging-in-Publication Data

Names: Higgins, Jason A., 1985–author.
Title: Prisoners after war : veterans in the age of mass incarceration /
    Jason A. Higgins.
Other titles: Veterans in the age of mass incarceration
Description: Amherst : University of Massachusetts Press, [2024] | Series:
    Veterans | Includes bibliographical references and index.
Identifiers: LCCN 2023013416 (print) | LCCN 2023013417 (ebook) | ISBN
    9781625347534 (paper) | ISBN 9781625347541 (hardcover) | ISBN
    9781685750367 (ebook)
Subjects: LCSH: Veterans—United States—Social conditions. |
    Prisoners—United States. | Veteran reintegration—United States. |
    Veterans—Mental health—United States. | Criminal justice,
    Administration of—United States. | Alternatives to imprisonment—United
    States. | Marginality, Social—United States.
Classification: LCC UB357 .H53 2024 (print) | LCC UB357 (ebook) | DDC
    362.860973—dc23/eng/20230828
LC record available at https://lccn.loc.gov/2023013416
LC ebook record available at https://lccn.loc.gov/2023013417

British Library Cataloguing-in-Publication Data
A catalog record for this book is available from the British Library.

Some material from the text has been published in a previous form in chapter 11 and the epilogue
from *Service Denied: Marginalized Veterans in Modern American History*, ed. John M. Kinder and
Jason A. Higgins (Amherst: University of Massachusetts Press, 2022). Used by permission.

For justice, for peace, and for our children

CONTENTS

List of Figures   ix

Preface and Note on Methodology   xi

Acknowledgments   xxi

INTRODUCTION

Locating Incarcerated Veterans in American History   1

CHAPTER 1

"Less than" Veterans
Discrimination, Discharges, and Disabilities during the Vietnam War   18

CHAPTER 2

War, Drugs, and the War on Drugs
Heroin and Vietnam Veterans during the Rise of Mass Incarceration   45

CHAPTER 3

Another War, Another Drug
Military-Carceral Punishment in the Reagan Era   68

CHAPTER 4

Leave No Vet Behind
Memory of the Vietnam War and the Founding of Veterans Treatment Court   86

CHAPTER 5

Generation 9/11
Incarcerated Veterans of the Global War on Terrorism   114

CHAPTER 6

Another Signature Wound
Substance Use Disorder and the Opioid Epidemic   136

CHAPTER 7

"Justice for Vets"
A New Veterans' Movement   157

CHAPTER 8

. . . And Justice for All
Women and Families of Veterans Treatment Court   183

CONCLUSION

No Peace, No Justice   209

Notes   217
Index   261

FIGURES

FIGURE 1. David Carlson   16

FIGURE 2. Henry D. Burton   22

FIGURE 3. Ari Sesu Merretazon   40

FIGURE 4. Haywood Fennell Sr.   49

FIGURE 5. Patrick Welch   103

FIGURE 6. Jack O'Connor   111

FIGURE 7. James Marciano   154

FIGURE 8. Timothy J. Wynn   169

FIGURE 9. Vanessa Guillen Memorial Mural   187

FIGURE 10. Alyssa Vasquez   193

PREFACE AND NOTE ON METHODOLOGY

Content warning: This book includes numerous first-hand accounts of traumatic experiences, including but not limited to combat and death, racial violence and injustices, sexual assault, suicide, and other topics that some readers may find disturbing, harmful, or distressing. Confronting the past, as difficult as it can be at times, is our collective responsibility to future generations. Readers should proceed only with caution and deliberate reflection.

Prisoners after War is a social history of veterans in the age of mass incarceration. It explores the complex relationship between foreign wars and the domestic war on crime, studying effects of the carceral turn on military veterans as they readjusted to civilian society. Since the war on drugs, the number of veterans in prison more than doubled between the end of the war in Vietnam and 9/11. This prison growth occurred during an era when policymakers criminalized and punished people with behavioral and social problems, especially the poor, disabled, and marginalized. Amid economic recessions, policymakers cut social welfare programs, increased police budgets, and mandated harsher punishments and minimum prison sentences for drugs, casting a wide net that caught millions of Americans and hundreds of thousands of veterans in the criminal justice system.

This book uncovers a history of discrimination, trauma, and incarceration among two generations of war veterans. During the Vietnam War, thousands of African Americans were excessively punished for minor offenses, behavioral issues, acts of resistance, and drug use. As the military began to withdraw forces from Vietnam, a disproportionate percentage of Black soldiers received administrative discharges compared to whites, disqualifying them from Veterans Administration (VA) benefits, disability compensation, and the GI Bill.[1] Because a large percentage of African Americans served in combat roles in Vietnam, Black veterans were more likely to experience combat stress and what became known as post-traumatic stress disorder (PTSD) but lacked resources and services to readjust. Without access to VA care, disability benefits, or other veterans' entitlements, a disproportionate number of Black Vietnam veterans were imprisoned after the war. By 1978, one out of four people in prison had served in the military, and half were Black veterans with disabilities.[2]

But the history of incarcerated veterans is not exclusively a story of racial injustice. It may surprise readers that white veterans were much more likely to go to prison compared to white civilians, and Black veterans were slightly less likely to go to prison than Black civilians (even though African Americans are still far more likely to be incarcerated than any other group in the United States). [3] These statistics demonstrate the necessity of an intersectional analysis of race, disability, mental health, socioeconomic class, and gender. Without a doubt, institutional racism and discrimination have been integral to the rise of mass incarceration, but more broadly, the war on crime transformed American society, profoundly affecting poor, working-class people in places of limited opportunities, where, it so happens, the military drafted a majority of the US combat troops during the Vietnam War.[4] These populations were usually less likely to have access to health services, higher education, and other pathways to escape environments where violence, drugs, and poverty are rampant. Social engineering throughout the Cold War era—from incentives that fed the national defense industry to austerity politics that starved the social welfare state—has channeled certain populations of Americans into higher education and the workforce and funneled other groups into war and prisons.[5]

For the past fifty years, Vietnam veterans were the single largest population of incarcerated veterans, a number far greater than World War II, Korean War, and Iraq and Afghanistan veterans. [6] To be sure, there is nothing naturally criminal about veterans; quite the opposite, I have discovered—most veterans (despite their crimes) are deeply committed to service and their communities. Nor was it inevitable that so many Vietnam veterans went to prison. Aside from their individual actions, incarcerated veterans' lives were constrained by historical and social forces beyond their control, caught up in the escalation of war and the expansion of prisons that followed. Many faced unforeseen consequences of discriminatory policies at multiple levels from the military, VA, and the federal government. In 1981, the Department of Justice published its first report on veterans in prison and jail, concluding that the unique nature of the Vietnam War and "the controversy surrounding it produced a very different homecoming," and, thus, caused readjustment difficulties and increased the likelihood of incarceration.[7] In this thinking, incarcerated veterans were another example of the public's mistreatment of Vietnam veterans, part myth and part memory, which became popular in the early 1980s, as the nation sought to separate the warrior from the war and heal the Vietnam syndrome.[8] This explanation, however, does not adequately acknowledge how Vietnam veterans, especially Black men, were unfairly denied veterans' benefits after the war. According to the report, most incarcerated veterans had less-than-honorable discharges that denied them disability benefits, and they were serving "lengthy sentences." Combined with unique social problems in the 1970s and '80s—as the nation turned away from rehabilitation in favor of carceral punishment—war on crime policies made Vietnam veterans more likely to go to prison than World War II veterans.

The most formidable barrier to studying incarcerated veterans is identifying them. After all, veterans in prison and jail do not wear caps with their branch of service. Since the Carter administration, the Department of Justice conducted surveys with veterans in jail and prison, but only recently have court systems and arresting officers and jails started systematically asking questions about military history. The Department of Justice reports provide key demographic information on incarcerated veteran populations, but the methodology has significant limitations and likely underreports the total incarcerated veteran prison populations.[9] For starters, these surveys rely on veterans self-identifying. Former military members may not disclose veteran status for many reasons, including discharge status, personal shame, or fear that it might affect their VA benefits. I cite quantitative research to provide statistical context for more generalizable conclusions, but my research is primarily based on oral history interviews that I collected with formerly incarcerated veterans from the wars in Vietnam, Iraq, and Afghanistan.

From 2017 to 2020, I recorded the memories of nearly sixty military veterans involved in the criminal justice system. Most of them were formerly incarcerated, advocates, or other veterans who work in the courts, as volunteers, police, and even judges. The Incarcerated Veterans Oral History Project (somewhat a misnomer, as most were not incarcerated at the time) recorded the life histories of veterans to understand a range of challenges that can lead to incarceration. Individuals respond to mental health challenges in unique and various ways, I quickly realized, but their ability to readjust after war also depends on social, historical, and cultural context, which are often determined by race, class, gender, and legal status.

The central research question that guides this project asks: What is the relationship between military-related trauma, discrimination, and incarceration?

I believe that the relationship is often causal.[10] In many cases, traumatic experiences during childhood or teenage years were exacerbated during and after military service, such as experiencing death, violence, or injury. The military and prisons drew their populations from essentially the same communities, where access to higher education, employment opportunities, and the "American dream" is limited. Many enlisted in the military as a path out of poverty and inopportunity, but once their service was fulfilled, many veterans often returned to the same communities, sometimes forever changed by the experience of war and without the knowledge, resources, or access to social services necessary to readjust to civilian life. This was particularly true during the Vietnam War era but remained a problem for post-9/11 veterans. Coping with mental health issues, many soldiers and veterans drank alcohol, used drugs, or engaged in aggressive or violent behavior, too often leading to legal troubles. Jail, prison, and criminal records multiplied the mental health, social, economic, and family problems faced by veterans and their families, creating a cycle of poverty, crime, and incarceration.

Exploring this research question, I employ a rhetorical analysis of the language through which memories of trauma and experiences of disability were communicated during oral history interviews. I am interested not only in how veterans experience trauma but also how they remember, talk about it, and respond to it. I understand trauma as a social construction,[11] and as a physiological and psychiatric wound—not to be mistaken as post-traumatic stress disorder exclusively. PTSD is but one specific diagnosis of psychiatric trauma, first defined by the *Diagnostic and Statistical Manual of Mental Disorders* (*DSM-III*) in 1980 and since revised.[12] However, "trauma" refers to a much more expansive concept, meaning a "wound" in Ancient Greek and further developed by scholars of trauma studies in the twentieth century.[13] More recently, sociologist Jerry Lembcke analyzed the cultural and political context of PTSD as a "socially constructed category whose meaning is only partly derived from its medical context."[14] Lembcke argues that pop culture, media, and popular discourse exaggerated PTSD as part of the "betrayal narrative" that dominated the 1980s political and cultural landscape, framing Vietnam veterans as the primary victims of American war. Hollywood films often depicted all Vietnam veterans as social pariahs and mentally damaged. In this environment, PTSD was inflated in the public imagination, and, arguably, some veterans may have sought compensation and disability benefits for PTSD without having debilitating psychiatric disabilities. This is one of the objections that critical scholars will raise when studying the reintegration difficulties of Vietnam War veterans.

On the other hand, it would be a serious error of judgment for scholars to conclude that trauma is beyond the concern of historians or to dismiss psychiatric disabilities, mental health, or unseen wounds in their scholarship. As an oral historian, I am particularly interested in how discourse on PTSD, traumatic brain injury (TBI), and mental health shapes how these veterans understand, interpret, and make sense of their own past. To be clear, I do not seek to diagnose any veterans I interviewed with PTSD; nor am I concerned with the question raised above regarding the possible overdiagnosis or exaggeration of PTSD. That is far beyond the scope of my expertise and research. Rather, my research uncovers the systemic denial of disability benefits to certain groups of veterans, especially Black Vietnam veterans, those with other-than-honorable discharges, and women who experienced sexual assault in the military.

Social historians should not underestimate the tangible effects of mental health or dismiss trauma as anachronistic, especially when studying marginalized people. Moral injury names a specific type of trauma that occurs when individuals violate their fundamental sense of right and wrong.[15] It results from an injustice or a betrayal of "what's right by an authority" in a situation like war, according to psychiatrist Jonathan Shay.[16] Moral injury usually involves perpetrating or witnessing acts that violate one's moral convictions.[17] Antiwar activists, lawyers, and prisoners' rights advocates, Alice and Staughton Lynd investigated institutions that create the conditions in which moral injury occurs—the military and the prison system.[18] Their work shows how soldiers and incarcerated people responded to moral injury by becoming conscientious objectors, engaging in nonviolent civil disobedience, and organizing in prisons. In my oral history interviews, I asked questions about how traumatic experiences or injustices affected veterans' ideological beliefs or motivated them to engage in activism, organize for systemic reforms, or push the envelope of cultural change. I found that many veterans who experience war and incarceration often rededicate their lives to justice or service to their communities.

Military-related trauma also constitutes disability, as categorized by the Department of Veterans Affairs and the Americans with Disabilities Act.[19] Historian John M. Kinder argues, "When we move disabled veterans to the center of the American war story, we'll see that war is not a temporary phenomenon. . . . [I]ts human legacies are felt for decades, if not entire life-times."[20] The people whose stories are told in this book experienced varying degrees of psychiatric and physical disabilities. Therefore, it was necessary to document and analyze their memories before, during, and after military service, shifting my central focus from wartime to lifetime experiences. In doing so, this research uncovers the deeper history of discrimination in the military justice system and the VA, recording the impact of retaliation, marginalization, and punitive discharges on the lives of veterans with disabilities. The VA quantifies disability rating and calculates monetary compensation for psychiatric trauma, traumatic brain injury, and military sexual trauma (MST). Thus, disability can be an exclusionary construct by which state apparatuses deny certain groups the social benefits of veteranhood.

The ethical challenges of this research have been at the forefront of project planning, interviewing, processing, and writing this book. In 2017, the federal government explicitly excluded oral history and journalism from Institutional Review Board requirements, removing oral history from the Federal Policy for the Protection of Human Subjects. Oral history no longer falls under the category of research on human subjects and does not seek to produce gener-alizable knowledge. In significant ways, this change liberated oral historians from constraints imposed by an outsider review board when ethical codes of conduct more relevant to the field are more specific, such as the Oral History Association's Principles and Best Practices. However, this moment also requires that oral historians further define and expand ethical principles and think more carefully about how to protect narrators, especially marginalized people (such as formerly incarcerated, survivors of traumatic experiences, and others). Because this project was launched in that moment, I deliberately, reflectively, and critically assessed the ethical dimensions of oral history work with formerly incarcerated veterans. I drew inspiration, knowledge, and guidance from a variety of resources across disciplines, such as trauma theorists, disability scholars, scholars of race and gender, and advisers with experience, especially historian of the Vietnam War Christian G. Appy and veteran advocates like Mary Ellen Salzano.

Oral history with trauma survivors also has the potential to heal and do harm.[21] I am not a trained psychiatrist, and, therefore, I cannot and did not attempt to provide counseling services, but before agreeing to interview a veteran, I informed each one that talking about traumatic memories can and does bring them to the surface. I also asked if they had access to counseling services should they require it. To be sure, the participants had access to services through the VA, Vet Centers, or privately, and many of them were already in treatment. This process grants the narrators autonomy, agency, and informed consent. These steps help to ensure that in telling their stories, I am not making their problems worse.

Engaged in narrative storytelling, participants in this project (usually without prompting) recounted traumatic memories, disclosing experiences from their youth, during the military service, and afterward as veterans. In the pre-interview process and invitation letters, I explicitly reminded narrators that they should not share any personal details of their life that they would not like on public record, and I provided the opportunity for them to review, edit, or omit anything in the recording, upholding shared authority and principles and best practices established by the Oral History Association.

Narrating trauma can also open a channel through which survivors begin to recover. Oral history allows people to narrate, to take control, and to contextualize their traumas.[22] Psychiatrist Dori Laub states that people who experience trauma "not only needed to survive so they can tell their story" but also "needed to tell their story in order to survive [and] to deal with the experience."[23] This requires someone willing to listen intently, presently, and empathetically. The "history of trauma," Cathy Caruth writes, "can only take place through the listening of another."[24] "That is its danger," she warns, "the traumatization of the ones who listen."[25] Immersing myself into the worlds of trauma survivors— interviewing, transcribing, and writing their stories—at times had effects on my own mental health as a graduate student, but I believe that bearing witness is an act of solidarity.[26] The scholarly conversation on vicarious trauma is important, but oral historians should never lose sight of our primary concerns: the safety and well-being of the narrators. To that end, I have expended every effort to protect narrators from harm. If narrators showed signs of emotional distress, I would pause the recording, give them the choice to continue or not, and offer the opportunity to delete any audio or video.

There is an additional concern for people who are still entrapped by the criminal justice system. My project is not actually interested in determining the guilt or innocence of any participants; rather, it documented their lives before, during, and since their involvement in the military and the criminal justice system to understand the historical and social conditions that led to their incarceration. Before the interviews, I clearly explained the potential legal concerns of sharing information about crimes for which they have not been prosecuted and explicitly advised them not to share anything on record that they would not want the public to know. Disseminating oral histories in the digital age raises additional questions about consent since we cannot plan for every scenario, nor can we be sure of our audiences and their intentions.[27] As I continued this project, I learned, adapted, and further refined my practices as a public historian. Even with informed consent, before making their personal histories public, I considered very seriously the ethical considerations involved, in consultation with participants and advisers, and increasingly sided with caution, restriction, and protection over open access, dissemination, and public history.

Because both wars and prisons dehumanize people, this book is written from the perspectives of individuals, contextualizing their personal experiences to produce a multibiographical history of veterans in the criminal justice system. I value the privacy of these veterans and respect the fact that they shared intimate details of their lives. Some oral histories have been shared online, with the permission of the narrators, to raise awareness and engage the public. In the most sensitive cases, such as those still currently incarcerated, I have decided not to make many interviews publicly accessible, at least not yet. Nor could I include every story in this book—even though every oral history, letter, private conversation, and exchange has informed and influenced my understanding immensely.

The informed consent form gave me (and the chosen archive) copyright and permission to include their oral histories and names in this book, but these veterans did not give away the rights to their life stories. As I explained to them before signing releases, they may use the oral history interview and any photographs or recordings for their own purposes, and many have, as they engage in activism, write autobiographies, leave historical records for their family, or begin their own projects. Furthermore, I provided copies to narrators with the opportunity to review and make any final editorial changes. The choice was theirs alone to participate freely in this project. I acknowledged their agency and upheld shared authority to the best of my abilities.[28]

After serious consideration and consultation with the participants, I have retained the identities of many of the participants in the Incarcerated Veterans Oral History Project—with their explicit permission and with the underlying philosophy that their history matters. These are groups of people unwritten into the annals of American history, and I believe their place in our national story is significant. For those veterans whose stories are not told in this book, I hope they can find satisfaction and resolution knowing that their interviews will be preserved for posterity and that one day their stories may be known too. To be clear, the participants in this project consented to include their full names, and I am upholding our contract, amplifying their voices as much as possible.[29]

I have also retold their histories as accurately as possible, and responsibility for any errors is obviously mine alone. I attempted to confirm historical accuracy with other sources whenever it was possible or in doubt. Undoubtedly, some critical readers may question the honesty or factual validity of the oral histories, particularly if they are unfamiliar with the fields of oral history and memory studies.[30] In courts, prosecutors have frequently dismissed the testimonies of survivors of genocide, rape, and war crimes, because trauma can distort the details of memory.[31] But, as Alessandro Portelli reminds us, oral history "tells us less about *events* than about *meaning*."[32] Obviously, we must verify and critically analyze all of our sources, for the purpose of historical documentation. But I am equally interested in how the past—particularly traumatic memories—shapes how people make sense of their experiences, understand their place in the world, and interpret their involvement in historical events.[33] Finally, I want to acknowledge that the conclusions I reach may differ from their own views. Veterans are not monolithic populations, nor do they all share the same views, beliefs, or interpretations of history. Toward that end, I have attempted to distinguish between the opinions of the narrators and my own historical analysis.

When the project first started, I made the initial efforts to solicit interviews, but quickly in the process and with the power of social media, the veterans often found me and volunteered to help tell this story because it had never been fully told. Many of these veterans engage in various forms of activism, advocacy, and education, raising public awareness on veterans' issues. During and after interviews, the narrators often expressed gratitude for this work because no one had asked these types of questions. Most had never talked in depth about their experiences at war or afterward, not with civilians and not even with family. Therefore, the stories written in this book are almost all previously untold.

This oral history project uncovered systemic inequality in the punishment of veterans over the past fifty years. In the beginning, based on preliminary research, I expected to find a disproportionately large number of African American veterans in prison and make a connection between the American war in Vietnam and the rise of mass incarceration. During the research process, the project expanded into a larger story beyond the Vietnam War era and into the twenty-first century. Despite considerable differences between Vietnam veterans and the post-9/11 generation, recurring themes emerged in the interviews with remarkable similarities. For example, most of the veterans did not talk about traumatic experiences for years after service, if ever.

Even after mental health care was available to post-9/11 service members, most veterans I interviewed did not seek treatment while actively serving in the military. Most of them feared the stigma of looking weak or incompetent. Some believed that reporting mental health concerns would negatively impact their careers. Others repressed grief and buried guilt, not fully recognizing the depth to which their minds, bodies, and personal lives had changed at war. These issues typically resurfaced afterward. Many self-medicated with alcohol or drugs. They experienced symptoms now commonly associated with PTSD: aggression, hypervigilance, anger, and other behavioral problems. In time, delayed onset PTSD or other repressed mental health issues resurfaced in civilian life, leading to involvement with the criminal justice system. Their stories are not identical, but they speak the same language and follow a familiar path. Most commonly, they hope to break the apathy of the American public toward wars and mass incarceration.

The Incarcerated Veterans Oral History Project grew organically. The snowballing effect of oral history allowed me to retrace the cultural ties that bind a community of veterans to their pasts and to one another. Constructed from these oral histories, this book is written in a way that amplifies the voices of these veterans, centering their lived experiences and retelling this history in their own words, while contextualizing the oral histories with rigorous historical analysis. This book is a snapshot of a cast of people, whose lives were constrained by historical forces often beyond their control. But they refuse to be victims. The narrators tell unexpected stories of hardship, resiliency, and advocacy. Together, their stories teach us about survival, second chances, and reparative justice.

ACKNOWLEDGMENTS

First, and most important, I acknowledge Danyelle, my spouse, partner in life, and the mother of our children. We are both first-generation college graduates from the delta of Arkansas, and together we have grown, moved many times, and struggled to create a better future for our children. Maya was born two weeks into my master's program, and Ian was born after the first semester of doctoral coursework. I thank them for their patience and understanding every time I worked late, wrote during the weekends, and when it was most difficult to focus on the present. Nearly fifteen hundred miles away, we lived beyond the ability of our families to offer support other than occasional holiday visits. In absence of extended family, we created our own traditions, imparted our own moral values, and opened new worlds of possibility.

A word of thanks to my immediate family—Tony, my stepfather, who fostered my independent thinking; Mary, my mother, who showed me the value of hard work; and Steven, my brother, who always had my back. The text messages kept me grounded even if our conversations centered on the weather. (I did complain an awful lot about living in the "tundra.")

I stand on the shoulders of many. Christian G. Appy, my dissertation director, sets the highest standard of excellence through his scholarship and teaching. He first read an early draft of this book, and his influence on it is boundless. My committee members Barbara Krauthamer and Jennifer Fronc challenged me to think more deeply about the past, read more broadly, and enrich my analysis. John Higginson, a field adviser, helped me see connections between global history and the present. David Kieran, whose scholarship significantly influenced my thinking about mental health and reforms, served as an outside committee member; I hope to pay forward this kindness to another grad student someday. I also want to acknowledge Kara Dixon Vuic for her willingness to uplift students within the field of war and society. The History Department at UMass taught me the value of writing history for the public, and this is my best effort to bridge academic expertise for the public good.

Coming from the South, I had to leave that place to really understand its history. But I would have never made it to this point were it not for the kindness, investment, and support of many educators along the way. At the

University of Arkansas at Monticello (UAM), the offices of my professors were always open. Professors in the English Department taught me to dissect and diagram language; Kay Walter taught me to care for it. With the History Department, I trained to become an academic, presenting original research at conferences and joining a cohort of other ambitious history majors. From Clinton D. Young, I learned the craft of history. At UAM, I first fell in love with oral history and storytelling.

At Oklahoma State University, I gained professional training at the Oklahoma Oral History Research Program and grew as an interdisciplinary scholar. John M. Kinder remains a mentor, collaborating partner, and significant influence on my writing and thinking about veterans. Elizabeth Grubgeld carefully guided me through the English grad program, served as my thesis adviser, and encouraged me to seek a PhD in history. I fondly remember sitting in her office, talking for hours, and losing track of time. A gift made in memory of her brother Lester Edward Grubgeld Jr., who experienced traumatic brain injury and paraplegia, helped to make this book possible.

I benefited from many grants, awards, and resources from UMass Amherst and beyond, which enabled me to complete much of this work. I turned the Oral History Lab into a writing space of my own during the pandemic. (Shout out to Sam Redman.) I learned to think like an archivist of social change at the W. E. B. Du Bois Library. (Thank you to Aaron Rubinstein and special acknowledgment of Robert S. Cox.) Beth McLaughlin, at Adept Word Management, generously donated transcription services. Even with all this support and opportunity, I still took out massive student loans to get where I am. (Thanks, Public Service Loan Forgiveness!)

Special thanks to Laura A. Belmonte for inviting me to Virginia Tech and providing me an opportunity to grow as a teacher, scholar, and editor. Colleagues in the History Department and University Libraries welcomed me into the world of digital humanities. Sylvester Johnson, director of the Center for Humanities, has emboldened me to imagine new possibilities for the humanities through technology. It has been a special privilege to work with and learn from Peter Potter, (former) director of Virginia Tech Publishing. With the generosity of Virginia Tech and a TOME (Toward an Open Access Monograph Ecosystem) grant, an e-book version of *Prisoners after War* will be open and available to the public for free. As a public historian, I believe that open access to credible information is essential to the work of democracy.

Matt Becker, editor in chief at UMass Press, has supported this project from its very beginning. Over coffee and lunch over the years, he has become a trusted mentor in the world of academic publishing and carefully guided me through the publication process of two books. I am exceedingly grateful for the critical feedback from the peer reviewers who helped me see this manuscript's full potential. Thanks to the Veterans series editors, Brian Matthew Jordan and J. Ross Dancy, for welcoming my work with incarcerated veterans and publishing our past coedited volume (with John Kinder) on marginalized veterans. Creating space within the field of veterans studies for unheard, forgotten, and dissident voices sets UMass Press apart.

I want to thank all the veterans who trusted me with their life stories. There are too many to name here, but I want to extend my sincerest gratitude to veterans and advocates who participated in this project—Ari Sesu Merretazon, Timmy Wynn, William Delaney, Haywood Fennell Sr., Henry D. Burton, David Carlson, Judge Patrick Dugan, Marie Demarey, John J. Sullivan, David Moffett, Heath Phillips, Brian Lewis, Bob Hunter, Penny Lee Deere, Kim Bailey, Nicole Dawson Corrin, Elvia Huirez, Matt Steiner, Melissa Fitzgerald, Christopher Deutsch, Judge Robert Russell, Jack O'Connor, Dr. Patrick Welch, Manuel Welch, Alyssa Vasquez, Joani Higgins, Leslie "Rock" Whitted, Donald Adkins, Gregory Nini, Matt Nicholas, Donna Sickels, Jacqueline Baum, Crystal Asia Wheeler, Dr. Margaret Seymour, Glen Douglas, Gil Vergara Colderon, Hector Barajas Varela, James Marciano, Andrew Kubacki, Neal Mays, Kevin Ogo, Robert Porter, Andre Torres, Scott Brewster, Anthony Stirlacci, Joshua Girard, Torin Traynor, William Babcock, James Duff, Edward Chip Powell, William Sloyer, James Torrey, Shawn Small, John Causton, Rico Nieves, and James Allen Wright. Special thanks to advocates for incarcerated and women veterans, including Mary Donovan, Diana Danis, and Lynn Newson. From the very beginning, Mary Ellen Salzano, a tireless advocate for women veterans, advised the Incarcerated Veterans Oral History Project. Thank you to the dozens more veterans who wrote letters. Many veterans I interviewed have passed away since I first started doing oral history in 2011. Rest in peace to Leslie Hoppers, Larry Forrest, Bob Loomis, Len Gardner, Dennis Magnusen, and Holocaust survivor Sol Berg, may his memory be a blessing.

I also want to acknowledge the people who risked their lives, bodies, and freedom for justice. I wrote this book during a time of great instability and social unrest. I wrote as the world witnessed George Floyd murdered. I wrote as thousands protested and marched for Black lives. I wrote as cities burned and police rioted. I wrote as armed white supremacists stormed capitols. I wrote while watching an attempted overthrow of the US government. I wrote as coronavirus infections surged and waned in waves. More Americans have died from COVID than all US soldiers killed in the Civil War, World War II, the Vietnam War, and the Global War on Terrorism combined. While I wrote from the safety of quarantine, the real work of justice happens in the streets, in the courts, and in the halls of power.

Last but not least, I want to acknowledge the countless civilians who died in wars, the Vietnam veterans serving life in prison, and the people who defended, fought, and died with moral courage.

PRISONERS AFTER WAR

Locating Incarcerated Veterans in American History

Iraq War veteran David Carlson lives in the wake of intergenerational trauma, American wars, and incarceration.[1] "My dad is from Mississippi. He's my Black side," Carlson says. "He was also an infantryman. After Vietnam, he got into a criminal lifestyle."[2] David's father, Abra Hayes, had a brutal life in the Jim Crow South, living under the yoke of white supremacy. Carlson vividly recalls his father's cautionary tale, warning him of the inherent dangers of being a Black man in America. During his childhood, young Abra witnessed the lynching of a Black man who—along with more than forty-four hundred victims of racial terror—was denied the constitutional right of due process and equal treatment under the law. This conversation between Black parents and children shatters their youthful innocence but lifts the veil to reckon with the double consciousness of unfreedom in the land of the free.

Born in Mississippi after the Second World War, Hayes grew up amid the intergenerational poverty and hardship of the sharecropping system with few opportunities for education, separate, unequal, or otherwise. Like most Black families in Mississippi in the nineteenth and twentieth centuries, children went to segregated schools outside of the harvesting season, if at all. Most worked the cotton fields from dawn to dusk, with calloused hands, laboring away their most formative years in the blistering Delta sun. Because their families were perpetually indebted to white landowners, Black children were funneled into a system of economic exploitation that functioned, in practice, like plantation slavery, creating generation after generation of poor, landless farmers with few rights and little opportunity.

Historically, the military could provide a path toward liberation. Along with tens of thousands of other poor, semiliterate Black men, Abra Hayes was drafted into the military during the Vietnam War, under the guise that the Army would provide opportunities for education, careers, and socioeconomic uplift. Project 100,000 enlisted men who, like Hayes, had attended segregated schools, scored lower than average on entrance exams, and desperately needed the bonuses awarded for combat service.³ Like 94 percent of men recruited under Project 100,000, the Vietnam War provided Abra Hayes neither specialized training nor further education.⁴ Instead, he returned to the Delta Mississippi where all the old systems of racial inequality and caste remained. But after Vietnam, Hayes carried home more problems than before.

Abra Hayes had been wounded in combat, but he received neither a hero's welcome nor the social and political capital of veteranhood. Carlson recounted his father's experience: "They were extremely poor. He went to Vietnam and got shot. He had a hard time coming home." After his discharge, Hayes returned to Jackson, Mississippi, where he was harassed by local police and still treated as a second-class citizen. Repressing the memories of combat in Vietnam, Hayes self-medicated. "He moved to California because it was a little better for Black people," Carlson says, but "he could never beat the alcohol and drug addiction." Like previous generations, after the war, Hayes migrated out of the South, seeking work and opportunities, but, as many other African Americans discovered, he could not completely escape the structural barriers that restrict Black life in America. He survived outside the law, hustling and inevitably harming his own family.⁵ Abra's son David Carlson would be incarcerated by age fourteen and imprisoned again after two combat tours in Iraq.

Prisoners after War identifies the Vietnam War as an inflection point in the history of mass incarceration, showing how veterans experienced, responded to, organized against, and were affected by war and incarceration at a formative moment in the American carceral state. To define the nebulous relationship between war and prison, this book tells a multibiographical history of veterans in the criminal justice system through an intersectional analysis of race, disability, trauma, memory, class, and gender. This scholarship brings into conversation two areas of historiography that rarely speak directly to one another: military history and carceral studies. At their intersections, I seek to establish previously unrecognized connections between American wars and mass incarceration, by recording the untold stories of those caught between them. From Vietnam to Iraq and Afghanistan, this book documents the consequences of foreign and domestic policies over the lifetimes of two generations of US military veterans and their families.

Spanning the past sixty years, *Prisoners after War* traces the history of incarcerated veterans from the Vietnam War to the Global War on Terrorism, outlining the backdraft of forever wars and identifying twin systems that perpetrate violence abroad and perpetuate inequality at home. Put another way, this book seeks to understand the consequences of punitive domestic policies on the agents of US foreign policies, veterans, and their families; conversely, it also seeks to understand the effects of militarism on domestic life, liberty, and democracy in the United States. Combined, these forces define what I call the American "military-carceral state," a framework to reconsider how wars and prisons together shape, restrict, and confine lives in the United States from the Vietnam War era to the age of "forever wars" in the twenty-first century.[6]

Many scholars have studied the carceral state at the federal, the state, or the local level, but *Prisoners after War* is an intimate carceral history, deeply invested in understanding how power at multiple levels affects the personal lives of otherwise ordinary people who went to war and prison afterward.[7] Rather than a geographical focus or traditional chronology of mass incarceration, my analysis follows the lives of people who crossed international boundaries, experienced and perpetrated violence, and navigated the difficulties of home-coming to show the effects of war, punishment, and reforms on communities, families, and intimate personal memories.

Through oral histories, I document the social history of punishment among veterans with mental health conditions, including post-traumatic stress disorder, substance use, traumatic brain injury, military sexual trauma, and other unseen wounds, such as moral injury. Any combination of these mental health problems and socioeconomic straits can contribute to reintegration difficulties and lead to involvement with the criminal justice system. A small population, particularly susceptible to mental health and social issues, US military veterans may experience homelessness, suicidal ideations, and incarceration, and while PTSD, homelessness, and suicide are popular today in common discourse about veterans' readjustment difficulties, incarceration is still taboo because it contradicts national narratives about veterans as symbols of strength, valor, and patriotism. To challenge these stigmas and myths, formerly incarcerated veterans spoke out and shared their personal experiences before, during, and after military service—to help the public understand how the criminal and military justice systems disproportionately punish people with mental health disorders, disabilities, and survivors of trauma, particularly those from impoverished and minoritized communities.

* * *

Even though incarceration affects veterans of all racial groups in the United States today, the central location of incarcerated veterans in the twentieth century is African American history. Nearly forgotten in national consciousness, the history of incarcerated veterans takes root in the violent past between white authority and Black resistance. Wars—and the power vacuums they create—produce tipping points in American social history, generating great geographic and social movement among Black families. In the twentieth century, generations of Black men volunteered or were drafted in the tens of thousands to serve a nation that treated them as second-class citizens. To those denied citizenship, wars were rites of passage, battlefields upon which manhood was proven and destroyed. More often than not, youthful hopes of equal treatment and opportunity were choked against the walls of white supremacy in the military and beyond. But, with bullets and ballots, Black veterans fought back for democracy; they returned from military service, determined to exercise citizenship in the courts and at the polls. Reimagining new uses for the skills and knowledge gained in the military, many practiced armed self-defense and trained others to defend themselves from racial terrorism. Yet many others became misfortunate martyrs to the cause of liberation, targets of police brutality and victims of lynch mobs, their bodies stripped, dragged, burned, shot, hanged, mutilated, and collected as souvenirs.

At these flash points in American history, Black veterans were caught in a crossfire of state-sanctioned violence, pinned down within the historical and political conflicts between federal power and local white authority from the Civil War to the civil rights movement. After the abolition of slavery, a new era of racial terror, convict leasing, and Jim Crow dominated the social and political landscape of the South for the next century. The First and Second World Wars enabled the great migrations but were followed by the Red Summer and the Red Scare, both of which targeted African Americans who demanded jobs and equality. The internationally publicized stories of Black World War II veterans—who were being beaten like Isaac Woodard, executed by police like Timothy Hood, or lynched like John C. Jones—forced the federal government to desegregate the armed forces, yet institutional racism and injustices continued throughout the Cold War.[8]

African Americans were unfairly arrested, faced excessive charges with inadequate legal counsel, were courts-martialed, and were sentenced to lengthy sentences, sometimes life, in military prisons, or executed.[9] Thurgood Marshall and the National Association for the Advancement of Colored People (NAACP) investigated racial injustice in the military in the 1950s. They found that segregation continued, in practice, in the Army, and Black troops were held to a different and nearly impossible standard. For example, both white and African American troops retreated in battle during the Korean War, but 90 percent of the soldiers accused of cowardice were Black, and 25 percent of the accused were sentenced to death or life in prison.[10] Facing racism on both fronts, many Black people became disillusioned, rejecting the idea that the military served as a path toward equality. A watershed moment in the civil rights movement, the tragic murder of Black Navy veteran Sammy Younge, who was shot in the face in Tuskegee, Alabama, for using a whites-only restroom in 1965, compelled the Student Non-Violent Coordinating Committee (SNCC) to become the first civil rights organization to publicly oppose the Vietnam War.[11]

The military did not completely uplift African Americans from the racial, social, political, and economic inequality they faced on the home front. In fact, institutional racism in the military and Veterans Administration exacerbated it. The demographic makeup of urban poverty and crime that still remains today is the result of generational racial and socioeconomic inequality, inherently connected to discrimination of Black families in the VA. As the GI Bill helped to build middle-class America, Black people were largely denied the social and economic capital earned by veterans in the twentieth century. Through redlining and the systematic denial of home loans to Black World War II veterans, state-sanctioned segregation expanded into the federal levels and across the continental United States.[12] The postwar urban crisis results from inherent economic inequality generated by capitalism, and African Americans have disproportionately felt the consequences of that inequality.[13] By the mid-1960s, the living conditions in urban areas had deteriorated so much that Black people rose up in rebellion.[14] In 1965, rather than looking at structural inequality, policymakers like Lyndon B. Johnson and Daniel Patrick Moynihan sought to explain the roots of urban poverty as pathological. Simultaneously, the Johnson administration escalated the war in Vietnam and launched a new war on crime, fueling conflict between police and Black communities and worsening the problems faced by Black families in the 1960s and beyond.

In the afterlife of segregation, mass incarceration was born out of a decade of state violence, poverty, and rebellion.[15] In the 1960s, President Lyndon B. Johnson sought to fulfill the promises of democracy and justice for all. Like Dr. Martin Luther King Jr., he understood economic uplift and civil rights as two sides of the same movement. His Great Society programs were, perhaps, the most radical transformation of American society since Reconstruction. In the first years of his presidency, Johnson ushered in the Civil Rights Act, the Voting Rights Act, and the Economic Opportunity Act, addressing both racial injustice and poverty. But the war on poverty ultimately did not completely eradicate economic inequality, and Johnson never fully embraced the idea of economic security as a civil right.[16] At the same time, Black youth rebelled in cities across the United States, a reaction to over-policing, abuse, and poverty. President Johnson understood that high unemployment, poor education, and poor housing were underlying problems at the root of urban violence in Harlem, Brooklyn, and Watts, but privately he felt that the rebellions were part of a "communist conspiracy" and feared political backlash from opponents who believed the civil rights movement fomented lawlessness and disorder.[17] In the fallout from the Watts Rebellion, the Johnson administration began redirecting funds away from the war on poverty to escalate the war in Vietnam.[18]

As civil rights leaders pointed out, the Vietnam War exacted an unequal toll on poor people of color. Eighty percent of combat troops in Vietnam were working class, and the draft disproportionately targeted poor communities.[19] Spearheaded by Secretary of Defense Robert McNamara, Project 100,000 lowered the standards on examinations for admission into the military, allowing less privileged and undereducated men, like Abra Hayes, to serve. Liberal policymakers believed the military would uplift the "subterranean poor," and "downtrodden men could be forged anew, retrained and salvaged for a lifetime of productive citizenship."[20] From 1966 to 1971, more than four hundred thousand men served in Army and Marine combat units in Vietnam under Project 100,000.[21] McNamara and Daniel Patrick Moynihan claimed that military service would provide a model of patriarchy denied to African American families, thus enabling the nation's Black youth to overcome what was, in fact, centuries of political, economic, and legal discrimination.[22] A 1985 study sought to prove McNamara's theory correct, but "very much to [their] surprise the comparisons" did not show an advantage.[23] Project 100,000 veterans were worse off educationally, socially, and economically than nonveteran counterparts with similar aptitude levels.

In reality, the military offered little civilian job training and few opportunities for social advancement. Instead, it sent "many poor, terribly confused, and woefully uneducated boys to risk death in Vietnam," writes historian Christian Appy.[24] As a result of their lower test scores, African Americans were disproportionately assigned to combat units and twice as likely as whites to die in Vietnam in 1965–66.[25] These disparate casualties influenced Dr. Martin Luther King Jr. to speak out publicly against the war in 1967. The government "was sending their sons and their brothers and their husbands to fight and to die in extraordinarily high proportions relative to the rest of the population. We were taking the black young men who had been crippled by our society and sending them eight thousand miles away to guarantee liberties in Southeast Asia which they had not found in" their own hometowns and communities in the United States.[26] By the late 1960s, many African Americans understood their disproportionate casualties in Vietnam as the result of political, economic, and racial inequality, and they resisted the war as such.

Like previous generations of Black soldiers, African Americans in the Vietnam War experienced discrimination in the military justice system and harsher punishment than whites.[27] As icons of Black culture, like Dr. King and Muhammad Ali, protested the war, Black soldiers in Vietnam engaged in daily acts of resistance, often refusing combat and going AWOL (absent without official leave). By 1970–71, a majority of Americans opposed the war, and the antiwar movement among US soldiers in Vietnam reached its apex, but Black soldiers were punished more harshly than white troops. Clarence Fitch, a soldier imprisoned in a military jail in Vietnam, recalls that "the overwhelming majority were black, much like the jails were back in the World. It just made you more bitter, more conscious, more hard, more militant, gave you more of a reason . . . to resist and fight."[28] In 1971, the Army reported that it was in a state of "collapse, with individual units avoiding or having refused combat, murdering their officers and non commissioned officers, drug-ridden, and dispirited where not near mutinous."[29] The "problem of race" and drugs deflected from legitimate criticism of policies in Vietnam.[30]

In response to GI dissent and resistance, the Army began the process of withdrawing troops and transitioning to an all-volunteer force and initiated stricter regulations, mandatory urinalysis, and issued punitive discharges for minor offenses. African Americans were given less-than-honorable discharges at disproportionate rates, and these administrative punishments caused lasting social and economic problems after service.[31] Less-than-honorable discharges excluded veterans from VA services and disability benefits.[32] After Vietnam, Black veterans experienced excessively high unemployment rates and often could not afford college.[33] By the late 1970s, a majority of veterans in US prisons had received less-than-honorable discharges, and most were African American veterans.[34]

In 1971, the Nixon administration declared a war on drugs, arguably, to distract the public from political scandals, the widespread unpopularity of the war, and the United States' failures to achieve either military victory or political stability in South Vietnam.[35] In his now infamous "public enemy number one" speech, President Richard M. Nixon essentially blamed heroin-addicted soldiers for losses in Vietnam, thus manufacturing a link between antiwar activists, dissenters in the military, and drug users. "America's public enemy number one in the United States is drug abuse. In order to fight and defeat this enemy, it is necessary to wage a new, all-out offensive," Nixon declared. He rationalized this new, global drug war, claiming that "it is essential for the American people to be alerted to this danger, to recognize that it is a danger that will not pass with the passing of the war in Vietnam which has brought to our attention the fact that a number of young Americans have become addicts as they serve abroad."[36] Since the Second World War, the United States developed increasingly punitive responses to illicit drugs,[37] but Nixon's emphatic use of "war" rhetoric created a sense of crisis, which sought to justify militarized policing, surveillance campaigns that targeted Black communities and encroached upon civil rights, and an expansive budget to build the infrastructure of the carceral state. As Donna Murch put it, "The declaration of war increased resources to fight the 'drug crisis' while initiating a conflict without end."[38] The war on drugs punished thousands of Vietnam veterans coping with readjustment difficulties, combat stress, and untreated symptoms that are now associated with post-traumatic stress disorder.[39]

The war on crime counteracted the war on poverty policies. Welfare programs were intended to provide job training, employment, and education to African Americans and Hispanic communities as well as poor whites. After Johnson's landmark decision not to seek reelection, the Nixon administration disinvested from the Great Society programs and funneled federal money into police departments and prison systems, building the infrastructure for mass incarceration in the United States, as historian Elizabeth Hinton argues. "'If the conviction rate were doubled in this country," Nixon claimed, "'it would do more to eliminate crime in the future than a quadrupling of the funds for any governmental war on poverty.'"[40] By reallocating federal funding to states, the Nixon administration increased the budgets of local police and courts. Consequentially, the courts and prison systems expanded, judges extended prison sentences, and legislation introduced mandatory minimum sentences for drug crimes commonly associated with African American communities.

The end of the Vietnam War marked a historic turn toward carceral punishment.[41] The government defunded social welfare programs, and policymakers in both major political parties adopted Nixon's "law and order" approach, each side embracing "tough on crime" politics and promoting carceral punishment over rehabilitation, especially when it came to marginalized groups.[42] During the second half of the twentieth century, as the criminal justice system expanded, the deinstitutionalization of state mental hospitals led to the confinement of people with psychiatric disabilities in prisons and jails instead of mental health facilities.[43] These policies accelerated the surge of mass incarceration, sweeping up a disproportionate number of Black people with disabilities.[44] By the late 1970s, one out of four people in prison was a military veteran, and most incarcerated veterans were Black men.[45]

In 1973, Ari Sesu Merretazon and other Black veterans imprisoned at Lorton Reformatory in Virginia organized for disability rights and founded the first Veterans Administration office inside a prison staffed by incarcerated veterans. The Incarcerated Veterans Assistance Organization assisted incarcerated veterans filing disability claims from within the prison.[46] Their efforts caught the attention of the Carter administration and spurred congressional hearings on incarcerated veterans in 1979. Merretazon testified alongside others, pointing out the consequences of other-than-honorable discharges and the denial of disability benefits to incarcerated veterans.[47] A General Accounting Office study found that there were no concerted VA outreach programs in prisons and jails. The Congressional Committee on Veterans' Affairs recommended a comprehensive study to determine the extent of the population of incarcerated veterans. At the directive of President Carter in 1978, the Department of Justice began to collect information on incarcerated veterans because at the time, "nothing was known about veterans in prison."[48]

In the clouded collective memory of the Vietnam War, prisoners after war were mostly forgotten by the public. But Vietnam veterans' organizations understood all too well how veterans came home from war and went to prison and jail. The Vietnam Veterans of America organized and advocated for disability benefits, the acknowledgment of the carcinogenic effects of Agent Orange, and recognition of PTSD.[49] In 1983, the VVA established a legal services program for veterans in the criminal justice system, providing assistance to veterans filing for disability benefits and legal advice. In the early '80s, the *VVA Veteran* also published letters from veterans in prison, highlighting their needs, and shared vital, up-to-date information on PTSD and how it could be employed in court cases or appeals. The second part of this book argues that the collective memory of the Vietnam War motivated veterans to engage in protest, advocacy, and justice reform.[50] Despite their notable efforts, however, the Vietnam War generation was caught up in the rise of mass incarceration, the total number of incarcerated veterans more than doubling between the end of the Vietnam War and the start of the Global War on Terrorism.[51]

Just as Vietnam veterans were gaining recognition for their reintegration difficulties in the 1980s, the war on drugs reached unprecedented proportions under the Reagan administration. Ronald Reagan campaigned on healing the Vietnam War syndrome, claiming that America's reluctance to engage foreign enemies had allowed communism to spread into the Western Hemisphere.[52] Linking communism and the Central American cocaine trade, Reagan saw drug use as symptomatic of national decline and vouched to fight a renewed global war on drugs at home, in the military, and abroad.[53] The Reagan administration redirected the drug war against cocaine, while intensifying domestic enforcement in predominately Black neighborhoods.[54] Simultaneously, Reagan repealed the Mental Health Systems Act of 1980, and his Economic Recovery Tax Act of 1981 decreased taxes for the wealthy and slashed government spending on social welfare programs, education, rehabilitation services for substance use, and housing programs.[55] Under Reagan, campaigns sought to depict welfare programs as criminal, robbing hardworking Americans to redistribute wealth to lazy poor people, "welfare queens," and drug addicts.[56] After cutting government spending on rehabilitation, Congress passed the Anti-Drug Abuse Act of 1986, increasing the number of offenses with mandatory minimum sentences, most notably for simple possession of crack cocaine, a drug more commonly associated with Black communities.[57]

Caught in a cycle of disinvestment, defunding of social services, and draconian drug laws, communities dealing with crime, drugs, and poverty in the

1980s became the primary targets of the Reagan administration's global war on drugs. The state of California aggressively carried out Reagan's drug war and developed a militarized law enforcement apparatus, including elite tactical squads, SWAT teams, airborne police units, and surveillance and eradication campaigns that removed large populations of Black and Brown youth from communities and confined them in jails and prisons.[58] By framing gangs as responsible for the "crack crisis," officials sought to justify militarized policing and civil rights violations as necessary to protect communities.[59] These policies turned cops into soldiers and criminalized young, poor, minoritized people. Law enforcement associated daily life among Black and Brown people as inherently gang related and criminal. Despite funneling billions of dollars into militarized police forces, more prisons, and longer sentences, violent crime increased during the second half of the 1980s.[60]

Further escalating the war on crime, President Bill Clinton signed the most punitive crime law in American history. The Violent Crime Control and Law Enforcement Act of 1994 mandated life in prison for third violent felony convictions, known as the "three strikes and you're out" law; expanded the number of laws punishable by death; and provided billions of dollars to build and expand prisons. The legacies of this bipartisan commitment to punishment over rehabilitation and funding for policing over social services drove mass incarceration from nearly 1,150,000 people in prisons and jails in 1990 to nearly 2 million by the end of the decade.[61] Even though African Americans were only 12.9 percent of the total US population, nearly half of the people in prison were Black. Michelle Alexander aptly calls this era "the new Jim Crow."[62] As a result of bipartisan federal, state, and local drug policies, the modern war on drugs entrapped entire families and their descendants in an intergenerational cycle of poverty and prison.

Half a century since the war on drugs, the population of incarcerated Americans has swollen from 200,000 in 1970 to an all-time high of 7.1 million Americans in prisons, jails, and on parole in 2010.[63] Criminal justice reforms have slightly deflated the prison populations over the past ten years, but in 2021 alone, there were still 1.8 million Americans incarcerated, 6.9 million annual admissions (that is, the number of people booked into and housed in jails), and nearly 4 million on parole—and millions more living in what Reuben Jonathan Miller calls the "afterlife of mass incarceration."[64] Carceral punishment has become a way of life in the United States, an integral part of

American culture and infrastructure. Heather Ann Thompson notes, "Between 1970–2010 more people were incarcerated in the United States than were imprisoned in any other country, and at no other point in its past had the nation's economic, social, and political institutions become so bound up with the practice of punishment." Ten times more Americans were imprisoned in the 1990s alone than the total number of American soldiers killed in the war in Vietnam.[65] Between the end of the Vietnam War and dawn of the war on terror, the total incarcerated population in the United States multiplied tenfold.

These statistics, well known today, do not—and cannot—tell the social history of mass incarceration. Studying incarceration from the bottom up necessarily requires listening to the disbelieved and recording the intimate, personal, and inherently traumatic memories of the human beings caged in and dehumanized by the American carceral state. So far, very few historians have peered under the veil of the prison system to look into the worlds of ordinary people. Through oral histories, *Prisoners after War* provides a glimpse into the complex underworld of confinement through a small collection of oral history interviews with formerly incarcerated veterans, revealing how American society punishes people with mental health conditions and disabilities, including the men and women who served in the military.

* * *

A microcosm of the complex history of incarcerated veterans, the story of Abra Hayes and his son David Carlson gives rare insight into the historical and social processes that shaped the lives of incarcerated veterans from the mid-twentieth to the twenty-first century. A more detailed digression into Carlson's life will help tie together the threads of American history from the Vietnam War to the Global War on Terrorism and begin to fill in missing gaps in the more recent historiographies of the military and carceral state in the twenty-first century. From his childhood, David's father transmitted the trauma of Jim Crow and the Vietnam War onto him, but those legacies merely formed the backdrop of Carlson's own struggles with poverty, gang violence, juvenile detention, the Iraq War, and his transformational journey from prison to justice advocate. His oral history offers a preview of the recent history of incarcerated veterans in the twenty-first century, showing both continuity and change over time.

David Carlson grew up amid instability, domestic violence, and drugs. He says, "When I was born, he was a pimp, and my mom was a prostitute."

Carlson's mother eventually fled her marriage to Hayes and became an advocate for survivors of domestic abuse, substance use, and sexual violence.[66] But the life of crime, into which Carlson had been born, followed him into his teenage years. At age thirteen, he joined a gang. By age fourteen, he was incarcerated in a juvenile detention center. By age twenty, not long after September 11, Carlson enlisted in the Army National Guard to serve and to escape, believing, like his father, that the Army would offer a way out and a new start.

To meet the manpower needs of the Global War on Terrorism, the Army lowered its entrance qualifications, admitting people with criminal records and issuing waivers to recruits without high school diplomas or who scored low on entrance exams, similar to Project 100,000.[67] Carlson deployed to Iraq from 2004 to 2005, where he experienced intense combat, near-death encounters, and survivor's guilt. On October 17, 2005, Sergeant Alwyn Cashe's Bradley Fighting Vehicle hit an improvised explosive device (IED), exploding in flames. Cashe's uniform caught fire, but he managed to rescue six other men. Within three weeks, he died of his wounds.[68] (After years of petitions, on December 16, 2021, Alwyn C. Cashe became the first African American awarded the Congressional Medal of Honor since the Vietnam War).[69] "That was two weeks before we left country," recalls Carlson. "It was like we betrayed them. In the moment that they needed people . . . we were back on base." He remembers, "That's the end of my tour, and that's it. There was no retribution for it. That happened, and then I'm home." He explains, "That's why I volunteered for my second tour."

In 2007, while deployed in Iraq, untreated mental health problems led to behavioral issues and misconduct. Carlson became increasingly isolated, aggressive, and rageful, exhibiting symptoms of post-traumatic stress disorder. He did not trust inexperienced or incompetent soldiers. One day, he assaulted a subordinate. The leadership conducted three separate Article 15–6 investigations of Carlson's misconduct. "Those could've landed me anywhere from demoted to private, to locked up," realizes Carlson. Then he fell into a cycle of depression and hypervigilance.

While in the Army, Carlson considered mental illness a failure of manhood. "I didn't believe in PTSD at that time," he says. "I had one buddy. During the first two weeks in Iraq, he got hit by an RPG [rocket-propelled grenade]." Carlson recalls, "The shrapnel went through both his feet, and he got sent back. I found out later that he had all these issues." His friend became an alcoholic and suffered from depression. "I thought he was just weak. And then after my second tour, I started having those same issues." At the time, Carlson believed, "If you're a man, you're not going to have issues with this. Period."

After Carlson returned to the United States, he quickly spiraled and got into fistfights, binge-drank, and had suicidal ideations. One night during an armed confrontation with police, he contemplated suicide by cop. "I had no self-worth left. I wanted to die," he says coldly. "The VA called it passively suicidal. I didn't care what was happening to me. I was so far at the bottom that being in jail or being homeless didn't matter to me." After this incident, Carlson was confined in a VA psychiatric ward and started a treatment program for PTSD.

While seeking mental health services, Carlson was discharged from the Army National Guard. He received an honorable discharge, thanks to the advocacy of his leaders, citing his distinguished service in Iraq. Afterward, however, his mental health conditions worsened without a support system. "Once I was released from active duty, I lost all purpose," Carlson recalls. "All the stuff that happened on both tours finally caught up with me. By the time I got arrested [again], I did not give a shit." He reverted to an anterior life of crime.

After being charged with burglary, Carlson was put on probation and ordered to complete Veterans Treatment Court. The law required a successful completion of a yearlong program of intensive therapy, urinalysis, and weekly court appearances. Defendants must plead guilty, and if they complete the program successfully, the judges often expunge the charges and dismiss the fines. However, during the program, Carlson was arrested for operating under the influence (OUI). The presiding judge expelled him from the treatment court and sentenced him to three years in state prison.

After twenty-two months of war, Carlson served four years in prison. While incarcerated, he became hardened and more violent and undermined prison authority. "Prison turned me into the worst person," he admits. "I was a predator. My plan whole was to get out and hurt the community. I wanted to destroy it. I hated the United States, and I hated everybody." After getting out of prison, Carlson recidivated. "I only lasted a few months," he recalls. "I ran from the cops. I was combative. I'm fortunate to not have life in prison or be dead."

In total, Carlson spent nine months in solitary confinement. For people dealing with mental illness, solitary confinement can be torturous. "I thought it was going to destroy me." He decided, "I had to either kill myself or change." While in prison, Carlson started writing about his life experiences and eventually got connected with the VA representative who helped him get the counseling and treatment he needed. Through his recovery process, he found a calling for advocacy work and justice.

Today, Carlson advocates for a nonviolent model of rehabilitation for veterans and engages in reparative justice projects. "I've had too much violence indoctrinated into me throughout my life," he realizes. "Violence is the number one thing you've got to take out of your life if you want to make any other changes." His story suggests moral injury and a type of ideological shock or cognitive dissonance that can make one lose faith in leadership and even American exceptionalism. "Policymakers have not been held accountable for the violence they cause," Carlson notes. "There has to be retribution for that." Motivating his service to the community is the need to repair the damage he caused. "I owe for the rest of my life. I have taken lives," he acknowledges. "I am in debt. If I don't live up to that debt, and I don't keep paying back towards it—then I am not a man."

Presently, Carlson is a law school student, father, and advocate for mental health care and justice reform. He also volunteers at the Eau Claire County Veterans Treatment Court in Wisconsin. Since his recovery, he has dedicated himself to helping other disadvantaged youth in his community. Through education and community activism, Carlson is breaking the cycle of trauma, imprisonment, and recidivism and charting a new course for his own son. Transformations like this were the most astonishing recurring themes in the oral history project.

A legacy of American violence, David Carlson's life is entangled in a tapestry of intergenerational trauma in the United States, intersecting, overlapping, and reflecting the major historical and cultural forces identified in the chapters that follow. This story follows an undercurrent through American history and reveals insightful lessons about war, veterans, and justice. The family history of David Carlson and Abra Hayes transects global, national, and social history, from US foreign policy to domestic politics, and it shows how sometimes the agents of state violence become the "collateral damage" of it. But David's remarkable story also shows the reparative power of advocacy and inspires hope that others can recover from the intergenerational trauma of war and incarceration.

FIGURE I. Photograph provided by David Carlson, ca. 2020.

* * *

Prisoners after War tells a unique cross-generational story about the relationships between veterans from two different eras in American history. Even today, collective memory of the Vietnam War continues to shape people's lives, especially Iraq and Afghanistan war veterans. The second half of this book documents the recent history of Veterans Treatment Courts while telling the stories of the veterans involved in them. Spearheaded by Vietnam veteran volunteers, Veterans Treatment Courts are a grassroots, multigenerational veterans' movement for reparative justice. A hybrid drug and mental health treatment court, Veterans Treatment Courts provide access to counseling services, support for housing, education opportunities, job programs, and disability benefits through the VA. As a result, Veterans Treatment Courts have the lowest recidivism rates in the nation. Treatment courts could serve as a model for greater criminal justice reform because they recognize the relationship between mental health and incarceration and provide alternatives to carceral punishment. Their proven successes also provide tangible evidence that treatment can prevent recidivism and break the pattern of trauma and incarceration among families by utilizing federal, state, and local community resources.

Despite reforms, justice is not equal. Veterans Treatment Courts vary according to state laws and exclude most violent crimes, disqualifying most incarcerated veterans. The courts mandate weekly attendance in court and urinalysis, even those with prescriptions for medical marijuana. The programs last at least one year, and many fail to complete treatment. Remember, Veterans Treatment Court did not save David Carlson from prison. Treatment courts are a step in a positive direction, but justice reforms that benefit only a small percentage of the population cannot solve the problems of mass incarceration. But, perhaps, the stories of formerly incarcerated veterans can promote bipartisan support for more systemic reforms and spur cultural change on how police, jails, and courts interact with people with mental health disorders. For equal justice, though, we must first reckon with historic and endemic racism, socioeconomic inequality, and the drug and mental health crises in the United States today.

Located in the shadows of the prison system, incarcerated veterans are removed from society, outside of national consciousness, and forgotten in public memory. Oral histories of formerly incarcerated veterans show the radiating effects of discrimination and traumatic experiences on veterans of war and their families. This intergenerational framework calls attention to the decades-long consequences of trauma passed down through military families. It helps us better understand the legacies of war and prison and their combined social costs. Equally important, their experiences challenge us to acknowledge structural inequality and ongoing injustices in the United States that affect us all, even without our knowing it. Military veterans are venerated as symbols of strength, honor, and patriotism, so if the public can see how veterans are vulnerable to the interrelated crises of mental health and mass incarceration, then perhaps this understanding can spark greater change in cultural attitudes toward incarceration, punishment, and the stigmas of conviction. The intimate history of incarcerated veterans, I hope, will enlighten some readers to see the intrinsic humanity of people in the criminal justice system.

CHAPTER 1

"Less than" Veterans

Discrimination, Discharges, and Disabilities during the Vietnam War

"In prison, you don't have *veterans*," says Henry David Burton, "only convicts and inmates."[1] Born the son of a coal miner in West Virginia, Burton joined the Marine Corps for the promises of career opportunities and social benefits. In 1967, he deployed to Vietnam. Two years later, he reintegrated from the war with all the problems that veterans face today with none of the resources. He did not know about the Veterans Administration or disability benefits. African American veterans with disabilities were especially vulnerable after the war. Burton came home during a time of high unemployment rates and few opportunities. He believed that his only "marketable skills were working in a grocery store and setting ambushes." His wife and infant had been waiting on him back in the world, but unrecognized symptoms of post-traumatic stress disorder permanently damaged his ability to provide financial and emotional support for his family. First, he robbed a grocery store and then a bank. No one was injured, but he was sentenced to fifteen years in a federal prison in Atlanta. In the criminal justice system, Henry Burton was judged as a Black male, first and foremost. If his veteran status mattered, it did not help his case. If anything, it made him look more dangerous.

Before the war, however, Burton had never been in trouble with the law. Like hundreds of thousands of teenage boys before and since him, he underwent the Marine Corps' rite of passage into manhood. "They break you down to nothing. I mean, you're not even an individual." The Marine Corps becomes a brotherhood—like family. It provides and protects. "They broke me down," recalls Burton. "When they gave me a pair of socks and pants, I thought I had a tuxedo. They looked good! I remember coming out of the camp, thinking I could take on the whole wide world." After graduating boot camp, "my chest stuck out so bad. . . . I couldn't wait to get to Vietnam to kill me some gooks." Apologizing for the racial slur, he explains, "That's how my mind frame was" at the time.

In late 1967, Henry Burton arrived in Da Nang; it had a "peculiar smell that I'll never forget," he recalls. "I can still smell it—the atmosphere was different. I know what it was now," explains Burton. "It was death that I was smelling. And the people were smaller, and they looked strange to me, but death was in the air," he recollects. "It still lingers today of death." Burton arrived by himself, the only one from his platoon to be shipped to Vietnam, with orders to join the Second Battalion, Seventh Marines (2/7). "I had to wait because they was out in the bush. And while I was waiting, that's when my father died, and I came back home."

Henry Burton's father died of "black lung disease" just weeks after Burton deployed. He flew home to attend the funeral. While back stateside, Burton met the woman who became his wife and mother of his child. Mourning and concerned for the family, he filed for "a hardship discharge from the Marine Corps because [he] was the oldest one of the family . . . but the Tet Offensive started" and General William Westmoreland was demanding more bodies. The appeal was denied.

When Burton returned to Vietnam, he joined the First Battalion, Fifth Marines, on the eve of Tet 1968. He first experienced combat near the city of Hue. "I fell in love with [the rush of combat] and I stayed there," he reflects. "I stayed a total of nineteen months, and in Vietnam, I became a different person." Burton underwent an extreme transformation in which his body and behavior adapted to the conditions of war—periods of boredom or searching for an elusive enemy, shattered by intense moments of violence, killing, and loss. At war, Burton learned to survive by isolating himself. He created emotional distances between himself and other marines. "When I got to Vietnam, I was the only one in my platoon, so I had to make friends from the men that I met, and I met quite a few." As he became conditioned to the suddenness of death by ambush, Henry started to isolate himself and sever emotional bonds with others. "When we got new men in the platoon, we really didn't care about them because they wouldn't survive long enough. . . . I lost that compassion for human beings." Facing the immediacy of death, he repressed the natural response to grieve. "I can remember the face of death," Henry says hesitantly. But memorializing is a conflicting process. "If my friends died . . . I couldn't think about them. All I could think about was the living. The dead had no meaning." The strategies that helped Burton survive in combat—isolation, numbing, hypervigilance—later prevented him from being able to reconnect to civilian society.

Henry Burton joined the Marine Corps in search of purpose but found killing and death in Vietnam pointless and unjust. It took decades for him to talk about one horrific memory.[2] "They hit us on the bridge on the way to Hue," he recounts. "After the combat, they asked me to go up to a place where all the dead bodies was to identify the men from our platoon. I get there, and it's like a football field of bodies, from one end to the other." He explains, "There wasn't a path in between, so you have to step on the bodies to get to the people to identify them. I remember stepping on the bodies, I kept saying 'excuse me, excuse me.' But yet, I had no feelings for them at that time. All kinds—races and different countries—had been killed. That still haunts me today." Occasionally, Burton still wakes up confused and trembling from the recurring nightmares of wading through inseparable remains of organs and mangled body parts.

After receiving a third Purple Heart and a Bronze Star with a *V* for Valor, Henry Burton was administratively discharged by the Marine Corps despite his appeals to stay. Burton says he was not ready to go home. "They give them three chances to kill you," Burton believes. "If they can patch you up, they send you back into combat. But if you lose an arm, leg, or something critical, then they send you home." After being wounded a third time, the Marines discharged him. Burton was suddenly booted out of the Marines with no time for adjustment, no job training, and no support. On April 15, 1970, he was back in the United States, but "was stuck with a wife, a child, no job, nothing—stuck." Without disability benefits or the support of the military, Burton struggled to reintegrate into civilian society. He explains, "I didn't know anything about disability. I didn't know anything about the VA."

After the war, Burton and his wife moved to Detroit. He got a job at a motor company in Wayne County, Michigan, installing upholstery in Ford station wagons. "I was putting the floorboard in there with twelve screws and an air gun. I had just come from Vietnam. I didn't last six months." He explains, "I just could not adjust to having an air gun in my hand because it reminded me too much of combat." In 1972, Burton left his family. "I abandoned my home in Detroit, and that's how I ended up in Roanoke," Virginia. Feeling like a failure and a burden, he asked his wife for a divorce. Afterward, Burton bounced around from employment services and various jobs but hit a dead end. "I had only two marketable skills, combat or the supermarket," he thought, "and this is how I ended up turning to crime."

In desperation, Burton robbed a bank, and today he's thankful that no one was hurt. Although it was his first offense, based on the nature of his crimes and his military service record, the court sentenced him to fifteen years in a federal penitentiary for armed robbery. Henry recounts the trial. "The judge gave me life, and my lawyer said, 'Your Honor, he never killed nobody.'" The judge responded, "'He's dangerous. Get him out of my courtroom!' It looked like my military service became my enemy. Everybody said, 'All he did was take the money,' but that still didn't matter. 'His military record makes him dangerous.'" It was not that Henry Burton was simply a combat veteran from an unpopular war. He was a Black man, an agent of state violence who committed a violent crime against the state. "I joined the military because I believed in our country . . . and almost died three times," he remarks. "You would die for a country and then come back and break the laws you're ready to die for? 'What happened to me?'" he keeps asking himself. "But that's not a question" that was asked. "I broke the law . . . but why do I get life?" "Give me another life," Burton pleads. "Give me another life."

Henry Burton survived the Vietnam War, but he was permanently marginalized in society. Over the next few decades, Burton would become institutionalized. "I think in the early part of prison, I became a prisoner of war [POW]. In my mind, that's how I coped." As in Vietnam, he learned to survive in prison by isolating himself. "My post-traumatic stress went dormant. It went to sleep on me." After serving fourteen years in prison, Burton was released to society unprepared and unaware of how much he had changed. Once more, the veteran came home to the world. Then, the PTSD resurfaced, and he recidivated. Since then, while incarcerated, Burton and his family have fought for recognition of his status as a veteran, and he now receives 100 percent disability benefits for combat-related PTSD and a lifetime of trauma. Last we talked, Henry Burton had found inner peace but lived in a state of unfreedom. He laments, "I've been buried in prison the last forty years."

Postscript: As an emergency precaution during the COVID-19 pandemic, Henry D. Burton was released on parole to live with his brother on March 5, 2020. "I look forward to this new journey," he wrote in his final letter to me. "This is the first time since Vietnam, I will start a future with a right mind and heart."

Oral histories provide a unique perspective into the lasting effects of war. Following the American War in Vietnam, oral historians published a plethora

FIGURE 2. Photo of
Henry D. Burton, ca. 1967,
courtesy of Burton.

of accounts of Vietnam veterans, providing an intimate glimpse into life on the
front lines. However, many of these compilations focus exclusively on battle
experiences and conclude with the veterans' homecoming.[3] These temporal
constraints limit our imagination to the possible ways oral history can be used
to historicize traumatic experiences, analyze collective memory, and study the
enduring consequences of war. Through oral history, this chapter documents the
reintegration experiences of disabled combat veterans during the Vietnam era,
analyzing the effects of military-related traumas on the lives of Black veterans
over several decades to understand why so many went to prison.

Henry Burton's oral history reveals one of the many ways that "undesirables" were administratively discharged from the military during the Vietnam
War and then treated as "less than" veterans. In chapter 1, I show how disability
is a social construct that has been determined in discriminatory ways by the
military and VA, causing lasting harm, especially on Black Vietnam veterans,
by denying much needed compensation, acknowledgment, and benefits for
service-connected disabilities. In the Vietnam War era, service members were
punished unfairly with less-than-honorable discharges, for sometimes petty
offenses or misconduct, and then subsequently kicked out of the military. The

military justice system also wielded considerable power with biased policies that disproportionately and more severely punished Black soldiers and people with disabilities. A misconduct discharge excludes former service members from veteran status and all the care and benefits that come with it. A DD 214, a certificate of release or discharge from the military, also contains codes that identify discharge status, a permanent record that could affect employment opportunities and stigmatize veterans long after military service.

Veteranhood in the United States is not simply a marker of social identity; it's a classification determined by the legal system and defined by the service record of military personnel, excluding some from its social and economic entitlements. During the Vietnam War, there were (and still are) five categories of offenses from which service members were disqualified from veterans benefits.[4] Among these were high crimes against the state—mutiny or spying—as well as "conscientious objectors who refused to perform duty, wear the uniform, comply with lawful orders."[5] It also included vaguely defined crimes such as "an offense involving moral turpitude" and "certain homosexual acts." Discharges with a statutory bar, rendering them ineligible for benefits, also included court-martial discharges, desertion, absence without official leave, and resignation for "good of service," a so-called "undesirable discharge." Between 1966 and 1969, the military issued only a couple hundred administrative discharges per year. But during the Nixon administration, undesirable discharges multiplied exponentially—6,911 in 1970, more than 12,000 in 1971, and more than 25,000 in 1972—tapering off as US forces withdrew from Vietnam in 1973.[6] Not coincidently, the increase of less-than-honorable discharges parallels the rise of Black resistance, the GI antiwar movement, and the "collapse" of the Army in Vietnam.

The military justice system used less-than-honorable discharges as a plea deal for members seeking to avoid courts-martial and bad-conduct discharges. In the Vietnam War, soldiers would accept an undesirable discharge to avoid criminal prosecution or get out of combat without usually realizing the lifetime consequences of "bad paper." The military then shifted the burden of care onto the civilian health-care market rather than the Department of Defense or Veterans Administration. Today, some veterans with other-than-honorable discharges may still receive VA care for the limited purpose of treating service-connected injuries, but those reforms are the result of several decades of veterans' activism since the Vietnam War.

Veterans kicked out of the military with less-than-honorable discharges often dealt with mental health problems without access to services, and although there were procedures to appeal discharge status, it took access to resources, time, and knowledge of the system to upgrade a discharge, privileging certain groups of veterans and preventing others. As such, most less-than-honorable discharges have never been upgraded. Before 2013, Discharge Review Boards granted only 3.7 percent of petitions.[7] In 2014, the "Hagel Memo" initiated reforms to the process, giving "liberal consideration" to "bad paper" veterans with PTSD and related behavioral issues.[8] These reforms were spearheaded by NABVets (National Association for Black Veterans) and the Vietnam Veterans of America, which has lobbied and petitioned for clemency to bad-paper veterans since the Carter administration. But for many veterans—during the forty-year period between the end of the war and the 2014 reforms—they faced severe consequences for less-than-honorable discharges, without access to care, entitlements, or benefits of veteran status. Without governmental support or VA care, tens of thousands of Vietnam veterans were incarcerated after the war, as the United States enacted harsh carceral punishment.[9]

In the 1960s and '70s, fear of violent crime drove up excessively long "life sentences" and reinforced structural racial inequality. Jonathan Simon argues that this fear of violence led to the expansion of prison sentences for drugs and nonviolent crime as well as violent crimes.[10] Much of the scholarship on mass incarceration, and efforts to reform the justice system, focus on drug-related crimes. But most veterans in prison were charged with acts of violence and served life sentences, according to a 1978 Department of Justice survey of sixty thousand veterans in prison. They were also more likely to have less-than-honorable discharges.[11] To understand these differences, this first chapter focuses on the historical and social conditions in which Vietnam veterans committed violent crimes and served excessive time in prison after the war.

Although they faced all the common problems of the Vietnam War generation, Black veterans were often excluded from conceptions of disabilities (seen and unseen) and denied veteran status. Less-than-honorable discharges operated in the military justice system as administrative punishment that denied claims of service-connected disability and veterans benefits. In the Vietnam War era, Black men were disproportionately punished in the military and beyond, given less-than-honorable discharges, and consequentially were more likely to go to prison afterward. Like generations before them, Black men joined or were drafted into the military, expecting opportunities of social advancement, job training, and the privileged status of American military veteran. Instead, many returned to the United States, marginalized in their communities, discriminated against, and, in severe cases, institutionalized by the state.

THE HISTORIC ROOTS OF MILITARY INJUSTICES

The disproportionate incarceration of African American veterans is rooted in the deeper history of institutional discrimination of Black families by the federal government, through the military justice system and the Veterans Administration. The Federal Housing Administration (FHA) and the VA excluded African Americans from good housing during the second wave of the Great Migration.[12] While the GI Bill built middle-class white America, the exclusion of Black World War II veterans perpetuated intergenerational wealth inequality and urban poverty. To be sure, a number of Black World War II veterans attended historically Black colleges and universities and advocated for fair and equal access to veterans' benefits.[13] Despite these limited advances, more often than not, African American families were rejected from government-backed mortgages and denied access to educational opportunities afforded to white families. During the postwar period, the federal government also expanded structural racism and segregation in the United States.[14] By 1965, over-policing, redlining, and unemployment created the conditions for social unrest, protests, and rebellion in cities on the West Coast and Midwest.[15] During the Vietnam War era, income inequality, racial discrimination, and state-sponsored segregation led to high unemployment and violent crime rates among African American men in urban cities.[16]

When these underlying tensions erupted into violence in Watts, California, in the summer of 1965, the Johnson administration began to blame the root cause of violence on the matriarchal family model of Black families, drawing from the work of Daniel Patrick Moynihan's 1965 report, *The Negro Family*. In the absence of strong men, Moynihan believed, African Americans were more likely to be unemployed and commit crime. The military would supposedly provide the model of patriarchy denied to young Black men, while providing technical skills, job training, and educational opportunities.[17] Moynihan proposed that the military lower its entrance standards, a recommendation that President Johnson must have thought would help solve the double-edged problem of racial unrest in the United States and the need for more American bodies in Vietnam. This logic, however, was deeply flawed, as it stemmed from a white supremacist school of thought that explained disproportionate crime rates through racialized theories, arguing that Black men were criminal by nature.

In actuality, the high crime rates among Black men were the result of at least a century of inequality in the legal system. After Reconstruction, southern states passed Black Codes that targeted formerly enslaved people, made it a crime to be unemployed, and severely punished petty crimes such as stealing chickens or vagrancy. Arrests soared, and the planter class profited. The state would auction convicted people to the highest bidders, like Nathan Bedford Forrest, former slave-trading oligarch, notorious traitor and murderer, and grand wizard of the Klan. Then convicts were leased to former slave owners and forced to work on plantations. Southern states exploited a loophole in the Thirteenth Amendment and practically overruled emancipation. This generation of freedmen and -women were entrapped in a state of unfreedom and usually worked to death. The convict-leasing system generated a perpetual demand for more convictions and new sources of labor. By the 1890 US Census, statistical evidence indicated that African Americans constituted 12 percent of the population of the United States but made up 30 percent of the prison populations.[18] Taken out of historical and social context of the Jim Crow legal system, statistics on Black criminality created the ideological justifications that fueled the rise of mass incarceration in the United States in the twentieth century.[19]

In the same vein, the Army channeled poor Black men into its ranks to meet the manpower needs of the Vietnam War, justifying it as a Great Society program. In 1965, as draft quotas soared, the military began lowering standards. Through Project 100,000, Secretary of Defense Robert McNamara led efforts to recruit more economically and educationally disadvantaged men, believing, like Moynihan, that the Army would provide training and job skills to poor Black men and help them avoid crime. From 1966 to 1971, more than four hundred thousand men served in Army and Marine combat units in Vietnam under Project 100,000. Many of the recruits were semiliterate Black men, mostly from the South. As a result of their lower test scores, African Americans were disproportionately assigned to combat units and in 1965–66 were twice as likely as whites to die on the battlefields of Vietnam. In 1968, Black men made up only 8 percent of military personnel, but 16.3 percent of combat troops in Vietnam were Black. Despite the neoliberal rhetoric, the military did not provide much job training or educational opportunities in Vietnam.[20] Tragically, many of the men never survived to see those promises broken.

Institutional racism led to excessively high casualty rates and injuries.[21] The NAACP decried the system that endangered Black lives, arguing that white soldiers were given exemptions and rear-echelon assignments as "'a bonus for growing up white.'"[22] The military also incentivized poor people to serve in combat roles, paying them a fifty-five-dollar monthly bonus, which many soldiers sent back stateside to help their struggling families.[23] In the face of rampant inequality and high unemployment rates in the States, many Black men faced the uncertainty of deployment and risks of death in Vietnam for the steady monthly income and the promise of equal opportunity.

During the early years of the American involvement in Vietnam, most civil rights organizations and their leaders still considered the military one of the few American institutions of racial equality, an opportunity for social mobility, job training, and equal citizenship. Black Power movement leaders like Robert F. Williams and Malcolm X had denounced the war in Vietnam and Black support for it early on. Yet many others still supported the Johnson administration, especially since it had ushered in the 1964 Civil Rights Act. Three days after the 1965 Voting Right Act, however, an African American Navy veteran named Sammy Younge Jr. was shot and killed in Alabama for attempting to use a segregated restroom. This incident sparked a wave of protests, and John Lewis, on behalf of the Student Non-Violent Coordinating Committee (SNCC), spoke out publicly against the Vietnam War.[24] Privately, Dr. King also condemned the war, but he remained hesitant to speak out, fearing it would alienate President Johnson and derail progress through the Great Society programs.

As the death tolls rose, civil rights leaders became increasingly critical of the war. In 1967, Dr. Martin Luther King Jr. broke his silence on Vietnam, highlighting the disasters of Project 100,000. "There was a real promise of hope for the poor—both Black and White—through the poverty program. . . . experiments, hopes, new beginnings," declared Dr. King. Then, "I watched the program broken and eviscerated, as if it were some idle political plaything of a society gone mad on war."[25] Dr. King increasingly saw the limitations of the war on poverty programs that, by then, included the criminalization of poor people, the turn to carceral punishment that followed urban rebellions, and the disinvestment of social welfare to pay for the Vietnam War.[26] As civil rights leaders combined forces with the antiwar movement, Black soldiers in Vietnam also resisted the war but were disproportionately punished for misconduct.

MILITARY-CARCERAL PUNISHMENT

African Americans in Vietnam fought alongside white soldiers in the "bush" but often faced overt racism in the rear, where some white soldiers proudly displayed Confederate flags. Beyond individual acts of prejudice, Black troops experienced institutional racism in Vietnam. Racial divisions were palpable. Many took notice that Black soldiers seemed to get more dangerous assignments, such as walking point. Herman Graham III writes, "Some outspoken African Americans believed that their white superiors gave them hazardous assignments because they equated blacks' complaints about discrimination with racial militancy. Others felt that they were more likely to receive dangerous assignments whether they voiced radical views or kept their politics to themselves."[27] The visible disparity between the number of white and African American officers made these beliefs only more widespread and potentially volatile.[28] In these times, Black people turned to one another in solidarity.

Black resistance took a variety of forms in the Vietnam War, as soldiers found new ways to express a more militant Black manhood: elaborate handshakes, growing out hair, coded language, music, art, and clothing, which white officers resented.[29] Clarence Fitch said, "We were growing Afros, expressing ourselves through ritualistic handshakes, black power handshakes, African beads, hanging around in cliques, trying to eat up as much of the black music as we could get our hands on. We kind of segregated ourselves; we didn't want to integrate into what we considered a white man's war."[30] These expressions violated the Uniform Code of Military Justice. Few in the field cared, but when infantrymen returned to rear-echelon areas, they came into conflict with white commissioned officers and career soldiers (known as lifers), who were offended by the apparently cavalier attitudes and general disregard for military decorum. As a result, Black soldiers were reprimanded for breaking arbitrary rules, leading to resentment and downright hostility. By the time Dr. King had been assassinated, racial conflict in Vietnam erupted, and military jails and brigs became breeding grounds for violence.

Compared to whites, Black soldiers were more likely to be court-martialed and receive longer sentences, so the percentage of military prison populations were disproportionately Black throughout the war.[31] Nicknamed LBJ, Long Binh Jail, on the outskirts of Saigon, exploded in violence in August 1968, mirroring the unrest and rebellions in cities across the United States that summer. Although African Americans made up just 11 percent of troops in Vietnam, Long Binh Jail was filled with more than 50 percent Black soldiers. Greg Payton admitted, "I had three courts-martial, and I went to the stockade [at Long Binh Jail], and it was all these black people."[32] The racial disparities were abundantly obvious to Black soldiers incarcerated, and many rebelled against the injustices. "I've never been as violent as I was in Vietnam," confesses Payton. "There was a lot of rage; it just began to build and build. I did so many things that were unnecessary and hurt some people" he says regretfully. "It wasn't necessarily their fault." He reflects, "Today I work on not becoming violent; I'm scared of violence."[33]

As public support for the war plummeted, incidents of fragging, combat refusal, and AWOL escalated. Soldiers deserted in record numbers.[34] These acts of resistance disgraced the Army's reputation. Fragging (the killing of officers) undermined military authority and the functionality of the command structure.[35] Soldiers usually only targeted officers who were clearly prejudiced, "gung-ho," and inexperienced, or who got soldiers needlessly killed. But the threat of fragging and the rumors around it limited the Army's capabilities of fighting the war indefinitely. Arguably, GI resistance in Vietnam hastened the withdrawal of American forces and helped bring the war to an end. Managing the tarnished image of the US Army, the Nixon administration abandoned the draft and established an all-volunteer Army, while still at war in Vietnam.[36]

As the Army initiated these reforms, it sought novel and more sophisticated ways to punish soldiers and kick them out with less-than-honorable discharges. Just as the Army had engaged in elaborate efforts of social engineering to fills the ranks, it developed tactics to rid itself of "lower-quality troops," code words for African Americans drafted under Project 100,000. The so-called crisis of quality became a watershed moment in the history of the all-volunteer force. The Army relied on aptitude tests to gauge recruits, and it had extensively studied the effectiveness of troops with low aptitude. Army leadership "was frustrated by the use of the military as an engine of social welfare and it was highly aware of the problem of race," writes historian Beth Bailey.[37] Addressing the interrelated problem of race and resistance, the Army employed an arsenal of punitive discharges to purge the military of "undesirables." Avoiding the process and paperwork of a court-martial and dishonorable discharge, the military justice system could issue less-than-honorable and administrative discharges quite efficiently. As a result, African Americans were more likely to be punished and discharged from the Army without benefits.[38] The Defense Manpower Center files on Project 100,000 did not record information on punitive discharges, but according to a congressional hearing on the *Readjustment of Project 100,000 Veterans*, based on the limited data collected, the "new recruits" were administratively disciplined 75 percent more and court-martialed 50 percent more often than other groups. "Less-than-honorable" discharges not only disqualified veterans from veterans' benefits and disability rights, but they carried a lifelong stigma that could prevent gainful employment and access to higher education.[39]

To avoid a court-martial or dishonorable discharge, many soldiers readily took a less-than-honorable discharge to get out of the field, but, at the time, few understood its long-term consequences. Historian James Westheider notes that African Americans received a disproportionate number of less-than-honorable discharges, but the "problem was not that blacks were less suited than whites for military life or more inclined to criminal activities."[40] Rather, the policies were unfairly applied in these cases. In 1972, the Department of Defense concluded that "in all services, blacks received a lower proportion of honorable discharges" compared to "whites with the same educational levels and aptitude."[41] In the civilian job market, less-than-honorable discharges came up on background checks and stigmatized veterans. Thus, the stated goals of Project 100,000 were completely abandoned under Nixon's administration, and those who believed the military would lead to job opportunities were gravely disillusioned by the war's end. Only 23 percent went to college under the GI Bill.[42] A congressional hearing in 1990 raised unresolved questions about how many Project 100,000 veterans were incarcerated. "I have no information on that," answered Dr. Janice Laurence, a research scientist who had conducted a years-long study. She speculated that they could not locate many of the surviving Project 100,000 veterans because they were presumably in prison.[43]

In punishing soldiers with less-than-honorable discharges for behavioral problems, the military denied VA benefits to veterans with disabilities. As Veteran Affairs addressed a massive increase of casualties during the Vietnam

War, disabled veterans were caught up in a bureaucratic crisis. Advancements in flight and medical technology resulted in a substantial increase of disabled veterans during the Vietnam War. In the Second World War, soldiers could expect to wait an hour between being wounded and receiving medical aid at a station. In Vietnam, medical evacuation helicopters reduced the average to fifteen minutes.[44] The Vietnam War produced a greater "wounded-to-killed ratio than any previous war."[45] But, as a result, disabled Vietnam veterans survived with debilitating and often emasculating wounds.

According to a Senate hearing on the readjustment of Vietnam veterans, nearly four hundred thousand disabled Vietnam veterans were discharged; 31 percent were physically disabled with bone and joint disease, and 18 percent were amputees.[46] These men overwhelmed the VA hospitals. Among Vietnam veterans, the VA had such a bad reputation for inadequate care that some vets avoided the VA entirely. Others, lacking disability benefits, never had the option to seek treatment. Unable to afford private doctors, many Vietnam veterans self-medicated with alcohol and drugs.[47] Dealing with a combination of physical, psychiatric, social, and behavioral problems, disabled Vietnam veterans were particularly vulnerable to the legal system. In 1976, the VA conducted a survey involving forty-four thousand people incarcerated at 325 prisons, finding that a quarter were veterans, and half of the incarcerated veterans were Black.[48]

The unpublished memoir of Louis Charles McNair illustrates the combined effects of military-related trauma, discriminatory punishment, and racial exclusion of veterans from categories of disability. "I was your average Black teenager from the sixties—rebellious and full of wonder," McNair wrote.[49] "I was heading for trouble." McNair was drafted into the US Army in March 1969. He heard stories about military life from family members who had served in World War II and Korea. But the discipline and lifestyle he encountered at Fort Polk, Louisiana, caused him great "anxiety," and he had difficulty adjusting. "Running, harassment, push-ups" served to build unity and discipline among fresh recruits, and eventually he adapted. McNair went to "Tigerland"—a nickname for Fort Polk, Louisiana, where he trained in guerrilla warfare. "The days got longer, the training got more intense, and the drill sergeants got meaner—I loved it!" McNair even signed up for Airborne training. He recalled, "After we earned our jump wings, we knew we were the toughest guys in uniform." He volunteered for Vietnam. But before shipping out, McNair went AWOL for twenty-eight days to spend time with his infant son.

When he arrived in Vietnam, McNair was mystified by the people. He watched them carry bags of rice in "perfect rhythm." He wrote, "I was in awe of the beauty of the country and the people were mysterious." His fascination quickly turned to suspicion. "I remember the stare that some of the older people would give you: 'Go home. You don't belong here,'" he imagined them thinking. "'You don't live here. We will kill you if we can, and you don't know who we are—but you will learn and you will leave.'"

Louis McNair recounted his first encounter with death. On a search-and-destroy mission, "I was very tired, physically and mentally." He closed his eyes for a moment. Suddenly, he awoke to a sound and reached for his M-16. The men opened fire. Afterward, "we surveyed the damage—lying in the stream is a young boy," fifteen years old, he guessed. "Dead as hell." The soldiers then used the corpse to set an ambush. When the enemy came back to retrieve the body, a claymore mine exploded, killing three more. "Instant death," McNair wrote. "Their bodies were blackened, twisted, and shredded limbs." "Then we left," he said frankly. "That's how we operated until I began to see that we were the bad guys," reflected McNair. "These people were defending their homelands, and we were destroying it."

The sudden experience of violence, death, and the killing of civilians can cause a form of trauma that psychiatrists call moral injury.[50] Moral injury is a "betrayal of what's right" by someone in a position of authority in a high-stakes situation.[51] It can happen when someone witnesses or participates in a violent act that violates a core moral belief or identity.[52] In some ways, moral injury shares distinct symptoms with a disorder known as post-Vietnam syndrome. In 1973, psychiatrist Chaim F. Shatan reported that symptoms were "delayed in onset," a key characteristic of post-traumatic stress disorder. Post-Vietnam syndrome, however, also involved betrayal, guilt, feeling scapegoated, alienation, rage, psychic numbing, and delayed massive trauma. "We know very little about the enduring moral aftermath," noted Dr. Shatan in 1973.[53] More recently, mental health professionals think of moral injury as distinct from PTSD, but it describes a timeless wound of war that soldiers have written about over the ages.[54] Veterans who experience moral injury are likely to be "homeless, unemployed, poor, divorced, and imprisoned."[55]

The deaths of McNair's friends and the unjustifiable violence he perpetrated were irreconcilable with his moral beliefs and reason for fighting, leading to behavioral problems, combat avoidance, and involvement in the military justice system. His memoir mentioned the deaths of two friends by name: Johnnie Allen and Sherman Poindexter. "I learned everything I knew about surviving those nightmarish conditions from them." They were killed in an ambush, and "I was never the same after that." Search-and-destroy missions often ended in ambush, causing American troops to feel like bait. After the ambush, McNair went AWOL. He sneaked off base for "marijuana, beer, and women" as a temporary escape from the war. But, as Jonathan Shay writes, "veterans carry the weight of friends' death *in* war and *after* war."[56]

Louis McNair served in Vietnam from January 24 to September 28, 1970. After eight months of combat, he received an "undesirable discharge" for "the good of the service," his DD 214 describing him as "unfit for military duty." The consequences of "bad paper" from a "bad war" felt especially stigmatizing to Vietnam veterans. Over the next three decades, McNair appealed to have his discharge upgraded in order to seek treatment for combat-related post-traumatic stress disorder. "I fought my undesirable discharge from November 1970 until I was finally able to win my case. In 2006, I received an honorable discharge." After thirty-six years, McNair was diagnosed with PTSD and finally awarded 70 percent service-connected disability. In 2012, the VA granted him 100 percent disability benefits. He earned a college degree forty-five years after the war.

INCARCERATED VETERANS ORGANIZING

Wallace Terry's *Bloods: Black Veterans of the Vietnam War, an Oral History* remains the most cited oral history collection of African American Vietnam veterans. Even today, *Bloods* still has enormous influence on Vietnam War scholarship and popular memory, inspiring the title of Spike Lee's *Da Five Bloods* (2020). This collection is also the first location of incarcerated Vietnam veterans in historiography.[57] Haywood "the Kid" Kirkland's story from *Bloods* dramatically illustrates the effects of combat trauma, disability, racism, economic inequality, crime, and incarceration. Kirkland changed his name while incarcerated, renouncing what he considered to be a slave name, so I will now refer to him as Ari Sesu Merretazon, meaning "guardian servant chosen to do the will of the creator." His story was imaginatively rewritten by the Hughes brothers and adapted in the 1995 film *Dead Presidents* (featuring Larenz Tate, Chris Rock, and Keith David). The film depicts horrific and grotesque scenes of war violence, including the disembowelment and castration of a fellow American, but the film climaxes when a group of Black veterans rob an armored vehicle. Unfortunately, *Dead Presidents* does not show the most important aspects of Merretazon's experiences: how he became radicalized during the war, the birth of his political consciousness, and his organizing incarcerated veterans after the robbery.[58]

During the war, Merretazon grew increasingly militant, making connections between Vietnam's fight for independence and the freedom struggles of Black people in the United States. In 1967, he was compelled into military service by the draft and served in a reconnaissance platoon in South Vietnam where he carried out search-and-destroy missions. In *Bloods*, he recounts witnessing atrocities, torture, rape, and burning down villages with women and children inside their homes.[59] More than forty years later, Merretazon was officially diagnosed with PTSD attributed to the anger, betrayal, and resentment of "fighting two wars while in Vietnam, one against the Viet Cong and North Vietnamese and the other against racism in the military."[60] After the war, Black consciousness became infused with traumatic memories and readjustment difficulties.

Coming home from war, Merretazon returned to a nation afire in the summer of 1968. "They killed Dr. King just before I came home. I felt used."[61] Dr. Martin Luther King Jr., an icon of nonviolence, was murdered while in Memphis supporting striking sanitation workers as part of the Poor People's Campaign. Dispirited and disillusioned, Merretazon felt betrayed by his government for sending him to war in Vietnam while the fight for civil rights continued in his own community. "It was very traumatic for me," he remembers. "When I came home D.C. was on fire. . . . I couldn't handle it."[62] For the first sixty days, he stayed at his parents' home and isolated. "I was still dealing with Vietnam in my head."[63] The psychiatric effects of the war were combined with the ideological shock of fighting for a nation that treated Black veterans as "less-than" citizens.

In Vietnam, Merretazon would talk with other Black soldiers about plans if they ever made it back to the world. "We were going to come back and help our communities out," he said. "When I saw an opportunity to do that, that's what I did. I got back involved in my community and the culture of being a descendant of African slaves in the United States."[64] Merretazon had been working at the post office and that's how he learned about how the Treasury

Department incinerated old currency. In December 1969, Merretazon robbed an armored truck delivering $382,000 in cash en route to be destroyed. After the robbery, he donated stolen money to impoverished families, bought food and toys for children, and donated supplies to the student medical center at Howard University. "I saw it as an act of repair," Merretazon reflects.[65] Today, he is an activist for reparations to the descendants of enslaved Africans in the United States.

The robbery of an armored car was sensationalized in the media, but the actual crime was not uncommon. In the 1970s, the most common offense among Vietnam veterans in prison (like Henry D. Burton) was armed robbery. One report showed that 50 percent of Vietnam veterans in prison committed armed robbery or drug-related crimes, or both.[66] For context, the end of the Vietnam War also coincided with a global economic recession, when the unemployment rate of African American veterans was three times higher than average.[67]

Even though no one had been physically harmed during the mail-truck robbery, Merretazon was sentenced to ten to thirty years in federal prison. A wounded World War II combat veteran, the judge showed little sympathy toward a Black Vietnam vet who broke the law.[68] Merretazon explained that there was a generational and racial divide. "The Vietnam War was unlike any other war," he says. "There was no assistance for us when we came home. We had to advocate" for the recognition of combat-stress reaction, post-Vietnam Syndrome, and post-traumatic stress disorder to be recognized in the *Diagnostic Statistical Manual-III* in 1980. "That was a big success for us Vietnam veterans," he states. However, at the time, the court did not take combat stress into consideration in sentencing. Making an example out of Merretazon, the judge condemned him to life in prison for armed robbery.[69] But the war and the heist are only half of the story.[70]

While incarcerated at the infamous Lorton Reformatory—a federal prison with a 99 percent Black population[71]—Ari Sesu Merretazon started organizing and advocating for VA benefits for incarcerated veterans. That was the first time he began to identify as a veteran.[72] He realized the power of his veteran status and that he could effect change from inside the prison. At the time, the VA "wasn't coming down to the prisons," he realized.[73] Merretazon was absolutely correct. A Government Accountability Office (GAO) study from December 1974 indicated there were no "systematic efforts to reach veterans in penal institutions."[74] With other incarcerated veterans, Merretazon set up the Incarcerated Veterans Assistance Organization. He recounts, "We went all way to the White House."[75] Staffed entirely by incarcerated veterans, the Incarcerated Veterans Assistance Office was approved by prison officials at Lorton as a self-help and rehabilitation program. Their efforts eventually gained national attention. "News got out that veterans were organizing in Lorton reformatory. That hit the *Washington Post*" and eventually reached the desk of the Oval Office.[76] In March 1975, the *Washington Post* ran a story on the Incarcerated Veterans Assistance Organization, highlighting its efforts to obtain educational and health benefits through the VA, file for discharge upgrades, lobby Congress for legislation, and petition the president to grant clemency to "bad paper" veterans.[77]

With an introduction from a fellow Black Vietnam veteran, William Edward Lawson who was working for the White House at the time, Ari Sesu Merretazon met with President Jimmy Carter and urged the White House to address the denial of disability benefits to incarcerated veterans. On October 10, 1978, the Carter administration issued a Presidential Directive to the Bureau of Justice Statistics (then the National Criminal Justice and Statistics Service) to collect data on incarcerated veterans, pointing out the complete lack of information about veterans in prisons. In 1979, the first survey given to a sample of incarcerated veterans revealed shocking information, offering a glimpse into a pivotal moment in US military-carceral history. That year one-fourth of the prison population were military veterans, and more than 60 percent of them were Vietnam era.[78] In 1975, Merretazon petitioned the appeals judge for a reduced sentence, and in recognition of an error in the life sentence and the work he had done advocating for incarcerated veterans, he was released after only five and a half years.

Over the next four years, Merretazon collected data on incarcerated veterans across the United States with key support from Congressman Ronald V. Dellums (a vocal critic of the Vietnam War, civil rights activist, member of the Congressional Black Caucus, and the first African American to serve on the Armed Services Committee).[79] "We were able to move in and out of prisons," explains Merretazon. "People from the president's office came down to visit us. That gave us a lot more protection and freedom to move around within the administrative processes and procedures of the prisons."[80] With support at the highest levels of political office, Merretazon began building a network of incarcerated veterans across the United States and gathering evidence that he would present to Congress in 1979. During that time, they discovered at "almost every prison in the United States, they had like 20–25 percent Vietnam veterans."[81] Merretazon engaged with prison administrators at other institutions and attempted to replicate the model first established at Lorton Reformatory with VA offices staffed entirely by incarcerated veterans. He would advocate for this model before Congress as a way to redress the inadequate VA outreach efforts to prisons at the time. He testified, "Not until incarcerated Veterans' Affairs offices are established within prisons, staffed and operated by incarcerated veterans . . . will the little assistance that the Veterans' Affairs and penal officials are giving to incarcerated veterans be of any significance."[82]

In July 1979, Congress held hearings on incarcerated Vietnam veterans before the Committee on Veterans' Affairs, highlighting key issues and the structural barriers they faced.[83] After the 1974 GAO study concluded that there were no systemic VA outreach efforts to prisons, the VA adopted a policy to conduct semiannual outreach efforts to every federal and state prison in the United States.[84] A major task before the congressional committee was to evaluate the effectiveness of the VA outreach programs since the reforms. The results of the 1979 study, titled "Veterans Administration Outreach Program for Incarcerated Veterans," revealed inconsistent efforts and regional disparities. Fundamentally flawed, the guidelines put the responsibility for outreach and awareness programs in the hands of the prison administrators. One of four wardens in this investigation downright opposed the VA providing counseling services to incarcerated veterans.[85] The VA had not visited some penal facilities at all, "because no requests were made from institutions served on an on-call basis" or because officials believed few veterans were incarcerated. The report concluded that VA prison outreach was a "low priority."

Available data on incarcerated veterans collected under the Carter administration outlined the long-term effects of racial disparities in military punishment during the Vietnam War. Based on GAO studies, VA records, and direct access to prisons, Ari Sesu Merretazon estimated, "We got over 500,000 Vietnam era veterans in prison, jail, on parole, or awaiting sentence. . . . Over half of them are Black."[86] A GAO report estimated that sixty thousand veterans were incarcerated in federal and state prisons and that 50 percent incarcerated in federal prison were convicted of armed robbery or drug-related offenses.[87] Chairman of the Committee on Veterans' Affairs Alan Cranston noted that "educationally disadvantaged veterans constitute a large segment of the incarcerated prison population."[88] Many veterans also believed they automatically lost disability benefits in prison. An estimated 40 percent were ineligible due to less-than-honorable discharge status.[89] According to the Government Accounting Office, forty-four thousand incarcerated veterans were denied disability benefits in 1975.[90] By 1978, another study found that more than half of incarcerated veterans had received less-than-honorable discharges and that half of them were Black Vietnam veterans.[91]

Many veterans, like Henry D. Burton, did not know how to file disability claims or seek VA services while in prison. In April 1979, the Veterans Administration printed pamphlets to make veterans in prison and on parole aware of VA benefits and how to file claims.[92] It remains unclear how widely distributed these pamphlets were or how effective they were in providing VA care to incarcerated veterans, especially to those without access to legal services, knowledge of institutional bureaucracies, and experience organizing. But nonetheless, using the federal government to provide health care, education, and disability benefits to incarcerated people was a powerful and historically important precedent in criminal justice reform. Representative Charles Rangel (D-NY), a founding member of the Congressional Black Caucus and Army veteran of the Korean War, envisioned a more rehabilitative form of justice for veterans: "VA benefits are an untouched resource in our efforts to rehabilitate prisoners," he stated in 1975.[93] More than thirty years later, the first Veterans Treatment Court in Buffalo, New York, successfully connected veterans in the criminal justice system directly to the VA from within a courtroom, proving Rangel's insight revelatory.

Ultimately, the 1979 congressional hearings spurred the VA to identify incarcerated veterans and help them apply for disability benefits.[94] The total number of incarcerated veterans was unknown, however, making it impossible to identify and connect all, or even most, veterans in prison to VA services at that time, even with a supportive presidential administration. During the hearing, VA director of the Veterans Assistance Service James J. Cox stated that the prison outreach efforts, as limited as they were, would be short-lived. Reduction of VA resources and manpower was "going to make it very difficult to maintain that prison visitation schedule. . . . [W]e can struggle through 1980. Beyond that, I would be hesitant to predict."[95] These hearings reveal how inherently dependent VA outreach efforts to prisons were on politics. In fact, after the Second World War, the VA had a well-established outreach program to prisons until the early 1960s. As the Vietnam War escalated, funding was cut from the VA, and representatives were reassigned to military hospitals to deal with the influx of casualties. Through the petitioning and organizing efforts of incarcerated Vietnam veterans like Merretazon, the VA reinvigorated its prison outreach services but only temporarily.

In 1979, incarcerated veterans stood for a brief moment in the sun, then receded into the shadows of the rising carceral state and faded in memory of the Vietnam War. When Ronald Reagan ascended to the presidency, he made massive cuts to federal spending to social programs, reducing the VA budget by $700 million in the first year of his presidency, and those cuts continued throughout the 1980s.[96] After 1979, the number of incarcerated veterans known in US prisons more than doubled, from an estimated 65,500 to 154,600 in 1985.[97] Despite this backlash, there were at least two major lasting results from the early efforts of incarcerated veterans' organizing: the Department of Justice continued to collect data on incarcerated veterans, publishing its surveys with veterans in prison and jail in 1981, 2000, 2007, 2015, and 2020; and in 1979, the federal government established a nationwide system of outreach and counseling centers. At Vet Centers, veterans would engage in group counseling sessions with other veterans and could seek treatment regardless of discharge status—a notable victory for activists against less-than-honorable discharges.

After testifying before Congress, Merretazon moved to Little Rock, Arkansas, to help start a Vet Center. He earned a certificate as a legal technician from Antioch School of Law in 1980 and decided to take his knowledge where it would be more useful. He explains, "I didn't want to stay in the major cities because they have so much more resources. I felt that based on my experience inside of prisons . . . that the worst conditions for veterans to exist was in the Southern prisons: Angola, Arkansas State Prison, and Parchman Farm in Mississippi."[98] But he came into conflict with a psychiatrist at the Little Rock Vet Center. Merretazon laments, "I went there with expectations that I could continue to work with veterans in prison. . . . He refused to allow me to go into the prisons and assist veterans."[99] In 1984, Merretazon helped revitalize the *Arkansas State Press*, a historically Black newspaper that had not published an issue since 1959. At the newspaper, he worked with Daisy Bates, a longtime serving president of the Arkansas chapter of the NAACP, who helped integrate Little Rock Central High. *JET* magazine ran a featured story on Merretazon and Daisy Bates in April 1984.[100] Throughout his life, Merretazon has continued to be an advocate for incarcerated veterans, education, and reparations. His organizing undoubtedly played a pivotal role in incarcerated veterans becoming a priority for national veterans organizations. Beginning in the summer of 1979, the Vietnam Veterans of America, a national organization made up of and dedicated to the needs of Vietnam veterans, would take the lead on raising awareness to post-traumatic stress disorder, and in 1983, it established a legal-services program for veterans in the criminal justice system.

THE OFFICIAL DIAGNOSIS AND STATE DENIAL OF PTSD

The most striking difference between veterans and civilians in prisons is that most incarcerated veterans committed violent crimes. In 1981, the Department of Justice published its first study on veterans in prison and jail, which found that Vietnam veterans were more likely to be convicted of a violent felony and to serve excessively long sentences.[101] After the Vietnam War, the imprisonment rates of veterans increased over the next four decades despite more awareness on PTSD. From 1985 to 1998, the number of incarcerated veterans rose from approximately 155,000 to 225,000.[102] In 2004, 61 percent of incarcerated

FIGURE 3. Ari Sesu Merretazon on January 2023 in his home at Wyncotte, Pennsylvania, getting ready for remote oral history interview. Photo courtesy of Merretazon.

Vietnam veterans were still serving time for violent offenses (13 percent were drug-related crimes), indicating a systemic and cultural problem that continued into the twenty-first century.[103]

In 1988, the National Vietnam Veterans Readjustment Study (NVVRS) found that thirty percent of all male Vietnam veterans who served in-country had experienced PTSD, nearly 1 million. Most significantly, the study indicated that PTSD can be lifelong. Half of the men (and one-third of the women) who reported PTSD "still have it today."[104] The NVVRS also reported that half of Vietnam veterans with PTSD had been arrested at least once, and nearly 37 percent committed at least six acts of violence in the previous year.[105] Despite this evidence and long after the American Psychiatric Association and the *Diagnostic and Statistical Manual of Mental Disorders* officially recognized post-traumatic stress disorder in 1980, court officials often refused to consider PTSD in the cases of violent crimes committed by Black Vietnam veterans.[106]

Capital punishment of Vietnam veterans with mental illness shows unequal treatment under the law, specifically regarding PTSD and violent crime. Amnesty International has documented the cases of at least nine Vietnam veterans executed by the US criminal justice system. Each one was diagnosed with post-traumatic stress disorder. Among those executed for murder were David Funchess, Manuel Babbitt, Wayne Felde, Herbert Richardson, Leonard Laws, Robert Black, Larry Johnson, Joseph Atkins, and James Johnson.[107] In one of the most horrific cases, Vietnam veteran Manny Babbit brutally murdered a seventy-eight-year-old white woman while under the influence of drugs in 1980.[108] Babbit had fought at the battle of Khe Sanh and suffered a head injury. Mistaken for dead, his body was loaded onto a helicopter full of corpses; he regained consciousness under a pile of limbs and pieces of bodies.[109] After Khe Sanh, he also suffered from severe psychiatric trauma. He spent eight months in a mental hospital where he was diagnosed with PTSD. But he never received treatment. Babbit drank alcohol and used drugs. A leading expert on PTSD testified that he had been experiencing a combat-related flashback while under the influence of hallucinogenic drugs when he killed Leah Schendel.[110] He was found guilty of capital murder by an all-white, twelve-member jury and sentenced to death. Babbit finally received a Purple Heart before dying in prison. He refused his last meal and asked that its cost be donated to homeless Vietnam vets. Fifty years and one day old, Manuel Babbit was executed by lethal injection in San Quentin, California, on May 4, 1999.

The tragic life of David Livingston Funchess underscores the discriminatory treatment of Black veterans with PTSD. As a marine in 1967, Funchess experienced intense combat in Vietnam. He served honorably and received five decorations. He was injured when a land mine detonated. Afterward, he experienced depression and mental illness. The military discharged him dishonorably. In 1982, a psychiatrist diagnosed his symptoms as post-traumatic stress disorder with chronic depression, characterizing his ailments as "massive internalized stress, which could erupt on occasion into uncontrollable outbursts of aggressive behavior." He had complex PTSD caused by combat and the murder of his brother. Funchess also used heroin to cope with symptoms, which included insomnia, nightmares, and flashbacks. According to his sisters, he dug foxholes in his yard. He "slept in cars" and resorted to petty crime. During a 1974 robbery, Funchess killed two white people. He was found guilty and sentenced to death. Funchess's lawyer later testified that he had been "unaware of the existence of PTSD and had had neither the information nor the resources" to save his life.[111] At the time, at least two other Vietnam veterans had been acquitted of murder, by employing the diagnosis of PTSD as a legal defense.[112] After the US Supreme Court voted seven to two, denying his stay of execution, David Funchess was electrocuted to death by the state of Florida in 1986.

In 1982, *Playboy* magazine published an article on incarcerated Vietnam veterans, titled "The Unrelenting Army," by Philip Caputo, a Vietnam veteran and author of *A Rumor of War*.[113] In the essay, Caputo tells the story of Wayne Robert Felde, a Vietnam veteran who suffered from post-traumatic stress disorder. In 1980, Felde was convicted of killing a police officer in Louisiana. At Felde's trial, a psychiatrist testified that the veteran was "not in touch with reality." At the trial, Felde asked for the death sentence: "'I hate everybody, I hate myself most of all,'" and "'I don't feel society needs to welcome me back. Just give me help,'" he begged. "'I'm a sick man. If society doesn't want to help me, I want to die, because death means the nightmare will be over.'"[114] His lawyer appealed the conviction but lost, and Felde's sentence was carried out at Angola state prison. A former slave plantation and convict-leasing site, Angola is notorious for its inhumane treatment of prisoners. A lawsuit in 2013 charged that Angola's death row violated the cruel and unusual punishment clause of the Eighth Amendment. During one summer, the heat index averaged above 126 degrees.[115] Alone with his thoughts, Felde was locked down twenty-three hours a day in solitary confinement without human contact, suffering from PTSD. On a concrete deathbed, he lived the remainder of his days in a sweltering hotbox, exposed to inhospitable conditions. Wayne Felde was electrocuted in Angola state prison in Louisiana on March 15, 1988.[116]

Herbert Richardson's execution is dramatically depicted in the 2019 film *Just Mercy*. He had returned from Vietnam in 1966 with severe psychiatric illness. While recovering in a veterans hospital, Richardson experienced symptoms of PTSD, including reenactments, flashbacks, and headaches related to a possible brain injury.[117] During this time, he developed a romantic attachment to a white nurse, whom he pursued back to Alabama. Delusional and wanting to be a hero, Richardson constructed a bomb and placed it on her porch. He planned to "save her, like he had saved people in Vietnam."[118] Tragically, the bomb exploded, killing a young girl and injuring another.

Richardson had been discharged from the military due to psychiatric illness and had a history of mental health disturbances. However, the Alabama court ignored Richardson's military records and dismissed post-traumatic stress disorder. The prosecution depicted him as a dangerous "outsider from New York, an evil person, and an intentional killer."[119] Richardson was convicted of capital murder by an all-white jury. His attorney never even appealed the death sentence. Bryan Stevenson, founder of the Equal Justice Initiative, filed for a stay of execution because of racial bias in the court and the failure of the defender to present any evidence of Richardson's history of military service and mental illness. Hours before the scheduled execution, the US Supreme Court denied the stay, making him the sixth person executed in Alabama since the reinstatement of the death penalty in 1976.[120] At forty-three years old, Herbert Richardson was blindfolded and shackled to an electric chair and shocked with eighteen hundred volts of electricity until pronounced dead at 12:14 a.m. on August 19, 1989.[121]

CONCLUSION

Incarcerated veterans were erased in public memory of the Vietnam War. Ironically, in the 1980s, forsaken prisoners of war, abandoned in Vietnam, became one of the most pervasive myths about the Vietnam War, but the public virtually ignored prisoners *after* war—American veterans in US jails and prisons. No credible evidence was ever uncovered to support the idea that

POWs had been abandoned in Vietnam,[122] but veterans' groups recognized the problems of incarcerated veterans and made the connection between PTSD and crime. The *VVA Veteran*, a monthly publication of Vietnam Veterans of America, distributed legal information and advice to incarcerated veterans about employing PTSD as a legal defense and proposing alternatives to punishment.[123] Vietnam veterans spearheaded efforts for gradual reform, easier access to the VA, and veterans' benefits for incarcerated veterans. But veterans, alone, could not generate systemic reforms or fix inequality in the court system, and Black veterans often faced unforgiving judges and unmoved juries.

Mass incarceration skyrocketed after the end of the Vietnam War, as thousands of veterans attempted to reintegrate and readjust to "the world." During the first ten years after the Vietnam War ended, veterans were more likely than nonveterans to be incarcerated in US prisons. In 1978, one in four prisoners in the United States were military veterans, a majority of whom were Black.[124] Many African Americans had been drafted or had volunteered to fight in the military—to prove their manhood, to earn equal treatment from white Americans, and to enjoy the economic rewards of veteran status. They had good reason to believe this. Many of their fathers, uncles, and grandfathers had encouraged them to enlist in the military, because despite the strict discipline and harsh punishment, Black men could fight for equality, earn a career, and walk with dignity, like first-class citizens.[125] In Vietnam, however, many experienced a world of moral and psychological trauma and were punished disproportionately for their behaviors and issued less-than-honorable discharges. As they reintegrated from the war, their military experiences became a handicap, not a hand up. Treated as "less-than" veterans, disabled Vietnam veterans like Henry Burton were discarded by the state, buried alive in prison, and nearly forgotten in history.

CHAPTER 2

War, Drugs, and the War on Drugs

Heroin and Vietnam Veterans during the Rise of Mass Incarceration

It is not coincidental that the jails and the army and the needle claim so many.

—JAMES BALDWIN, *No Name in the Street* (1972)

The best scale to measure the effects of war and incarceration is a lifetime. From 1959 to 1964, Haywood Fennell Sr. served in the US Army. He was influenced by a strong family legacy of military service. His uncles were Korean War vets; one retired after twenty-three years in the Air Force. Haywood joined the Army at seventeen years old, believing it was a path toward social equality and economic uplift. "Why the hell not go into the military and serve to be able to come back and get an education and own a home—why not?" he asks rhetorically. "I'm not getting here. Maybe it is true. Let me try it and see. I've seen some. My uncle did it, but my uncle is not me," he states. "I'm a generation from him. I tried it his way and it didn't work. I was exposed to a lot of covert/overt racism."[1]

While stationed in Okinawa, Fennell was attacked by American soldiers. Towns and prostitution districts outside the base were still segregated in practice. The US military exported Jim Crow to bases across the empire.[2] One night Haywood crossed the color line. "I was traumatized. I was attacked—beat up real bad in the nighttime and pissed on by my attackers," recounts Fennell with a look of shame and anger in his eyes. "When I reported it to the company commander, the first thing they told me was I was out of bounds. 'You weren't supposed to be down there in that area,'" scolded the commanding officer. "I was down by the hooches," Fennell explains, "trying to buy some sex, and that was out of bounds."

Although officially desegregated since 1948, the US military often continued to enforce color lines, and the military justice system excessively punished African Americans who crossed boundaries.[3] It also protected white perpetrators of racial and sexual violence against Asian women.[4] His assailants were not reprimanded, but Haywood Fennell Sr. experienced retaliation afterward.

The commanding officer denied his scheduled promotion. "I thought it was reprehensible." The injustice was "eye-opening."

The assault was the fulcrum point in Fennell's military career. Like his uncles, he planned to complete twenty years in the military and retire. Prior to this incident, the soldier had not gotten into any trouble in the Army. Afterward, "I was stationed right next to a morgue and was seeing body bags every day," recalls Fennell. As a distraction, he began using drugs. Heroin was available in Okinawa in the 1960s. By the time he was discharged, his drug use was habitual, and Fennell went home with more problems than he had when he first left New York City. By the time Dr. King was assassinated in April 1968, he was sitting in a jail cell.

Haywood Fennell experienced an institutional betrayal, which led to behavioral and psychiatric disorders, including what is now called "moral injury."[5] Reintegration "was very traumatic because I was unable to communicate the things that occurred over there," he recounts, "because I thought that it was so horrendous. To be beat up. Degraded. I couldn't talk to my wife. I tried to heal myself. I started using." After his discharge, the veteran "shied away from any affiliation with the military because of the shame." "I got caught up in the drug game. I tried to work, but drugs became overwhelming, so I became a full-time addict." By the mid-1960s, heroin was already readily available in New York City.[6] "The insidiousness of the drug just takes over. You have absolutely no control to the point that your freedom is in jeopardy." It destroyed his family relationships, and he decided it would be better to leave. "I was first incarcerated when I was twenty-eight years old as a direct result of my addiction," says Fennell. "It creeps in, and nothing really matters but me and the drug. The family takes second or third place. I did love my family. I do love my family. But it was up and down—jails, bails, fails for me."

Haywood Fennell Sr.'s experiences followed a pattern of what would happen to tens of thousands of other Vietnam-era veterans. From 1964 to 1968, in the four years between Fennell's military discharge date and his subsequent incarceration, heroin quickly spread in US cities and the military. In 1965 heroin use was estimated at "57,000 known addicts in the entire country, and most of these were out of sight, out of mind in black urban ghettos," writes Alfred McCoy. By 1969 the estimated number of heroin users jumped to 315,000; by 1971 it multiplied to 560,000.[7] Consequentially, the drug laws became harsher and prison sentences longer. In the twenty-year span of Fennell's incarceration, the United States embarked on a new war on drugs, undergoing an extreme social transformation in the process, what sociologists and historians call the carceral turn.[8]

Between 1968 and 1983, Haywood Fennell Sr. served time in and out of jails and prisons, caught in the revolving door of substance use, confinement, and recidivism. At Massachusetts Correctional Facility Norfolk, he formed a group of disabled veterans and then extended that group at Baystate. This group organized for disability rights and coordinated with the Disabled American Veterans (DAV). Group members developed a list of contacts, collected resources, and provided guidance as other incarcerated veterans filed for VA care and disability benefits. "There is some respect for veterans from the veterans that are correctional officers," Fennell says. "But there is no solidarity in the relationship that would put them in an advocacy position—house them by themselves" or bring in counselors who "can deal with the trauma." Carceral institutions customarily medicate prisoners instead of rehabilitating them.

After prison Fennell lived in transitional housing and homeless shelters. But finally, at age fifty-six, he stopped using heroin. For years he resented the military and wanted nothing to do with the VA until 1996, when he checked himself into a detox program.[9] "'Now, I want to live,'" Fennell told the nurse. "I went through the withdrawals and got myself thinking that I could stand on my own two feet. I didn't have anything left to lose because I had lost everything: my family; I've got a record; I've been to prisons. What else is there for me to do but to stand up? That was twenty-one years ago." He wrote his first play while living in VA detox facility.

Living in Boston today, Haywood Fennell Sr. is a writer, educator, and community activist.[10] "It took me twenty-eight years to get my college degree," he says triumphantly. He studied urban planning at UMass Boston and engages in community organizing. Fennell frequently gives lectures on African American history and literature and still visits jails and prisons to advocate for mental health and social services. Most recently, Fennell led a grassroots campaign to build a memorial in Boston for Edward O. Gourdin, an Olympic medalist, commanding officer of the 372nd Infantry Division in World War II, and first African American supreme court justice of Massachusetts.

Haywood Fennell Sr. underwent a traumatic experience that reconfigured his ideological understanding of the United States, forming political consciousness and international solidarity with victims of American wars. The immediate act of racial violence was the catalyst, but when he experienced retaliation after reporting it, the military justice system betrayed his sense of trust and nation-hood. "You have to careful about this United States of America—land of the brave and the slave," he cautions. "In other countries, they're giving food in one hand, and they're taking minerals and resources with the other hand—to strengthen us and weaken them. People don't want to accept it, but the truth will set you free." Fennell's critique of American imperialism echoes Dr. Martin Luther King Jr. when he broke his silence on the Vietnam War and spoke out against the "giant triplets of racism, extreme materialism, and militarism."[11]

In the 1967 Riverside Church speech, King worried about the long-term effects of the Vietnam War on veterans: "I am as deeply concerned about our own troops there as anything else," explaining that "what we are submitting them to in Vietnam is not simply the brutalizing process that goes on in any war. . . . We are adding cynicism to the process of death." US soldiers experience firsthand the contradictions between the rhetoric and reality of war. "Before long they must know that their government has sent them into a struggle among Vietnamese, and . . . that we are on the side of the wealthy, and the secure, while we create a hell for the poor."[12] Fennell warns of the dangers of American militarism. "They make veterans pawns. The government could decide not to build three bombers. You know how much money that is for helping veterans?" The answer is over $2 billion. Veterans of the Global War on Terror need to "know the history of how they got there," concludes Fennell. "Today, you're getting a backlash of ISIS and all these other groups that come from generations of war for oil. For the displacement of humanity. For going into other people's nations with so-called foreign aid and exploiting those people. Those things come back like a boomerang."

Over the span of a lifetime, the consequences of these wars are genera-tional. Incarcerated veterans and their families experience intergenerational harm—seismic effects on the lives of spouses, children, and grandchildren.[13] Haywood Fennell Sr. explains, "If you had 100,000 veterans from the Vietnam War era that were parents that got incarcerated, leaving the kids at home. And say they got a long stretch of ten years. Leave a kid at eight and come back at fifteen. You try to come back as a father—you're trying to reclaim the collateral damage of your being incarcerated." He thinks, "A lot of these people today in their twenties, thirties, and forties had veterans as parents and grandparents. They didn't get that wholesomeness that's needed, and that prevents them from being parents. So now, you've got these Vietnam-era veterans, their children,

FIGURE 4. Photo taken by the author on July 7, 2017, at the Mattapan branch of the Boston Public Library.

and their grandchildren caught in a cycle." Fennell's incarceration had an immeasurable impact on his family. His son, Haywood Fennell Jr., served a short prison sentence at just eighteen years old. His life was cut tragically short by complications of HIV. Fennell's daughter is a captain at Rikers Island. Their lives are caught in an undertow, pushed and pulled by the forces of the military and prison industrial complexes.

VIETNAM AND THE WAR ON DRUGS

The end of the Vietnam War marked the beginning of the war on drugs. Both wars impacted African American communities and poor people disproportionately. According to the Department of Justice, African American veterans constitute a disproportionate number of the veterans in prison and jail. Apart from violent crimes, veterans are imprisoned on drug charges more frequently than any other crime.[14] These studies also record a sharp increase in incarcerated veteran populations among Vietnam veterans. None of this is coincidental. In 1971 the war on drugs fueled the rise of mass incarceration, a consequence of harsh drugs laws, mandatory minimum prison sentences, and police surveillance that unfairly targeted Black communities. Thus, both wars entrapped a generation of Vietnam-era veterans and their families.

The infrastructure of the carceral state took shape during the Vietnam War. Great Society programs were the priority of the Johnson administration in 1965, but policymakers invested increasingly more of the national treasury maintaining the South Vietnamese government and funding the escalating war. Paradoxically, Lyndon Johnson ushered in the Voting Rights Act while also waging a new war on crime. In the political fallout from the Watts riots in 1965, the Johnson administration began redirecting funds away from the war on poverty while also lowering draft requirements.[15] As Elizabeth Hinton argues, social welfare programs started under the most significant liberal social experiments of the 1960s were used to build the modern police state.[16] These shifts in foreign and domestic policy happened synchronously.

The Nixon administration, then, disinvested from the Great Society programs and enacted legislation to make policing more militarized in predominantly Black urban areas.[17] State authorities began funneling federal funding away from community resources in order to fund police forces and build more prisons. John Ehrlichman, one of the coconspirators of the Watergate scandal and adviser to President Nixon, admitted in a 1994 interview: "The Nixon campaign in 1968, and the Nixon White House after that, had two enemies: the antiwar left and black people. . . . We knew we couldn't make it illegal to be either against the war or black, but by getting the public to associate the hippies with marijuana and blacks with heroin, and then criminalizing both heavily, we could disrupt those communities. We could arrest their leaders, raid their homes, break up their meetings, and vilify them night after night on the evening news."[18] In drugs, right-wing politicians and media found a new menace, a dog whistle coded to appeal to the so-called silent majority and reactionaries against cultural changes, racial integration, the women's rights movement, and antiwar sentiment. Black people, of course, disproportionately felt the impact of the conservative backlash.

The year 1971 is pivotal in the history of the military-carceral state. The full weight of federal, state, and local power descended on Attica prison in September 1971. The conflict between officials and prisoners at Attica had been building for years due to poor living conditions, medical neglect, racial discrimination, and officers' suspicion of militant African Americans and Puerto Ricans.[19] During the summer of 1971, prisoners at Attica grew more politically conscious, making connections between their immediate environment and the lives of poor people of color around the world. A small study group read and debated ideas about colonialism, imperialism, capitalism, and Marxism, drawing connections between the Black freedom movement and Vietnam's war for independence.[20] This moment of political awakening created solidarity across racial, class, and religious divisions. All that summer, prisoners at Attica had been demanding improvements to their living conditions. Then, on August 21, 1971, prison guards at San Quentin, California, killed George Jackson, a prison organizer, activist, and author of *Soledad Brothers*.[21] Jackson's death generated a groundswell of multiracial coalitions among prisoners across the country and led to a hunger strike at Attica.[22] A group of prisoners at Attica sent the "July Manifesto" to the governor of New York, petitioning for a number of reforms, including religious freedom, improvements in living and working conditions, access to education, and better medical care.[23] Exercising nonviolence, their demand for basic human rights was an inherently democratic process, but the authorities at Attica cracked down on the prisoners' activities, punishing them with segregation and censorship.

The punitive response added fuel to an already volatile situation. In September 1971, the prisoners of Attica rose up in rebellion and overran the prison, taking guards hostage. One of the leaders was Richard Clark, a Vietnam veteran with a history of drug use, who became a devout Muslim in prison. He protected the injured correctional officers during the rebellion and saved some of their lives.[24] National leaders of the Black Panthers, Young Lords, and civil rights lawyers rushed to Attica, hoping to help negotiate and advocate for the prisoners' demands. Immediately, with approval from the Nixon administration, the FBI's COINTELPRO disseminated misinformation and sabotaged the negotiations.[25] Historian Garrett Felber argues that the state viewed prisoner uprisings as a continuation of urban rebellions.[26] Framing the uprisings as senseless acts of spontaneous violence, rather than a continuation of the Black freedom struggle, officials sought to justify state violence as warranted.

On September 13, the negotiations ceased suddenly, and from helicopters the National Guard dropped tear gas and the state police breached the prison, openly firing on the people inside and killing ten correctional officers and thirty-three prisoners, including bystanders. Governor Nelson Rockefeller relayed the gruesome details to John Ehrlichman and the president. "It was a beautiful operation," reported Rockefeller.[27] Nixon praised the governor's decisive actions, stating that "'it's the black business . . . he had to do it.'"[28] Two years later, Rockefeller led the charge on mandatory sentencing for drugs and went on to serve as the vice president under Gerald Ford. The Nixon administration saw the Attica uprising as part of a revolutionary plot against the US government, and therefore, any state violence was warranted and the losses acceptable. Beyond accountability, the state-sanctioned violence unleashed on prisoners at Attica exercised a growing, militarized carceral power and illustrated how the state delegitimized and openly attacked political opponents. Attica was a microcosmic event in the sustained program of state violence against dissidents under the Nixon administration, including violent crackdowns, FBI surveillance, illegal activities, and National Guard attacks on American citizens.[29]

The conditions for prisoner uprisings and Black rebellions in the United States extended into Vietnam as rear-echelon areas and military jails became sites of racial conflict, violence, and resistance. The most infamous incident occurred at Long Binh Jail in August 1968 in the aftermath of Dr. King's assassination. Black prisoners revolted against the mostly white guards and attacked other white prisoners, leading to one death and more than one hundred injuries. Mainstream media focused exclusively on the Black prisoners, depicting them as violent criminals.[30] But most of the prisoners had not been convicted of violent crimes. As historian Gerald F. Goodwin points out, they were incarcerated for offenses that would "not have warranted any type of prosecution in the civilian world."[31] During its investigations of the uprising, the Army found that prisoner abuses, overt racism, solitary confinement for arbitrary accusations, and overcrowding were all underlying causes for unrest.[32] In the weeks leading up to the violence, prisoners had been subjected to humiliating strip searches for possession of marijuana and other daily degradations.

The uprising at Long Binh Jail was the first widely reported incident of intramilitary racial violence in Vietnam, with mainstream media describing the violence as part of a larger "social revolution." Black newspapers pointed out that Black GIs resented being labeled as a militant for expecting equal treatment.[33] Between 1968 and 1971, the underlying conditions that led to racial violence only worsened. Between July 1970 and March 1971, there had been twenty-seven incidents of racial violence in the region near Saigon and numerous more across South Vietnam.[34] Time and time again, Black soldiers reported discrimination and protested their disproportionate punishment, but the Army generally ignored the evidence, denying Black troops a channel to air grievances and report injustices.[35] As an act of resistance, violence was the last resort. Like authorities back home, military officials increasingly viewed the organized activities of Black men as inherently threatening or even revolutionary. In 1970–71 Army Counterintelligence conducted surveillance programs on Black soldiers, fearing the rise of militancy and Black power in the ranks.[36] Similarly, in the United States, the FBI under Director J. Edgar Hoover sought to "preemptively destroy organizations the FBI deemed prone to revolutionary violence."[37] But the FBI, Nixon administration, and Army officials alike saw any Black organizing—especially prisoners of the state—as inevitably revolutionary and a dangerous threat to the social order.

This moment in 1971 is critical context to understanding the interlinked motivations behind the war on drugs, increased administrative discharges, and the transition to an all-volunteer force. By 1971 the war in Vietnam had become widely unpopular across the spectrum, from Left to Right, civilian as well as military. Today the antiwar movement is misremembered as a small group of hippies and campus radicals, but it was actually the most diverse coalition of Americans opposed to war in US history—involving civil rights leaders, women, and veterans as well as active-duty GIs. According to a March 1971 Gallup poll, seven out of ten Americans believed the war was a mistake. Sixty-nine percent believed Nixon was lying about the war (a slightly wider credibility gap than even Johnson's).[38] By June Americans' mistrust was confirmed when Daniel Ellsberg leaked the "Pentagon Papers" to the *New York Times*. According to this Department of Defense history of US involvement in Vietnam (1945–67), the Johnson administration had believed that the war was unwinnable as early as 1965; at best, it would become a protracted stalemate by 1967. The Johnson administration publicly stated that American boys were being sent to defend freedom and prevent a communist takeover of Southeast Asia, but secret documents revealed that the primary US objective in Vietnam was "to avoid humiliation" and preserve America's reputation.[39] The Pentagon Papers exposed the secrecy and dishonesty of the US government in its conduct of the war from its very beginning.

Antiwar activists and draft resisters helped expose an unjust system that imprisoned thousands of Americans for draft resistance, while war criminals were practically beyond accountability. In April 1971, President Nixon ordered the release of Lt. William Calley from prison, three days after he was convicted of the premeditated murder of 109 civilians at My Lai in 1968. (The Army had covered up the slaughter of 504 unarmed mostly women and children for twenty months.) The only American convicted for the war crimes, Calley served only three and a half years on house arrest. Testimonies from Vietnam veterans revealed that atrocities were not isolated incidents. Earlier that year, at the Winter Soldier investigation, more than one hundred Vietnam Veterans Against the War testified to witnessing and participating in war crimes.[40] On April 18, 1971, more than 2,000 Vietnam veterans descended on Washington, DC, many casting their medals on the steps of the US Capitol, a symbolic rejection of their military service and sacrifice in Vietnam.[41] Later that week, John Kerry testified before a Senate panel, warning, "The country doesn't know it yet, but it has created a monster, a monster in the form of millions of men who have been taught to deal and to trade in violence, and who are given the chance to die for the biggest nothing in history; men who have returned with a sense of anger and a sense of betrayal which no one has yet grasped."[42] The willingness of soldiers to dissent, to resist, and to risk imprisonment also placed enormous pressure on military leaders and the Nixon administration to end the draft and to withdraw American soldiers from Vietnam, even as it escalated the bombings of Vietnam, Cambodia, and Laos.[43]

President Nixon responded by seeking to delegitimize the antiwar movement and critics, including veterans and whistle-blowers like Daniel Ellsberg.[44] Nixon used federal agencies to spy, target, harass, and discredit a list of political opponents, journalists, antiwar veterans, and activists who spoke out against the expansion of the Vietnam War.[45] The so-called plumbers even broke into the office of a psychiatrist to use Daniel Ellsberg's mental health history against him. Illegal operations like these eventually became the president's undoing during Watergate. In these campaigns to silence dissent and attack opponents, Nixon broke the law, abused the office of the presidency, and lost the support of most Americans, even though he won the 1972 election against George McGovern by landslide. Secret recordings released during Watergate revealed that Nixon was a paranoid, cynical, and manipulative man.

In the meantime, drugs provided a scapegoat to deflect criticism of US policies in Vietnam, to punish soldiers who resisted the war, and to redirect attention to social issues at home. The Nixon administration associated drugs with the decline of American values and called for a return to law, order, and "respect for our police from our young people," as he put it after the Ohio National Guard killed four unarmed college students and wounded nine at Kent State.[46] Heroin became a convenient distraction from the reality of the Army in Vietnam. Morale was at an all-time low; desertion rates were at an all-time high.[47] By 1970 heroin became widely available to US troops in Vietnam.[48] A congressional study found that heroin was sold openly in Saigon, and American troops were a lucrative customer base in the drug trade.[49] In June 1971, Col. Robert D. Heinl Jr. published an article in the *Armed Forces Journal*, describing the US Army as "drug-ridden" and "dispirited." Heinl claimed, "Our Army that remains in Vietnam is in a state of near collapse, with individual units avoiding or having refused combat, murdering their officers and non-commissioned officers."[50] The GI resistance movement reached its apex in 1971 and was partly responsible for the withdrawal of troops.[51] But the military blamed drug addicts for the inability of the United States to achieve its goals in Vietnam, drawing on stereotypes about drugs, racism, and the antiwar movement.

On June 17, 1971, President Nixon officially launched the war on drugs, marking a pivotal moment in the history of the American military-carceral state. In the infamous "Public Enemy Number One" speech, Nixon stated that "young Americans have become addicts as they serve abroad whether in Vietnam, or Europe, or other places," he warned. He claimed that veterans would return to small towns and cities across the United States and infect their communities with heroin addiction. These myths served to justify the new war on drugs. Jeremy Kuzmarov argues that mass media "fixated on the pathologies of American veterans" and "helped to refocus public debate away from the consequences of the war itself and to harden social attitudes toward drugs, binding them in the public consciousness to the tragedy of Vietnam."[52] As Susan Stuart puts it, "the poster boy" for the war on drugs was the US soldier who used heroin in Vietnam, but "law enforcement had become the centralized goal of the war on drugs and the Vietnam veterans fell—and are still falling—victim to the increased criminalization of drugs and drug abuse."[53] By linking national defense to public safety concerns, President Nixon presented the failures in Vietnam as a pretext for a new global drug war, simultaneously stigmatizing and stoking public fear of Vietnam veterans, while also severely criminalizing behaviors associated with psychiatric disorders.

As stories of the "addicted Army" circulated in media, a congressional study indicated that 10–15 percent of soldiers in Vietnam were addicted to heroin. In another study, the Department of Defense estimated as many as "30 percent or more personnel used heroin" in 1972.[54] According to this report, service members were customarily kicked out with administrative discharges for possession of heroin or other drugs, and those convicted of selling drugs were court-martialed and given "stiff sentences."[55] In a follow-up study, Lee Robins studied heroin use among a sample of 450 GIs who had returned from Vietnam within the year and had screened positive for opiate use. Most surprisingly, among those who had used heroin in Vietnam, only 10–15 percent reported heroin use in the year after coming home.[56] These findings both conflicted with the popular narrative of the addicted Army and were also contrary to conventional understanding of heroin addiction as a chronic disorder. Even though the actual number of drug addicts in Vietnam is widely disputed, the Army initiated antidrug campaigns to restore its reputation.

The US military responded with a notably sharp turn in punishment in 1971, introducing mandatory urinalysis for the first time. Administrative discharges for positive urinalysis increased in all four branches from 1970 to 1971.[57] A deceptively ludicrous name for a consequential drug policy, "Operation Golden Flow" processed soldiers out of the military expediently.[58] As many as two thousand soldiers were dishonorably discharged each month.[59] While many soldiers in Vietnam must have felt relieved to go home immediately, veterans with less than honorable discharges were systematically excluded from VA care and military entitlements. The Nixon administration created detox programs and methadone clinics via the VA,[60] but discharge status could bar veterans with substance-use problems from those services. The military's antidrug program in Vietnam produced "the biggest boon in the history of urinalysis," notes historian Kathleen Frydl.[61] Soon afterward, employers in the United States started drug-testing employees. Urinalysis in the civilian workforce remains as one of the legacies of the military-carceral state.

As the Army targeted drug use in the military, it did so in racially discriminatory ways, disproportionately punishing Black troops. In response to crimes, racial conflict, and drug use, the Army blamed its deteriorating state on a lack of "quality" troops, especially those recruited under Project 100,000. Military discourse on "quality" carried certain assumptions about race and ultimately obscured the language of racial discrimination. Army policies prohibited recording the racial data of soldiers punished, but among enlisted men, stories of arbitrary punishment, prejudice, and racial injustices spread throughout the ranks and emboldened GI dissent and resistance.[62] "The Army was in crisis," writes historian Beth Bailey. "Drug addiction, combat refusal, fragging, and racial conflict undermined the Army's image." To salvage its reputation, the Army kicked out soldiers associated with the "problem of race." With an arsenal of standardized testing, quotas, and punitive discharges, the military could "reject those deemed undesirable" and compel those it wanted.[63] Courts-martial and nonjudicial punishments steadily increased between 1968 and 1972.[64]

The military had developed a complex system of social engineering and punishment—confinement, administrative discharges, personality disorders, less-than-honorable discharges, bad-conduct discharges, and courts-martial. Military punishment often depended on the discretion of commanding officers, leaving considerable room for bias to reproduce inequality. "That discretion," writes Elizabeth Hillman, was "wielded by an almost exclusively white corps of commanding officers who were advised by almost exclusively white judge advocates."[65] With few African Americans in positions of authority, unsurprisingly, military jails were disproportionately Black, and the majority of less-than-honorable discharges were given to minorities.[66]

Administrative and bad-conduct discharges for drug use barred veterans from benefits.[67] Civil rights activists were quick to advocate on behalf of "bad paper" veterans who had gone to war but were prevented from recognition of their service. In 1973 the *Baltimore Afro-American* reported that Black GIs arrested for a "minor offense" were "more likely to be punished . . . more severely, than the white GI."[68] Despite this advocacy, African Americans were disproportionately incarcerated in military jails, discharged without benefits, more frequently hospitalized for drug use, and they were more likely than white veterans to be clinically diagnosed with substance use disorders. Compared to whites, Black veterans were also more likely to be convicted as felons and serve lengthy sentences in prisons.[69] Administrative punishments followed veterans into the civilian world, creating a paper trail that often led to unemployment and prison after war.

Vietnam veteran Lee Slemmons Ewing describes his life as "a story of paradoxes."[70] He grew up in Louisville, Kentucky. In 1965 he received his draft notice. To avoid the Army infantry, he enlisted in the Marine Corps for four years. He was at Parris Island, South Carolina, on his twentieth birthday. He graduated boot camp and had a thirty-day leave. The commanding officers said, "We're going to allow you to go home and see your families. The reason being is because 90 percent of you are going to get orders for Vietnam, and most of you will never see another Christmas—you'll come back in a body bag."

Before deploying to Vietnam, Ewing was arrested with marijuana. An African American from the South, he was labeled as a troublemaker and was punished more severely than the other white marines. He was court-martialed, sentenced two years in a naval prison, and issued a bad-conduct discharge. "I didn't want that bad-conduct discharge. I really didn't have any idea what that meant" at that time, Ewing admitted, "but I knew it didn't sound good." Ewing accepted a plea deal; the bad-conduct discharge would be dropped after eleven months in military prison and a twelve-month deployment to Vietnam. Ewing served his time. "Military authorities cracked down on marijuana consumption only to discover that they had a more serious problem on their hands," stated Eric Schneider: "increasing numbers of GIs were using opiates."[71]

Going to war in Vietnam felt like punishment. After being released from jail, Lee Ewing attended "truck driving school," but by then, he had been labeled. "On my orders, it says I volunteered for Nam," Ewing claimed. "To this day, I don't know if I actually volunteered, but I know things wasn't going well at Camp Lejeune." He was passed over for promotion twice. When he asked his sergeant about it, the two got into an argument. "I got my PFC [private first class] ranking back," elaborated Ewing. "But I was shipped to Vietnam." In total, Ewing spent "eight months and nine days in Nam." He said, "I didn't even get to do a total tour because . . . I got wounded twice over there."

As a Black man from the South, Lee Ewing "sympathized" with the Vietnamese people. "I tried not to be prejudice towards anyone." But over time, he learned not to hesitate. War made him callous. During one mission, Ewing witnessed another marine step on a land mine. "I would not feel from that day forward, and I remember thinking that I was going to die in Vietnam—I believed that to the depths of my being." At war fear could lead to morally questionable and even reprehensible actions. Ewing said, "There were some atrocities and things that happened over there. I've seen times when we'd be out, and we'd lose a guy wounded or killed or something, and the next day the guys would be so angry they'd do things to get even," he remembered. "Even though I knew it was wrong, you . . . look the other way because you know the feelings that motivate it."

On a search-and-destroy operation, the marines ransacked a village. "It took me a long time to admit." Ewing entered a hooch and suddenly, "Something caught my eye." He heard movement, swung around, and "just whaled." Instinctively, Ewing fired his M-16. "I emptied a clip," killing three people. "One was a three-year-old child," he said reluctantly. The other marines heard the gunfire. "I will never forget it. One of them said, 'What happened? What happened, Ewing?' I said, 'Let's go.' He repeated, 'What happened, Ewing?' I said, 'Let's go, goddamn it, let's go.'"

War veterans usually try to bury the memories of killing, but the past has a tendency to resurface later in life. "I carry that," said Ewing. "These were civilians," he admitted. "I live with all of it." Throughout his life, Ewing has experienced flashbacks, reenactments, and nightmares of the memory. "It took me twenty-four years to tell that story," he said. Moments after the killing, Ewing was wounded in action.

Under attack Ewing rushed to recover the body of a wounded marine, not yet realizing he was already dead. Ewing darted across a bridge and "grabbed the body." "It's John Wayne crazy!" he exclaimed. "I start back. I get hit." He remembers thinking, "If I stay here, I'm going to die here." He belly-crawled for cover. When he moved, a sniper shot him in the back and twice in the legs. The next thing he remembers is being picked up by his flak jacket. "It was Lieutenant Johnson, a redheaded white boy out of Chicago, Illinois, and I could have kissed him."

Ewing was medevaced to a field hospital where doctors operated. They "graphed a vein from my right leg and put it in place of the artery that I'd lost." The memories are visceral: "I got four inches of femur artery shot out of this leg, and I got two bones shot out of my right foot." He remembers, "They left the wounds open." Later that night, the hospital was attacked. "They had mortars coming in, and I remember them coming around dumping people out of the beds . . . and throwing mattresses on them." Ewing was finally medevaced to Yokohama, Japan, where his wounds were closed. He said, "I laid in the hospital for five months."

Then one day in recovery, Ewing tore his staples and reinjured himself. "Marines don't use bedpans," he thought arrogantly. Determined to prove his manhood, he stood up and tried to make it to the restroom. "I'm getting tough now," he recalled. "I muscled my way up out of my bed into my wheelchair, and I was going to use the head—like men did." He fell and reopened his wounds like a "damn fool." He had to undergo a second set of surgeries.

In St. Alban's Naval Hospital, Lee Ewing developed a drug dependency. "From the day I got hit," he said, "I had a drug . . . called Demerol, and I could get it every four hours, on the four hours." Patients being treated for pain may anticipate the next delivery, marking the hours of the day by their doses.[72] "Before I realized it, I was strung out on Demerol." He recounted a conversation with his doctor: "Dr. Ball . . . looked me over to assess my wounds and told me I was no good to the Marine Corps." The doctor asked about his plans. "I'd like to get up and go back to school," Ewing answered. The doctor recommended him for 30 percent disability rating. "I was getting out of the military due to my wounds, but by then, I was strung out on Demerol, and I was afraid to tell the doctors." He had already been excessively punished and served time in a brig for marijuana. "I just didn't want the stigma, so I just muscled my way off" the Demerol.

In his autobiography, disabled Vietnam veteran Lewis Puller Jr. describes coming to terms with the amputation of both legs. Puller writes, "Without the morphine to dull my senses, I had to face both the physical pain and the reality of my loss, and for several days I was nothing more than a bundle of jagged nerve endings." In addition to the physical pain, he came to terms with the fact that his life would never again be the same. His military career was over, and he could not yet imagine a fulfilled life in a wheelchair. "It was a period of my life during which I lost all self-respect for not having the strength to carry myself with dignity, and I loathed my country and the Marine Corps for having brought me to such depths."[73]

Similarly, Lee Ewing felt ashamed of his experiences in Vietnam. Afterward, his mother asked about his time in Vietnam. "I started to tell her a couple of things about what had gone on in Nam, and she said, 'I can't take it—don't tell me no more.' And I knew then, if my mother, who loved me and brought me into this world, could not stand to hear it, then it wasn't supposed to be talked about, and I did not utter a word about Vietnam for the next 24 years."[74]

The dates and lengths of time are prominent in veteran narratives. Soldiers in Vietnam counted down the days of their tours, and most knew exactly how much time they had left. Much like a prison sentence, tours in Vietnam had fixed start and end dates (so long as they were not killed or wounded in action). GIs in Vietnam kept track of their time served, daydreaming of the "freedom bird" that would take them home. These dates and the memorable deaths or injuries in between plot a psychiatric road map in Vietnam veterans' narratives, and they help us understand how GIs interpreted their service in Vietnam. They checked off the days on calendars, wrote in journals, and crossed through the months on their helmets—like prisoners who etched lines into the walls of their cells to keep track of the days.

Ewing got out of the Marine Corps on June 17, 1968, and got married

July 27. "When I came home, life just wasn't what I left." He said, "I had me a good job, but wasn't nothing the same." He had left while others seemed to move on without him. "All the guys and ladies and girls that I come up with through high school . . . went on to college or got jobs or got married," he said grudgingly. "I was so serious, and I was so angry." Ewing had gotten married too quickly. Over the following decade, his substance abuse caused marital problems and readjustment difficulties. "I got into a bunch of trouble, drug-related trouble. I went to prison. I've been to prison three times total," Ewing admitted, "once in the Marine Corps and twice on the streets, and all of it was drug related—drug and alcohol related."

More than twenty years later, Ewing checked himself into a "psych ward." "I was at the end of my rope when I went to the VA." Recently, he had heard about post-traumatic stress programs. "I was the prime candidate for it, but they wouldn't even recommend me for it until I [stopped] my drinking and drugging." "That's how I got in the process." Ewing started an alcohol and drug treatment program in Marion, Indiana. He completed a ninety-day program, and for the first time since his injuries, he didn't use drugs.

Without the numbing effect of drugs, Ewing was forced to confront long-repressed memories from Vietnam. While working through the steps of an Alcoholics Anonymous (AA) and Narcotics Anonymous (NA) program, he relapsed after seven months of sobriety. "I got high, and I got totally crazy for another two years." He admitted, "I really didn't want to stop drinking and drugging—that was my only escape from . . . my own head." During those two years, Ewing became "hopeless." On two separate occasions, he contemplated suicide. "I sat on the edge of my bed with a pistol in my hand and put it up to my head." Intrusive memories of corpses in Vietnam flashed through his thoughts. "I didn't want my family to come in and see me splattered all over the wall," he said, "because I know what a bullet can do to a human body."

With nowhere else to go, Ewing went back to the VA, not knowing "if they would even accept me because I was violent." He admitted, "Some of the staff admitted they were afraid of me." After Vietnam he resented the VA and the federal government for what he viewed as a betrayal. He felt ashamed for what he considered to be a failure of mental function and manhood. "I still got a little resentment for that," he explained, because "they sent me to a psychiatric hospital." He resented the label of mentally ill and the stigma of "crazy vet." Eventually, though, Ewing completed the rehabilitation program and has been "clean and sober ever since June 8, 1991." Yet the account of Lee Ewing is not entirely unique.

In 1971 the *Hartford (CT) Courant* ran a series of investigative articles on incarcerated veterans and the problem of drugs, featuring stories of disillusioned men who coped with the reality of the war by escaping with drugs. Just one month after Nixon declared a war on drugs, journalists were exploring ideas on how the public could help reintegrate and rehabilitate Vietnam veterans with drug problems. These ideas stood in stark contrast to the punitive response championed by the Nixon administration, allowing us to imagine an alternative history. "The new ideas are there," Barbara Carlson writes. "Get the troops out of Vietnam. Create halfway houses for returning men. Stop calling drug use a crime. Pump funds into the war on poverty instead of the war in Vietnam." Major Peck, an unorthodox military psychiatrist, stated, "You can't treat a disease that's illegal to have."[75] He naively expected marijuana to be legalized within ten years. Unfortunately, as we know, the opposite occurred over the next decades as policymakers in both major parties criminalized drugs and mental illness and invested in carceral punishment over social programs and treatment.

In 1976 the *Boston Globe* reported on some of the earliest surveys with incarcerated veterans taken in New England. A census of Massachusetts and Pennsylvania state prisons found that between 11 percent and 13 percent of the incarcerated population were Vietnam veterans. That year the Federal Bureau of Prisons recorded similar numbers. The article featured the story of Russell Morse Jr., a disabled Army veteran and combat infantryman who was wounded near the border of Laos in March 1971. Moore had casually smoked marijuana in Vietnam, but after the injury, he developed a substance use disorder. Recovering from his wounds, Moore became dependent on morphine and Demerol. "I didn't have to deal with my colostomy. It was a complete escape." When he first returned to the United States, he stayed clean and sober for only a couple of weeks before turning to heroin. "After a while, I was on the needle and it was downhill from there."[76] There tended to be a formula in the narratives of drug-addicted Vietnam veterans. They had mostly served honorably, witnessed atrocities, suffered injuries, and developed addictions either in Vietnam or afterward. By the 1980s, media began to attribute the drug problems to post-Vietnam syndrome or PTSD, or both, focusing not on the brutality of the war but on the victimhood of the veteran.

Into the late 1970s and into the early '80s, stories of veterans self-medicating with heroin continued to make the headlines. In 1979 the *Hartford Courant* reported, "Of all the men in jail in Connecticut prisons, one in every four has served in war," which was consistent with the 1981 Department of Justice report on veterans in prison. The article also highlighted the racial and economic disparities of incarcerated veterans. "These young veterans who land in jail seem to have a lot in common," notes the author intuitively.[77] "They come from poor families. They are mostly black or Hispanic. And many never went to high school.... While in Vietnam, many started using drugs." The columnist tells the story of Steven Noel, a Black veteran from New Hampshire. "He came back in 1970 with a drug problem. Noel said he began using drugs so he would not be scared of getting killed in Vietnam." While in the military, he tried "many times to get help to end his drug problems. But nobody did anything." After coming home from Vietnam, "he turned to stealing to support his drug habit and to survive." Although Noel had no prior arrests, he was sentenced to seven years for burglary. By the 1980s, the Vietnam veteran homecoming narratives focused on damaged veterans navigating careless institutions, which used and abandoned them after their service was no longer needed or appreciated. There was, undoubtedly, some historical truth in the collective memory of abandonment.

In 1981 the Department of Justice published its first study called *Veterans in Prison*, reporting that an excessive percentage of state prisoners were military veterans—one out of four. Among 65,000 veterans surveyed, 39,500 served in the Vietnam War era (1964–75). Forty percent of veterans in prison had received less-than-honorable discharges. The report hypothesized that this was "undoubtedly related to their criminal history while in the service."[78] But only 25 percent of those with less-than-honorable discharges had been previously incarcerated in or before the military. The data suggest a few takeaways: the conditions of the Vietnam War itself, discriminatory practices in the military justice system, and the sharp turn to criminal punishment over treatment in the United States in the 1970s and '80s created a generation of veterans more likely to become prisoners after war.

Despite their limitations, the Department of Justice reports reveal a pattern among incarcerated veterans, which allow us to study change over time. For starters, between 1978 and 1998, the number of veterans in prison more than doubled, and the vast majority were Vietnam veterans. M. J. Boivin estimated that between 69,000 and 200,000 Vietnam veterans were incarcerated in 1987 alone and 500,000 were on parole.[79] Some studies differ in estimation of the total veteran prison population. In 1985 the Department of Justice estimated that 154,600 veterans were prisoners.[80] By 1998 it estimated more than 255,000 veterans in prisons.[81] Each of these studies provides only an imperfect annual estimation of the actual number of veterans in prisons. Together, the series measures the magnitude of the readjustment difficulties faced by a generation of veterans, charting decades-long consequences of drug policies first enacted in 1971. In sum, the problems of Vietnam veterans did not simply go away over time even by the twenty-first century.

More important than their total figure, however, the available data suggest some underlying conditions of criminality in veteran populations. A quantitative study involving 129 veterans incarcerated in jails identified a strong correlation between post-traumatic stress disorder and veterans arrested. Almost 40 percent of these veterans screened positive for PTSD. Almost all of them had reported traumatic life experiences (87 percent). Even more significantly, those who screened positive for PTSD reported a variety of different traumas and more severe criminal history, "more lifetime use of alcohol, cocaine, and heroin," more psychiatric symptoms, and poorer overall health.[82] Another study with a group of Vietnam veterans conducted over a twenty-five-year period found a causal relationship between PTSD, drug dependence, and suicidality over the course of a lifetime.[83]

The data available also confirm that a disproportionate number of incarcerated veterans are African Americans. The 1981 Department of Justice study found that white veterans were much more likely to go to prison than their nonveteran counterparts. Of course, prisoners are disproportionately Black in both groups: civilians and veterans. Black men, in general, constituted half of the state prison population; comparatively, African American veterans were one-third of the incarcerated veteran population.[84] This might suggest to some that military service provides more opportunities and social rewards to many veterans. After all, we should not ignore the agency of these men despite their circumstances and barriers. Nonetheless, African Americans only constituted 11 percent of the US population during the Vietnam War era and were disproportionately incarcerated afterward. One study from 2013 found that Black veterans were 34 percent more likely to go to prison during their lifetimes than their white counterparts. It also showed that 59 percent of Black Vietnam vets involved in PTSD programs in 2013 had a history of incarceration.[85] The findings outline a relationship between PTSD, race, and histories of incarceration among Vietnam veterans.

This relationship is at once racial, social, and psychiatric. Benjamin Fleury-Steiner argues that the war on drugs "plunged marginalized African American veterans deeper into unemployment, poverty, and other manifestations of structural violence. Taken together, the drug war's focus on arrest, conviction, and incarceration has undermined African American veterans' ability to transition positively back into civilian society."[86] In *Disposable Heroes*, Fleury-Steiner narrates the experiences of "Carl," an African American combat veteran who was incarcerated on drug charges. "PTSD bled into his entire life." After the Vietnam War, this veteran's "social network eroded and catalyzed his struggles with addiction and . . . HIV," writes Fleury-Steiner.[87] "'I got deep into the lifestyle and was sharing needles," admitted Carl. "'I actually got infected with HIV, so I'm dealing with all those medications. And also smoking crack.'" Over three decades, the combined problems Carl faced—unemployment, substance use, untreated PTSD, and poor health—caused an intergenerational cycle of trauma and crime in his family. Like Haywood Fennell Sr., Carl's incarceration had immeasurable effects on his son. Carl believes, "'There was a price to be paid for that in the way he turned out—he's locked up for drugs now.'"[88] Histories like Carl's and Fennell's help convey the depth of issues faced by Black veterans and their families in the criminal justice system.

CONCLUSION

The rise of the modern carceral state can be traced back to policies enacted during the Vietnam War era. The Nixon presidency signified a historic shift in American politics, when policymakers in both parties began to embrace an increasingly militarized "tough on crime" approach to address drug addiction throughout the 1980s and '90s. In 1973 Nixon created the Drug Enforcement Agency (DEA) to conduct drug investigations within and beyond US borders. During the war on drugs, Black veterans who self-medicated were disproportionately punished and spent years in prison for petty drug use. The Nixon administration endorsed mandatory minimum sentences for drug-related crimes, and police primarily targeted African American communities. In March 1973, Nixon proposed legislation to reinstate the death penalty, deny bail to drug users, and create mandatory minimum laws for heroin (five years to life). This legislation also made it more difficult to employ legal insanity as a defense.[89] According to the Federal Bureau of Prisons, when Congress mandated longer prison sentences for drug offenses, the federal prison population grew from 24,000 to more than 214,000.[90] A US Sentencing Commission report to Congress stated that Black people were more often convicted of crimes that carry a mandatory minimum sentence.[91] Between 1970 and 2000, the total number of people in state and federal prisons multiplied sevenfold, from 300,000 to more than 2 million.[92] Heather Ann Thompson notes that "between 1970–2010 more people were incarcerated in the United States than were imprisoned in any other country."[93] Fifty years since Nixon's war on drugs, the total population of incarcerated people in the United States has reached astronomical levels, with as many as 2.5 million people in prison, a majority of whom are minorities, with millions more in jail and on probation and parole.

Vietnam-era veterans have consistently been the largest group of incarcerated veterans over the past fifty years. In 2000 the Department of Justice reported that among veterans in state and federal prisons, Vietnam veterans were still 35 percent of state and 43 percent of federal prison populations of veterans. As a comparison, World War II veterans were only 1.3 and 1.2 percent, respectively.[94] These generational differences resulted from drug laws first passed in the 1970s, which criminalized poverty, Blackness, and mental illness. Rather than rehabilitate, the state punished and incarcerated hundreds of thousands of people for substance use. Amid the rise of mass incarceration, veteran populations in prison more than doubled.[95] But these data tell only a partial story about Vietnam veterans in the age of mass incarceration.

Through the intimate oral histories of formerly incarcerated veterans, we can learn a deeper truth about military-carceral history. They served believing that the US military was a fair, meritorious, and just institution where, regardless of class, race, or status, any man could serve the nation and reap the rewards of the military welfare state afterward. But their expectations were traumatically shattered by reality. Political consciousness was born out of an American reckoning—the mass killing of poor Asians for a government that treated descendants of enslaved Africans as inherently criminal. In the ideological aftershocks of state violence and injustice, their sense of institutional betrayal transformed into militancy, resistance, and disorders. Many attempted to escape the violence, literally by going AWOL or figuratively with drugs. The military-carceral state punished their dissidence and behaviors as criminal, judging them undeserving of veterans' benefits and unworthy of the very freedom they swore to defend.

CHAPTER 3

Another War, Another Drug

Military-Carceral Punishment in the Reagan Era

Entrenched into the landscape of the National Mall is the memory of 58,318 Americans who died in the Vietnam War. A black mirror, the Vietnam Veterans Memorial reflects back the silhouette of those who stand before it, overlain across the engraved names of the fallen, to invite deep introspection and reckoning with the past. Following the walking path, visitors descend below the ground. The names loom over us, quickly becoming too many to bear. Where the two sides converge, the wall stands beneath the earth at 10 feet, 3 inches, towering above the crowds. A family accompanies a grandfather; heads are bowed, reverently. At the vertex, the memorial embraces the Vietnam veteran, welcoming him into the heart of the nation. Like open arms, at a 125-degree angle, the sides of the wall extend 246 feet and 8 inches each way, reaching for the Lincoln Memorial and, in the other direction, outstretched toward the obelisk of George Washington. Moving forward, the path arises from the earth, carrying us back into present-day but oriented toward a storied past. Along the way, we are left with a somber, ghostly feeling that this history lingers among us, shaping our distinct national identity today.

In 1980, Ronald Reagan assumed the presidency, riding a wave of economic anxieties, anticrime rhetoric, fear of America's enemies, and calls to honor veterans and heal the wounds of the Vietnam War. Efforts to build a national memorial to Vietnam veterans had been approved under the Carter administration, but Reagan made Vietnam veterans a central element of his campaign strategy. During a speech made at the Vietnam Veterans Memorial, Reagan erased the tragic lessons of the Vietnam War: "We remember the devotion and gallantry with which all of them ennobled their nation as they became champions of a noble cause."[1]

The president proclaimed that the only lesson of the war that mattered was that "young Americans must never again be sent to fight and die unless we are prepared to let them win."[2] Although the memorial was designed in the spirit of healing, Reagan promoted a revisionist history of the Vietnam War, claiming the US military had been victorious in Vietnam, winning every battle it ever fought, but leftist radicals, drug users, and undesirables had undermined the war effort and betrayed the brave men who sacrificed their lives for freedom. Glorifying the war rather than acknowledging the actual experiences of Vietnam veterans, Reagan attempted to recast America's war in Vietnam as a noble crusade, as he secretly waged a new war to "roll back" communism in Central America.[3]

Memory of the Vietnam War loomed ever presently in policy decisions during the 1980s. An anticommunist ideologue, Reagan promised to heal the Vietnam syndrome and reassert American military dominance around the globe. He argued that guilt, shame, and reluctance to get into "another Vietnam" strengthened America's enemies and enabled communism to spread throughout the Western Hemisphere.[4] Despite Reagan's best rhetorical efforts, according to polls from 1975 to 1990, the vast majority of the public still believed the Vietnam War was not only a mistake, but it was fundamentally and morally wrong.[5] In fact, the more Reagan espoused fervent anticommunism and threatened to intervene in El Salvador, the more skeptical and distrusting the people became of "another Vietnam."[6] Therefore, the Reagan administration secretly and illegally engaged in covert operations in Central America and the Middle East.

Reagan saw drug use as symptomatic of America's decline and a pernicious threat to the fabric of society and global order. The next war on drugs reached new heights as the United States asserted itself in the economies and conflicts of Central America. The Reagan administration "tapped into deep-rooted anxieties surrounding the ramifications of drug use in post-Vietnam America," linking it to the "spread of violence, crime and an erosion of national strength and power." Historian Jeremy Kuzmarov argues that "Vietnam and the enduring myth of the addicted army influenced social attitudes toward drugs in the 1980s." Following Nixon's precedent, in 1986 Reagan declared drugs a threat to national security and intensified domestic enforcement.[7] The Reagan administration harnessed the power of Vietnam War memory to ascend to political power and to rebuild US hegemony, while carrying out a global drug war and militarizing law enforcement.[8]

Under the Reagan administration, cocaine poured into American cities partly because of the Contra drug trade and the willingness of federal agencies to look the other way. In 1996, Gary Webb published a series in the *San Jose Mercury News*, called the "Dark Alliance," linking the crack cocaine boom in California to the Contras. National Security Council documents declassified by a Freedom of Information Act request prove that high-ranking officials, including Oliver North, knew that drug money funded the Contras and that cocaine was being trafficked from Honduras into New Orleans in 1985.[9] Two years later, Senator John Kerry (D-MA) launched an investigation that revealed Oliver North's involvement in a triangle of attempted bribery between cartels, the DEA, and the Contras. These covert operations and convenient, if uneasy, alliances partly enabled crack cocaine's boom in the United States, which devastated Black communities from the mid-1980s to the early 1990s. At the same time, the Reagan administration simultaneously expanded the war on drugs at home.[10]

Reagan's war on drugs radically changed the nature of policing, punishment, and imprisonment in America. These draconian drug laws unfairly punished poor people of color and people with disabilities, including mental health disorders. To combat the so-called crack epidemic, the Justice Department launched, in the words of Doris Marie Provine, a "new—blacker—war on drugs."[11] Mandatory minimum sentencing laws removed the discretion of judges on sentencing. Drug laws criminalized crack cocaine (a drug commonly associated with Black and Brown communities) more severely compared to powder cocaine. Mandatory minimum laws punished drug users as well as distributors. The 1986 Anti-drug Abuse Act introduced mandatory minimums for possessions of small amounts of crack cocaine. It also established drug surveillance and mandatory urine tests on employees of the federal government, law enforcement, and military personnel.[12] From 1985 to 2000, the number of veterans in prison increased by 53 percent, from 100,200 to 156,400, as the United States became the most punitive nation in the world, with the largest and most expensive prison system in history.[13]

"ANOTHER VIETNAM"

A veteran of the US Army, Shawn Small had a childhood innocence short lived in a neighborhood destroyed by drugs. "Growing up was not fun," he states

bluntly. "When people say, 'I wish I was a kid again,' I never would say that."[14]
Drugs and gang violence were a constant threat during his youth. He recalls,
"Every day, it was a shooting, ducking, coming home from school, can't go
outside, police all over." "Like I said, I'm from New York City." Shawn Small
spoke with a thick accent. "I grew up in a housing project called Baruch. Poor-
dirt poor family. Mother wasn't really there. Father wasn't there. I was raised
by my grandmother, aunts, friends of the family and such."

Small moved around a lot, staying with different family members. Life
was unstable. His mother would leave for weeks at a time. "I had an aunt. She
died," Small states soberly. "I loved her to death. Me and her were real close."
His aunt took him to Coney Island and bought him "popcorn and cokes." As
a first-grader, he stopped by her house every morning on the way to school.
The dealers in the neighborhood knew his aunt. "I would go to them, and they
would give me what she was using." Small would unknowingly deliver heroin
to his aunt each morning and then wait for her to walk him to school. "This
particular morning, I brought it to her," he remembers. "'Come on, Auntie,
I've gotta go to school,'" he called out. "I went into her room, and she was out.
I thought she was sleeping. I shook her and shook her." She had overdosed
on heroin. He called his grandmother. After the ambulance came, "I got my
butt whooped for not going to school. Grandmother was very harsh," he adds.
Small would blame himself for years.

When he was fifteen years old, Small met his "real father and went to live
with him." His father served in the Army. Life at Fort Bragg "was better" than
avoiding the gangs and drugs in the projects. "He sat me down and gave me
the talk. 'This is not New York,'" warned his father. When he was living on
Bragg, another student had called him the N word on the bus, but only Shawn
got in trouble. His father was upset at him for bringing unwanted attention.
It was a formative lesson in surviving and navigating institutional racism in
the Army. While staying at Fort Bragg, his father deployed to Germany, so he
moved back in with his grandmother. "I had trouble in school," he recalled,
so "when I turned 17, I joined the Army." He was searching for an escape and
the possibilities of a brighter future. "I had no skills. Nobody even talked to
me about college, even in school." He said, "It wasn't no other options. The
Army was the best option."

Shawn Small served the Army from 1982 to 1989. His first discharge was
honorable, but his second discharge was "other-than-honorable." He currently

has VA benefits and access to care thanks to the first discharge being honorable. "I started out as 11 Bravo," infantry, says Small. He considered getting out after the first three years, so he turned down the option to extend. When he got back home, "the first week was great—hanging out partying, but it was the same old thing," he quickly realized. During the 1980s, the US Army had mastered recruitment tactics and relied on economic incentives, commercials, and propaganda to fill the ranks of the all-volunteer Army.[15] Small talked to a recruiter and requested a different assignment. He negotiated a cash bonus and reenlisted for three years.

In the first year of Reagan's presidency, the United States began a covert campaign to weaken the Nicaraguan government, training counterrevolutionary forces, supplying helicopters, weapons, and military training. By 1982, the Central Intelligence Agency (CIA) program was disclosed to Congress, and it provoked widespread fears of "another Vietnam."[16] Despite Contra's human rights abuses and only a 20 percent public approval rating for any US military or economic aid in Central America, Reagan escalated a new, clandestine, global cold war, beyond public accountability.

Shawn Small volunteered as part of a special envoy of advisers to Honduras in 1986. "The US was there supposedly to train the Honduran Army," he explains, "to beef up their Army to protect the border in case it spilled over. But we were also there training the Contras," a group of right-wing militias, who fought against the Sandinistas in Nicaragua. "Train them in everything," he went on, "so they can be an efficient fighting force." The lines between observer, adviser, and combatant could be more porous in the field. "You take them out on an actual patrol," he elaborates, "now you've gone from an advisor to an observer. And if they're going into combat, you're not just going to stand there. . . . You're going to be getting down with them."

The first time Small received enemy fire was during a cross-border operation with Contras, "a platoon sized element, maybe twenty guys" he recalls. "Real jungle—it's dark in the daytime. We're on a patrol, and we start taking fire. To hear bullets from automatic weapons in the woods is nuts because they're hitting trees. The sound is," he searched for the right words. "I can't even describe it to you. It's like ten thousand people with hammers hitting trees. Knock, knock, knock, knock, knock. You got bullets bouncing off everything."

Small and another adviser had been training this platoon, but they were all untested in combat. "These guys broke and ran. They scattered," claims Small.

"They took off in all directions, and this left us in a bind." He realized, "We're really not supposed to be there. We needed to get out of there before something bad happened to us." Small continues, "We fought a running gun battle for about four hours. Scared! It's like do you want to get killed, get captured?" But he realizes, "I was more scared afterwards. We got away. That was a real big mess after we got back and had to explain it to the CO [commanding officer]. We was not supposed to be across that border. It would've been a terrible incident. That was the first time I experienced that," but it would not be his last. Since Honduras, he has been diagnosed with combat-related post-traumatic stress disorder.

Benjamin Fleury-Steiner retells a similar story of an African American man called Gerald, a sniper who served in secret operations in Honduras during the Reagan era. "'Honduras came to define me,'" said the veteran. "Gerald found himself in the bizarre position of defending from abroad the very drug war he witnessed tearing away at the fabric of his community," writes Fleury-Steiner.[17] Gerald experienced symptoms associated with PTSD, nightmares, and bitter disillusionment. He was given a medical discharge after going AWOL. Without access to VA care and dealing with untreated PTSD, this veteran's life fell apart. His sister died in a drug-related murder. His father died months later. Then his older brother went to prison. Without a job, Gerald became involved in the very drug economy that destroyed his neighborhood. It was not lost on him that he had fought in covert drug wars in Honduras.

Serving in black ops under the Reagan administration, Sgt. Shawn Small experienced firsthand the contradictions between Cold War rhetoric and US foreign policy. He had deployed as a member of a USSOCOM (Special Operations Command) team on a classified mission in the Middle East. Small purposefully omits the name of the location. After returning from one such deployment, Small had the unfortunate burden of contacting the wife of a soldier killed in action. "Because of the secrecy of the operation, we had to come up with another story," he says. "This was my soldier. He had six kids. . . . I used to play with his kids. Now, I gotta lie to his wife."

Multiple deployments took a toll on Small's home life. "I was married at the time. I would go nuts in my sleep. My wife was like, 'what in the hell happened to you?' It got to the point . . . if she wasn't in the bed with me holding her, I could not go to sleep without dreaming. I would hold onto her arm, and I would be all right." Small had no access to mental health services in the Army. "It was no such thing," he thought. "I started drinking more and more. If I drank enough, I'd pass out." He acknowledges, "I had a bad attitude. I didn't care no more. This is all bullshit." After the last deployment, he went on drinking binges. "Finally, at the end, I was AWOL for a while. I went on a three-week drunk. It's all day. I'd wake up drinking. I'd get the shakes."

Then a new company commander arrived on base. "He didn't really know me. He was out for blood. He was going to court martial me." Small believes the commanding officer punished him excessively for drinking and going AWOL, even though he had no prior incidents. "It was a prejudiced, racist CO," claims Small. "I'd been a super soldier. I didn't get not one Article 15. I didn't get one adverse statement. I got six Army achievement medals," he boasts proudly. But "this other CO, he just wants to put me out. He doesn't care why." After experiencing combat and the secretive nature of a soldier's death, his behavior had changed abruptly. "I chaptered out of the military," accepting an other-than-honorable discharge to avoid prosecution.

Since the Cold War, the US military had been developing sophisticated systems for removing "undesirables" from the ranks, while also saving money on a lifetime of VA benefits. In the post–Vietnam War era, the US Army worked to rehabilitate its image, as it faced another so-called crisis of quality. Questions of quality in the military continued to be inextricably bound to matters of race. The all-volunteer Army "was having trouble with its recruits—disaffection," historian Beth Bailey notes. As Ronald Reagan assumed the presidency, "AWOL and desertion rates were climbing. Drug use was common; alcohol abuse more common. . . . Crime was rampant."[18]

In the 1980s, the Army rebranded itself, advertising good pay, educational opportunities, and career prospects, and young people enlisted as an economic investment. Youth unemployment in the 1980s reached more than 17 percent, and the Army recruited from communities hit especially hard by the recession.[19] Unemployment was twice as high for young African Americans, at 35 percent. Unemployment rates for Black men on average have been consistently twice as high as whites over the past sixty years, according to Pew Research.[20] The highest gap occurred during the 1980s. But at the same time, the Army had also sought to rid itself of problems with race, drugs, and poor-quality troops, using economic incentives to fill the ranks and less-than-honorable discharges to weed out "undesirables."

Service members who were kicked out with other-than-honorable (OTH) discharges carried a lasting stigma and faced record-level unemployment.

"Unfair enough at the time," the *Baltimore Afro-American* reported in 1973, "the punishment becomes part of the permanent record . . . and follows him throughout his life." The author railed, "This is an unfair violation of his civil liberties, and a terrible form of subtle discrimination that increases the anger so prevalent among veterans today and increases the unemployment rolls."[21] Similarly, those kicked out of the Army in the 1980s with less-than-honorable discharges were systematically denied the economic rewards for which they had enlisted and the benefits of veteran status.

Shawn Small had received an honorable discharge from his first enlistment, so he qualifies partially for service-connected disability. He explains, "They would give me a claim for anything that happened during the first four years, but 'we're not going to give you anything for the second,'" he was told. "The second one, I got hurt too. I've been hurt three times." He lashed out at the system: "You can't file a claim on an injury if you've got an OTH, which is bull crap. If you get hurt in the line of duty, that should be it. Period." At the time of our interview, Small had been in the process of filing for a discharge upgrade in order to receive compensation for injuries. While excessive consumption of alcohol is widely condoned in military culture, low-ranking enlisted men, particularly men of color, are more likely to be punished for it. Because one commanding officer wanted to make an example out of Small, he accepted the uncertainties of an OTH discharge and the unforeseen consequences of it.

In 2014, Shawn Small finally visited the VA. "I didn't want nothing to do with the military after I got out." Bitterly, he says, "There was no support then like there is now. I remember going to the unemployment office and the guy looked at me and said 'Well, Mr. Small there's no jobs out here jumping out of planes or running through the desert.'" After his discharge, he continued to experience behavioral problems commonly associated with post-traumatic stress disorder.[22] He self-isolated. "I went to truck driving school. I didn't have to be around people. I didn't want to be around people." He remembers, "I tried working in a factory; I think I lasted thirty minutes. I had anger problems," he admits. "It was hard. It was *real hard* when I first got out."

Between county jail and state prison, Shawn Small has spent more than four years behind bars. He was convicted on the intent to distribute drugs. During SERE (Survival, Evasion, Resistance, and Escape) school, Small had been trained to evade and endure captivity. "I put it in my mind 'I'm a POW and I've been captured. Now I got to do this, this, and this, and act like this.'

That's what got me through jail." Prison is an inherently traumatic environment especially for someone dealing with combat-related PTSD. The prison-industrial complex "criminalizes the experience of disability and creates new experiences of disability both within and after people get out."[23] Incarcerated veterans with mental illness experience a type of double trauma of military and prison experiences.

A short-timer, with only twenty-eight days left, Small was charged with "maiming with the intent to kill." It's not as bad as it sounds. A younger man had been harassing Small. After repeated warnings, he defended himself. "I did use what I learned in the Army on him," Small confesses. "But he kept threatening me. I begged him to leave me alone." But "I'm not going to let this young man hurt me. He was twice my size and half my age. He kept on, and I clicked," Small says. "I'm bringing the whole Army now." Defending himself, he gave the man a "broken nose, major concussion, 17 stitches in the face, and two black eyes." There was "blood everywhere. I picked him up, carried him out, and laid down and said, 'the man needs help.'" Afterward, "I sat down on the ground. Meanwhile, the riot squad was coming in. I was just sitting there, calm."

Under the "three strikes law," Small faced life in prison. He recalls the lawyer saying, "'These injuries were so extreme. The timeframe was short—one minute.' She said, 'you were in the Army. This is not good.'" Special forces had trained him in lethal hand-to-hand combat, and his training helped him survive in prison. Small had mostly kept to himself, and the correctional officers testified on his behalf that he had taught some of the others to read and write. He got lucky because "prison staff is generally untrained and unqualified to identify or understand physical and mental disabilities." Incarcerated people with mental illness "are often seen as troublemakers and end up being further punished through institutional charges and administrative segregation."[24] Solitary confinement can be especially cruel to people with PTSD and other psychiatric disorders. After the fight, "they put me in the hole for ninety days. That didn't bother me either. I knew how to deal with that mind-wise," he adds. "Thank goodness for SERE. That's the one time I was glad I was a vet. I went in with my mind and came out with it."

When he was released on parole, Small searched for jobs, but very few industries were willing to hire a felon. "I'm fifty-four years old. I'm disabled." He washed dishes for a while, but it never paid the bills. "I tried for years to get a job, and nobody would help me. Some of these places that are supposed to help veterans get job placement, and then they can't help because of the violent felony. 'I tried,'" they would say. "I got sick of hearing that." His mental health began to spiral quickly.

Small became suicidal. He had been living in Baltimore. The nightmares started to occur more frequently. "As you get older, it can get worse," he said. "I was locking myself in the house. Dreams was killing me. I wouldn't sleep for three or four days. I didn't want to sleep because I didn't want to dream this dream. I had attempted suicide back in 2013, and in 2015, I was thinking about it again." He started visiting a case manager through the VA at the Baltimore Crisis Center.

Then he got pulled over for driving on an expired license, a minor misdemeanor. When he was arrested, the officers asked questions about his history. When they asked if he was suicidal, he replied, "Yes. I'm a vet. I got PTSD." Incarceration now triggers severe anxiety for him. "They took me downstairs to the holding cell, and it was like I was captured." After that arrest, he started a program at the Baltimore Veterans Treatment Court, which provides alternatives to incarceration and connects veterans with the VA, mental health services, and housing. "My case manager suggested it because at the time, I was also homeless," he explains. He started the long recovery process first by seeking counseling and then confronting the deeper moral injury of clandestine military operations.

The covert nature of his military experiences and the secrecy around the deaths of US soldiers produced a psychiatric trauma precipitating serious behavioral issues and affecting his marriage, military career, and civilian life afterward. "That's why I got out of the Army because I got disheartened by the whole thing. Some things just really pissed me off at the end." As he studied history, Small grew increasingly disillusioned. "The United States always wants to go somewhere and intervene." It took time and distance, but he started to contextualize his own experiences within a greater history of American violence. Three decades after his involvement, Small is vocal in his opposition to US-sponsored coups and covert intervention. "This Afghanistan thing—should've never been there in the first place. When the Russians were in Afghanistan . . . I even trained to go to Afghanistan back then. The war in Afghanistan's been years in the making," he realizes. "In the 1980s, we were looking at Afghanistan. Big mistake. That's why we're stuck there now. Another quagmire. They're stuck, and the reason they don't want to get unstuck is they don't want to lose face now," he says insightfully. "Because if they just pull out, they'll say, 'This is like Vietnam.'"

In the summer of 2019, after one year of intensive counseling, Small graduated from the Veterans Treatment Court and found housing in Martinsburg, Virginia. At the time of our interview, he was seeking a discharge upgrade in order to receive disability compensation for injuries incurred in the Army. Only recently has Small identified as a veteran. "For the longest time, I wouldn't even tell people." He felt shame after the other-than-honorable discharge. Now, "I'm starting to acknowledge it." He explains, "Look at where I came from. Look at what was going on, not just that I went AWOL and got an other-than-honorable discharge." He urges people to consider the underlying conditions of criminality. "I was AWOL. I was getting drunk every day. Do you know why I was doing that?" His case manager even said, "'Look at your service record. You go away on a deployment and come back like that. Something happened.' But back then, they didn't want to admit that." Today, Small is thankful that things are changing, even if it has taken decades. "That's why they're starting to change. Research and people like you are starting to ask questions, 'how'd he get kicked out?'"

SURVEILLANCE AND PUNISHMENT

Senator John Kerry asked a similar question in a congressional hearing on Drug Abuse in the Military in 1985: "Punitive remedies have proven effective in lessening the drug abuse. But does this address the real problem?" asked Kerry. "We must investigate the fundamental problems inherent in the whole military system."[25] The former member of Vietnam Veterans Against the War blamed the drug problem on low morale. He said, "During my tour in Vietnam, I witnessed soldiers uncertain of their military missions; platoons unsure of the cause for which they were fighting. . . . Lacking sense of mission and commitment, American soldiers overwhelmingly reverted to drug use." Yet Kerry embraces a punitive response in his testimony. "We must eradicate any drug use in our Armed Services," he stated, and "from urinalysis tests and surprise inspections there has been a dramatic decrease in drug abuse." But during this era, policymakers focused exclusively on surveillance and punishment without efforts to promote rehabilitation or recovery.

During Reagan's war on drugs, the US military reinstated urinalysis as part of its efforts to rebrand the post-Vietnam Army. By the 1980s, "crack had the nation in a panic," writes David Farber. It struck bipartisan fear. "Black and white, liberal and conservative, a bevy of politicians . . . fought to prove they were the most zealous soldiers in the latest iteration of the war on drugs."[26] The war metaphors were apt. One Democratic state representative named John Broujos, a veteran of Vietnam and Korea, declared, "We are at war with drug dealers, and we must marshal all our national assets in the conduct of that war."[27] For the first time since the end of the Vietnam War, the Pentagon again implemented mandatory urinalysis testing. Military personnel found with traces of opiates or marijuana "faced likely discharge or punishment (but not rehabilitation, which was a lower priority)," notes historian Jeremy Kuzmarov. Ronald Reagan championed punishment and portrayed drug testing and administrative discharges as a "resurgence of American military power."[28]

The antidrug campaigns in the military in the 1980s were heightened by widespread fear of the "crack epidemic," but were also part of the Reagan administration's efforts to distance the military from its Vietnam-era reputation—to "cleanse it of its most toxic associations."[29] Senator Paula Hawkins (R-FL) opened a 1985 congressional hearing on drug use in the military: "The U.S. citizens are fortunate, indeed, to have the finest fighting forces in the world. They are the best trained, the best equipped, and the best disciplined."[30] She asserted, "They are the most courageous military troops on Earth. They have proven US superiority in every way from minor skirmishes to world wars for more than two centuries." An allusion to Vietnam War stories, Hawkins warned "an enemy has crept into camp. . . . The enemy leaves in its wake, a military that cannot be ready and cannot respond." She stated, "The enemy is substance abuse—both the use of illicit narcotics and the abuse of alcohol." Drug use served again as a convenient excuse for history's lessons on American exceptionalism. In the 1980s, rhetoric like this cast the United States as the victim of outside forces that destroyed the military from within, through no fault of its own policies, by an enemy that could not be defeated on traditional battlefields, even though, as Hawkins claimed, the US military is the greatest, bravest, and most superior force in the world.

Interestingly, the 1985 congressional hearing on drug use in the military attempted to establish a relationship between drug use, welfare, and threats to national security. Senator Hawkins asked how enlisted-level members could pay for cocaine while eligible for food stamps. No one apparently thought to ask why a military family of four might require food stamps to survive on an E-4's salary. Hawkins then asked if members who used drugs on deployment were vulnerable to espionage. "Absolutely," answered Andy Laplante, a retired Army officer who worked with the Alcohol/Drug and Prevention Control Program. He explained that dealing drugs could pay for personal use, adding that Miami is a major port of entry for cocaine from Central America.[31] In the era of "welfare queens," the "crack epidemic," and massive cuts to government spending on social programs, this discourse influenced the military's punitive response to drugs within the late–Cold War context, stretching the imagination to see a connection between the global drug trade, communist infiltration, and "undesirable" troops.

Against this backdrop, the *1984 Military Readiness Report* showed a substantial increase in drug-related discharges.[32] In 1984 alone, more than one hundred thousand military service members tested positive for drug use. Senator Hawkins stated, "The Navy does the bulk of the military urinalysis testing—viewed as the greatest single deterrent to drug abuse in the military." These policies shaped the demography of the all-volunteer force, channeling the ideal citizen-soldiers into the branches with economic incentives and enforcing "quality" control through drug testing. More than eighteen thousand personnel were dismissed from the military for drug and alcohol problems in 1984. In a 1986 speech, President Reagan stated, "The U.S. military has cut the use of illegal drugs among its personnel by 67 percent since 1980. These are a measure of our commitment and emerging signs that we can defeat this enemy. But we still have much to do." The nation faced a new drug epidemic: crack cocaine, "an explosively destructive" and lethal drug, he warned. "It is an uncontrolled fire."[33] The Reagan-era policies to fight drugs in the military were surveillance, punishment, and expulsion for drug use. Service members caught using drugs were kicked out without veterans' benefits and returned to communities as users without job prospects, access to services, or futures outside of crime and prison.

Ricardo "Rico" Nieves Jr. served in the US Navy from July 1981 to October 1987, but got kicked out with a "less-than-honorable" discharge for drug use. He had grown up around drugs. A child seeing his older brothers using heroin,

Rico thought drugs were normal or even cool. "I was raised in Brooklyn, New York," he says. His mother and father are from Puerto Rico. His mother had only a sixth grade education, and his father left the family in 1971. "I was the seventh child of eight. . . . I have four sisters and my three brothers, Carlos, George, and Samuel, who are no longer here. They died between 1993 and 1994 from the complications of HIV and AIDS because my brothers were crushed heroin addicts." His brothers died too young. They were thirty-seven, thirty-nine, and forty years old, respectively. Two brothers died ninety-one days apart, and the third died within the next year. His stepfather died while Rico was in prison. "Using drugs in my home was a normal way of life," he reflects. "The disease of addiction is genetic. It was passed down to me."

A Puerto Rican from New York City, Nieves never felt like he belonged in the mostly white Navy of the Reagan era. His lived experiences made him different. But Nieves excelled at first. His first tour was outstanding and honorable. He earned E-5 in six years. When his enlistment was up in 1985, he accepted an honorable discharge, took a short vacation, and visited a recruiter and reenlisted. He leveraged his options and applied for Navy Recruiter School. "I wanted to be master," Nieves explains. He had always planned to retire from the military.

During his second tour, while on leave, Rico tried cocaine. "I tested positive," he admits. "I chose a court martial, and I was found guilty." He lost rank and pay. But the immediate consequences were incomparable to the ostracism and shame. "I tested positive twice on two different occasions." He developed a substance use disorder. "I didn't realize that I had a problem because I was in denial. There was never no treatment offered whatsoever—just punishment." He had no previous legal troubles.

After testing positive for cocaine, Nieves was court-martialed and then outcasted. "I was ostracized by my fellow shipmates there [in Groton, Connecticut] because I was labeled." He admits, "I did cocaine. But guys are passing out drunk, drinking bottles and bottles, but I was a druggie. I was a doper." He was under strict surveillance. "They made me do 26 weeks of mandatory urinalysis—no treatment." His commanding officer said, "'I'm going to make sure you get kicked out of the Navy.'" Rico responded, "I made a mistake. I just want help." His tests were negative twenty-five weeks in a row. "The last week I came to New York City." He used again and tested positive. He was kicked out in October 1987.

Nieves planned to retire from the Navy after twenty years, but after the less-than-honorable discharge, his life fell apart. Guilty and ashamed, he hid the truth. "I told my family that the Navy let me out early. I didn't know how to tell them I got kicked out." Without the structure and support of the Navy, he returned to the lifestyle he once fled. He bounced around jobs, driving trucks. He used drugs recreationally. In 1990, he started selling cocaine. He had gotten married while in the Navy. "I went down South to visit her in Norfolk, Virginia, and I carried a ball of cocaine with me." He intended the drugs for personal use. But his wife didn't use and said, "'We could sell that.'" Nieves recalls, "I was off to the races. That started my journey." He says, "I was pushing weight." Today, he understands and regrets the harm he caused. "I can never take back [what] I put into my community," he acknowledges.

In 1995, Nieves was arrested in Virginia Beach and was facing a mandatory minimum sentence for distribution, so he fled but got caught. Ashamed, he says, "I got kicked out of the military. I buried my three brothers from the disease of addiction and the complications of HIV/ AIDS. Three of my four sisters were fucked up from the disease of addiction—and now I'm incarcerated." Once caught in the cycle, it can be nearly impossible to break the habit, but the deaths of family members gave him reason to find a new purpose in life.

While in prison, Nieves started a rehabilitation program. He admitted that he was an addict and started the twelve steps of a narcotics anonymous program. While incarcerated he competed a thirty-six-month program and became "the first inmate in the state of New York to receive apprenticeship certification as a substance abuse counselor through the Department of Labor." He served as a peer counselor to others in prison. At the advice of his brother, he avoided gangs and helped others as a "grievance clerk." After forty-nine months in prison, Nieves was released on good behavior.

Since then, Rico rebuilt his life and broke the cycle of substance use and recidivism. He warns, "You can get caught up in the invisible quicksand of recidivism and keep coming back. . . . It's a way of life for many people because you get conditioned." Rehabilitation is "a joke. The system is not designed . . . to rehabilitate you." He earned an education and eventually wrote his master's thesis in public administration on "chemical dependency and prison recidivism in a Latino population," studying the increase in penal institutions in New York since the 1970s.

The deaths of his brothers inspired Nieves to advocate for incarcerated people infected with HIV, one of the most marginalized populations in the United States. "I came home November 1999. I got my first job in April 2000 as an HIV peer educator. He had worked "as an HIV educator for inmates." According to a 1997 UN report, prisons are "'breeding grounds'" for HIV.[34] Nieves says, "I watched many inmates that were co-infected in HIV die in prison because they were beaten—because they didn't want to be labeled." Nieves believes education can save lives by tearing down stigmas and raising awareness to problems that disproportionately harm Black and Brown communities.

Within three years, he earned a bachelor's and a master's degree. During this time, the World Trade Center was attacked. "I started school just before 9/11 happened." Nieves graduated from Metropolitan College in New York, formerly known as Audrey Cohen School of Human Services. "My alma mater was right in Ground Zero," says Nieves, "less than a quarter mile away." Exposed to toxic chemicals from the debris, Nieves developed cancer. "After the first week, the mask came off of me. It was normal for me to go around that smell—that stench. You got used to it." He developed cancer of the bladder, prostate, and esophagus. "My throat was broken by the chemicals." As a member of the World Trade Center Health Organization, Nieves has access to medical care, Social Security, and disability benefits.

It took him twenty-five years to seek treatment through the VA. "I didn't believe I was entitled to anything." In 2011, he visited the VA for the first time. "'What took you so long?'" they asked. "I couldn't tell anybody I was a veteran." He didn't realize he was entitled to disability benefits from his first enlistment. Nieves qualifies for 80 percent disability rating.

Today, Rico Nieves engages in reparative and rehabilitative work, advocating for alternatives to incarceration through a "Vets to Vets" program and volunteering in his community. At the time of our interview, Nieves was running for mayor of Woodbridge, New York. (He narrowly lost the election by thirteen votes.) "Win, lose or draw, I've already won," he explains, "because I've been labeled for so long as a degenerate—as a doper, as less than—but I'm already a victory." He's twenty-five years clean. "Let's talk about that," he says. "I'm not using drugs since October 1995. Let's talk about that. I'm not breaking laws today. I am a productive member of society. . . . Let's talk about how I help people empower themselves. Let's talk about that," he repeats emphatically.

"Let's talk about how I'm a good man trying to be a better man and taking a good community and making it a better community." Nieves concludes, "our past doesn't have to define our future. . . . We don't always have to get stuck in the muck and the mire. We don't always have to be held by invisible quicksand."

CONCLUSION

The cycle of intergenerational poverty, trauma, and incarceration entraps poor Black and Brown communities, draining the lives of children and grandchildren and generating a cyclone of lifelong harm. Since the "anticrack initiatives," the prison population multiplied to more than 2 million people by 2001. Black youth were six times more likely to be incarcerated than white and twice as likely as Hispanic. A drug relentlessly racialized in media and political discourse, crack cocaine drew "lawmakers into a frenzy of legislative" action that punished minorities disproportionately. The criminal justice system targeted Black and Brown males, and increased police forces in urban communities, enforced mandatory minimum sentences, and assigned felony status for every offense, and built "a well-funded enforcement apparatus."[35]

Two decades into the twenty-first century, the results of generations of legal, economic, and social inequality are quantifiable. In the fifty years since the first war on drugs, the population of Americans incarcerated in US prisons has swollen from 200,000 to 2.2 million.[36] A 2017 report indicated that 7.7 million Americans have been incarcerated, and 12.1 million are convicted felons.[37] Incarceration can reflect, reify, and reproduce low education levels, unemployment, and lifelong poverty, while preventing many from voting or receiving social support services, health care, food programs, student loans, and housing.[38] Criminal records exacerbate wealth inequality between Black, Latino, and white communities. At the root of this economy of incarceration is extreme inequality. Between 1973 and 1989, wages in cities fell by 16 percent, while the top 1 percent acquired a greater concentration of wealth than the bottom 95 percent. From 1980 to 1990, the size of police forces doubled and became increasingly militarized.[39] Maintaining the world's most expensive prison system costs the United States hundreds of billions of dollars per year spent on police, court systems, and prisons.[40] Its budget is surpassed only by the Pentagon.

But the numbers alone cannot convey the total, lifelong costs of intergenerational trauma and mass incarceration. At the root of the problems faced by veterans—rates of suicide, homelessness, violence, and crime—is the expansion of the military- and prison-industrial complexes, conjoined systems of state violence that are inherently traumatic and destructive to marginalized communities. These problems, however, are not beyond human agency; they are produced by presidents, policymakers, and legislators whose power ultimately encroaches on civil rights, human rights, and democracy. Black veterans are all too familiar with how militarism and carceral punishment continue to shape and restrict American life. But the history of incarcerated veterans also teaches us the redemptive power of second chances and future possibilities.

CHAPTER 4

Leave No Vet Behind

Memory of the Vietnam War and the Founding of Veterans Treatment Court

It began the moment a Vietnam veteran shared his story for the first time. "Slumped" over the podium, an elderly African American man absently gazed at the courtroom floor, mumbling beneath his breath. "'You've been attending your group counseling sessions,'" the presiding judge cautiously waded into the conversation. "'I'm very happy and pleased that you're going to counseling.'" With a warm voice, the judge speaks deliberately. "That's a good thing, but . . . they don't think that you're really engaged. What's going on?'" "'Hmph,'" the man grunted. After years of frustration with the system, he must have looked defeated on that day. This man had, in fact, given up and stopped trying. For good reason, he was distrustful of the entire system. After all, the judge may have sounded compassionate and looked more like himself, but the Hon. Judge Robert T. Russell Jr. represented the law, and treatment was punishment.[1]

Earlier that day in Mental Health Court, Judge Russell attended a case conference regarding this participant's refusal to take part in group therapy. Counseling had not worked. He had completely shut down in groups. Punctually, he attended every meeting but never engaged. Since launching the new hybrid court in 2002, Judge Robert Russell was convinced that with counseling services and access to community resources, treatment courts could transform the lives of people in the criminal justice system. Why wasn't it working this time? Russell needed to know.

After looking more closely into his file, Judge Russell discovered this man's service record in Vietnam. Fortuitously, two other Vietnam veterans, Jack O'Connor and Hank Pirowski, were also present in court that day. From past conversations, Russell knew that both Jack and Hank had served in Vietnam. During court, the judge pulled the two vets aside. "Would you go out to the hallway and talk to this guy?" Russell asked. "I'll recall the court case in about twenty minutes," the judge said, not knowing what to expect.[2]

86

The next time the defendant reentered the court, he approached the podium with purpose. "This veteran is now standing in front of me at parade rest. He's standing erect. His hands are behind his back, and he looks directly at me . . . and said, 'Judge, I'm going to try harder.' To see someone who was barely responsive, standing in a slump posture," remembers Judge Russell, "now standing erect, looking at me eye-to-eye and making that promise—I was totally floored by it." Jack O'Connor adds, "I was there that day in the courtroom. Hank and the Judge looked at each other like 'what happened?' That was the start, in my opinion, of veterans' court."[3]

Bewildered but equally inspired, Judge Russell asked Jack and Hank to stay late. "What did you do to this guy?" the judge remarked.[4] Nothing particularly extraordinary; when they walked out in the hallway, the veterans simply struck up a conversation. They each shared memories of war, where they were located, which units they were with, and what years they were in Vietnam. Although each of the three had gone different directions after Vietnam, these men found commonality in their shared history. Jack and Hank realized that this veteran felt deeply uncomfortable in group settings with civilians. "All that man wanted was to be around other veterans," they realized. It was a pivotal moment of clarity. Drug treatment wasn't working because of underlying mental health problems, but counseling wasn't working because of mistrust, deeply embedded in memory of the Vietnam War. Judge Russell wondered how many more veterans were in the courts. No one had thought to ask. During the following year, Hank Pirowski discovered more than three hundred veterans in the Buffalo court system.[5] Jack O'Connor recounts, "They asked me to set up the mentor program because of what happened in the hallway."[6]

Over the next year, Judge Robert Russell and three Vietnam veterans, Hank Pirowski, Patrick Welch, and Jack O'Connor, founded the first Veterans Treatment Court in Buffalo, New York, in 2008.[7] Judge Russell is not a military veteran, but he recognized the unique mental health needs of a subculture and responded with intuition and creativity. But even more importantly, Russell had the knowledge and experience necessary for breaking new ground in criminal justice reform. Since 1995, Judge Russell has been a pioneer in Drug Treatment Courts. In 2002, he had also successfully launched Buffalo's Mental Health Treatment Court, so he knew how to navigate barriers and carry out new ideas. Equally important, Judge Russell recognized the importance of building relationships with communities and making the most of his resources.

The Department of Veterans Affairs proved instrumental in the development of Veterans Treatment Court, as the courtroom became a nexus for connecting defendants to federal, state, and local resources. As fortune would have it, Jack O'Connor happened to be "on the Board of Directors at the VA hospital at the time."[8] With the introduction from O'Connor, Judge Russell pitched the idea of a new court specific to the needs of veterans to the Buffalo VA Medical Center. Surprisingly, the board voted unanimously in approval. "The veterans around the room," Judge Russell recounts, "they would say, 'if you're serious, I would like to volunteer . . . and help people.'"[9] The response of overwhelming support from the board surprised Russell, at first. "Usually, if I'm in the forum talking about a concept of doing something new," he explains, "there's a zillion questions: 'What do you mean? Who are you going to accept, who won't you accept, what kind of cases?' It wasn't one question with regards to that." But they quickly came into conflict with law enforcement.

Authorities in the criminal justice system felt threatened by these reforms, for veterans or not. The police and court authorities in Buffalo were not supportive of the Veterans Treatment Court in the beginning. "No one accepted this court here," states Jack O'Connor. "Cops thought it was a get out of jail card. There's 14 judges in the building. Nobody was referring cases to us." Over time, with stories of successful completion and exceptionally low recidivism rates, the court began to articulate a cogent argument for why veterans needed a separate treatment court that met culturally specific needs, making the most of resources provided by the VA and social services to offer treatment over punishment. "Now, every judge in this place refers every single veteran to [Judge Russell], but there are doubters all over the country," states O'Connor. Despite the initial pushback, the Veterans Treatment Court ultimately proved its efficacy, and success stories of veterans recovering from lifelong mental health and substance use disorders won the hearts and minds of the doubters.

Success stories of veterans like Manny Welch, who graduated from the Buffalo Veterans Treatment Court and avoided recidivism after a decades-long struggle with substance use disorder, eventually garnered national attention and generated popular approval for Veterans Treatment Court. Manny became the first graduate to join the team of veteran mentors.[10] Within six months after the launch of the Buffalo Veterans Treatment Court, *USA Today*, the *New York Times*, and National Public Radio spotlighted the promise of a new future for veterans in the criminal justice system.[11] *USA Today* broke one of the first of many national stories on the Buffalo Veterans Treatment Court. It profiled an incident between a Vietnam veteran with PTSD and Buffalo police.[12] Tom Irish served in the US Army in Vietnam. He had been drinking vodka. When police arrived at his home, the vet brandished a shotgun. He was experiencing a type of reenactment, a flashback to fighting "Vietcong." Instead of jail time, the Buffalo Veterans Treatment Court diverted Irish to treatment, potentially saving his life. This was the first time in forty years that he had ever sought help or spoken out about Vietnam. The program connected Irish with the VA and eventually expunged the crime after successful completion. The *USA Today* article also highlighted how potentially widespread these issues were in the United States. After all, Judge Russell was not the only judge to recognize the alarming number of veterans in the courts. A new law at the time in California had also permitted judges to offer alternative sentencing to veterans. In that moment, the Veterans Treatment Court was on the precipice of breaking new ground in criminal justice reform.

The underlying reasons for the remarkable successes of Veterans Treatment Court can be uncovered in the recesses of memory. The enormous growth of Veterans Treatment Courts since 2008 was spearheaded by grassroots efforts of Vietnam veterans volunteering in their local communities. Jack O'Connor has personally traveled to hundreds of courts over the past ten years, training hundreds of veteran mentors. "I sure remember over 1,000 mentors I've talked to in the last ten years and learning from them. Most of them are Vietnam vets."[13] Out of widespread concern for the next generation of veterans of American wars, Vietnam veterans organized a grassroots movement to reform the criminal justice system. The founding members of Veterans Treatment Court were directly influenced by personal traumas of war and collective memories of betrayal during the Vietnam War era. They created a new model for criminal justice reform based on veteran culture that provides mental health, drug treatment, and rehabilitation to criminal offenders. Today, thousands of Vietnam veterans volunteer in local courtrooms across the United States as trauma-informed peer mentors, providing meaningful support, a sense of community, and solidarity with veterans of America's recent wars. Together, Vietnam veterans serve to ensure that no other generation of veterans feels left behind.

This chapter explores the communal spirit of the Vietnam generation to volunteer, advocate, and organize for systemic change. To do so, at this point in the book, we must take a step back in time and journey through the contested collective memory of the Vietnam War, departing from the traditional chron-ological organization of historical analysis. The Vietnam War continues to shape the lives of surviving veterans, and its influence on American national identity, remembrance, foreign policy, and military-civil relations has incredible longevity at a time of "forever war."[14] My interpretation situates the history of the Veterans Treatment Court within a rich historiography of Vietnam War memory, while excavating the oral histories of the Vietnam veterans who founded the first Veterans Treatment Court and led a new grassroots veterans movement for criminal justice reform.

The motto of the court, "leave no veteran behind," is loaded with multiple historic meanings, born out of the collective memory of abandonment. At once, the symbolism is literal, generational, and mythological. It originates with the creed of soldiers leaving no American bodies behind on the fields of battle. This time-honored tradition stood in contrast to the generational divide between World War II and Vietnam veterans. As veterans reintegrated from Vietnam, many felt abandoned by their fathers' generation who relished in victory culture.[15] Generally, Vietnam veterans reintegrated from war largely without victory parades, public fandom, and the level of entitlement provided in postwar America.[16] Many veterans began to imagine themselves the forgotten victims of governmental neglect and public apathy.[17] In the wake of reintegra-tion difficulties, the Vietnam Veterans of America organized for institutional changes and recognition of psychiatric disorders. "Never again will one gen-eration of veterans abandon another" became their founding principle.[18] After the war's end, "Leave no veteran behind" took on a new meaning, politically charged with the popular, but debunked, myth that prisoners of war had been abandoned in camps in Vietnam.[19] In this context, it makes sense that Vietnam veterans would become advocates for prisoners *after* war.

BETRAYAL IN MEMORY OF THE VIETNAM WAR

A longtime member of the Vietnam Veterans of America, Dr. Patrick Welch is one of the founding veteran mentors at Buffalo Veterans Treatment Court. In 2008, he was the director of the Erie County Veterans Service Agency in Buffalo. Alongside Jack O'Connor and Hank Pirowski, Patrick Welch helped lead a new reform movement, "aiming to leave no veteran behind."[20] The moti-vations for his advocacy are rooted in a lifetime of service, personal loss, and traumatic experience in the Vietnam War. To some, Welch may look like an unlikely advocate for criminal justice reform. But he's a member of a generation of activist veterans, who formed powerful advocacy groups in the aftermath of the Vietnam War. One such group, the Vietnam Veterans of America, organized for veterans' benefits, lobbied for reforms to the VA system, and provided legal services to veterans in prison and jail, beginning in the early 1980s. In a sense, the Veterans Treatment Courts are the offspring of this ongoing history of veterans' advocacy since the Vietnam War.[21]

Born of a "whirlwind marriage" from the Second World War, Patrick Welch is an all-American baby boomer who grew up with the privileges of postwar prosperity. His father served aboard a submarine in the Atlantic theater. After a six-week romance, his father married Patrick's mother during the war. His mother's family has a long tradition of military service. Four of Patrick's uncles were marines; one uncle served in the Army. Three of his uncles fought in World War II and one in Korea.

After the war, Patrick's father carried on in silence, drinking heavily to dull the memories of terror under the sea. He looked for comfort in the company of other World War II veterans at the bars of the Veterans of Foreign Wars, where they cheered to victory over fascism and bonded over a shared traumatic experience. It seemed better than drinking alone. "My father basically was a functional alcoholic," Patrick admits. "I inherited a culture of drinking." Patrick grew up in the current of intergenerational war trauma.

Patrick's relationship with his father was based on a military lifestyle, and their adventures trained him for a career in the Marines. "My father was my idol," Welch says. "He knew my desires to go into the military, so he was prepping me, training me with boxing, and scuba-diving." They bonded intensely through camping, hunting, and boating. At six years old, most kids wanted to be a "teacher or fireman," but Patrick Welch planned to be a "career Marine." "It's all [he] ever wanted to be." He says, "I wanted to be a leader of marines."

Then tragedy struck. Patrick recounts the day his father died. "We were scuba diving, and we had an equipment malfunction. I watched him drown and couldn't help." During our interview, Welch paused and digressed to explain the long-term effects of his father's death. "That was my first instance of PTSD." But unfortunately, it would not be his last. Welch bears the unnatural burden of having survived his father and his child. Severe survivor's guilt has shaped his entire life, keeping him awake at nights and keeping him in bed for years at a time. In the most formative moment of his early life, Patrick Welch was forced to watch his father die, powerless to save his life.

At fifteen years old, Patrick was suddenly expected to become the man of the family and fill the enormous shoes of his father. Looking for a place to "vent [his] anger at the world," he rebelled against authority. In hindsight, Welch reflects, "I was a teenager, suffering from PTSD—an extremely traumatic event in one's life—when you watch your father die right in front you, screaming for help. And the more *I screamed for help*, the more they punished me and treated me as a delinquent." Naturally, "the more they punished me, the more I rebelled against them." This tragic moment informs Welch's advocacy for people in the criminal justice system today. "I look back at that now, in the work I've done with veterans since then, it's provided an educational base for me to understand." He views mental health as a primary reason people break the law.

On his seventeenth birthday, Patrick asked his mother to sign a waiver for him to join the Marine Corps. Still grieving his father's untimely death, Patrick embarked on a new adventure, as he had always planned. The Marine Corps would become his new family. In the summer of 1964, Welch arrived at Parris Island, South Carolina. Acclimating to the humidity and heat of the South was a challenging adjustment, but beyond the wooden barracks and lack of air-conditioning, Welch was "exactly where" he wanted to be. "Everything that we went through—the verbal and the physical abuse that you took in Marine Corps boot camp back in those days—there was nothing that happened to me that was unexpected because my uncles had told me what to expect."

During the first weeks of boot camp, drill instructors effectively broke in the recruits and turned them into a deadly fighting force. "The brotherhood starts in boot camp," Welch recalls with a sense of nostalgia. Through a gauntlet of physical and mental abuse, the Marines deconstructed the individuality of the recruits and rebuilt them as a member of a unit, each willing to sacrifice his body for the corps. When one of them consistently made mistakes, the instructors would customarily punish the whole group. "There was some retribution taken against them, blanket parties," Welch admits. These incidents were tolerated and even encouraged by the instructors because, at war, mistakes can cost lives. Midway through basic training, the recruits became more hardened, conditioned for killing, and ready to die for each other. If one man fell behind, the platoon struggled together and uplifted one another. "That's part of the esprit de corps that's built into boot camps." This formed the most enduring lesson: Leave no man behind.

Graduation from boot camp is a rite of passage into manhood, when "maggots" become marines. "The day I officially became a United States marine" was the "greatest achievement of my personal life," says Welch proudly. "Two days later, we were on a bus to Camp Lejeune to begin infantry training. The time to celebrate was rather limited." He had known very little about Vietnam back in 1964. "I went out to the First Marine Division in Camp Pendleton, California. There were hints of what was going on. I started taking Marine Corp institute courses on guerrilla warfare and jungle tactics." Determined to rise the ranks of the Marine Corps as an infantryman, Welch saw the potential escalation of war with Vietnam as a career opportunity. "My whole scheme was to be a squad leader," he states. "I worked very hard at my profession."[22] More than anything else, Welch wanted to be a leader of men at war, and soon he got his chance. Also among the first marines in Vietnam, Philip Caputo reminds us, "War is always attractive to young men who know nothing about it."[23]

The first major betrayal of Vietnam veterans occurred before the invasion, when President Lyndon B. Johnson lied on national television about the Gulf of Tonkin incident. On August 4, 1964, he reported that the United States Navy (just miles off the coast of North Vietnam) had been attacked on the "high seas" without provocation. North Vietnamese vessels allegedly fired torpedoes at the USS *Maddox* on August 2, and again, two days later, patrol boats attacked the USS *Turner Joy*. "Repeated acts of violence against the Armed Forces" had compelled the United States to "take all necessary measures in support of freedom and in defense of peace in southeast Asia," Johnson announced.[24] The administration claimed that these attacks were unprovoked, even though the United States had been operating secretly against North Vietnam since 1961, launching commando raids and gathering intelligence.[25] The president also lied about the second incident, which was unconfirmed at the time and later proved false beyond a doubt. This deception was more premeditated than a simple sonar blip. In fact, the Gulf of Tonkin Resolution had been drafted months prior to the alleged incident, essentially giving the Johnson administration a "blank check" to wage war without congressional declaration. Johnson claims, "It's like mother's nightshirt—it covers everything."[26] Just months before the 1964 presidential election, the Gulf of Tonkin incident also bumped Johnson's approval ratings by thirty points over his anticommunist hard-liner opponent, Barry Goldwater, and it provided the official justification for escalating war against Vietnam.[27] And so began the bombing campaign against North Vietnam and the US invasion of

South Vietnam that followed in March 1965. By the end of the year, more than 185,000 American combat GIs were in Vietnam.

The Third Marine Division based in Okinawa was preparing to deploy in January 1965. "We were told early on we were probably going to Vietnam," Welch remembers. At the tip of the spear, the Marine Corps landed in Da Nang on March 8, 1965. American troops were greeted as liberators, and Welch recounts Vietnamese women celebrating their arrival. His real introduction to war happened two nights later. "Within 48 hours, we had taken defensive positions at Da Nang air base," recalls Welch. "We were attacked the second night we were there." American troops began to realize that "defending freedom" in Vietnam was more complicated than they had been told.

In 1965, before most Americans could identify Vietnam on a map, the first wave of combat troops marched to war, heralded by the revelry of American exceptionalism and faith in the domino theory. Philip Caputo describes it best: "we had also been seduced into uniform by Kennedy's challenge . . . and the missionary idealism he had awakened in us. America seemed omnipotent then. . . . and we believed we were ordained to play cop to the Communists' robber. . . . we saw ourselves as the champions of 'a cause that was destined to triumph.'" Caputo writes, "So, when we marched into the rice paddies on that damp March afternoon, we carried, along with our packs and rifles, the implicit convictions that . . . we were doing something altogether noble and good. We kept the packs and rifles; the convictions, we lost."[28] Similarly, at the time, Welch thought, "I was there to save them. That was my mentality. I looked at the United States as being the bellwether for the world. We know everything. . . . We were the strongest economic and military power in the world. We can solve things." After war, Vietnam veterans who carried out these missions struggled to reconcile their idealistic beliefs with their memories of violence.[29]

The conditions of war in Vietnam contradicted the Americans' sense of themselves as saviors. Welch recalls, "Our job during the day was go out and pick a fight. That was the job, the concept being to send out a small unit, entice the Viet Cong or the NVA to engage, and then send reinforcements. A lot of it was going out, picking fights, and encouraging them to take shots at you." Under ambush, US forces would call in artillery or sometimes napalm the area. This strategy proved woefully ineffective in waging guerrilla warfare and, in turn, produced massive casualties.

Combat in Vietnam came at great costs to both sides, but early in the war, the Vietnamese realized they didn't need to win battles—only prolong the war, survive, and outlast the United States, much as they did the French. To the frustration of US troops, the Vietnamese typically controlled the terms of battle.[30] As early as 1966, one study reported that 79 percent of engagements were initiated by the enemy. Again in 1972, the US Joint Chiefs of Staff concluded that in three-quarters of engagements, Vietnamese forces chose the time, location, and duration of fighting.[31] The enemy would strike quickly and flee using a complex series of underground tunnels. By the time the bombs dropped, the enemy seemed to disappear into the land. These tactics inevitably made American soldiers feel expendable, causing low morale and widespread disillusionment. American combat soldiers began to feel like victims of a mismanaged war, trotted into the jungles and rice paddies to wander aimlessly with little sense of mission, purpose, or power to win the war. As a result, combat experiences in Vietnam formed this collective memory among veterans as disposable.

The US tactics in Vietnam produced mass civilian deaths, especially with permanent free-fire zones and body counts. Waging a counterinsurgency, the United States developed new ways of measuring victory against enemies in Vietnam. Land had been the conventional metric to gauge military success, but in Vietnam, General Westmoreland devised the strategy of attrition and counted corpses to calculate victory. "Body counts," states Welch, "became the way of determining the how successful operations were. 'Give us a body count. Give us a body count,'" the demand increasing evermore. "That was the way of prosecuting it." In a war measured by body count, every body counted as the enemy. But if body count alone were the primary criteria for military success in Vietnam, however, then the United States would have won the war—ten to one.[32] Over time, sustaining the war came at unacceptable losses. Vietnamese casualties were estimated as high as 80 percent. Large populations from the South Vietnamese countryside were displaced and removed to poorly managed strategic hamlets. Many either fled to urban areas in search of work or simply returned to the free-fire zones. The city of Saigon swelled from 500,000 to 3 million people. As many as 5 million people were forced off their ancestral lands. Once cleared, the land was declared a free-fire zone, and the United States claimed the right to destroy anything that moved. As a consequence, the American war killed an estimated 3 million Vietnamese and produced innumerable psychiatric casualties and environmental damage.[33] Brutalizing and indiscriminate death became a defining feature of the Vietnam War.

The conditions of the war led to indiscriminate violence against civilian populations. As the casualties trickled in, the GIs grew increasingly paranoid of an elusive enemy that seemed to hide among the people. All Vietnamese became suspect. Soldiers "struggled to find meaning in these deaths and the losses of their comrades," writes Christian Appy. "They sought to reconcile their direct experience of the war with the official explanations of American intervention in Vietnam."[34] This caused a significant drop in morale among US troops by the early 1970s,[35] and veterans would confront these contradictions for years as they tried to memorialize the dead.[36] Welch recalls, "After it's all over and done, you say, I don't believe I could have done those things because it's just not within the realm of daily living, which is what a traumatic event is all about." This is the language that psychologists employed when defining post-traumatic stress disorder: "'It results from a psychologically traumatic event that is generally outside the range of usual human experience.'"[37] As news of atrocities eroded US public support for the war, the People's Army of Vietnam (or NVA) and People's Liberation Armed Forces/National Liberation Front (colloquially known as the Vietcong) needed to outlast the American resolve to continue fighting indefinitely. And as US public support for the war declined significantly over the years, Vietnam veterans felt betrayed by the government for sending them to fight an unwinnable war and abandoning them afterward.

For many veterans, the shocking realities of life and death in Vietnam shattered their faith in American exceptionalism and caused many to testify to witnessing and committing war atrocities. Psychiatrist Robert Jay Lifton famously described the Vietnam War as the conditions under which "evil is born." Testifying before a Veterans Affairs subcommittee in 1969, Dr. Lifton predicted that Vietnam veterans would experience "'psychological effects specific to the Vietnam War,'" what would be called post-Vietnam syndrome.[38] The specific symptoms were "rage, guilt, and protest," as well as feelings of betrayal.[39] By the early 1970s, "America's guilt over what they had done (and were still doing) in Vietnam and their guilt over how they had ignored their veterans had been intertwined." Post-Vietnam syndrome formed the basis for post-traumatic stress disorder, but it had been stripped of its social "intangibles," such as, the feelings of social ostracism, betrayal, and disillusionment that characterized many homecoming experiences. Those feelings were the effects but not the cause of PTSD. Fred Turner argues that the new diagnosis described traumatized veterans as having "passively 'experienced'" or had been in the presence of combat. In doing so, the *DSM-III* presented veterans "exclusively as victims," whereas Robert Jay Lifton described veterans with post-Vietnam syndrome as neither victims nor executioners.[40] Beyond the specific diagnosis of psychiatric disorder, violence in Vietnam contradicted many Americans' worldviews and sense of morality.[41] At the time, most soldiers in Vietnam did not possess the clinical language to articulate what they understood as fundamentally unjust—it was a gut reaction. In response, Vietnam veterans became less trusting of government institutions, more outspoken, and more willing to organize politically.[42]

At war, however, soldiers rarely consider larger matters of foreign policy or history; their daily lives consist of moments of sheer terror followed by long periods of waiting and searching for the enemy. The stress and physical exhaustion of combat in Vietnam could lead to fatal mistakes.[43] Patrick Welch and his squad of marines had not slept the night before the morning of September 18, 1965. They had been out in the bush on an ambush assignment. Welch's men were exhausted and hungry after a night of high anxiety. At daybreak, the marines returned to base camp and sat down for breakfast, when a call came urgently requesting reinforcements. "My Marines were tired, they were grumpy, they were hungry," he says, "but I was gonna save the world." Against their protests, Welch volunteered his men to go back out into the bush. On their way, the Americans swept through a village and captured a suspected enemy. "In the past, we normally did not take prisoners," states Welch. "But for some reason, that day I decided that bringing a prisoner would be a good thing." Frustrated and impatient, Welch's second lieutenant continued forward, despite orders to secure the prisoner. "I'm calling for him to wait for us," remembers Welch, but it was too late. Lieutenant Levi "exposed himself to small arms fire and was gunned down." Harold Bird, the corpsman, rushed to save Levi but was also killed in action. By the time "we caught up with them, I directed my squad to start returning fire." He didn't yet know if they "were alive or dead."

Dashing to the rescue, Patrick Welch "tripped a booby trap." A hand grenade bounced into the air and detonated "between [his] legs and disintegrated about five inches of femur. The shrapnel cut though [his] leg and cut the nerves." As the marines engaged the enemy, they "called for air support and medivac," but the "helicopters were waved off numerous times because of the intense ground fire." Everything went dark. "I was brought to a field hospital where they administered debridement for the wounds and put me in a body cast from [my] armpits all the way down. Totally immobilized me except my arms and my head."

The physical injuries were compounded by unseen wounds. Welch reflects, "That experience that day has led to life-long survivor's guilt because I felt that had I not made a mistake—and my mistake was taking a prisoner—that Levi and Bird would have lived. The survivor's guilt has overwhelmed me for many, many years." Welch seeks counseling and treatment for PTSD. He explains, "I had the discussions with the psychologists, the psychiatrists, and the social workers about survivor's guilt. At war, people die. Not necessarily somebody's fault . . . and intellectually, I can rationalize that. But in my heart, I will never believe that it's not my fault that they died." In his mind, he traded the lives of his own men for an enemy captive, which causes internal conflict and blurs the lines between wrong and right.[44]

At any other point in the history of American wars, Patrick Welch would have lost his legs or died on the spot. Thanks to the advancement of medical and flight technology, he survived the evacuation to a field station, where he was stabilized long enough to make it to Clark Air Force Base in the Philippines. Fortunately, he survived the flight across the Pacific to San Francisco and finally made it to St. Albans Naval Hospital in New York. There, a young, ambitious doctor named Richard Lukens performed an innovative operation, saving Welch's leg. But the recovery process took much longer than a typical amputation. "They put me in traction—drilled a hole through my leg, put a pin in, and put my leg up on a skeleton device, hung weights off the end of it, and I laid in bed for another nine or ten months." The aftermath of being wounded remains a blur. He was heavily sedated for the next few months. By the time Welch could comprehend the reality of his injuries, his life, as he previously knew it, was over.

In the hospital, Welch quickly developed a dependency to Demerol. "I became a clock watcher. Every three and a half hours, I'd yell to the nurse, 'Get my shot ready!' and right at four hours, I'd get a shot. That lasted six months or so until . . . they started weaning me off the Demerol." He lost a significant amount of weight, down to approximately 120 pounds. "My doctor put me on a beer ration," and "the guys could go off the hospital grounds with liberty at night; they would come back with little mini bottles of booze." Late at night, Welch would chase vodka, bourbon, and gin with cans of beer. "I'd be pounding down the liquor and the beer, plus the Demerol."

In a haze of drugs and alcohol, Welch could not fully grasp the full damage yet. "A lot of my recovery time is a fog. It wasn't until I finally got off the drugs that I finally became more and more cognizant." He reflects, "Maybe keeping me on the drugs was a good thing. I don't know that I would have survived that long of a time being confined to a bed. It's sometimes hard to describe to somebody what it's like to lay in bed fourteen months and never touch the ground." Welch tries to explain: "Your whole existence is this little mattress—You urinate. You defecate in these stainless-steel pots and pans. I think if it weren't for the drugs and the booze—I think I might have done something to harm myself."

As the doctors tapered off the Demerol, Welch slowly realized his life would never be the same. Lewis B. Puller Jr. expresses the feeling best: "I had been forever set apart from the rest of humanity."[45] Welch recalls, "My lifelong dream is now gone. . . . I started getting suicidal ideations. What am I going to do with my life?" he asked. "No education. Crippled. Where am I going?" He digressed, explaining, "That perspective gives me insight into working with the veterans today that have suicidal ideations—because I was there. My life was over." For soldiers, at war, their bodies were "the ultimate embodiment of national ideals" and masculinity, argues historian John Kinder.[46] But, quite the opposite, wounded bodies after the Vietnam War became permanent reminders of the war's waste.

After experiencing poor treatment at the VA hospital, Patrick Welch rededicated his life to advocating for veterans. "I'm lying in a hospital bed. It's September 8, 1966. A nurse comes to draw some blood," he recounts. "She put the strap on. And the nurse starts sticking. And sticking. And sticking. And sticking. Can't get a vein." He responded, "'Take it easy. Work at it to find the vein. Don't keep sticking and poking, hoping to find one. Work at finding one.'" The nurse scolded him, "'You better understand something, Welch. In this hospital, it's mind over matter. We don't mind, and you don't matter.'" In his autobiography, *Born on the Fourth of July*, Ron Kovic states that the VA treated disabled veterans "like a bunch of cattle, as if we don't really count anymore."[47] More significant than one nurse's poor bedside manner, this memory illustrates how Vietnam veterans felt mistreated and unappreciated during the Vietnam

War era. Welch remembers, "That was my introduction to VA healthcare . . . and the more I thought about it, the more my blood boiled. Here I am, having served my country, having bled for my country, having become a cripple for my country, and the government organization that's supposed to be take care of me is telling me I don't matter," he recalls. "That's when I became a veterans' advocate." Maltreatment at VA hospitals formed a powerful cultural memory among Vietnam veterans that generated gradual reforms. Yet within the first decade after Vietnam, many veterans refused to visit the VA out of sheer spite or wounded pride. This collective memory of mistreatment at the VA manifested as institutional betrayal among the Vietnam generation.

For many Vietnam veterans, especially in the late 1970s and early 1980s, the VA represented the federal government's impersonal, bureaucratic disregard for veterans. Veterans felt frustrated and too often ashamed to seek care at VAs, knowing that if they asked for help, they would be subjected to a litany of questionnaires, psychological examinations, and stigmatizing diagnoses. Rather than disentangling the red tape and navigating the embarrassing conversations, many veterans in the 1970s simply avoided the VA, at least until after the Vietnam Veterans Outreach Program was started in 1979. Once Vet Centers became more widely available after 1980, more Vietnam veterans joined "rap" group counseling sessions with other Vietnam veterans and engaged in peer-to-peer counseling.[48] This would serve as the model for the Veterans Treatment Court mentor program.

In many ways, Patrick Welch's experiences were similar to fellow Marine Corps veteran John Musgrave. After being wounded, Musgrave joined the Vietnam Veterans Against the War. He participated in Operation Dewey Canyon III, rejecting his war medals. But Musgrave never let go of the idea that his sacrifice had some greater purpose. He eventually grew disenchanted with the direction of the VVAW and the members who apparently partied more than they protested. For more than a decade, he also dealt with untreated PTSD, suicidal ideations, and debilitating pain. The VA prescribed morphine, Demerol, and Percocet, but his tolerance for drugs led to substance use disorder and chemical dependency. Like many, Musgrave detested the VA, associating it with the government's betrayal of Vietnam veterans. In 1980, when the first Vet Center opened in Kansas City, a skeptical Musgrave joined the first peer-counseling sessions. And eventually the Vet Center proved to be the exception to what many saw as a callous, careless institution because it was led by Vietnam veterans. Musgrave asked, "How many veterans out there, part of their PTSD is that sense of betrayal, the sense of a country that didn't care about them when they were there and doesn't care about them when they're home?"[49] Popular culture fixated on the idea that the antiwar movement betrayed the troops, but in reality, veterans joined the movement and directed their organizing at institutional reforms. The Vet Center provided Vietnam veterans an opportunity to heal among a community of like-minded vets, all dealing with similar feelings of estrangement and mistrust.

Betrayal is a characteristic of what was previously called post-Vietnam stress syndrome, until it became incorporated into PTSD in 1980. A pioneer in psychiatric trauma, Robert Jay Lifton understood that Vietnam veterans formed a unique bond with one another, recognizing that they were more likely to open up about their experiences with other Vietnam veterans. In the 1970s and '80s, Lifton facilitated rap sessions with Vietnam veterans, where they engaged one another in group counseling and spoke openly about the war. Vet Centers were founded on this model. Patrick Welch states, "Our generation said, 'This needs to stop. You need to seriously take a look at mental health issues: Civil War soldier's heart, WWI shellshock, WWII and Korea combat fatigue,'" listing off the various manifestations of combat trauma. World War II veterans tended to be dismissive. "'You guys are fine.' Bullshit, we're not fine!" exclaimed Welch. "We did things. We saw things that have affected us and our ability to proceed and have a normal life, so the VA needs to step up. . . . We were very vocal about it." Vietnam veterans often felt rejected by the World War II generation and the traditional veterans' organizations like the American Legion.

The collective memory of veterans being shunned after Vietnam has generated real changes in public policy, as many organized politically, filed lawsuits, and testified before Congress. In 1979—the same year as the congressional hearings on incarcerated veterans—a group of activists founded the Vietnam Veterans of America, an organization solely composed of and dedicated to the needs of Vietnam veterans. Since then, the Vietnam Veterans of America has lobbied Congress for greater access to disability benefits and VA treatment, spurring cultural change on mental health treatment and disability rights. The VVA promoted reforms by organizing more than eighty-five thousand members in pursuit of legislative action.[50] A member of the VVA since its beginning, Patrick Welch explains, "I was vocal in the areas of treatment for those who served the country because I felt the government had broken its promise to us." Banding together in service of one another, the Vietnam Veterans of America exposed mistreatment in the Veterans Administration and offered legal services to veterans seeking disability benefits, compensation, and better treatment.

The VVA has advocated for incarcerated veterans since its founding. In 1983, it launched the Vietnam Veterans of America Legal Services, dedicated to helping veterans receive VA care, disability benefits, and treatment for PTSD.[51] A publication of the Vietnam Veterans of America, the *VVA Veteran* covers veterans-related news and shares information for Vietnam veterans. Circulated widely through prisons, it became a vital source of communication for and about incarcerated veterans. In 1984, Robert E. Jackson, a Vietnam veteran identified as prisoner #337194, wrote to the *VVA Veteran*: "All I want to know is *who* is looking into the problem of incarcerated Agent Orange victims."[52] The VVA Legal Services would have enabled incarcerated veterans like Jackson to file a disability claim with the VA and seek VA care while in prison.

The next month, the *VVA Veteran* provided detailed legal advice to veterans for employing PTSD as a defense in court cases. It suggested, "If a judge is convinced that Stress Disorder contributed to a defendant's criminal behavior, he might impose a sentence that requires . . . a treatment program rather than prison term." The article continued, "To be successful, however, the defense team (the lawyer and defendant) must begin planning a 'rehabilitation program.'" This was a crucial step, the author warned, "because it will be necessary to educate the judge about Stress Disorder."[53] Vietnam veterans themselves were largely responsible for raising recognition on PTSD in military culture and fighting for its recognition in the VA and the criminal justice system.[54]

In 1985, the VVA Legal Services team produced *The Vietnam Vet Survival Guide: How to Cut through the Bureaucracy and Get What You Need—and Are Entitled To*. Like its title suggests, this book offered Vietnam veterans a clear, easy-to-follow guide to navigating civilian life in the post-Vietnam era—from filing disability claims through the VA and appealing a less-than-honorable discharge to seeking compensation for PTSD and exposure to Agent Orange. The survival guide included an entire chapter on veterans in the criminal justice system, designed to help them employ post-traumatic stress disorder in the courtroom to avoid or appeal a prison sentence. It was not meant as a get-out-of-jail-free card; quite the opposite, it was meant to help veterans in the criminal justice system understand their rights and seek proper treatment for PTSD. The chapter walks the veteran through the legal system, step by step, from before and during the trial, to navigating the VA and seeking disability while in prison. It also offered expert counsel to veterans on parole, advising them on how to avoid recidivism, seek educational benefits, and get care at the VA. Within the first year of publication, *The Vietnam Vet Survival Guide* had sold more than 150,000 copies, and since then, it has been revised, updated, and made available to download for free, helping the next generation of veterans navigate the VA, civilian world, and legal system.

Veterans Treatment Courts became the latest extension of the Vietnam Veterans of America's advocacy for incarcerated veterans. Veterans in jail and prison were the embodiment of the forgotten veteran. This collective memory of abandonment among the Vietnam War generation takes on new life today. For the past twenty years, Vietnam veterans have made special efforts to welcome home veterans from the wars in twenty-first century. More than a "thank you for your service," the Vietnam generation exemplifies a new model of veteranhood that promotes mental health, holds the VA accountable, and supports the next generation of incarcerated veterans. The grassroots spirit of the Vietnam War era carries on today in courtrooms across the United States. A new veterans movement, Veterans Treatment Courts are attracting a groundswell of Vietnam veterans who serve as mentors, volunteers, and

FIGURE 5. Photo provided by the author and taken on July 9, 2019, outside Welch's home near Buffalo, New York.

advocates to post-9/11 veterans. Patrick Welch concludes, "What has been created through Veterans Treatment Courts is the most profound change in our criminal justice system . . . in the history of this country. Nothing like it elsewhere exists."

"WELCOME HOME"

For Vietnam veterans, these two simple words carry the weight of national memory. Fifty years after the war's end, Jack O'Connor still makes it a point to welcome home Vietnam veterans. "Whenever I speak in front of large crowds . . . I ask all the Vietnam veterans to stand up. I thank everyone for their service," he says proudly.[55] The reasons that motivate his advocacy for veterans are more complicated than readers might imagine. It stems from the collective memory of the Vietnam War. Authentic, imagined, or exaggerated, the abandonment of Vietnam veterans has *real* impacts on the veteran community in the twenty-first century. Bonded by this collective sense of abandonment, Vietnam veterans joined together and organized for veterans' benefits, disability rights, and support services. A half century later, Vietnam veterans are still pushing for greater access and equal justice.

Jack O'Connor is perhaps the single most influential Vietnam veteran responsible for the development and growth of Veterans Treatment Courts. Given his dedication to welcoming home Vietnam veterans, one could be forgiven for mistaking his zealousness for an uncritical faith in the US government or even a defense of the Vietnam War. "I'm proud to be a soldier," explains O'Connor, "but I hate the Vietnam War. . . . I am not *ashamed* of Vietnam, but I'm not proud of it." After the war, he tried to move on and forget about it. But decades later, after his retirement, O'Connor launched a second career dedicated to supporting veterans. Founding director of the Buffalo veteran mentor program, O'Connor has helped establish more than 250 veteran treatment courts and has trained hundreds of Vietnam veterans who volunteer as peer mentors.

O'Connor's advocacy, however, is also deeply rooted in a legacy of service. After immigrating to the United States, Michael O'Connor, Jack's father, served in the Army during the Second World War but "never said a word" about it. After World War II, Michael O'Connor worked as a foreman for a gas company, and they "had a nice life in Buffalo," New York. "We started in the projects, which we didn't think was poor then," Jack says. "No car or anything but lots of military families. The projects were built for the World War II military. We eventually got out of there. He built his own home. We had a nice life. He died—they both died in their eighties."

Jack's mother, Susan O'Connor, ensured he went to college. His parents were poor farmers born in Ireland who wanted to provide their children with opportunity. When she came through Ellis Island, Mrs. O'Connor could barely speak English. Jack was the first person in his family to go to college. He majored in sociology at Canisius College in Buffalo. "I quit college in my senior year," he remembers. "My mother went berserk. She made me complete it before I joined the Army."

In 1968, just weeks after graduation, O'Connor got his letter from Uncle Sam, so he "volunteered for the draft." If he had known then what he knows now, he might've gone to Canada. Living only miles from the border, he thought briefly about evading. But "I knew I had to go," O'Connor realized, "because my father served." He reflects, "I don't know how I made it. I wasn't a tough guy"—just a "skinny kid with glasses." Humbly, he admits, "I'd be too afraid to go back. Pure fear." But at the time, O'Connor told himself, "My father got through it. Other guys got through it." Therefore, he had faith he would survive too.

At twenty-one years old, Jack O'Connor was already an "old man" compared to most combat soldiers in Vietnam.[56] "I got married before I went in," says Jack. Ten days after the honeymoon, he reported for basic training at Fort Dix, New Jersey. "I probably could've got out once she was pregnant. But . . . I went to Vietnam about 14 days after my daughter was born. They let me stay home for that, which was an extra three or four weeks." It must have been difficult for his wife, Patricia, to care for their colicky baby by herself, not knowing if she would ever see her husband again alive. "I got lucky with my wife," Jack reminisces. "I don't know why she stayed with me fifty years."

Despite the circumstances, Jack O'Connor considers himself fortunate. He was stationed in a relatively secure area outside of Saigon in 1969 with the 82nd Airborne. "That was good duty. I didn't know it then," but "I lucked out." He explains, "I was very, very fortunate that I didn't go over a year earlier when the Tet Offensive hit." The scariest part was "you never know when you would die." It's difficult to capture that feeling of uncertainty. "You went out on patrols and didn't know if you would come back." Other than occasional sniper fire and mortar attacks, however, O'Connor avoided major combat. During the Vietnamization stage of the war, Army of the Republic of Vietnam (South Vietnam) (ARVN) forces began preparing for the imminent withdrawal of American forces. "We weren't going out looking for the bad guys," says O'Connor. By then, "the Vietnamese were doing all the work."

When the 82nd returned to the States, Jack O'Connor joined the Quarter Cav (Fourth Cavalier Regiment). He was stationed outside Saigon. "I had about two months left," recalls Jack. "I went into the 25th by helicopter. They had a major battle going on. There were body bags coming back, and I go, 'this is it! I've avoided crap for ten months, and now it's all gonna hit.' I'll never forget." The captain asked, "'Does anyone here know how to type or have a college degree?'" O'Connor explains, "They needed someone in the rear. My hands flew up. He said, 'if you're lying to me, you're done!' And I did—I had a college degree. My mother made me," he reminded me. "I tell that story to my grandkids to show how important school is," he laughs, "never know when it's going to come in handy!" For the last two months, "I had a very easy time in a place called Củ Chi with the 25th Infantry, while the other poor guys were out in the field," remembers Jack, with a countenance of guilt. He thought he would be safer in the rear. But little did O'Connor know at the time, the chemicals he worked around were slowly poisoning his body.

During the Vietnam War, many soldiers believed that Agent Orange would help win the war by destroying the enemy's food supplies and denying them territorial advantage by defoliating the forests. From 1962 to 1971, during Operation Ranch Hand, 19 million gallons of herbicide were sprayed in Vietnam. Agent Orange was the most common herbicide used in the war, consisting of chemicals known as dioxins, which can cause cancers and birth defects in the descendants of those exposed. Jack O'Connor recollects, "We were glad of Agent Orange" at the time. "It burned this foliage down, but obviously—and they knew it, these bums! I hope DOD [Department of Defense] is watching us." O'Connor blames the Pentagon for exposing American soldiers to dioxins even though there were doubts about the effectiveness of chemical defoliates during the war. The Kennedy and Johnson administrations were deeply worried about global perceptions of the United States using chemical defoliates in Vietnam, fearing a loss of American prestige. In 1967, the RAND Corporation reported that Operation Ranch Hand undermined the goals of pacification through the "hearts and minds" campaigns. Not only did Agent

Orange cause political fallout, but the RAND reports also refuted the myth of its military effectiveness.[57] The studies emphasized that most villagers felt inescapably trapped between global forces beyond their control, with the air war causing innumerable civilian deaths, destroying crops, and disrupting the traditional Vietnamese way of life.

To this day, the US government has never apologized, offered reparations, or acknowledged the enormous environmental destruction caused by Agent Orange in Vietnam. It only reluctantly and belatedly acknowledged the long-term effects of dioxin on Vietnam veterans. Jack O'Connor says, "There's so many guys my age, guys right here in this [Veterans Treatment] Court, that have stomach cancers, leg neuropathies, feet neuropathies, all because of that— it's unbelievable." He has survived cancer many times but fears its inevitable return. "It hits the muscle, lasts for about four months," and moves to a new muscle. "You can't rebuild the muscle because the nerves are dead. I haven't lost much: fifteen–twenty percent" muscle mass. At the time of our interview, the cancer had returned six times already. "Why it waits 30–50 years, I don't know," O'Connor states, but "it's got me." Between the first reports of Agent Orange–related cancer in 1977 and the passage of the Agent Orange Act of 1991, the onus of responsibility for proving exposure to Agent Orange fell on veterans, leaving many without much-needed early intervention and care. The government's delays and bureaucratic barriers in granting disability benefits for exposure to Agent Orange have created yet another collective memory of betrayal among Vietnam veterans. [58]

Many Vietnam veterans felt that the government had abandoned its responsibility by asking soldiers to fight for a lost cause and then failing to welcome them home or care for them afterward. The Pentagon Papers revealed that the government had lied about Vietnam. As a result, a generation of veterans grappled with their sacrifices in a war that most Americans believed was immoral and a mistake. After coming home, Jack O'Connor "was glad it was over." He remembers, "I was starting to dislike the things I heard about the war. . . . It didn't accomplish crap. Lost 58,700 men. For what?" He struggled to find any meaning in his service and others' sacrifice. "I drank a lot when I came home," O'Connor admits. "I rode a motorcycle through a fence at 100 miles per hour." While in a body cast, his wife issued the following ultimatum: "Stop or bye-bye." It was a wakeup call. "I straightened out," he says. Then, "I had three kids. Life got good." O'Connor worked at social services for the next thirty-eight years.

Vietnam veterans felt alienated in society, so most felt deeply uncomfortable talking to civilians about military service. When they first came home, most found it hard to identify with former friends and family members. This can be a source of conflict in memory of the Vietnam War. "The civilian world seemed alien," writes Philip Caputo. "We did not belong to it as much as we did the other world, where we had fought, and our friends had died."[59] Many memoirs and oral histories of Vietnam veterans express this feeling of estrangement, especially compared to the World War II generation. These accounts formed a collective memory of abandonment by the government and betrayal by an unwelcoming public. Scenes of protesters at airports served as a metaphor for the rejection many veterans felt during their homecoming. Sociologist Jerry Lembcke sought to debunk the myth of what he calls "the spitting image," pointing out a lack of physical evidence that Vietnam veterans were actually spat upon in airports.[60] Nonetheless, this collective memory dramatically symbolizes how a generation of Vietnam veterans felt isolated, unwelcome, and estranged.[61] When Jack O'Connor came home from the war, family and friends treated him differently and found it difficult to relate. "They didn't understand, but it was okay with me," O'Connor explains. "I didn't want to talk about it anyhow." He clarifies, "They wouldn't yell at you. Mostly, people would avoid you."

This collective memory of abandonment was epitomized by the fall of Saigon when the US government refused to intervene. April 30, 1975, marked the end of an era, and many Vietnam veterans blamed media and Congress for abandoning ARVN forces. The memory of helicopter evacuations of desperate people from a rooftop in Saigon signified a final betrayal.[62] Like many Vietnam veterans, Jack O'Connor watched Operation Frequent Wind unfold live on television and felt humiliated, ashamed, and immensely guilty. "They were picking them off the roof of the embassy. Is that a way to leave a war?"[63] Photographs of helicopters being shoved over the side of aircraft carriers not only illustrated the poor planning to evacuate allies, but in climatic fashion, these scenes also captured the essence of the war's waste. Having fought alongside ARVN forces, many Vietnam veterans felt resentment about how the war ended. "What did we accomplish there?" asks O'Connor rhetorically. "Nothing."

A foundational moment in the history of the VVA, the memory of Saigon's fall became a rallying cry for a generation of veterans that felt abandoned by the federal government. "We're not going to let you walk over us the way you walked away from the Vietnamese!" Patrick Welch exclaims. "We're gonna hold you accountable." The VVA pressured the federal government "to provide adequate support—better treatment at VA hospitals, testing and compensation for possible Agent Orange–related health problems, improved educational benefits, effective treatment for war-related psychological problems."[64] The aftermath of the war in Vietnam and the refugee crisis faded in public memory, however, as the media fixated on the myth of American POWs and the poor public reception of Vietnam veterans.[65] Far from a myth, the homecoming experiences of Vietnam veterans were often traumatic, and it's certainly true that, during the Vietnam War era, there were few ritualistic rites of passage from war to civilian life, no national homecoming parades, and few acknowledgments of veterans and their readjustment difficulties. The focus on who should be remembered, and therefore who would be forgotten, remains a central paradox at this moment of national reckoning.[66] Amid the formation of this hierarchy in Vietnam War memory, veterans' organizations took it upon themselves to remember incarcerated veterans.

Letters from incarcerated Vietnam veterans published in the *VVA Veteran* in the 1980s provide rare insight into their needs and the cultural battles of the time. The January 1984 issue featured a newly organized chapter of incarcerated Vietnam Veterans of America, with a photograph of imprisoned Vietnam vets meeting in their rap group counseling sessions. A large pull quote next to their image reads, "'When the Iranian Hostages came home everyone had parades and wore yellow ribbons. I came home at midnight and my family wasn't even there to greet me.'—James W. Armstrong." Many Vietnam veterans resented their homecoming and the lack of public acknowledgment. Historian Christian G. Appy notes, "The heroes' welcome for the hostages triggered a major transformation in public perceptions of Vietnam veterans."[67] The website of the VVA marks this event as a turning point: "When the American hostages were returned from Iran in January 1981, it was as if America went through an emotional catharsis that put the issues of the Vietnam era on the table for public discussion. The question was asked why parades for the hostages but not for Vietnam veterans?"[68]

This spirit drove efforts for a national Vietnam veterans memorial and belated efforts to welcome Vietnam veterans home. In 1995, after more than two decades, Jack O'Connor finally acknowledged his service in Vietnam while visiting the National Vietnam Veterans Memorial.[69] "I loved it. Some people didn't like it. I thought it was unbelievable. It took that long to get there." During those lost years, O'Connor tried to forget about Vietnam and refused to talk about the war. "Even today, I don't talk to anyone that's not a vet, but if I go to a different town like Galveston, and I meet a Vietnam vet, we just talk. I don't talk to anybody else like that. I don't even talk to my wife like that," says O'Connor. Vietnam veterans' reluctance to talk openly with civilians and authorities stems from the collective memory of betrayal and abandonment. This is essential context for understanding why the Vietnam veteran in Judge Robert Russell's Mental Health Court would not engage in group counseling with civilians and at least part of the reason for his distrust of authorities.

Memories of the Vietnam War weighed heavily on Jack O'Connor until he started giving back to veterans. "I thought when I retired, life was over. I think it just started," remarks O'Connor. "I don't remember anything I did as Director of Medicaid. I sure remember over a thousand veteran mentors I've talked to in the last ten years and learning from them." He explains, "Most of the mentors I see now, Vietnam vets, they love doing this because it's their chance to give back. I hear that all the time—all the time. All over the country. They couldn't give back in 1970." But now, "They're sixty and seventy years old. They run companies. They got money."

Veterans Treatment Courts seek out local community resources, sponsors, donors, veteran-friendly businesses, and volunteer mentors. Not only do hundreds of Vietnam veterans volunteer in the courts, but they also donate their money and provide vital community resources. One of Jack O'Connor's proudest accomplishments is compiling a book of resources for veterans in Buffalo. "All these guys now run companies. We have a record. We call it 'veteran-friendly employers.' One owns a steel company, oil company, car dealerships. They're all Vietnam vets. And they trust this court now." When he visits other courts, O'Connor teaches the coordinators to make similar connections with community partners. "Start putting together a resource list from day one. . . . You need some contacts in welfare, Medicaid, food stamps, child assistance," employment services, and educational programs. When veterans came home from Vietnam, few understood how to file disability claims or apply for governmental assistance; today, in Veterans Treatment Court, navigating the governmental bureaucracies is the first step in the long process of recovery, rehabilitation, and reintegration.

Veterans Treatment Court serves as a nexus between local, state, and federal government, providing access to VA care, disability benefits, and counseling services. The courts tapped into the entitlements of the military welfare state

FIGURE 6. Photo provided by the author and taken on July 9, 2019, in Buffalo, New York, at the Veterans Treatment Court.

to rehabilitate people in the criminal justice system and prevent recidivism.[70] On any given court day at Veterans Treatment Court, representatives will be present from a range of community partners, state resources, employment service agencies, volunteers, advocates, and legal services, all working together to ensure veterans avoid jail and prison. One of the most vital community partners, the Vet Centers provide counseling services to "bad paper" veterans who are ineligible for VA care. This service remains one of the most enduring legacies of Vietnam veterans' activism and advocacy for "less than" veterans.

CONCLUSION

What started in 2007 outside the Buffalo courtroom as a private conversation between Vietnam veterans eventually grew into a grassroots movement to provide mental health, drug treatment, and rehabilitation services to veterans in the criminal justice system all around the United States. But, as this chapter shows, Veterans Treatment Courts are a continuation of a Vietnam veterans' movement that advocates for disability rights, expanded VA care, and treatment for mental health disorders. Although largely forgotten in public memory and historical scholarship, incarcerated veterans were a crucial focus and core component of this movement since the early 1980s.

In May 2008, the National Association of Drug Court Professions promoted the initial successes of the Buffalo Veterans Treatment Court. Founded in 1994, the NADCP serves to provide training to and develop drug courts nationwide. There were more than twenty-one hundred by 2008. Judge Robert T. Russell Jr. had been a pioneer of Drug Treatment Courts since the 1990s and served as the NADCP Board Member Emeritus when he conceptualized a specialty court for veterans. "The Buffalo Veterans' Treatment Court presents a unique opportunity to help veterans in trouble with the law," writes Russell.[71] In 2009, Judge Russell published an article in the *New England Journal on Criminal and Civil Confinement*, laying out the details of his revolutionary model for criminal justice reform. In October 2008, the Buffalo Veterans Treatment Court was the only specialized court for veterans in the nation, but "it will certainly not stand alone for long," noted Russell prophetically.[72] The following year, seven more Veterans Treatment Courts had followed suit, including Tulsa, Oklahoma; Orange County and Santa Clara, California; and Rochester, New York.[73] Judge Russell had recognized something unique in the veteran mentor program, "something about the beauty of service," the bonds among veterans, and their unwavering support for one another.[74] But this bond is neither an intrinsic trait nor an inevitable outcome of military service; it was actually a terrible lesson learned during the Vietnam War and a core collective memory of betrayal among veterans.

Veterans Treatment Courts were carried on the shoulders of Vietnam veterans, who refused to leave the next generation of veterans behind. In the beginning, members of the Buffalo Veterans Treatment Court, Judge Russell, Hank Pirowski, and Jack O'Connor visited, provided training, and set standards for best practices in each new Veterans Treatment Court. Jack O'Connor has personally trained more than 250 courts, but that model was unsustainable. The National Association of Drug Court Professionals developed a standard curriculum, facilitated a training process, and implemented the key components and best practices based on Judge Robert Russell's Veterans Treatment Court model.[75] Founded in 2010, Justice for Vets, a branch of the National Association of Drug Court Professions, provided the national infrastructure to replicate the Buffalo court as the model for Veterans Treatment Courts on a nationwide scale. In collaboration with Jack O'Connor, Hank Pirowski, and Judge Robert

Russell, Justice for Vets expanded the number of Veterans Treatment Courts across the United States. The number of Veterans Treatment Courts grew exponentially: 1 in 2008, 11 in 2009,[76] 24 in 2010, 80 in 2011, and more than 100 by 2013.[77] Justice for Vets has trained more than three thousand court staff and thousands of volunteer veterans as peer mentors. Today, there are more than 600 Veterans Treatment Courts and many more in planning stages.[78]

Veterans of the "forever wars" benefit from the cultural currency of the Vietnam War in American memory. Vietnam veterans volunteer in their local communities, greeting Iraq and Afghanistan war veterans at airports and providing the type of support that they wish World War II veterans had shown them after Vietnam. The collective traumas of American wars have accumulated across two generations of veterans in the United States, producing a backdraft of social problems today.[79] While distant from American soil, the consequences of our wars can be felt in a small community of American veterans and their families. The wounds of wars in the twenty-first century—PTSD, traumatic brain injury, moral injury, substance use, suicide, and various untreated mental illnesses—can lead to homelessness, family crises, unemployment, arrests, and incarceration. Concerns for Iraq and Afghanistan veterans were a central priority for the Veterans Treatment Courts, and the intergenerational relationship between veterans provided the cultural bonds and community support necessary to enable rehabilitation, recovery, and reparative justice.

CHAPTER 5

Generation 9/11

Incarcerated Veterans of the Global War on Terrorism

The Army National Guard brands itself as "hometown heroes," citizen-soldiers who "protect the weak, save lives and restore neighborhoods."[1] On the home page of the US National Guard website, soldiers in camouflage carry pickaxes and shovels instead of armor and rifles. One could easily believe joining the Army National Guard is basically community service. Its former slogan, "One weekend a month, two weeks a year," created the expectation that the Guard's job in fighting terrorism would be part-time and temporary. Despite the recruitment propaganda, however, the Army National Guard and Reserves have played an outsized role in carrying out combat missions in the Global War on Terrorism. Most of these veterans had joined to pay for college or support their families—never expecting to deploy to Iraq or Afghanistan—and certainly not multiple combat tours. After all, during the Vietnam War, the National Guard and Army Reserves did not deploy to combat zones. However, during the first ten years since the invasion of Afghanistan, the number of National Guard and Reserves deployed totaled more than 540,000 troops.[2] Without a draft to compel men into service, the professional military activated part-time soldiers to fight the Global War on Terrorism.

Since 1973, the ranks of the all-volunteer force have been filled by an increasingly smaller percentage of the US population, marking historic shifts in the demographics of the military. For starters, minoritized populations are overrepresented in the military. As of 2010, service members who deployed to Iraq and Afghanistan were 65 percent white (compared to 75 percent of the general population).[3] Sixteen percent were Black, compared to 12 percent of the civilian population. Asians were equally represented between military and civilian populations at 4 percent. Hispanics made up 10 percent of the military but 12.5 percent of the civilian population. But the largest difference between the Vietnam War and the Global War on Terrorism is the number of women deployed to combat zones. Fewer than 7,500 women deployed to Vietnam, but more than 200,000 women had deployed to Iraq and Afghanistan by 2009. The average age of service members deployed is also considerably older today compared to the Vietnam War era, meaning they are more likely to be married and have children. Of those who deployed to Iraq and Afghanistan, nearly half were married, and 43 percent have two children, on average. These historic changes gave rise to significant and unique challenges among Iraq and Afghanistan war veterans compared to previous generations of American veterans.

Multiple deployments are the defining feature of post-9/11 veteran experiences, leading to a mental health crisis in and beyond the military. With only a fraction of the population serving active duty, the Department of Defense required service members to deploy multiple times during the Global War on Terrorism. As of 2009, 40 percent of active members had deployed at least twice. More than 263,000 deployed more than twice.[4] Multiple deployments also created more readjustment challenges between tours, causing unforeseen hardships on families and untold stress. More frequent deployments and extended combat tours also led to an increase in the number of psychological casualties of the wars in Iraq and Afghanistan, the so-called signature wounds: post-traumatic stress disorder, traumatic brain injuries, and cases of suicide.[5] Studying the recent history of mental health care in the Army, David Kieran argues that the Army was both "more progressive and more aggressive to address mental health issues."[6] Despite increased awareness on mental health, one study found that only one-third of soldiers who "needed psychological help actually sought it."[7] Even as more services became available, many feared retaliation, cultural stigmas, and looking weak if they asked for help.

The mental health crisis in the post-9/11 military also created residual social and behavioral problems among veterans, including homelessness, suicide, substance use, and incarceration.[8] The US Department of Justice special report *Veterans in Prison and Jail, 2011–12*, estimated that 181,500 veterans were incarcerated in the United States.[9] More than half of veterans in state prison were incarcerated for acts of violence. Approximately half of incarcerated veterans had been diagnosed with mental health disorders, including PTSD, TBI, depression, and substance use disorder.

Two historic changes emerged after the Vietnam War relevant to incarcerated veterans of the post-9/11 generation: a lower percentage of the population serves in the military,[10] and a greater percentage of the population is incarcerated. Since 1978, the Department of Justice's studies on veterans in prison have documented significant trends in incarcerated veteran populations over time.[11] In 1978, nearly a quarter of the prison population were veterans.[12] In 2011, only 8 percent were veterans.[13] The percentage of veterans in prison has declined since the post-Vietnam era. But that is because the total percentage of the population that served in the military has steadily declined since the end of the draft. On the other hand, the number of Americans incarcerated in jails and prison has risen exponentially since the war on drugs.

Despite certain methodological limitations, the Department of Justice studies reveal the long-term effects of military service on veterans and help us understand why some groups of veterans are more likely to go to prison. Surprisingly, given the racial disparities in the US criminal justice system, African American and Hispanic veterans were slightly less likely to go prison than their nonveteran counterparts.[14] Oppositely, white veterans are incarcerated at more than twice the rate of white nonveterans (50 percent to 23 percent). Nonetheless, Black veterans were still 5.5 times more likely and Hispanic veterans were 4.3 times more likely to be incarcerated than white veterans.[15] These studies suggest that some of the economic and social rewards of military service uplift some marginalized communities, but military service can also cause social and behavioral issues among veterans after war, leading to trouble with the law. The number of incarcerated veterans doubled after the Vietnam War, and for the next fifty years, the Vietnam generation remained the largest percentage of veterans in prison, until the newest Department of Justice study from 2016 reported that Iraq and Afghanistan veterans combined now outnumber Vietnam veterans in prison.[16]

For most veterans, their stories are unique, their personalities are complex, and their mental health challenges are deeply personal. Through a holistic analysis of three oral histories, I explore memories before, during, and after war to understand the relationship between mental health, punishment, and incarceration. A snapshot in time, this collection of oral histories portrays readjustment problems symptomatic of the nature of war in Iraq and Afghanistan to help explain why post-9/11 veterans end up in the criminal justice system. It also shows how some veterans fall through the cracks, even at a time of significant mental health and criminal justice reforms.

MENTAL HEALTH, MANHOOD, AND MULTIPLE DEPLOYMENTS

The paradox of the 9/11 generation is that despite increased mental health awareness and access to services, many soldiers still do not seek treatment in the military for fear of potential consequences.[17] Hundreds of thousands of veterans experienced the "signature wounds" of American war in the twenty-first century: post-traumatic stress disorder, traumatic brain injury, and suicidal ideations. One study found that only one-third of soldiers who "needed psychological help actually sought it" because they feared career consequences or cultural stigmas.[18] According to a 2007 RAND study, three hundred thousand Iraq and Afghanistan veterans experienced PTSD or depression, but only half sought mental health care.[19] In response, the military promoted greater access to mental health services, as historian David Kieran has argued, producing gradual but more enduring cultural change in the Army at the grassroots level.

But cultural changes in the military justice system are still needed to reckon with the practice of punishment of soldiers with psychological disorders for misconduct and the subsequent denial of care. VA psychiatrists had a history of diagnosing mental health problems as "adjustment disorders," which denied veterans disability benefits. Since the Vietnam War era, the Army preferred to kick soldiers with psychological or behavioral issues out of the military rather than deal with them.[20] During the Global War on Terrorism, as evidence mounted that the wars in Iraq and Afghanistan were producing mass psychological casualties, Army leadership promoted cultural change on mental health as a way to improve mission readiness. But the deeper tradition of suspicion, cultural stigmas, and practice of punishment prevented many service members from seeking mental health treatment. The accounts of formerly incarcerated veterans show that many feared the stigma, retaliation, or weakness associated with mental illness and did not get help until it was too late.

Multiple deployments intensify mental health problems, disrupt reintegration to civilian life, and harm family relationships. Less than half of 1 percent of the US population actively serves in the military today. Nearly 80 percent of service members come from military families; 30 percent had parents who served, creating a divide between the military and civilian world.[21] Afghanistan War veteran Kevin Ogo's family history with the US military is deeply complicated. His maternal grandfather was Japanese American, too young to remember much about the internment camps. From a camp in Arizona, Kevin's great-grandfather enlisted in the US military among a group of Japanese Americans (Nisei) known as "yes-yes" soldiers, those who answered yes on loyalty tests and volunteered to fight for the US Army. Ogo served in the famed 442nd Infantry, one of the most decorated segregated units in World War II.

On the other side of the family, Kevin's father, Luis, is a member of the Army Special Forces. Luis has completed multiple combat tours in Iraq and Afghanistan. Kevin's father immigrated into the United States illegally from Mexico. After being deported, Luis enlisted in the Army as a path toward US citizenship, a so-called "green card" vet. The military recruits on average five thousand "aliens" per year to help fill the ranks of the all-volunteer force.[22] Between deportation and deployment, Luis was absent from Kevin's life for years at a time. "I moved around a lot," he recalls. "It wasn't until I moved to Ft. Bragg with my dad as a teenager—that was the most stable living I had ever experienced." The father-and-son duo share the unique experience of both having fought in Afghanistan.[23]

Like many among this generation, 9/11 dramatically altered the trajectory Kevin Ogo's life. He had been living on Fort Bragg with his stepmother while his father was deployed to Bosnia. One day in science class, his teacher walked into class and turned on the television. Shocked and confused, the students gathered around the small television, watching smoke pillaring from a tower. Then, suddenly, an airplane struck the second tower. "I didn't understand what was going on" at the time. "I was young." He says, "Then we watched the towers fall." In the first shocking moments, most Americans were confused about what was happening; media were slow to speculate, but by the time a third plane hit the Pentagon, most people understood that the US homeland, for the first time since World War II, was under attack.[24] Ogo recalls, "I didn't realize it was a terrorist attack until later that day," as Fort Bragg scrambled to "mobilize and went completely on lock down." Suddenly, this young man was launched onto the world's stage, swept up in the rising tides of war.

Shortly thereafter, his father Luis deployed to Afghanistan, so Kevin moved back to West Covina, California, to live with his mother. Most of his life, he had been raised by a single mother. She had gotten pregnant at sixteen years old. "Her family was not supportive of her getting pregnant that young, so she really struggled." By high school, Kevin joined the football team, craving structure and discipline and to get away from neighborhood gang violence and drugs.

The military often recruits from high schools and shopping malls in poorer communities.[25] "We struggled," admits Ogo. "I remembered thinking back on my time at Ft. Bragg—a lot of the people that my dad lived near, in the housing area, they were young people. They had just joined the military and they all had houses and nice cars. They weren't struggling at all." He says, "College wasn't really an option—and a war was happening. Soldiers were needed. A lot of my buddies had joined even before they graduated." Many of his teammates had gotten sign-on bonuses. His father had encouraged him to join the Air Force, but the recruiter turned him away because of his tattoos. Next door, the Army recruiter eagerly welcomed him. "All the recruiters are in the same office," he recalls. "They all wanted to snag everyone up as they're walking in." Proudly, he reflects, "I'm glad I joined the Army and not the Air Force."

After passing basic training, freshly minted soldiers continued their advanced training and integrated into units, forming bonds with other scared, eager young men and women on their way to a war zone. Ogo explains, "I don't think anyone could ever fathom what war is really like, so it was easy for me to just see it as a word." He felt anxious to deploy and prove himself on the field of battle. "I didn't have any cohesion with any of my peers," he recalls. "Everybody had already gone. I felt like I was the only person who had not deployed yet." The reality hit him on arrival in Afghanistan. "I took it very seriously because it was a life-or-death situation."

During his first deployment to Afghanistan, Kevin Ogo experienced a horrific amount of death, which had a lasting effect on his mental health. When he first arrived, a non-commissioned officer (NCO) named SSG Eric Lindstrom took him under the wing. "He really saved me because I felt like I was on my own," says Ogo. On July 12, 2009, Staff Sergeant Lindstrom was killed in action near Barge Matal, Afghanistan.[26] "To have someone who was my mentor—he had just had twins—that shook my whole perception and reality. That shook everything. How could somebody leave who was doing so well? He was a religious person . . . and his life was taken in an instant." His emphasis on fatherhood and religion indicates a moral injury. Ogo wondered why he survived while another soldier died, a new father, a leader, and a model soldier who did everything by the book. Lindstrom's sudden death caused survivor's guilt. He would ask, "'Why not me?'" Psychiatrist Jonathan Shay writes, "The death of a special friend-in-arms broke the survivor's life into unhealable halves, with everything before his death radically severed from everything after."[27] Ogo remembers, "We lost a lot of people on our deployment—that destroyed me. It took away everything that I was and made me, whatever I became after that, which is really isolated and confused."

At war, soldiers had neither the time nor the distance to memorialize the dead. "We didn't grieve—I didn't," says Ogo. "I don't remember ever really grieving. I remember getting angry and maybe shedding a tear. The mission was tomorrow." The soldiers would organize a makeshift memorial or wear a bracelet to remember the fallen, but then quickly repress the natural response to grieve while deployed. "When we came back, we would try and see their family at the homecoming ceremony and shake their hand, and that was it. I never really did put too much emphasis on grieving." He tried to bury his feelings. "I figured *this is war.*"

Kevin Ogo was only twenty years old when he returned from Afghanistan the first time. In 2009, "I was in three different IED blasts—that was the worst deployment for me. But that also set me up for the rest of my career. No deployment after that was hard for me, in a sense. I knew what the worst was going to look like." Even though he knew what to expect, Ogo "still struggled." The accumulated effects of PTSD and traumatic brain injury led to mental health and behavioral problems, ultimately derailing his military career.

Over multiple deployments, mental health problems culminated among members of the 10th Mountain. Ogo says, "A lot didn't make it to the third" deployment. "Most of the buddies that I know that have committed suicide were from my first unit in 10th Mountain. So that really deterred me" from connecting with other soldiers. Afterward, "I didn't really search for any friends, at all." Ogo also experienced suicidal ideations. "The biggest challenge for me, was not seeking help—not acknowledging that I had a mental health issue."

By the end of his second tour, he would feel more comfortable in Afghanistan than the United States. "Once I hit boots on ground in Afghanistan, it was like— I'm home. I'm good." He thought, "It feels better to be here in Afghanistan— because I'm always on guard anyway. I'm always high anxiety anyways, so this feels . . . like I'm putting my stress to use, in a place where this is needed." Hypervigilance is a reaction to post-traumatic stress, which can help soldiers survive at war, but it also makes it more difficult to cross the military-civilian divide. Ogo explains, "It just did not feel right to be in America. I felt more at home every time I went back to Afghanistan."

During his second and third tours, Ogo deliberately self-isolated and became increasingly hypervigilant. He lost contact with friends he made during his first deployment with the 10th Mountain. "One by one, other soldiers, who are going through their own missions and going through their own losses—everyone was isolating in their own way. It made it easier for me to isolate," as a type of self-imposed exile and self-preservation. After transitioning out of the 10th Mountain, Ogo felt intense survivor's guilt. "I cannot think of any person that's still alive because a lot of them deployed a second and third time with 10th Mountain," he says sadly. Nancy Sherman calls this "luck guilt and betrayal," a distress that comes from detachment from a unit.[28]

Despite more cultural awareness of PTSD in the Army today, military training conditions soldiers to bear discomfort in silence and put the mission first. Ogo believes, "Mental health is never encouraged because it takes away from the mission." Army psychiatrists were available on bases, but many still believed they would be stigmatized or labeled for seeking help. "They're not going to say that you can't do that. They're not going to say that's a bad thing, because they'd be wrong. But they discourage it, a lot." Suspicion and mistrust of the Army mental health professionals deterred soldiers with PTSD from seeking services. He feared retribution for seeking mental health care. "I thought it was going to affect me being an NCO," says Ogo. "I thought I wouldn't progress" or get promoted to "specialist if I actually go to the therapist three times a week." This mentality becomes internalized and self-enforced. He felt guilty for needing help, while others had died or were still fighting, so he found excuses. "We're about to deploy again," Ogo recalls. "I'm trying to get my rank up . . . so I never went," regretfully. "I didn't actually seek help until I had to, until it was command-referred." During his second deployment, the mental health problems became such a problem that the chain of command ordered him to seek counseling because his behavior had become a liability to the Army's mission readiness.

After combat deployments, it can be challenging to readjust to civilian life, especially for parents and spouses. Ogo had gotten married before deploying. "By the time I came back from Afghanistan, I was somebody that she didn't know." She said, "'This isn't who I met. This isn't who I married.' I didn't know how to fix that," realizes Ogo. They would eventually divorce. Manhood might compel some to seek help and others to deny a problem altogether. After coming home, his wife said, "'You need to get help. It's affecting you at home. It's affecting you being a husband. It's affecting you being a father.'" As a father, he needed to be strong and take care of the family, but his behavior was toxic to those relationships.

This veteran could not perform the traditional roles of fatherhood.[29] "I couldn't walk into a store. I couldn't. I had to wait in the car. I couldn't go into Walmart and wait in a line. I couldn't go into [restaurants] . . . just because my anxiety would race so high. I knew there was an issue there," but he told himself, "It's normal. That's part of war. That's part of what you do." Ogo had anxiety attacks in cars. "I had to be in control," he explains. "Anything in the middle of the road" would activate a stressor, and "I would have to pull over, and I was turning around." Daily routines were unbearably stressful, making the responsibilities of fatherhood impossible to uphold. "There was no way we were going to get through the day after that. It had a really big impact on my life—on me being a dad—on me being a husband, and everything else."

After coming home from Afghanistan, Ogo would drink alcohol, hoping it might help him reconnect with people. He never really liked to drink, even in high school. "But I remember my wife, at the time, she was a little bit of a drinker. She would encourage it." When he turned twenty-one, his wife told him to loosen up and drink with her. "I think she thought, maybe that would help," explains Ogo, "and maybe things would start to get better." But when mixed with untreated psychiatric trauma, the drinking made his problems more volatile. "I was connecting more with other combat veterans, who were also drinking. Then, we would get together and drink together, all day and all night." He admits, "I just became an alcoholic after that." The Army did not typically punish members for drinking alcohol after deployments unless it led to serious behavioral issues or misconduct. The military tested for drugs regularly, so many would drink to dull the effects of combat trauma instead of using drugs.

In 2015, Ogo was discharged from the Army, but afterward he lost a sense of purpose and started using drugs, which led to a substance use disorder and criminal lifestyle. "I had nowhere to go," he says. "I wasn't working. I had a little bit of money from the Army. I was now a drug addict." He became more isolated from society. "The only people I knew were my drug dealers and other people who used drugs. That's the life I got into, doing various things for drug dealers. . . . [I]t wasn't too long until I started learning the tricks of the trade."

Over the next year, he became suicidal, homeless, and violent. Ogo was arrested three times and had twenty-eight felonies pending. "My bond was set really high," he remembers, so "I couldn't bond out, which was good. It allowed me time to sober up—physically and mentally sober up." For the first time since coming home from Afghanistan, he started to face the mental health problems that had ruined his marriage and led to jail.

Incarcerated veterans are also at increased risk of suicide.[30] When Ogo left the Army, he felt lost. "I felt like I had lost everything," he says. "I just felt like I had no more purpose in life." In 2016, he attempted suicide. A combination of factors led to the attempt, especially guilt, shame, hopelessness, untreated PTSD, and substance abuse. Today, he recognizes that other friends from the 10th Mountain were dealing with similar issues. "A lot of my friends who have committed suicide, we were all in the same boat. We had just gotten out. I remember drinking with them heavily. When were in the States, and some of them might've picked up substance abuse issues." Discharges sever the connection among soldiers, and for many, it can be like losing family.

After the attempted suicide, Ogo finally faced his underlying mental health problems. "I chose to use my time in prison as recovery, for me mentally and spiritually, as far as, finding out who I am and what I want to become in the future, because I was lucky enough to get such a short time, seeing all my crimes, I should've gotten a lot more. I really did take the second chance, and I really did focus on myself." Ogo isolated while in prison. "There was a lot of traumatic things that did happen. I happened to see people killed" while incarcerated. "Unfortunately, I did what I did during war, and it's just shoved in the back of my head, but now I know that I need treatment."

Colorado Springs has a veterans' pod, where military veterans are jailed separately from the general population. Bernard Edelman notes, "By housing veterans together in an environment that inspires military culture, values, and a sense of brotherhood or sisterhood, these units are not only promoting safety improvements, but also restoration, healing, and growth in a way that may not have been possible via general population housing."[31] Colorado also has a Veterans Treatment Court, but like the vast majority of veterans in prison, Ogo did not qualify for the Veterans Treatment Court. He was sentenced to four years in prison.

While incarcerated, Kevin Ogo first contacted the VA and started receiving disability benefits. "I actually got them in prison." Previously, "I didn't ask for help. I hadn't ever spoken to the VA." In county jail, Ogo founded an advocacy group called Warriors First and started learning about disability benefits for incarcerated veterans. When he went to prison, he contacted a VA liaison, who visited the facility to identify veterans and provide services. "He gave me all the paperwork I needed to file for my disability." The disability claim was processed very efficiently. The Colorado VA had a well-established program for veterans in jail and prison. "They got clearance to come into the facility and interview me and do everything they needed to within 45 days," says Ogo. "I actually got my payment in prison, but whatever percentage you get granted while you're incarcerated, serving a sentence, you only get 10 percent."

Post-9/11 veterans often find meaning not in the cause of the wars they fight, but in the bonds that they form with other men and women who served—shared experiences, unspoken language, and kindred past. Many veterans in the criminal justice system find a new mission in advocating for other veterans. "Everything I do now," Ogo says, "it's to try and help another veteran who's been down the same path." Bonding with other incarcerated veterans through Warriors First helped him reconnect to the military culture. "There's camaraderie when you're in, but you lose it when you're out," he realizes. "I missed that. I found that a lot of other people missed that. The fact that we had each other's backs, we knew each other's families, and we essentially became brothers. All of that has caused me to find my purpose in life—and that is to help other struggling veterans." In turn, advocacy helps some veterans deal with their own guilt, depression, and mental health problems.

For Kevin Ogo, the connection between PTSD and incarceration is self-evident. "That is a very direct, *very direct* relation. I don't think I ever would've done any of those things, had I not gone through what I did in the military. That's not any excuse," he clarifies. The underlying mental health issues led to substance abuse. "They are directly related," he states unequivocally. "As soon as I got out, I went to jail and then prison. There was no break in time."

In addition to the common issues most Americans in prisons and jails face today, veterans face unique circumstances stemming from their experiences at war and the military justice system. These conditions may warrant a real need for specialty courts, veterans' pods, and other services that can help them reintegrate into civilian society with military-related problems, mental health disorders, and less-than-honorable discharges. With proper treatment, social services, and opportunities for self-improvement, education, and job training, formerly incarcerated veterans can recover and avoid recidivism. Their stories illustrate how all people in the criminal justice system with a fair opportunity and infrastructure to support their recoveries could similarly become engaged citizens, community leaders, mentors, teachers, and advocates for reform too.

MENTAL HEALTH, MISCONDUCT, AND PUNISHMENT IN THE MILITARY

As the casualties of the Global War on Terrorism trickle back into the United States, their invisible wounds are shaped by cultural discourse on psychiatric trauma, gender, and rehabilitation.[32] In *Signature Wounds*, David Kieran argues that lasting cultural change in the Army "happened from the bottom up."[33] In 2007, high-ranking military officials spoke out publicly about PTSD, but most enlisted soldiers looked to platoon leaders as an example. At this level, the quality of leadership tends to vary. At Fort Carson, for example, service members were "'humiliated if they had problems,'" called "'weak'" and a "'shitbag.'"[34] Encultured masculinity in the military commands soldiers to never show weakness. Even as mental health treatment became more available, despite the Army's efforts, some service members were reluctant to report mental health concerns, fearing stigmas, retribution, or career consequences.[35]

In 2007, the *Nation* published an explosive article by Joshua Kors, exposing the Army's policies that punished combat veterans with behavioral issues. Army doctors misdiagnosed PTSD as a "personality disorder" or PD. As David Kieran has pointed out, diagnosing a soldier with a preexisting personality disorder "had historically been used as an expedient way to discharge someone who was problematic or not adjusting to military life." Since "personality disorder" is vaguely defined, it "could be used indiscriminately."[36] After incidents in 2007, Congress held a series of hearings on the misdiagnosis of post-traumatic stress disorder as a personality disorder to uncover if the misdiagnoses were intentional. "The difficulty in determining how to treat 'bad paper' veterans fairly is that it can never be known whether their PTSD or related behavioral health condition is actually the cause of the misconduct," Major Bryant Boohar argued.[37]

In response to congressional inquiries, the Army reformed policies on issuing personality disorder discharges in cases of combat veterans but continued to punish them for misconduct. By 2008, PD discharges dropped significantly. In 2009, a congressional law prohibited the discharge of soldiers for mental health problems related to service. Yet top Army officials continued to express dismissive attitudes about the link between PTSD and misconduct. Lt. Col. Chris Ivany, a top US Army officer who oversees mental health, said in an interview that for some soldiers diagnosed with mental health issues (PTSD or TBI), "their condition 'subsequently improved' before the misconduct—so they can't blame the war for causing them to misbehave." Yet symptoms of PTSD are delayed onset and persist for long durations; in fact, that is the defining nature of PTSD. In 2013, researchers revisited the 1988 National Vietnam Veterans Readjustment Study, studying PTSD symptoms in male Vietnam veterans over a longitudinal study—forty years after the war.[38] The study concluded that PTSD remained stable over time. In the post-9/11 era, veterans discharged for misconduct usually continue to experience behavioral problems afterward without access to VA benefits. These injustices cause serious problems in civilian society. One study estimated that 40 percent of "veterans who suffer from PTSD . . . have committed a violent crime since" their discharge.[39]

Despite mental health reforms, the punishment of service members with mental health problems has continued, most notoriously at Fort Carson, Colorado. In 2014 SSG Eric James secretly recorded a private meeting with a psychiatrist. The Army had already threatened to kick him out for drinking and driving in 2011. After first experiencing abuse, James recorded twenty hours of sessions with doctors and officers, "berating him for suggesting he has mental health problems."[40] NPR reported that military psychiatrists "tried to convince him his experiences in Iraq were not too traumatic—and even seem to ignore him when he talks about wanting to commit suicide." After an internal investigation, two therapists were "reprimanded" for mistreatment. The Army concluded that this problem was "not systemic." But actually, the Army ignored evidence of mistreatment from nine other soldiers at Ft. Carson.

From 2009 to 2015, the US Army separated more than 22,000 soldiers for misconduct after coming back from Iraq or Afghanistan.[41] Securing hundreds of records via the Freedom of Information Act, an NPR investigation uncovered widespread punishment of soldiers with mental health disorders. According to the Department of Defense, those 22,000 soldiers discharged had also been diagnosed with PTSD, traumatic brain injury, or other mental health disorders. In 2017, a congressional report found that found that 62 percent of service members separated on misconduct discharges from 2011 to 2015—more than 57,000—had been diagnosed with major mental health disorders, including PTSD and TBI, within two years prior to misconduct.[42]

Of this number, 13,283 were issued other-than-honorable discharges, rendering them ineligible for VA care and benefits. Moreover, although the Department of Defense policies required the military to assess the impact of PTSD and TBI in cases of misconduct, those policies were inconsistently implemented across service branches, including the Army and Marines. Thus, while the military has made progress in mental health care, the institution still punishes members whose misconduct is related to mental health disorders, including PTSD and TBI, but none more severely and quickly than substance use disorder.

Andrew Kubacki was sitting in ninth grade history class when the World Trade Center collapsed. This memory led to his decision to request Airborne infantry. He was searching for a new sense of family. When he was only thirteen years old, his father died unexpectedly. Then, during senior year of high school, his mother died too. In grief, he started using drugs. It must have been unimaginably difficult to come of age amid such personal loss. "It took me a long time to process it," recalls Kubacki, "because it was nonstop for me from 13 until I got out of the military." He joined the Army. The risk of the Iraq War did not discourage him; quite the contrary, it compelled him. He thought, "I don't want to kill myself, but I don't want to be here. What better way to die than a hero?" he thought. But "I was naïve," then.[43]

While Army training at Fort Benning, Georgia is not as extreme as the Crucible, the basic process that transforms civilians into soldiers is identical. Andrew Kubacki tried not to stick out in the Army. "I stayed quiet and tried to blend in," he explains. "You don't want to screw up and get singled out." Before "we graduate, we do the big ruck march and spend the week in the field." "You get this huge sense of pride," he says. "I am a man now. . . . Now my life is really going to start." He completed Airborne training at Fort Benning and deployed to Iraq in August 2006. Over the next fifteen months, Kubacki would drive trucks on more than three hundred missions.

Not long after deploying to Iraq, Kubacki was wounded in a firefight. "I got shot in my hand and then hit in my vest" by a sniper. "Sergeant Christopher Roybal comes and like drags me and pulls me to safety." Kubacki received the Army Commendation Medal and a Purple Heart. He was still recovering on base when the sergeant got killed in action. "I wasn't going on missions," he says, but "I stayed a part of the team. I didn't milk [the injury] as much as I could." He got permission to return to duty as soon as possible. "The new sergeant major saw me doing that with my [injured] hand," he recounts, "so he made me his driver. I squired for him." That, in turn, made Kubacki unliked by the other men. "Nobody really liked a mouse. Everybody wanted me to get blown up." The new sergeant major, however, was unpopular. Some of the others wanted him to "die and get replaced. That's how bad people hated him." Kubacki believes, "He really wasn't a bad guy. But the sergeant major before . . . he was there for soldiers." When he died, "it sucked out the life out of a place."

Over time, the looming threat of danger in Iraq led to PTSD and behavioral issues. Kubacki drove security for the sergeant major on more than three hundred missions in Iraq. The Army extended the length of tours to fifteen months to meet the demands of the Global War on Terrorism with only a limited size force. The duration of his deployment took a toll on him. Kubacki never hit an IED, but they had several close calls. The threat was always present, and he never felt in control of situations. The tension and boredom of driving security combined, making him extremely hypervigilant.

In 2007, by the time Andrew Kubacki returned to the United States, the Army made coordinated efforts to raise awareness about PTSD and mental health.[44] He recounts, "I knew something was wrong, so then I asked for help, but that was the worst thing I could have done." These feelings are consistent with the criteria for PTSD, especially persistent and exaggerated negative beliefs about oneself, others, and the world. "I was a piece of shit because I was getting help. I was rehabbing my hands, and I was rehabbing my mind because I needed that help. I'm a piece of shit soldier according to the higher ups." Attitudes on mental health among NCOs and lower-ranking officials could vary. After Kubacki sought counseling, this platoon sergeant singled him out. One day, tempers flared. "I wouldn't piss on you if you were on fire," the sergeant taunted him. In response, Kubacki verbally threatened to kill him on the next deployment.

After returning from Iraq, Kubacki drank heavily with three other battle buddies. "When we got home, I knew something wasn't right," he recalls. "I wasn't sleeping, I was just drinking so much. I was just rowdy. I wanted to fight people." His anger turned to despair and "negative thinking," a common symptom of PTSD. He felt hopeless about the future and isolated. A combination of symptoms of PTSD, binge drinking, and behavioral problems led to misconduct within the first year after coming home from Iraq.

The Army threatened punishment or a court-martial to pressure soldiers with mental health problems to accept an administrative discharge. Administrative discharges required fewer records than courts-martial, which makes studying them harder because of a lack of court documentation. In 2008, the Army discharged Kubacki with a general under honorable conditions for misconduct, even with a documented history of seeking mental health care. "There was no trial, just paperwork." He says, "The whole process was a year from getting home to getting out." The US military justice system sometimes uses administrative discharges to get rid of undesirables or as a type of plea deal to avoid courts-martial and bad conduct discharges. Oftentimes not realizing the compounded consequences of "bad paper" on their lives after service, soldiers will accept a "less-than-honorable" discharge to avoid criminal prosecution.

Without the support system of the military or access to counseling services, Kubacki continued to drink, get belligerent, and get in trouble with the law after his discharge. He had gotten married while in the Army. But the more he drank, the more he and his wife fought. They finally divorced in 2010, and then he got into a series of toxic relationships. Alcohol enflamed the symptoms of post-traumatic stress disorder, making him more hypervigilant and confrontational. "It all goes back to the PTSD. I'm drinking because I'm depressed. But I'm depressed, [be]cause I'm drinking," Kubacki explains. "I would get really drunk almost every night—blackout drunk . . . so I can pass out, actually fall asleep." One night, he recounts. "I was violent towards my girlfriend when I was drinking. I had one domestic violence [charge]. I was put on probation." He served four months in jail for assault and battery and aggravated domestic violence. Without making excuses for his behavior, he reconciled his relationship and sought help.

Andrew Kubacki was sentenced to a Veterans Treatment Court, requiring weekly court attendances and mandatory urinalysis. "That was so overwhelming for me," he explains. "I didn't have a car at the time," so he missed court dates and failed to complete treatment. Eventually, counseling helped him identify the root cause of his behavioral problems. He realized, "I'm going through these symptoms. This is what caused it." Kubacki says, "You gotta find people that you can express yourself to." Although Andrew did not graduate from Veterans Treatment Court, the community of other veteran mentors helped him make sense of his experiences in Iraq and understand how his mental health affected his behavior after coming home. "I've seen some shit. Once I started telling people the whole story, it was like a relief—a weight off my shoulders. I came to terms with it."

Facing mental health disorders required some veterans to dispel prior notions of what it meant to be a man. "You're supposed to be in the Army. In the military, you're supposed to just put [emotion] in a box and keep it under your bed. But that's not healthy," Kubacki realizes. "You gotta be vocal about it. You gotta let people know, and there's no shame in getting help. No shame at all. It's probably the most honorable thing you could do for yourself." He offers this advice to other veterans: "Talking about it, whether it be with your family or another veteran . . . it's good to get it out—don't keep it in the box under your bed."

Since the war, Andrew Kubacki educated himself on US involvement in Iraq. "I was naive," he says. "I was just doing what I was told. But then when I got out, I started reading more things and other sides. . . . I didn't make a difference. If anything, I made matters worse. It was disappointing to . . . find out that we shouldn't have been there." These feelings compounded other problems in his civilian life. He states, "I never traded my humanity for patriotism. A lot of people did. I never did anything I shouldn't do." Referring to the torture of prisoners at Abu Ghraib, he says, "There are people that would beat up our prisoners or shoot the dogs—and forget that these people are human too—just fighting on the different side, fighting for a different belief system." David Wood notes, "Those who have experienced a moral wound [tend] to react with cynicism or bitterness, to distrust authority; to be more prone to anxiety, depression, . . . isolation, or self-medication of drugs, alcohol," and, most commonly, "to never talk about the war."[45] Kubacki resents being punished, marginalized, and stigmatized for seeking mental health care in the Army but now understands that he is not alone.

US Army National Guard veteran Neal Mays didn't kick in doors or fight building to building during his time in service from 2008 to 2016.[46] When Mays served in Operation Iraqi Freedom in 2009–10, his job was boring. As a gunner on the back of a Humvee, Mays would ride for hours across the desert from Kuwait to Baghdad, listening to Metallica songs to pass the time. "The first six to eight hours is pretty boring land in Iraq. It's pretty flat. It was all desert," remembers Neal Mays. "Not much happens there. Not a lot of action.

Not a lot of nothing." He says, "We would go all over . . . all up and down Iraq."
Mays explains, "We can't go very fast, so we'd push, and it would take a long
time sometimes, and we would get stuck because of an IED, or we'd have to
wait for EOD [Explosive Ordinance Disposal] to blow up an IED." To avoid
unnecessary risks, "we always traveled at night." That's not to say that being
outside the wire was safe. "It was 2009–10. Things calmed down a little bit."
Nonetheless, the fear of incoming, the expectation of dying, and a culmination
of acute stress could be damaging. "There were sometimes where definitely I
thought I was going to die."

Neal Mays believes he had been lucky to deploy to Iraq at the time he
did. "Mostly I missed home," he admits. "It was just the day-to-day—always
being super alert, always being on edge, always being super hypervigilant, all
the time, 24–7, and having mortars come in" on base. "You can't even sleep,
because you've got mortars coming in and blowing up buildings—and don't
trust," he says. "I'm still super hypervigilant, and can't seem to relax, and play
scenarios in my head." According to the *DSM-5*, directly experiencing combat
and death is only one cause of PTSD among many. Experiencing repeated or
extreme exposure to the traumatic event, such as living in a war zone, mortar
attacks, and the fear of dying, can also lead to PTSD.

After a year in Iraq, Neal Mays returned to the States and finished out his
enlistment in the Army. As they arrived on base in Fort McCoy, Wisconsin,
the unit went through demobilization. He remembers wanting "to get through
it. You just want to get home," he explains. "If you put down anything, they're
going to slow the whole process down." Impatient with the process, Mays preferred not to report any mental health concerns. "You've already been sitting
there for eight hours, trying to just get through this little, stupid thing." He
says, "You just check the box. You don't care. Whatever it is, you put zero. . . .
You put no issues, just so you can get through it."

The reintegration process was supposed to function efficiently. Mays says,
"That's how most of the military is—you just want to check the box." He
described an impersonal process: "you kind of go through a lot of PowerPoints
about suicide and all this stuff. They call it death by PowerPoint. 'click, click,
click, click,' we have to do this, 'click, click, click.'" He believes, "They just click,
click, click. They don't care."

Neal Mays was also kicked out of the Army with a general discharge under
honorable conditions. After coming back to Fort McCoy, he experienced

symptoms commonly associated with post-traumatic stress disorder. Even though mental health services were available, Mays feared retaliation for reporting issues. "What's going to happen?" he wondered. "Will they kick me out? You're not supposed to have that stuff in the military," believed Mays. "The military taught me to be strong and to be a man." He saw "mental illnesses" as "a sign of weakness." He admits, "I didn't want to be weak because all the other guys are handling it fine. Why can't I?" he asked. "I didn't get shot over there, so why would I have any issues?" Mays mistakenly believed, "It can't be from [the war]. I didn't see any of my friends die in front of me, so obviously, I don't have PTSD—that's what I thought at the time." In fact, Mays's behavior meets many of the criteria identified in the *DSM-5*, and he has since been diagnosed with PTSD. Media portrayals of "crazy vets" with PTSD distort the reality of war-related trauma. Partly in consequence of popular misconceptions, Mays lacked the language or self-awareness to understand what he was experiencing.

In 2011, Neal Mays drank alcohol to dull symptoms of post-traumatic stress disorder, but alcohol also made him violent and enflamed the underlying problems. When he came home from Iraq, Mays and another soldier drank heavily. "It was just a disaster waiting to happen," he realizes. "We didn't know how to handle coming back. We both came back, and all of a sudden, we were both angry and irritable—we would punch holes in the walls, and we would get into fights." These behaviors would lead to reckless and self-destructive behavior. "We were addicted to adrenaline. We would do dangerous things—drive cars really fast, get in fights—we were just always looking for that heightened sense," recalls Mays. They would get belligerently drunk and "would just end up crying. "Why are you acting like this?" he wondered. "We had some issues: a lot of drinking, a lot of fighting, a lot of breaking things, and just angry a lot." He adds, "Me and him both got in relationships, because I'm sure we were lonely." Feelings of detachment and estrangement led to angry outbursts and regrettable incidents. "We were both mean to our significant others."

For Mays, smoking marijuana seemed to relieve the depression, calmed his anger, and relaxed his hypervigilance. However, the National Guard required mandatory urinalysis. He got caught with THC in his system. "They were trying to kick me out," likely under a Chapter 9 for first-time drug use. But one commanding officer vouched for his service record. He sought treatment at a thirty-day inpatient rehabilitation program in St. Cloud, Minnesota. With only a minor infraction for smoking marijuana, Mays completed the rehabilitation program but discontinued counseling. "I stopped smoking pot," he explains, "but I'm still drinking." Then, in the summer of 2011, Mays got arrested for driving while intoxicated. "I was doing 137 miles an hour in my Mustang." He bailed out of jail, missed Guard duty, crashed the car two weeks later, and got another (driving under the influence) DUI (.07). This misconduct meets the criteria for Chapter 14, repeated drug and alcohol abuse. In 2016, Specialist Mays was administratively separated from the National Guard with a general under honorable discharge, which denied him certain veterans' entitlements. After that, Mays had a son and tried to "straighten up." Yet, sobriety was short-lived. His drinking worsened. Then, he started using methamphetamine, and everything went downhill from there. He eventually lost his job, his home, his car, and his freedom. Neal Mays spent two years incarcerated in prison on drug-related and theft charges.[47] Today, he has a good career, proudly working with an elevator union.

Despite more progressive attitudes in the Army on PTSD, TBI, and depression, the military continues to punish those with mental health and behavioral problems, especially for first-time drug use. Chapter 9 administrative separation involves the failure to complete drug or alcohol rehabilitation. This means that a service member failed to complete or relapsed after seeking help for substance abuse. According to a 2012 US Army report, Chapter 9 discharges doubled from 2006 to 2011. Chapter 14 separations for repeat drug offenses have steadily increased each year between 2001 to 2011, from 862 in 2001 to 3,116 in 2011.[48] The US Army takes great pride in its policies of punishing members for drug use, framing the increase in administrative separations as progress and improving mission readiness.

But from a different perspective, punitive policies for substance use disorder are draconian and regressive. Rather than providing treatment, the military kicks out personnel with mental health, substance use disorders, or behavioral problems that often result from fighting in the Global War on Terrorism. One study of VA health records showed that among 206,000 veterans, one-third were diagnosed with at least one mental health disorder, and 41 percent were diagnosed with a mental health, including depression, or a behavioral adjustment disorder.[49] In the first ten years after 9/11, misconduct separations accounted for a vast number of the Army's nearly 180,000 administrative

discharges. As double punishment, former service members with misconduct discharges are usually denied access to VA benefits, disability rights, and
health care. It costs less money and takes less time to discharge soldiers with
behavioral issues than to treat their underlying mental health problems. There
is a long, well-documented history of these policies. Over the past fifty years,
Vietnam veterans have been fighting against less-than-honorable discharges,
but despite protests and reforms, "bad paper" continues to punish the next
generation of war veterans.

CONCLUSION

As the clock stuck midnight on the Obama presidency, John Rowan published
a forceful op-ed in the *New York Times* calling for the outgoing president to
issue a full pardon to every veteran with "bad paper" discharges. Invoking the
memory of the Vietnam War, Rowan cited the precedent of President Jimmy
Carter, who "issued full pardons to Americans who had refused induction
via the Vietnam-era draft, erasing the felony-level offense of draft resistance
for thousands of people."[50] He writes, "Countless Vietnam veterans were also
separated from service unfairly with 'bad paper' administrative discharges
that denied them critical benefits." Since its founding, the Vietnam Veterans
of America has advocated on behalf of disabled veterans, "bad paper veterans," and incarcerated veterans. President of the VVA John Rowan says, "It
is unconscionable that our newest veterans are being discharged for similar
reasons." Without access to care, veterans with less-than-honorable discharges
are "more like to become substance abusers, homeless or incarcerated—or to
die by suicide."

In arguing for full pardons, Rowan retold the story of Kristofer Goldsmith,
who "photograph[ed] mutilated bodies" during a one-year tour in Baghdad.
Like many veterans in this chapter, when Sergeant Goldsmith returned to
the United States, he began to drink heavily, isolated himself, and had family
troubles. In 2007, he attempted suicide. Weeks later, the Army issued him an
"other-than-honorable discharge" for "serious misconduct." Rowan writes, "His
undiagnosed and untreated post-traumatic stress disorder was hard enough
for him to deal with—now he had discharge papers that looked like a criminal
record." For years, Goldsmith fought the discharge. He has since become a
national figure in the fight for veterans' benefits. The problem is systemic and

cultural: "that a suicide attempt amounts to a serious act of misconduct."[51] Rowan's op-ed cogently argued for the forgiveness of all bad paper discharges. But unfortunately, President Obama declined his big Carter-like moment.

Nonetheless, in 2017, the Fairness for Veterans Act was passed to reform the discharge appeals process for "bad paper veterans" who were diagnosed with PTSD or TBI.[52] It required Discharge Review Boards to "'give liberal consideration' to the former member that post-traumatic stress disorder or traumatic brain injury potentially contributed to the original characterization of the member's discharge or dismissal." John Rowan called the Fairness for Veterans Act a "reason for every American to celebrate."[53] This legislation represented a watershed moment in the history of Vietnam veterans' activism and the decades-long fight for expanded access to VA benefits. But this legislation acknowledges the problems of misconduct discharges only as an afterthought, without addressing the root cause of the problem within the military. And because appealing a discharge takes expert knowledge, resources, and time, it also permits systemic and social inequality among veterans.

CHAPTER 6

Another Signature Wound

Substance Use Disorder and the Opioid Epidemic

Visualize a Marine Corps recruitment advertisement: starch white caps, bold blue dress coats, polished gold buttons, and crisp, ironed white trousers. Front and center, one marine stands at attention, one of the few, the proud. Fearlessly, his dark, penetrating eyes glare indirectly toward the camera. His square jaws are clenched tightly. The distinctive contour lines of his clean-shaven face gradate from light into shadows, highlighting the texture of his deep Brown skin. The message is subtle but deliberate—"only one color matters in the Marines." Behind his figure, a group of marines are standing in formation, motionless, controlled breath, equidistant. "We got your six." Their shoulders are aligned, chests swollen, arms angular, bodies parallel, converging on a single vanishing point. Their identities blur together into a monochromatically navy-blue backdrop. The Marine Corps is a singular collective noun, one body, one accord, and one purpose.

The total percentage of the American population that serves in the military is at a historic low, so the military relies on marketing campaigns like this one to advertise the benefits of service, offering economic incentives to fill the ranks: cash bonuses and promises of educational opportunities.[1] But this image does not reflect real life; it is the artistic composition of a male fantasy, designed by a team of specialists, tested with a control group, and carefully curated to attract teenagers. Currently, if you click on the benefits tab on the Marine Corps website, you can navigate the various rewards of service: "financial security, advancements, benefits"; "professional development"; "leadership and management skills." Neoliberal discourse like this persuades potential recruits to believe that military experiences will translate directly to their job résumés as civilians. But the Marine Corps offers more than the standard entry-level job. In the Marines, you can experience "pride of belonging," "challenge," "courage, poise, and self-confidence," and, of course, "travel and adventure." The emblazoned symbol of the Marine Corps—the Eagle, Globe, and Anchor—is stamped across the web pages.[2] The Marines still takes great pride in being toughest and best dressed, a continuation of its storied past.

Despite the recruitment posters and popular images, military service members are neither homogenous nor guaranteed to enjoy economic success and prosperous careers. Those possibilities can be easily lost at war, when mental health becomes collateral damage. A 2010 study found that marines who deployed to combat zones in Iraq and Afghanistan between 2001 and 2007 were more likely to have PTSD, more likely to be charged with "misconduct," and more likely to be discharged without benefits. PTSD was a significant predictor of misconduct. The marines who deployed to war and were diagnosed with PTSD were 8.6 times more likely to be discharged for drug use. Consequentially, Marines Corps combat veterans with PTSD were more likely to be denied access to care. In other words, the first generation of Iraq and Afghanistan combat marines was extremely vulnerable to punitive drug policies even at a time of military mental health care reforms. Without veterans benefits, these marines were also more likely to be incarcerated after war.[3]

In this chapter, I tell the story of three formerly incarcerated Marine Corps veterans, exploring the recent history of mental health, punishment, and the opioid epidemic. After multiple deployments, post-9/11 veterans often became entangled in a nexus of military and civilian justice policies that punish deviant behavior, stigmatize mental illness, and criminalize drug use. Substance use disorder is another "signature wound" of the war on terror, but it receives neither the care nor the recognition of other veterans' issues because of cultural stigmas attached to drugs in the United States.

A NEW DRUG CRISIS IN THE MILITARY

After the September 11 attacks, a generation of Americans volunteered to serve the military, expecting to fulfill a timeless civic duty, to reap the social benefits of wartime service, and, for many, to seek revenge and kill terrorists. James Torrey saw the Marine Corps as an escape from his life.[4] He never met his father. One of his mother's boyfriends was the son of a chief of police in Ludlow, Massachusetts. "My mom had drug issues, drug problems, and I used to get beaten pretty heavily by all of her boyfriends." He lived with his grandmother off and on. In school, James was a disruptive, though bright, student. He excelled at mathematics, and his grades improved after he was diagnosed with ADHD and medicated.

On the day a Marine recruiter visited his high school, Torrey was only sixteen years old. Later that evening, he asked his mom for permission to sign up for the delayed entry program. "9/11 had happened a few years before, and it really pissed me off," Torrey recalls. He took a practice ASVAB (Armed Services Vocational Aptitude Battery) and scored in the top percentile. The recruiter said, "'You can have any job you want. What do you want to do in the Marines?'" Immature and crass, Torrey responded, "I wanted to throw grenades and fuck bitches." "'Infantry, you're signed up!'" Of course, the reasons most men enlist in combat infantry are more complicated and nuanced than that, but this shows Torrey's mindset at that time. Either way, he certainly did not join the Marine Corps just to pay for college. He wanted to kill terrorists.

At its most basic purpose, Marine Corps boot camp prepares humans to kill or die at war.[5] After turning seventeen, James Torrey was getting "smoked" at Parris Island in the sweltering summer heat. "It's soupy. It's so humid" that at the end of "the day you have salt stains on your cammies—and then the sand fleas." Recruits were forced to do PT (physical training) in the sandpits. "They make you march there and stir up all the sand fleas. They start biting you, and they make you stand in attention, and you can't move. If anybody is caught moving—time starts over." Exercises like these forced recruits to bear physical and psychological discomfort and to put the needs of the unit above one's own, or else everyone gets punished. Recruits must learn to trust and depend on one another. "You can't let anybody down." Torrey thought, "I don't want everybody else to get smoked for another hour. So you start thinking of others instead of just thinking of yourself." The psychological discipline of the Marine Corps is paramount. "They brainwashed me really quickly. In those three months, I was a machine for them." He reflects, "I would call it severe training because it severed any kind of thinking I had before that." Coming out of boot camp, Torrey says, "I wanted to kill. I wanted to go to combat, and I wanted to jump on the grenade for somebody else."

In 2004, James Torrey deployed to Iraq. Before deployment, Torrey completed infantry battalion training at Camp Geiger. He gained endurance, running and preparing for the imminent deployment to Iraq. But nothing could truly prepare him for the reality of combat. Torrey recounted one particularly traumatic memory. "We load up in the convoy and we're going on a mission. And we don't make it far," he recounts. "All of a sudden, boom, boom, boom, IEDs blow up all the trucks." The squad leader "lost his legs—boom—cut off, both of them." He remembers, "We're ripping people out of the trucks," trying to save them from burning to death. "I had screwed my back up very badly and screwed up my knee."

These injuries would eventually render him non-deployable, leading him down a path toward depression, drugs, and a dishonorable discharge. "We started pulling people out, and all we can smell is gunpowder, burning flesh . . . and I can still smell it sometimes today." But the danger was not yet over. "Not only did we just get hit by IEDs," explains Torrey, "ting, ting, ting—it's an ambush. They're trying to kill us all as we're getting out." He thought: "You can sit in there, burn to death, or die of smoke inhalation, or you can get out and fight." In the confusion of combat, Torrey felt "disoriented. When those bombs go off, you can't see or hear anything for a minute—the smoke, the dust, everything, and then your ears are" ringing. "You can't hear nothing—blood comes out of your ears."

Torrey graduated from boot camp with another Marine who was killed in action. "He was in front of me, and we went" into a complex. Torrey recounts, "There was someone in the left-hand corner behind a wall of sandbags. And you hear burrrrrrrr, bop, bop, bop, bop, bop. You can feel the bullets. I can feel the bullets bouncing off of him." The tempo of Torrey's speech increases as he describes the graphic memories. "We're working on my boy who got hit in his femoral artery . . . so we threw some tourniquets on him. They tried to throw quick clot in there just to see if they could stop the bleeding, and it wasn't working, and we had like no vehicles, all our vehicles were hit. It was a daisy chain, IEDs, bam!" Torrey recalls, "We just started running people back. . . . So, I carried this guy, and I'm screwed up. I'm hurt so bad. I'm running, I'm talking, I'm trying to keep him with it—he's not out yet." Torrey collapsed under the weight of the body. "He died on my shoulder." In disbelief, Torrey clung to hope, thinking if he pounded on his chest hard enough, like in the movies, his friend might regain consciousness. "I got back there, and I started shaking my corpsman, telling him, 'you need to fix him.' He was only 18." Witnessing the death of another marine forever changed Torrey's military career and personal life. "When he died, I was very cold. I didn't want no more relationships and I didn't want no more friends. I had a friend, so that's it. He died. Now, I don't have friends." Torrey blamed himself for years, a natural and common feeling among combat veterans. "I felt hopeless—I fucked up. I didn't run fast enough. These are the things I'm always battling."

The culture of the Marine Corps does not customarily encourage men to ask for help, and in 2004, military doctors still knew very little about the effects of traumatic brain injuries. James Torrey claims, "When we were getting ready to come home, they set up trailers, and they had some computers taking tests, they are mental evaluation tests." But after returning from a warzone, Torrey wanted to avoid the bureaucratic delays, psychiatrists, and examinations. During demobilization, he believed, "if you want to go home and see your family, you'll answer these questions right, and if not, you're going to go to a mental institution for thirty, sixty, ninety days and you're not going to get to go home and see your family." Marines are engendered to bear pain in silence. When asked if anything could have prevented his post-combat adjustment problems, Torrey says resentfully, "It would've been nice if they didn't make us feel weak if we told them we had any kind of problem."

Returning to the United States while comrades were still deployed could lead to survivor's guilt or depression, potentially causing behavioral problems. Torrey says, "I had torn ligaments in my knee and my back was really starting to give me problems after that. So I actually got surgery on my back, and I was not deployable after that, and I got really depressed." Being labeled non-deployable compounded the mental health problems he was experiencing. "I *wanted* to go back," Torrey emphasizes. He lost a sense of purpose and mission, falling into a cycle of drinking, drug use, and depression. "Me and a few other guys that had the same issues with some injuries and stuff, we started drinking a lot, and with that, we started doing co[caine]." To afford the cost of drugs, "we started trying to make moves where we would get some for somebody and then get some for free. And by doing that, NCIS [Naval Criminal Investigative Service] ended up getting involved." He explains, "That landed me in the brig with a couple of different options—BCD [bad conduct discharge] and ten years in the brig or a dishonorable discharge and three years." Torrey opted to serve the shorter prison sentence and accept the consequences of the dishonorable discharge.

Incarcerated veterans are often punished double by the military and the criminal justice systems. James Torrey served thirty months in the Navy brig and took the dishonorable discharge. "I was in trouble all the time," including for assault and battery. After a series of back surgeries, Torrey also developed a dependency to prescription opioids. Substance abuse also inflamed the underlying psychological and behavioral problems. "I had a doctor who was prescribing me Oxycodone, like 180 a month, with some OxyContin. That was for years," says Torrey. Eventually, the doctor stopped prescribing the drugs, and "I was left to find my own way of getting them." He turned to a criminal lifestyle. Then, when "there was absolutely no way of getting them, I decided to do heroin. From that point on, everything went downhill *real quick.*"

Trajectories like this—from prescription opioids to heroin—were not uncommon among Iraq and Afghanistan war veterans. In 2012, among 440,000 veterans prescribed opioids at the VA, more than one-third were "chronic users," and two-thirds of that number had comorbid mental health diagnoses.[6] That same year, according to the Department of Veterans Affairs, 55,000 military veterans were diagnosed with opioid use disorder.[7] After the Department of Defense and VA implemented stricter policies in the prescription of opioids, some veterans began to use heroin because it was more accessible and affordable.[8] In turn, heroin use increases the risk of overdose among veterans, especially when cut with fentanyl, an often fatal drug.[9] Iraq and Afghanistan war veterans were twice as likely to die of opioid overdose compared to civilians.[10]

In the summer of 2017, James Torrey had been living at Soldier On, at the Leeds Veterans Administration facility in western Massachusetts. In a small office without air-conditioning at the VA, he shared his oral history with me. Torrey had been involved in intensive therapy sessions as part of a treatment regimen. He spoke openly about his mental health problems. "I took a lot of therapy. . . . [O]ne of my therapists told me basically it's desensitizing. The more you talk about something the less it will bother you." He reflects, "It's like the first time you heard about 9/11, it was very devastating . . . but we've heard about it a billion times now, and we could say it without gasping for air and choking up in tears because we've heard it so much, and we've kind of been desensitized." Over the following year, James Torrey completed Veterans Treatment Court in Holyoke, Massachusetts and began the long process of rebuilding his life, working and seeking education, and establishing a healthy relationship with his daughter. But the daily struggle against substance use disorder is often a lifelong battle.

Drug use in the post-9/11 military constituted a "public health crisis." After a whistle-blower incident raised alarms in Congress about opioid use in the military, the Department of Defense launched a study with the Institute of Medicine to analyze policies in order to prevent and treat substance use disorder in the military. The findings were revelatory. Military doctors had prescribed 3.8 million painkillers in 2009 alone. The number of opioid prescriptions had quadrupled since 2001. More than half of service members also reported binge drinking.[11] Despite reforms in the military, alcohol and substance abuse among service members "remains unacceptably high," concluded the study. The Institute of Medicine also found numerous barriers that prevent service members from seeking care—"gaps in insurance coverage, stigma, fear of negative consequences, and lack of confidential services." It recommended expansion of health care and access to outpatient services for those seeking mental health care outside the military. Torrey's oral history reveals how combat-related PTSD can lead to substance abuse and punishment in the military, but it also shows how veterans are often caught in the opioid epidemic after service.

MANHOOD, MULTIPLE DEPLOYMENTS, AND SUBSTANCE USE

The instinct to deny mental health concerns and refuse help becomes ingrained in the mentality of service members during training. Boot camp culminates in the notorious rite of passage into the Marines, a fifty-four-hour training exercise known as the Crucible. Before the recruits graduate, they must pass a final test of endurance and deprivation, designed to push them to their breaking point. "The Crucible was tough," admits Matt Nicholas, "but it got you to work as a team." If one of the recruits struggled, others helped carry their packs. To leave anyone behind would violate the mantra and the sacred code among marines. At the end of the Crucible, the instructors would shake their hands and pin on their uniforms the coveted Eagle, Globe, and Anchor, a distinctive badge of honor symbolizing the Marine Corps' history of fighting in the air, on land, and from the sea. Graduation day was initiation into marine-hood. For many, it was the proudest day of their lives. Matt Nicholas says, "I became a man."[12]

Matt Nicholas served two tours in Iraq in 2005 and 2007.[13] He joined an Explosive Ordinance Disposal team. With that designation, he says, "I knew I was going to war. I didn't know what it was going to be like. You look at movies and you see the worst, but especially in my job—you were just waiting to get blown up." Nicholas provided security detail. "We worked 24 hours a day. Grunts would find an explosive device and call it in. Some days we'd be out all day." During those first nine months in Iraq, Nicholas went on 170 missions to detonate or disarm improvised explosive devices. The Marines were still learning to deal with the threat of IEDs in Iraq in 2005. "There'd be missions where nothing would go down. But there were places—I still think about this road today—called route iron," recalls Nicholas. "A bunch of our vehicles were getting blown up. Then we started getting better equipment. The first few months we were there, we were putting sandbags in Humvees. By the end of it, we had different vehicles that were pretty much bomb proof."

Disarming or detonating improvised explosives is not only incredibly dangerous but also an unpredictable, high-stress situation, a state of constant fear of instantaneous death. Nicholas explains, "You never know what's going to happen. There are a lot of unknowns." Providing security detail for the ones handling the devices meant being constantly alert, scanning for possible enemies, and assessing potential threats: snipers, suicide bombers, or small-arms fire. "You're just trying to stay alive and do anything to keep you and your buddy alive." Mistakes could be fatal. Usually, soldiers do not realize the extent of the psychological changes until afterward, when the calm settles in at night or in the monotony of life on base. Nicholas explains, "I don't think I really thought about it in the field. I didn't think about it at all, really. It was something that your mind and body was trained to do. Maybe, when I got back to Lejeune," he admits, but "I don't think even then I grasped what I just did for the past nine months. I just thought that was normal because I was in the Marines. When I look back now, some of those missions were crazy." He says, "I still think about days and the people—some of the bad stuff." In hindsight, Nicholas reflects, "I think that first tour changed me."

The stresses of combat accumulate over time. Nicholas's second deployment to Iraq in 2007 was not nearly as dangerous, but his mental health problems worsened. "People were still getting hurt and killed, but nothing compared to two years before that." Nicholas says, "We were there to win hearts and minds. We'd bring soccer balls to villages, food and water. The rules of engagement were a lot different," he explains. "The first deployment, you weren't letting anyone get near you. The second deployment, you had to let them live their lives. We were just in the way, really."

Nicholas never seriously considered reporting any mental health concerns. "Not at all. I don't even think it came up. I don't think until maybe year three or four I was in, people started getting diagnosed with PTSD." The Marines also conducted urinalysis to screen for substance use. "They started popping piss tests for drugs. A lot of people got kicked out. A lot of *good* people got kicked out. A lot of people ruined their careers because they failed a pop piss test because they wanted to mask whatever problems they had." The Marines justified urinalysis and punitive discharges in the name of mission readiness, but in Nicholas's thinking, many of those who self-medicated with drugs had served honorably and deserved treatment. An administrative discharge for misconduct prevented many veterans from receiving VA care, denying them mental health services and options for recovery.

Redeployments create innumerable burdens on military families and relationships, which can cause conflict when troops return home.[14] Nicholas says, "A girl stuck by me through the Marine Corps. We did the long-distance thing. It was tough. That's why I couldn't wait to get out." In the meantime, he started binge drinking, and "when I got out, I just continued" to drink. "I didn't need to work," he recalls. "I was taking time off. I was partying and drinking a lot. When I look back, thinking of it, I probably was drinking to hide some of those memories." He was honorably discharged from the Marine Corps in 2008.

Over the next ten years, Nicholas continued to drink, fight, and use opioids. "I remember getting arrested a few times," he says. "I was a bigger guy. It took the whole force to take me down. I wasn't just giving up" without a fight. The underlying PTSD became explosive after drinking alcohol and taking Percocet, a powerful opiate. Over time, he developed a substance use disorder. "It was reoccurring. I would stop for a year" and then start again. He checked himself into an in-patient facility. "I would go there for six months or eight months. I would sober up, come back, and last for a little bit, and then fall back in that same hole."

After being arrested in Sea Isle City, New Jersey, Nicholas got connected with the VA and began the long process of recovery. Today, the VA provides disability, counseling, and outreach services to veterans in prison and jail. Sitting in a jail cell, Nicholas reached out to the VA and made connections with social services. "This lady helped me out. It was a life-changer because . . . she understood. She gave me a couple numbers to get help through the VA. I didn't know nothing about it. I didn't know you could get help like that. She gave me these numbers, and I used them." The early intervention helped. After getting released, he visited the Coatesville VA Medical Center. "Once you're in the VA system, you see so many people—countless psychologists and therapists." He qualified for a 70 percent disability rating.

In 2017, Matt Nicholas was sentenced to complete a treatment program at the Philadelphia Veterans Treatment Court. After crashing his vehicle, he went to jail because he had marijuana in his system. "It was bullshit!" he exclaims resentfully. Participants in treatment courts often express frustration that the mandatory programs of treatment and urinalysis did not fit the nature of their life situation that led to involvement with the criminal justice system.[15] At the time, Nicholas had suicidal ideations and dealt with depression. "Money was a big stressor and becoming a father." In a sense, he was punished for suicidal behavior, but once part of the court system, Nicholas finally received treatment for depression and PTSD.

It's Memorial Day week in 2019, graduation day at the Philadelphia Veterans Treatment Court. The judge invited the graduates to address the court. For some, it's short and obligatory. For others, it's somber and cathartic. During the ceremony, a robust, dark-haired Marine Corps veteran approached the podium. Judge Patrick Dugan shook Matt Nicholas's hand, praising his courageous service in ordinance disposal and briefly describing the perilous dangers of the job. Nicholas spoke from prepared notes, first sharing that more than a year before, he had suicidal ideations. Then, he recounted a story about taking a road trip recently to Boston to memorialize a fallen battle buddy. He expressed deep gratitude for family and life. He quickly thanked the veteran mentors and stepped aside. In the audience, his family members rejoiced for second chances and future possibilities.

Today, Nicholas focuses exclusively on work, school, and his future. "I just try to keep to myself really. I don't really talk about much." He says, "I don't even try to think about it. I just try to throw it under the carpet because I know that mental health is a part of me now." Understandably, he would prefer to forget the past and live for the present. "I really don't think about it. I don't watch international news. . . . I don't really know what's going on with the military no more. Just a different chapter in my life," he says. "Move forward."

More than fifteen years after Iraq, Matt Nicholas feels conflicted about his role in the war and avoids talking about it. On the one hand, he still believes deeply in the idea of American exceptionalism. He saw it as a sacred duty to fight for the United States Marine Corps. Yet this veteran still struggles to move on. "I know what's right and wrong," says Nicholas. "While I was in, I chose to do something wrong, and then I choose to do something right. We didn't want to be there. We didn't want anything to do with these people." He did his job to the best of his ability, and that's what matters. Still, he mourns and feels stuck. Nicholas works overtime, goes to school, and takes care of his family.

Who has time to talk about the past? At the end of our interview, this stoic man, still wearing the grime from a hard day's work in construction, reflected: "You know, I was helping you out doing this, but I think it's helped me out. It's definitely helping me out because I don't try to talk about it. I try to keep it moving and see what happens. But every day is a fight for me," he admitted. "My mind is definitely changed, and I think it's from that first time in Iraq."

THE WAR ON OPIOIDS

The current opioid epidemic in the United States connects only indirectly to the Global War on Terrorism, but post-9/11 veterans are caught in the battlespace of a concurrent mental health and drug crisis in the United States.[16] The opioid pipeline crosses international drug markets, carrying the raw materials for the production of heroin from the poppy fields of Afghanistan to the streets of Europe and communities around the world. Although most heroin in the United States comes from Mexico, Afghanistan has been the world's leading producer of illicit drugs since 2001, the poppy harvest supplying 90 percent of the world's heroin. What started in 2001 as a military campaign to avenge the terrorist attacks on 9/11 transformed into perpetual warfare in the Middle East, which, consequentially, fueled the global drug trade through a network of poppy farmers in Afghanistan, Taliban leaders, and international drug syndicates. Since the invasion of Afghanistan, opioids have grown into a full-blown, worldwide pandemic.

At the dawn of the war in Afghanistan, the US military primarily targeted al-Qaeda and the Taliban leadership. Initially with high US public approval and rapid military success, the Afghanistan War transformed into a twenty-year counterinsurgency with little chance of US victory. The "Afghanistan Papers," a collection of intelligence reports, government documents, and oral history interviews with military officials acquired by the *Washington Post*, reveal the connection between the Global War on Terrorism and the war on drugs, showing how the latter severely undermined the former. Named similarly as the "Pentagon Papers" to amplify the distinct parallels between the wars in Vietnam and Afghanistan, these documents similarly expose a long-standing tradition of American officials publicly promising progress, but intelligence reports prove that policies in Afghanistan undermined and contradicted military objectives.

After the initially successful military campaign, the Bush administration fought a second front in Afghanistan, targeting the production of opium, exercising a war on drugs mentality while engaging a nation-building project.[17] Paradoxically, the Taliban had successfully eradicated the production of opium in Afghanistan by declaring it un-Islamic and banning poppies.[18] When the invasion disrupted the power of the Taliban, Afghan farmers returned to the cash crop to survive in a war-torn, arid land. By 2006, Afghanistan supplied 80 to 90 percent of the world's supply of opium. The drug trade paralleled the resurgence of the Taliban, so policymakers presumed that opium financed terrorism.[19] Policymakers asserted that fighting a war on drugs in Afghanistan would be necessary to fight terrorism.[20] Directed by the Drug Enforcement Agency and State Department, the United States waged a new war on opium in 2006, initiating Operation River Dance. Publicly, US officials boasted incredible progress in the effort to eradicate Afghanistan of opium, but the campaign quickly backfired. The war on opium actually drove Afghans into clutches of terrorists.

Destruction of poppy fields generated blowback, radicalizing poor farmers and turning them against Americans. They planted booby traps, flooded fields, and sabotaged the machinery of the war on opium. The United States also sprayed herbicides to eradicate poppy crops, despite the dangers of poisoning water and food supplies and the potential carcinogenic effects of herbicides. US military leadership had opposed the use of herbicides in Afghanistan, viewing opium as a law enforcement concern, not a legitimate military target. Many also feared the effects of herbicides on US troops, heeding the mistakes of the Vietnam War, when Agent Orange caused cancers among veterans.[21] Not only was Operation River Dance a strategic failure, but opium actually reached record levels of production in the following years. By destroying the livelihoods of Afghans, Americans recreated the conditions for a prolonged insurgency and practically guaranteed that the initial military and political successes during the first wave of the war on terrorism were undermined, contradicted, and bogged down by the war on opium. The failed counterinsurgency in Afghanistan lasted twenty years, affecting two generations of veterans and costing billions of dollars.

Waging a kinder, gentler war on drugs, the Obama administration invested billions of dollars to develop and diversify Afghanistan's agricultural sector, building irrigation systems, modernizing equipment, and creating an infrastructure to produce and export legal agricultural products. This, too, failed.[22] Decades of war, since at least the Soviet-Afghan War (1979–89) destroyed agricultural production, making poppies the nation's singular cash crop.[23] Narcotics outmatched the legal economy of Afghanistan by more than an estimated $1.3 billion.[24] The US occupation of Afghanistan further destabilized the region. Perpetual warfare and violence effectively ensured that Afghans would continue to produce opium as a means of survival.

The Obama administration built a carceral state in Afghanistan, investing $4.5 billion in drug interdiction and law enforcement, but confiscated only 2 percent of the nation's annual output of drugs. The US government created a legal system, constructed prisons, organized courts, and trained lawyers, judges, and prosecutors in Afghanistan.[25] But corruption was endemic to the Afghan justice system. Few drug traffickers were ever prosecuted, and fewer served prison sentences. In 2011, Genevieve Chase, a soldier with Pashtun-language skills who served in Afghanistan, testified before the US Senate Committee on Foreign Relations. She stated, "We threw billions of dollars at civil affairs and reconstruction projects that we thought would win the 'hearts and minds' of the Afghans." But many Afghans believed the US-backed government "contained nepotistic and corrupt officials. With the help of these same embezzling officials," the United States supported "the eradication of their rival tribe's poppies while failing to provide alternative crops to the poorest of farmers. We forced the farmers and drug lords to align with the Taliban and al-Qaeda in order to protect their livelihoods."[26] Even the Obama administration's "soft power" approach in Afghanistan failed too, entrenching opposition to the US occupation.

In 2017, with the full force of American airpower, the Trump administration bombarded Afghanistan with F-22 Raptors and B-52s, dropping two-thousand- and five-hundred-pound bombs on drug labs in Helmand Province. Operation Iron Tempest was praised in media as a no-holds-barred, total war on opium.[27] It was yet another colossal failure of American policy, misguided by hubris and misinformed with faulty intelligence. The United States spent inordinate sums of American taxpayers' dollars blowing up makeshift drug labs that produced only small amounts of opium, estimated in the thousands of dollars—not millions, as claimed.[28] The operation faded into quiet abandonment. Efforts to bomb Afghanistan's drug production into complete annihilation represent the futility of American policies in Afghanistan as a whole. The US spent $9 billion in the war on opium, but production of the raw materials needed for heroin tripled from 2002 to 2017.[29]

No amount of American might, money, or men could counteract the destabilizing and radicalizing effect of the US military presence and policies in Afghanistan. Afghanistan is now the world's leading producer of opium.[30] Rather than destroying, or even deterring, opium production in Afghanistan, US policies fueled the explosion of heroin in the twenty-first century. The United States' joint wars on terrorism and drugs only reinforced the ranks of terrorists and augmented the global heroin trade. It seems that the more Washington asserts its power on foreign nations, the greater the inertia of resistance and inevitable blowback. This, in turn, necessitated multiple deployments from the small percentage of Americans who fought the Global War on Terrorism, putting them at increased risk for PTSD and TBI and leading many down this cycle of substance use disorder and incarceration. In 2020, an article in the journal of *Military Medicine* found that combat veterans were at an alarming risk of opioid use disorder, fatal overdose, and heroin abuse. It described the opioid epidemic as a "threat to national security."[31]

James Marciano had completed four combat tours in Iraq and Afghanistan between 2007 and 2015.[32] His grandfather was a World War II veteran. The memory of admiring his grandfather's medals had a strong influence on the trajectory of his life. On September 11, Marciano was in eighth grade English class. He remembers that the teacher came in and turned on the television. The first tower had already been hit. James witnessed the second plane smash into the second World Trade Center tower live on television. When he turned eighteen, he enlisted in the Marine Corps, carrying on the family legacy of service.

In January 2008, Marciano received orders to mobilize for deployment to Iraq. "A lot of the guys had just come back from Fallujah," he recalls. "I was with Second Platoon." When he first arrived, "there were a few guys that looked out for me. But . . . you've got to prove yourself in order to gain their trust." Marciano says, "You can train all day—But until you fight, it's completely different. You never know who's gonna freeze or who will have your back in those situations." The stakes were high. "It's Iraq. We're going to go, do our job, and fall in with them." Some members of the Second Platoon felt disillusioned after being recalled after Fallujah. "The other guys just didn't give a shit," Marciano recalls. Stop-loss policies, which prevented members from returning at the end of their enlistments if their units were deployed, were extremely unpopular among troops.[33] After fighting and bleeding together, the Second Platoon became a brotherhood. "I got to the unit with three other guys I was in school with," says Marciano. "We watched each other's backs."

In 2008, Marciano completed a seven-month tour in Iraq. After experiencing combat, some marines developed a strategy of uncoping, denying the reality of traumatic experience. "You just remain emotionless. You stayed emotionally detached," Marciano says. "Because when your emotions get involved, you're in trouble." He explains, "It's horrible to say, but you just got to keep going." He says, "You can't stop and think about it because . . . lives are at stake." Marciano became conditioned to life in a combat zone, remaining in a constant state of fear and hyper-vigilance. "Your guard is always up. You're always on high alert. And it's hard to turn off." After living in a combat zone, he would be "jumpy, easily startled," and would "get angry." Even when he started realizing that the post-traumatic stress was affecting his behavior, he decided it was best to deal with it on his own, "whether it was going to the gym, alcohol, or just not even paying attention to your feelings," Marciano says. "In the Marine Corps, you [are] not really big on feelings." If he sought mental health service, he believed it would adversely affect his career. "Nobody went to mental health. Nobody sought help. They just suppressed it." He returned to the United States in September 2008 with little time for adjustment. By October, they were already preparing for a second deployment to Afghanistan.

Multiple deployments were the defining feature of forever war. More than 2.5 million US troops served in Iraq and Afghanistan, and 40 percent served multiple tours.[34] The likelihood of PTSD or other mental health problems increases substantially with the number of deployments to combat zones.[35] While the war in Iraq was winding down by 2007–08, the war in Afghanistan was escalating.[36] After four separate deployments, James Marciano also felt stuck between his life in the United States and his duties as a marine. It felt like "deployment was home. You just came back to the US to prepare to go back."[37]

The first time Marciano deployed to Afghanistan was in 2009. "There was nothing there," he remembers. It was entirely different from Iraq. "We did the invasion of southern Afghanistan," he recounts. "It was a bad deployment. Again, I was with Second Platoon. I pretty much spent the entire deployment outside the wire." He joined a wrecker crew, "which is glorified tow truck." The quick reaction force (QRF) team would be called out to provide fire support or tow vehicles that were hit by IEDs. "I got there in May," recalls Marciano. "There was a truck right inside the gate to the motor pool, that had just come off the road, hit an IED, melted the three-inch armored glass out of it. The doors were mangled. Nobody survived that." His first time outside the wire, they were on a resupply mission, and three trucks hit IEDs. "We were pinned down for quite a while by indirect fire and small arms fire after they hit our trucks." When he finally made it back to Camp Leatherneck, Marciano realized, "the shit is real. This isn't like Iraq at all."

An estimated one in three military personnel who deployed to combat zones experience traumatic brain injuries, which increases the risk of PTSD, depression, and other health problems.[38] In the first years of the Global War on Terrorism, the US military had still been learning to counter the threat of IEDs, and the doctors understood little about the long-term effects of traumatic brain injury.[39] The signature wounds of the war, TBI and PTSD, can cause behavioral issues in personnel and veterans, which, in turn, leads to punishment. In 2008, the RAND Corporation estimated that since 2001, out of more than 1.5 million troops, one-third had at least one mental health disorder and 320,000 experienced TBI.[40] Another study showed that incarcerated veterans of the Iraq and Afghanistan wars reported higher rates of combat PTSD compared to other generations.[41]

James Marciano has experienced extensive traumatic brain injuries. "I've been blown up four times, three times in 2009 and once in 2011," he claims. "Then being in blast [radius], I was probably in the percussion or within an arm's throw of 15–20 more." He states, "In 2009, our trucks didn't stop running. My truck platoon hit 42 IEDs. We got fucked up. We were blowing up trucks faster than they could get them to us off the ships." One time, his truck "ran over a pressure plate and blew the front of the truck up." The third time, he was on the ground level. Marciano recalls, "I was walking. I was guiding the wrecker back and a vehicle passed behind me about thirty feet behind me, to about my 7 or 8 o'clock and hit an IED. It was a huge blast. I got absolutely berated with rocks and shrapnel." It knocked him unconscious, for how long, he cannot be sure. The corpsman performed a field test called the Mace exam. He answered three of five questions correctly. "It definitely shook us up," says Marciano. In southern Afghanistan in 2009, "there were very minimal medical services," he explains. "Our battalion aid station was out of a twelve-man tent. . . . That's where our medical was," hardly the most state-of-the-art medical facility. "They didn't know the severity of the blast or whether I was having internal injuries or not, so the doc said to me, 'you can go back out against medical advice, but if you get hit one more time, we don't know if you're going to be a vegetable,'" the doctor warned. "That was a reality check. I'm not superhuman."

James Marciano got married to his high school sweetheart and had children while deployed. After coming home from his second deployment, his wife got pregnant. In August 2010, his first child was born. He redeployed in 2011. He was in Afghanistan from the time she started to crawl until she started to talk, missing those precious milestones. Before deploying again in 2013, his wife got pregnant again. "I was gone for the whole pregnancy," but returned just in time to see his second child born. Stoically, he reflects, "It's difficult. It is. But again, it's still a job. You gotta provide for your family, and you gotta be there for the guy to your left and your right."

Today, less than one half of 1 percent of the US population serves on active duty in the military, and recruits come from a small number of counties and are usually the children of military families.[42] Compared to the Vietnam War, veterans of the wars in Iraq and Afghanistan were also older on average and more likely to have spouses and children.[43] Deployments create hardships for families of service members, and when soldiers return from combat zones, their mental health problems affect their spouses and children. After coming home from Afghanistan, James Marciano always felt on edge in the States. "Your guard is always up. You're always on high alert." Marciano would become angry, anxious, stressed, or frustrated for reasons he did not understand at the time. "Things that typically wouldn't bother you, start to bother you."

Problems like these can become overwhelming in the event of a death of a family member. After getting out of the Marine Corps in 2015, James Marciano felt disconnected. "I was dealing with emotions and feelings and not having that bond around me." Then, his mother became terminally ill. "We—me, my wife, and two kids—moved into my parents' house . . . so my kids could be close to my mom." His father also had cirrhosis of the liver, from a lifetime of alcoholism. "My father started to get better; my mom started to get worse." His mother died in July 2015, and then his brother was incarcerated. "That's really when things started to unravel for me."

At the time, Marciano was still processing the effects of multiple deployments and untreated mental health problems. He struggled to control his "emotions and inability to control the outcomes of certain situations." He says, "I got into an argument with my father that resulted in me and him not talking anymore. So, it was within a short period of time—I lost my mother, my father, my brother was locked up." While going to school, he also took over the family business, but knew little about running a body shop. He admits, "With all that, and having a wife and two kids at home, things got tough."

Dealing with pain from service-connected injuries, Marciano took prescription opioids. Then the laws on prescription drugs changed. "I couldn't get pills anymore," he explains. "That led to heroin." The combination of family problems, mental health problems, and stress became insurmountable. "I used the pills and drugs to suppress the feelings." Marciano reflects, "being in the Marine Corps, I didn't have feelings. You operate at such a high level. Then, getting out, everything was a flood of emotion, using opiates for pain . . . which led to heroin, and then from there, the legal trouble started." During that time, "I was a functioning addict. I function at a very high level." He continued to work and attend classes full-time until 2018. "April of last year, I had lost a ton of weight, using a lot of drugs," he recalls, "so I went to rehab." He dropped out of school. "It was just all too much. I needed to focus on sobriety."

In 2018, Marciano completed a rehabilitation program in Texas called Warriors Heart. It was a program designed to treat veterans and first responders only. Patients needed a "dual diagnosis—you have to have PTSD and substance use." After rehab, he stopped using heroin but started drinking alcohol again. "I got in a car accident on I-91, where I crashed my car at a high rate of speed, and I didn't stay there. I took off, leaving the scene of an accident and causing bodily injury." Over the next three months, he continued to get into legal trouble. He was caught driving without a license twice and arrested for possession of a firearm without license.

After Marciano went to jail, the judge ordered him to complete Veterans Treatment Court. One day, during the summer of 2019, I met James Marciano outside of the Holyoke Veterans Treatment Court in western Massachusetts. He was wearing a dark gray Black Rifle Coffee Company T-shirt, smoking a cigarette, and looking characteristically anxious before a court appearance. He was slightly out of shape at the time, but he had the physique of a marine. I struck up casual conversation with him. As it turned out, we lived in the same area, and our children were the same age. I shared details about my oral history project and the goals of my research. He finished his cigarette, and before entering the court, he shared his phone number and told me to text him to set up an interview.

At the end of the oral history, Marciano hoped that by telling his story, it would help bridge the military-civilian divide. He wanted the public to understand that veterans in the criminal justice system are "human," but "don't just think that because we've been through stuff, we're using our traumas as an excuse to use" drugs. Marciano laments, "If I could, I would fucking take it all away and live a normal life. The shit I've seen, the shit I've done. Nobody wants to have to deal with that. So, for everybody out there that hasn't experienced trauma or experienced picking up your buddy's body parts," it might be impossible to relate. But interviewing James Marciano reminded me that veterans with substance use disorders are everywhere in the United States. They attend classes, go to work, and pick up their kids from school, just like the rest of us. But they are also invisible and isolated within civilian society. They deal with unique mental health problems stemming from war violence, unaware and unfathomable to most Americans.

Since getting out of the Marines, James Marciano has had time and necessary distance to reflect on experiences fighting two concurrent wars. "Iraq

FIGURE 7. Photo provided by the author, taken outside Marciano's home on July 1, 2019.

and Afghanistan weren't really, I feel, a direct threat to the United States, this being the longest that we've been at war." He questions the moral justification of the wars and the implications of his participation. "What did I do? Was it right or wrong? Am I to blame? Why not me?" he asks. "There were a lot of situations where things were questionable," but "I was just so detached from my emotions that it didn't really affect me until after I got out. There's always going to be collateral damage in war. It's unfortunate because there's a lot of people that didn't want us in their country—didn't want us in their backyard, driving through their poppy fields." In his opinion, there's a "hell of a coincidence" between the war in Afghanistan and the opioid crisis in the United States.

CONCLUSION

A direct relationship between the war in Afghanistan and the current opioid epidemic is circumstantial, at best. The correlation between them is not one-to-one. It's more like a chemical reaction. US policies in Afghanistan sowed the seeds of a prolonged insurgency, creating a demand for more American bodies. Without a draft, the armed forces required personnel to serve multiple deployments, separating them from their families and dividing them from the rest of the population. The conditions of fighting the forever wars produced signature wounds, PTSD, traumatic brain injury, and other mental illnesses. Returning to their families and communities, the veterans of the Global War on Terrorism carried the contagions of a dual mental health crisis and opioid epidemic.

Invisible and extremely stigmatized, substance use disorder is a comorbid signature wound of the Global War on Terrorism.[44] Today, more than one hundred Americans die from opioid overdoses each day, surpassing the total killed on September 11, 2001, each month.[45] In 2019, fifty thousand Americans died from opioids; that's more than seven times the number of US troops killed in Iraq and Afghanistan.[46] From 1999 to 2008, opioid prescriptions quadrupled, including oxycodone, hydrocodone, codeine, morphine, and fentanyl.[47] In 2012, medical doctors wrote 259 million prescriptions. At the same time, veterans of Iraq and Afghanistan were at a higher risk for opioid abuse, especially if diagnosed with PTSD and TBI.[48] The VA reported that 25 percent of veterans in outpatient care were prescribed opioids. As the nation faced the reality of an opioid crisis, the VA reformed its policies on prescribing opioids, and by

2016, prescription opioid use among veterans decreased 25 percent.[49] But after it became more difficult for Americans to get prescriptions, many turned to illegal drugs, especially heroin. Consequentially, opioid overdoses rapidly increased, and today drug overdose is the leading cause of death in the United States.

Ultimately, reforms in military mental health care, the VA, and the criminal justice system serve as a type of triage to the "collateral damage" of the American wars. At the end of a lost twenty-year war, we need an autopsy on the bipartisan policies that sustain perpetual warfare. For the military, the primary motivation for mental health care reform is mission readiness—the capacity to carry out war. But thousands of service members who fought in Iraq and Afghanistan were punished for behaviors related to mental health disorders, and substance use makes for an easy and convenient target. Across the divide, improvements to the VA allow the federal government to claim it supports the troops while continuing to deny care to "bad paper" veterans with substance use disorders. Still, meaningful progress, however slow, is undoubtedly better than none at all. Largely thanks to Vietnam veterans who organized, veterans in the criminal justice system today have greater access to disability benefits, treatment, and opportunities to recover and avoid recidivism. In local communities across the United States, Veterans Treatment Courts provide critical intervention amid the opioid crisis.

CHAPTER 7

"Justice for Vets"

A New Veterans' Movement

How we treat those who have made mistakes speaks to who we are as a society and is a statement about our values—about our dedication to fairness, equality, and justice, and about how to protect our families and communities from harm, heal after loss and trauma, and lift back up those among us who have earned a chance at redemption.

—PRESIDENT BARACK OBAMA, "The President's Role in Advancing Criminal Justice Reform," January 2017

In the summer of 2008, Iraq War veteran Matt Steiner was working in Tulsa City Hall, reading an article in *USA Today* about a new specialty court for veterans. After the initial success of the Buffalo Veterans Treatment Court, national new stories celebrated treatment courts as the "solution" to the problems of incarcerated veterans and called for greater justice reform.[1] Vietnam veteran Hank Pirowski, the founding project director of the Buffalo Veterans Treatment Court, said in an interview, "We knew we had to do something now because soon we're going to have 400,000 troops coming home. Veterans Court is a way to prevent the veterans' future contacts with the justice system, incidents of harm to self, and others (suicide or violence)."[2] Steiner recalls, "I thought about my own service, and I've known of some guys who got back home, had gotten in trouble, and I just really wondered, what kind of support is there for veterans in criminal justice?" Steiner remembers "looking out the window, wondering, 'How many veterans were in that jail right now that need help or [have] mental health or substance abuse issues?'" Apparently, nobody in Tulsa had thought to ask.

In 2003, Matt Steiner served as a marine during the US invasion of Iraq. After his tour, in 2004 he returned to Oklahoma and took advantage of the GI Bill. He first attended Tulsa Community College, then earned a bachelor's from Oklahoma State University, and later earned a master's in public administration from the University of Oklahoma. While going to school, Steiner also worked as an intern in the Tulsa mayor's office. He became the veterans' affairs coordinator at the municipal level, where he collaborated with various veterans' organizations. "We had this veterans center at the airport to welcome" troops home. "It's amazing how many resources are out there for veterans, but veterans just don't understand or realize" it, says Steiner. "Many people leading those entities—they just don't talk to each other." Steiner realized they could "use the power of the mayor's office to bring all these people together." They built a centralized infrastructure to assist veterans coming home from the wars in Iraq and Afghanistan. "We did that with the veterans' advisory council and veterans center at the airport. At the time, at Tulsa Community College, they had 1,200 veterans." In this role, Steiner coordinated local organizations, the mayor's office, and the VA to address veterans' issues in the greater Tulsa community.

Shortly after reading about the Buffalo Veterans Treatment Court, Steiner met with Sarah Day Smith, a municipal judge with experience in Drug Treatment Courts. But "Judge Smith was not really sold on that at the time." She asked, "'Why do we need another specialty court?'" They decided to visit the Buffalo Veterans Treatment Court. After meeting Judge Robert Russell and witnessing the transformative power of the court, Judge Smith was "hooked automatically," says Steiner. Returning from New York, they wondered, "How many veterans are getting arrested in Tulsa County?'" The first problem was "how to identify veterans within the criminal justice system," Matt explains. "We spent a long time on that. Veterans don't walk around with a V on their head, like, 'I'm a veteran.'" He says, "When I first got out, I didn't want to be identified, necessarily, as a veteran." The Tulsa court requested that the Tulsa County Jail start asking about military service during arrests on the intake forms. From September 2008 to June 2009, nearly twelve hundred veterans were arrested in Tulsa County. The new Tulsa Veterans Treatment Court admitted a third of that number into the treatment program.[3]

Launching it in December 2008, Tulsa established the third Veterans Treatment Court in the nation. Oklahoma had a significantly high number of National Guard members deployed in the war on terror at the time. The state also had one of the highest incarceration rates per capita in the world.[4] At the same time, studies suggested that Iraq and Afghanistan veterans were dealing with "dual diagnoses comprised of addictions, traumatic brain injuries, and suffer from post-traumatic stress disorder or major depression."[5] The Tulsa Veterans Treatment Court intercepted hundreds of Iraq and Afghanistan veterans in the system for mental health and drug-related problems. Steiner explains, "It wasn't all combat-related. Some of it was military sexual trauma," recognizing the large number of women in the military who experience assault.

Matt Steiner became an effective advocate and staunch believer in broad criminal justice reform. With treatment and access to resources, veterans in the treatment courts graduated and stayed out of jail. "We had like a 96 percent passage rate," states Steiner. "You're talking about men and women who—they're bad off. There are some really tough issues." But their lives "make a 180"-degree turn once they start receiving counseling services, getting disability benefits and veterans entitlements, "resources that they've earned and all those wraparound services and that veteran mentor," he explains. "That's why they work so well." Providing an expansive social safety net, Veterans Treatment Courts have remarkably low recidivism rates.[6]

The experiences of veterans in Tulsa shined a light on structural inequities and the need for greater changes in this country's approaches to mental health and drugs. The US criminal justice system costs about $300 billion each year,[7] but it does not prevent recidivism. Steiner asks, "Why are we throwing this person in prison who has a drug problem or a mental health problem? If you go to jail or prison . . . you're getting no treatment. You're going to be worse off," he realized. "Now you have a record. Now you can't get a job. Why shouldn't you get treatment?" With treatment and opportunities, offenders can avoid going back to jail or prison. "Taxpayers aren't paying for you to go stay in jail or prison, and you can work and contribute to society, and have a family."

Matt Steiner has been on the ground of this new veterans' movement for justice since its beginning. In 2008, Steiner served as the coordinator of the Tulsa Veterans Treatment Court, and in 2010, he started training other Veterans Treatment Courts as part of national team of "mentor courts." From 2011 to 2013, Steiner served as the first director of Justice for Vets, a national organization dedicated to the expansion of Veterans Treatment Courts. Afterward, he worked for VA secretary Eric Shinseki and later became director of military veterans affairs in the Executive Office of the President in the Obama administration. Still actively involved with Justice for Vets today, Steiner is an effective leader in the movement for criminal justice reform and, above all, a tireless supporter of veterans.

BUILDING A MOVEMENT

Veterans Treatment Courts are a multigenerational movement by and for veterans. Vietnam veterans faced many debilitating issues (PTSD, high unemployment, and substance use to name a few), but in addition to these, post-9/11 veterans faced distinctive problems. Multiple deployments increased the risk of PTSD, traumatic brain injury, and other mental health disorders. Veterans Treatment Courts sprang up in response to a military-related mental health crisis produced by the Global War on Terrorism.[8] Men and women returning from multiple combat tours in Iraq and Afghanistan constituted a serious public health and safety concern.[9] Signature wounds were a driving force behind the growth of Veterans Treatment Courts. At the time the courts were founded, one study indicated that 300,000 out of 1.5 million Americans who served in combat experienced PTSD, TBI, or co-occurring mental health and substance use disorders.[10] The founders of Veterans Treatment Courts sounded alarms for the next generation of veterans dealing with PTSD, TBI, substance use, and military sexual trauma. As the courts encountered these issues, veterans challenged prevailing cultural stigmas associated with mental health disorders, slowly changing the hearts and minds of people in the criminal justice system.[11] From 2008 to 2016, the Obama administration would mark a historic turning point in how the justice system treated people with mental health and substance use disorders.

It was a ripe moment for justice reform. In March 2008, then senator Barack Obama delivered one of his most powerful speeches on the history and legacies of racism in the United States, known as the "A More Perfect Union Speech." In a notable departure from "tough on crime" political discourse, he acknowledged systemic inequality in the United States: "Current incidents of discrimination, while less overt than in the past—are real and must be addressed, not just with words, but with deeds, by investing in our schools and our communities; by enforcing our civil rights laws and ensuring fairness in our criminal justice system."[12] During his first administration, President Obama called for "prevention, treatment, recovery, innovative criminal justice strategies" to address the problem of drugs as a public safety and health problem.[13] The Veterans Treatment Courts also gained the attention of the Obama administration, including early proponents Jill Biden and Michelle Obama. In May 2010, the Obama administration's National Drug Control Strategy marked a dramatic shift in federal drug enforcement away from carceral punishment and toward treatment and recovery. The veteran courts provided a concrete example of the efficacy of justice reform in action and could generate bipartisanship in an extremely divisive Congress.

In August 2008, Senator John Kerry (D-MA) and Senator Lisa Murkowski (R-AK) first introduced the SERV Act, which established a federal grant to fund Veterans Treatment Courts. In 2009, Kerry introduced additional legislation to authorize the NADCP to implement a nationwide training program designed to expand Veterans Treatment Courts based on the Buffalo city court model.[14] "You have to heal the hidden wounds of war too," announced Senator Kerry. "You can't be afraid to bring those issues out of the shadows. We need to be ready to help them readjust and deal with post traumatic stress so it doesn't consume their lives and lead to drug and alcohol abuse." With a strong endorsement from the Iraq and Afghanistan Veterans of America (IAVA), Veterans Treatment Courts received bipartisan approval in Congress. Soon thereafter, the National Association of Drug Court Professionals launched a new branch dedicated to Veterans Treatment Courts—Justice for Vets.

Veterans Treatment Courts also received timely support from the VA at the national level. In 2009, after visiting the Buffalo court, Secretary of Veterans Affairs Eric Shinseki established the Veterans Justice Outreach program. The primary role of the VJO coordinators is to identify veterans in local courts, jails, and prisons and facilitate their access to VA services as early as possible.[15] A memo in May 2009 required VA Medical Centers to provide outreach to veterans in prisons, jails, and courts within their regions.[16] The VJO helps to identify veterans in the criminal justice system outside of VA care and works with Veterans Treatment Courts (wherever they are available). Although there had been efforts to document the number of incarcerated veterans in jail or prison since the Carter administration, many courts and jails still had no idea how many veterans were in their systems. On a panel on community and military task-force relations, Matt Steiner stated, even though "a lot of law enforcement are veterans," police did not typically ask questions about military service at the time of arrest or in the jails.[17] Partnering with dedicated VA officers, Veterans Treatment Courts coordinated with the federal government to locate incarcerated veterans and train local law enforcement and corrections officers to understand veteran-specific needs. These efforts began the process of raising awareness to the relationship between mental health disorders and crime, while also demonstrating the effectiveness of treatment over carceral punishment.

In 2009, the National Association of Drug Court Professionals met to develop a curriculum for Veterans Treatment Court. As director of communications for Justice for Vets, Christopher Deutsch has been instrumental to the growth of Veterans Treatment Courts since the beginning. According to Deutsch, the NADCP was "really in a unique and fortunate position to provide some of that national infrastructure to help grow the programs. We had been involved in drug courts almost from the very beginning. We knew how to put curriculums together, to go out and develop training, and get it out to communities that are interested in launching these programs." In 2009, the Department of Justice provided funding to support the growth of Veterans Treatment Courts, so "we convened some of the early pioneers to develop a curriculum," remembers Deutsch. Among the curriculum development team were founders of the first three Veterans Treatment Courts in the United States: Judge Robert Russell and Jack O'Connor from Buffalo, Judge Steven Manley from Santa Clara County, and Judge Sarah Day Smith and Matt Steiner from the Tulsa Veterans Treatment Court.[18]

By 2010, just a year later, the National Association of Drug Court Professionals selected four courts to train and implement the curriculum for Veterans Treatment Courts.[19] These "mentor courts" served as national models to replicate Veterans Treatment Courts in communities across the country. Judge Sarah Day Smith, who presided over the Tulsa Veterans Treatment Court and helped launch the mentor court program, said, "We will not only be helping the men and women of Tulsa," she emphasized, "but all across the nation."[20]

At first the courts mostly operated without additional funding outside of their court systems.[21] As news spread of the early successes, advocates pointed out that Veterans Treatment Courts saved more money over time than the costs of incarceration.[22] At a Senate hearing, in July 2011, actor Martin Sheen and Chief Judge Jeane LaFazia of Rhode Island District Court attested that Veterans Treatment Courts were "saving money and saving lives," which has since become their unofficial motto.[23] The proven early successes of treatment courts helped generate excitement among Congress, which passed legislation, financing the proliferation of Veterans Treatment Courts across the United States.

In 2011, Matt Steiner became the founding director of Justice for Vets. Chris Deutsch recalls, "Matt had helped launch the Tulsa program . . . and had really been a high energy, high impact advocate for Veterans Treatment Courts." Steiner employed key lessons he learned organizing veterans' organizations from the office of mayor of Tulsa and expanded that concept with Justice for Vets. First, he introduced himself to the Veterans Service Organizations (VSOs) and the Veterans Justice Outreach in the VA.[24] "He built a relationship with them. And within a few months, we had resolutions from the big VSOs stating that they support Veterans Treatment Courts and Justice for Vets." This was important, according to Deutsch, because it "allowed us to . . . be at the table for some of the meetings taking place. It really gave us credibility."[25] After developing the training curriculum and launching the mentor court initiative, Justice for Vets became well known in the Drug Treatment Court community and on Capitol Hill.

Under Matt Steiner's leadership, the number of Veterans Treatment Courts multiplied from eleven in 2009 to more than one hundred by 2013. Then National Association of Drug Court Professionals hosted the first annual conference dedicated to Veterans Treatment Courts. At that time, "We didn't know what to expect," remembers Deutsch. To their surprise, "We had over 1,000 people show up." Deutsch says, "That was the moment that I think established not only Justice for Vets but Veterans Treatment Courts on the national stage." The enthusiasm seemed palpable. "We took our cue from that," realizing for the first time, "this is a movement."

A priority of this new veterans' movement was the urgent need for mental health and drug treatment in the criminal justice system. "Trauma is really at the heart of this from the very beginning," says Deutsch. Early on, the Buffalo court recognized that "what they were doing in their drug court wasn't quite enough because there was this underlying trauma [or] a mental health disorder." Mental Health Court did not always work either, especially with veterans. "When they were dealing with this mental health issue, with this trauma, they were self-medicating with drugs and alcohol," they realized. Mental health issues "can really be a driving force behind their behavior when they come home. And if we're going to change that behavior, we need to address that trauma." And that takes time, patience, and flexibility. Treatment courts are "long, and they're intense. This isn't 30 days. These are typically 12- or 18-month programs." He explains, "You have to really dig deep and address some of those underlying issues." Most important, the courts must be willing to accommodate and anticipate defendants with substance use disorder who relapse. These problems "called for a hybrid model," bringing expertise from the fields of drug and mental health treatment together to serve veterans. Veterans Treatment

Courts responded to multiple needs at once, providing social services in one setting and reconnecting defendants to the VA and military culture. But to bridge the divide between civilians and military veterans, the hybrid court required the advocacy and leadership of veterans willing to speak out about mental health, substance use, and incarceration.

THE NEW MILITARY MASCULINITY

Timothy Wynn currently serves as the veterans mentor coordinator for the Philadelphia Veterans Treatment Court and collaborates with Justice for Vets to train other Veterans Treatment Court members. Like Matt Steiner, in 2003, he also served in the Marine Corps invasion force of Iraq. After a six-month deployment, Wynn returned stateside. He had been a stop-loss, meaning his enlistment was extended to meet the demands of the war. After coming home, Wynn became socially isolated. Most of the marines in his unit were still in combat six thousand miles away. It was only twenty-four hours between living in a combat zone and his parents' home in Philadelphia.

In 2004, after returning from Iraq, Tim Wynn did not go through any formal reintegration program, nor did he consider reporting mental health concerns. "Coming back straight from Iraq and [then back to] Philadelphia, I didn't really even have time to decompress," Wynn recalls. "It was different back then." He had little opportunity to report mental health issues and probably wouldn't have said anything even if those services were available. Without the support of his unit or any readjustment program, this veteran struggled in civilian society.

Military masculinity prevents many veterans from seeking help.[26] "It's something we're taught when we're younger: Men don't cry. Men can drink and hold their liquor. Men are independent. This is all bullshit that we're taught as men when we're younger," Wynn laments. "These are all male myths that we live by. It took me years to realize that and years of talking to people. I think we're damaged when we're younger. It's one of them things. Men are not supposed to do that."[27] Marines are further conditioned not to complain or show weakness. "To not be stoic in the face of agony," writes Nancy Sherman, "was to fail as a warrior."[28] Even as the military screened for PTSD, many marines like Wynn were either unaware or unwilling to report mental health problems.

In June 2008, the *New York Times* published its first article on Veterans

Treatment Court, featuring the story of Anthony Klecker, a Marine Corps veteran who served in Iraq. "I was trying to be the tough marine I was trained to be—not to talk about problems, not to cry," says Klecker. "I imprisoned myself in my own mind."[29] The Veterans Treatment Court connected him with the VA, where he received treatment for PTSD. The article warned of rising concerns for the large number of veterans coming home from Iraq and Afghanistan with similar issues.

In absence of treatment, military veterans customarily drink alcohol or use drugs to repress mental health issues. Alcohol is the culturally acceptable coping mechanism while in the military because drug tests deter other substances.[30] But alcohol enflames symptoms associated with PTSD, such as anger, hypervigilance, or depression, increasing the likelihood of confrontation with the law.[31] After coming home from Iraq, Timmy Wynn drank alcohol, used drugs, and got into fistfights. Wynn was charged with felony aggravated assault. After being arrested, he went to the VA. "They gave me medication," benzodiazepines such as "Xanax and Clonazepam." The prescription pills made his behavior unpredictable and worsened his legal troubles.

In total, Tim Wynn was arrested seven times on charges related to aggression, violence, and substance use and incarcerated in state prison. Without appropriate mental health services, he continued to be combative and noncompliant with authorities. His "moment of clarity" came while incarcerated. He remembers, "I'm in shackles. I'm in the bowels of the prison." After the incidents with prescription pills, Wynn had been "cheeking" his medications, refusing to take them. One day, he got into an argument with the nurse about the meds. A Vietnam veteran who worked in the prison happened to overhear the confrontation and intervened. "This guy wasn't a doctor. He was just a Vietnam vet," recalls Wynn, "but that held so much weight with me, man." This was the first open conversation he ever had with another veteran. "I'll never forget what he said to me that day." He recounts, "'That person you were before you left is gone, and they are never coming back. You are forever a different person now. And these things that you're doing, they're not working for you, so let's start working on ways to combat this, different ways. Because all this anger and all that keeps getting you in prison.'" Without knowing the full situation, this veteran struck the heart of the problem, making a profound impact on the way Wynn understood his experiences in Iraq and the root of his problems.

In the Drug Treatment Court world, this relationship would be called peer counseling, when someone uses their own life stories to connect with and enable others to recover from substance.[32] Wynn says, "That was my first interaction with peer-to-peer support. That was a game-changer." Wynn was among the first troops to come home from Iraq. "Being the first to go and the first to come back, not too many of my peers were out here," he says. "They were still over there," amplifying Wynn's survivor's guilt. In prison, two generations of veterans from different wars shared a common bond, immutable across time. "He wasn't a doctor or clinician, nothing like that." He "was a Vietnam vet. He spoke my language. Although our stories weren't exactly the same, we had been through some similar things," explains Wynn. Over the next year, they would meet and form a mentor-mentee relationship. "He would send a slip to my cell block to get me off the unit. I'd come down and sit in that room with him. He'd sit at one end of the room. I'd sit at the other, and some days, we wouldn't say shit to each other, but he knew that was exactly what I needed," realizes Wynn. Peer-to-peer support proved instrumental in Wynn's recovery. "Finally, I had an outlet. I could talk to this man, and I knew he wasn't sitting here going, 'crazy vet again.' He understood it, and I felt comfortable with him." This memory shows the communal recovery process among veterans who often feel separated from civilian society and unable to cross the division after war.

When he was first released from prison, Wynn stayed sober for a year and a half. But then he was arrested again for "road rage." Sobriety had not resolved all of his problems, and prison did not rehabilitate him. After getting out, Wynn reexperienced those same residual mental health problems from the Iraq War. After that latest arrest, Wynn attended Philadelphia Veterans Treatment Court. The court requires at least a year to complete, and defendants must attend intensive counseling sessions, meet regularly with a probation officer, and pass mandatory drug tests. Once in the program, Wynn found kinship among other veterans and thrived under the hierarchical, military-like structure. This community of veteran mentors helped Wynn grapple with the underlying mental health problems, and after a year, he graduated and found a new calling for advocacy and justice.

After an appropriate amount of time, Judge Patrick Dugan, a veteran of the Global War on Terrorism, recruited Wynn to serve as a veteran mentor. He was eventually hired as the veteran mentor coordinator of the Philadelphia Veterans Treatment Court, one of the first graduates to be hired by the court. Wynn discovered a new mission in helping other veterans with similar readjustment problems. Serving as a mentor meant becoming a new model of veteranhood, disassociated from the more toxic characteristics of military masculinity. As a mentor, he creates a space for the veterans to express themselves safely and without fear of shame. "Number one: I share my experience. I tell them who I am. I tell them that 'I've been broken, and I've been able to rebound. It's okay to be broken. . . . It's okay to cry—It's okay to ask for help.'" He admits, "For the longest time, I thought I'm this big, bad Marine. I can walk through walls because that's what I was taught to do. But I tell them that 'it's okay to just let it all out, man. Let it out. What we talk about stays between us.'" Over time, the veterans in the system come to realize that the mentors and the treatment court members genuinely care even if the court itself is mandatory punishment with strict surveillance and urinalysis.[33]

I met Tim through Facebook. On May 15, 2019, another graduate of the Philadelphia Veterans Treatment Court, Pearson Kennedy-Crosby, posted a photograph of himself, Timmy Wynn, and Matt Hallman with the caption: "2 out of 3 are STILL alive because of vet court." Hallman served two tours in Iraq, but the opioid epidemic plagued his life afterward. In 2013, a journalist profiled his case, asking rhetorically, "Will his addiction consume him or will he fight back?" He had recently relapsed, but the article ends with a glimmer of hope. Hallman had been sober, and Judge Patrick Dugan encourages him to "keep it up."[34] Matt Hallman graduated from the Philadelphia Veterans Treatment Court but tragically died of overdose in 2018. Veterans Treatment Court can be a catalyst for recovery, but it's far from the perfect solution to the conjoined problems of mental health, substance use, and suicide in America. Veterans like Tim Wynn hope that their stories can help raise awareness in law enforcement, the courts, prisons and jails, and the public about how to interact empathetically with people with disabilities and disorders.

Today, with Justice for Vets, Tim Wynn serves as an advocate for criminal justice reform, raising awareness on mental health and substance use disorder. Wynn believes, "The hurt, the confusion, the pain, everything, sitting in jail for a year, seven arrests—everything that I've done . . . in the military or in the civilian world, with my arrest record—all that has brought me to this very point—sitting here talking to you right now." He recognizes an inherent value in sharing his story, hoping to inspire others to not give up. "I tell these vets when I work with them: lived experience is the most powerful thing that you can have." He adds, "Even you, sitting here today, asking these questions and with a camera, it's your experience in life that has brought you to this point." Veterans engage in storytelling to bridge the military-civilian divide because most Americans have very little understanding of the wars fought in our name or the experiences of those who survive. During de-escalation training sessions with police, Wynn frequently shares memories of the Iraq War, to provide advice and insight into police encounters people with mental health disorders.

Timmy Wynn transformed his traumatic experiences into advocacy for veterans and wider justice reform. He says, "I found myself when I started helping others." Wynn recently organized a grassroots campaign to build a memorial to the 290 soldiers from Pennsylvania who died in the Global War on Terror.[35] "My whole recovery revolves around what I do for others," he says. In 2018, Justice for Vets awarded him the Hank Pirowski Award, in honor of the late founding veteran mentor of the Buffalo Veterans Treatment Court. Wynn embodies the organization's mission of recovery, redemption, and restorative justice. With Justice for Vets, he has visited the White House under two administrations. He recalls, "I was standing right in front of President Obama." In his speech, the president quoted Mahatma Gandhi: "'The best way to find yourself is to lose yourself in the service of others.'" The words resonated deeply with Wynn. "Now here I am, I'm a drunk and a drug addict—I will be 'till the day I die because recovery is a lifelong process—I'm a guy who has seven arrests, spent over a year of my life in prison. Now, I'm standing on the White House lawn hearing the president of the United States talk. It felt like everybody else went away, and it felt like he was talking to me."

Tim Wynn's mentor is the Honorable Judge Patrick Dugan, an 82nd Airborne Army combat veteran. An Iraq and Afghanistan war veteran, Patrick Dugan knows all too well how America's longest war comes home and impacts families. Currently, Dugan serves as president judge of Philadelphia Municipal Court and presides over the Philadelphia Veterans Treatment Court. His family history is a legacy of military service. Dugan's grandfather was a World War I veteran, several uncles fought in World War II, and his father served as a marine in Korea. Following the family tradition, from 1981 to 1989, Dugan served in the US Army. After September 11, 2001, he reenlisted in the Army and served a second career from 2003 to 2016. In 2003, he deployed to Iraq as part of civil affairs. Afterward, he applied for commission as a JAG (judge advocate general) officer and deployed to Afghanistan in 2006. When he came

FIGURE 8. Photo provided by the author and taken on May 30, 2019, in Philadelphia at the Veterans Treatment Court.

home from Afghanistan, Dugan returned to his native city and became the presiding judge of the Philadelphia Veterans Treatment Court. A proponent of sweeping justice reform, Judge Dugan advocates for treatment and alternatives to punishment.

Today, the all-volunteer force increasingly relies on a small percentage of citizen-soldiers to carry out the Global War on Terror. Dugan says, "I know a lot of guys who served in Vietnam" and "it's now 40–50 years later, and many still struggle with it—from one deployment." The perpetual readjustments between a war zone and peace take a substantial toll on service members and their family life. "You come home. You're so glad to be home. You try to get back to normal," explains Dugan. "Get back with your family. Get back with your friends. Get [used to] being out of the war zone. You start figuring out how to get back to reality and life. You start learning coping skills, and then boom! Eight months later, you're on your way back" to war.

Multiple redeployments are the defining characteristic of military experiences since 9/11, causing long-term effects on American military veterans and their families. The psychiatric and social effects of combat increase relative to length of duration and frequency of deployments.[36] "I believe anybody that's exposed in a combat zone to the horrors of war—and yes, those young men and women who are kicking in doors and having hand-to-hand knife fights, absolutely. Back to those clerks . . . on a fortified base with mortars and bodies coming in and out—everyone's going to be affected," says Dugan. "I believe that any human being that is exposed to this has some form of it. Whether or not it's diagnosed or internal, it's there. I believe that anyone that is in this environment should definitely sit down and talk to therapists." According to the 2008 RAND study, 20 percent of Iraq and Afghanistan veterans reported PTSD symptoms, totaling three hundred thousand.[37] But that study relied exclusively on self-reporting. After multiple deployments, post-9/11 veterans were at an exponentially increased risk of traumatic brain injuries, complex PTSD, substance use, homelessness, suicide, and incarceration.

The US military has not yet overcome the stigma attached to mental health treatment. Dugan thinks, "The military, the reserves, the active-duty component, the VA hospitals, all need more therapists, psychiatrists, counselors. We need to make it 20-fold. There's not enough down range. There's not enough when we come home." He says, "They need to put a couple zeros behind the dollar amount that's spent at the VA." Dugan opines, "PTSD is a lot higher than anything they think it is now." But more money and more doctors cannot resolve the mental health crisis without cultural change on mental health care among veterans.

Although mental health services are more readily available in the military, cultural barriers still prevent many from seeking treatment.[38] Many fear repercussions, believing it could ruin their careers. Service members associate stigmas with mental health treatment. Judge Patrick Dugan thinks, "It definitely was a career breaker if you went and said you had issues." He believes, "There was a culture that you couldn't do it. I think that culture still prevails. Not as much as it did. I think leadership and policies" have changed, but "there still is some feeling that it's going to be a career killer."

Patrick Dugan discussed the influence of Gen. Carter Ham, who spoke out publicly about mental health problems. Carter Ham "rose to the rank of four-star general. He was actually the general in Mosul, when a suicide bomber walked into the chow hall one day and blew it up over on the airbase in Mosul." On September 21, 2004, a suicide attacker detonated explosives, killing twenty-three people and injuring seventy-two.[39] "It was the worst day of my life," recounts Ham.[40] The creeping death toll in Iraq and Afghanistan had a devastating effect on Ham's mental health. Dugan recalls, "It seemed like every day we'd get a casualty report, it would be one dead, four wounded; four wounded, zero KIA; 2 KIA and 18 wounded. It was drip by drip again. I remember seeing an article in a newspaper, and then seeing general Ham interviewed" about mental health.[41] In an interview with *Stars & Stripes*, General Ham states, "The way to get soldiers to open up is to remove the stigma that still exists within military culture to seek counsel and admit to what's still seen . . . as a weakness."[42] The Army promoted mental health care from the top down, but the most "enduring cultural changes" happened from the bottom up, argues David Kieran. When soldiers see leaders seeking mental health treatment, enlisted men are more likely to seek treatment too.[43] Dugan says, "He was just a very well-respected general who served in combat. He came out and admitted that he had PTSD." Ham's example of leadership inspired Dugan. "To me that was just a huge breakthrough." It took real courage "for him to come out and say that. It was huge. Because that's telling the corporals 'Look, don't be ashamed.'" Dugan carried those lessons from war home.

In 2007, Patrick Dugan returned from Afghanistan and became a judge in Philadelphia. "I was appointed to be a judge the day I got home from Afghanistan." Dugan's experiences in the military influence his thinking on criminal justice reform. Veterans Treatment Courts promote awareness and effect change on mental health treatment. When a veteran in court approaches the judge, a mentor stands with them. Veteran mentors serve as source of support and a point of contact between the court and the defendant. More than that, "veterans talk to each other," explains Dugan. Veteran Treatment Courts restore this military network and provide treatment to people in the criminal justice system. That is why they work so well.

Today, as a leader in Justice for Vets, Judge Dugan seeks to normalize mental health treatment. "It should be like PT, like physical training," he says. "It should be mandatory that we all go and talk to somebody. Because everybody needs it. I'm sitting here getting a little choked up thinking about some of this stuff. When you get a veteran to open up, there's going to be moments that we cry," he admits, "and it's normal. The biggest, toughest men and women that I've met" sometimes break down and need help. "It's upsetting, and it should be talked about." Dugan acknowledges, "It's getting better, but we're not there yet."[44] Mental health treatment is paramount to broader criminal justice reform.

Judge Dugan believes that "holistic treatment" is the single greatest lesson that civilian courts can take away from Veterans Treatment Courts. "There's a huge movement throughout the justice system to do these treatment courts, and Philadelphia is one of the leaders in that," says Dugan. Recently, Philadelphia launched an experimental treatment court for victims of sex trafficking. "In many of our courtrooms, we try to do other programs—not just for veterans. Veterans are a great subset of our citizenry to cherry-pick and bring us together because we have the VA," and the resources to support the treatment court. Veterans inspire people to get involved, and many believe that veterans inherently deserve a second chance. "We tend to have some discipline. We can find mentors" and people willing to volunteer. "We need that across the board." Dugan says, "You name the classification, and I'll tell you if we could do a treatment court." He listed examples: "18–25-year-old city kids. Damn right. Give me a bunch of 28–30-year-old mentors . . . who somehow survived it and are now productive citizens. Give me them as mentors. Give me some programs that can help them find jobs, give me some programs where I can send them for treatment." Provide them with "education and opportunity. Every court should try to do that."

Alternatives to incarceration for nonviolent drug offenses divert tax dollars away from private prisons and invest them in community resources. But treatment does not mean people are not held accountable. "The key is we don't want them to keep committing crimes, so we just keep putting them on probation and keep putting them in jail, but all we're doing is hardening them up. They're going to come back out, . . . and then, they're gonna go back," Dugan says. "No, we want to make sure they don't go back, so we need to treat people holistically. To find out, what's their problem? Why did they commit the crimes? And let's try to fix it." The national warlike responses to crime since the 1960s have not prevented or deterred people from breaking the law. Dugan says, "People have to think outside the box."[45] Leaders in treatment courts are resourceful, innovative, and imaginative in their approaches to healing the double wounds of mental health and substance use disorders.

"FORGOTTEN" VETERANS OF THE FOREVER WARS

Readers might wonder—despite the criticisms, moral injuries, and feelings of abandonment among veterans of the Global War on Terrorism—why didn't these veterans organize against the wars, and why did they instead become advocates for mental health and criminal justice reforms?

At least part of the reason is the misremembering of the Vietnam-era antiwar movement, but also, in absence of a draft, the all-volunteer force carried out the Global War on Terrorism for two decades with only a tiny fraction of the US population. Because so few Americans were directly affected by the wars, there were no mass civilian movements against the wars in Iraq and Afghanistan, no major student protests, no large antiwar GI movement, no civil rights icons who spoke out forcefully against the wars, no major social unrest in the United States directly related to the wars, and no major civilian deterrent from the US military waging war indefinitely. The Iraq Veterans Against the War enlisted fewer than a thousand members. Following in the legacy of the Vietnam Veterans Against the War, Iraq veterans testified at their own Winter Soldier hearing in March 2008.[46] Nearly two hundred veterans testified to the dehumanization of Iraqis, Islamophobia, and racism. They recounted stories of sexual assault, prisoner abuses, torture, disregard for the rules of engagement, the killing of civilians, and raiding the homes of innocent people.[47] These violations radicalized the people living under US occupation and allowed terrorist organizations to recruit more people into their ranks, creating a vicious cycle of endless war, military occupation, dislocation, and terrorism. Amid perpetual conflict, opioid epidemics, mental health crises, and mass movements against police brutality and racism, veterans of the Global War on Terrorism organized for justice and effected gradual but systemic change.

At a time when the military-civilian divide has never been wider, a central paradox in American society is that the division between militarism and the carceral state has never been narrower. "Americans are enthralled with military power," writes Andrew Bacevich.[48] American militarism is deeply imbedded within national identity and culture, and it infringes on democratic rights, citizenship, and civilian life. Increasingly throughout modern American history, the power of the executive branch has expanded at the expense of the democratic balance between the president, Congress, and the people.[49] The "shadow of war" created a culture of fear, anxiety, and heightened concern for national security that generated a more militarized American culture and a general willingness to accept the outsized power of the president to wage endless, undeclared wars.[50] In 2004, a Bush administration official reportedly said to journalist Ron Susking, "'We're an empire now, and when we act, we

create our own reality. . . . We're history's actors. . . . [A]ll of you will be left to
just study what we do."[51] Before the Society for Historians of American Foreign
Relations in 2011, Marilyn B. Young challenged historians "to make war visible,
vivid, an inescapable part of the country's self-conscious . . . as it is reality."[52]
Since 9/11, American civilians, for the most part, were physically unharmed
by distant wars, yet lived in a constant state of high alert to the ever-present
dangers of terrorism—an atmosphere in which the US military engaged in a
series of conflicts around the globe without mass resistance as a deterrent to
perpetual warfare. This culture enables "forever war."[53] The American public
simultaneously praised the troops while ignoring the lived realities of those
who experience endless wars.

In 2003, giving a speech before the United Nations, General Colin Powell
called for the invasion of Iraq, alleging that evidence of weapons of mass
destruction was an existential threat and that all diplomatic solutions had failed.
Following the Vietnam War, the Powell Doctrine had cautioned against "another
Vietnam." War should be waged only with broad public support and the overwhelming use of force, to achieve concrete goals with a clear exit strategy.[54] Before
the Security Council, General Powell said, "The facts speak for themselves. These
are not assertions," he swore. "What we're giving you are facts and conclusions
based on solid intelligence."[55] This allegation provided the primary justification
for the Iraq War. Yet the world awaits conclusive evidence of weapons of mass
destruction. Moral injury involves a betrayal by someone in a position of "legitimate authority."[56] For a generation of Iraq War veterans, the words of Vietnam
veterans like Colin Powell held great authority. In Vietnam, Powell had served
as a military adviser in 1963. He returned, in 1968, as a major and, after surviving
a helicopter crash and rescuing three soldiers, was awarded the Soldier's Medal.
"He was somebody that I would've voted for president," claims Dugan. "I always
believed that when a person raises his or her right hand and swore to tell the
truth, I gotta give them the benefit of the doubt—and Colin Powell was one of
my heroes." But "he [went] the United Nations and pretty much lie[d] at the
expense of men and women." Similarly, at least in that moment of time, "When
president Bush stood atop the pile at 9/11," Dugan recalls, "you could do nothing
more than believe in him."

Veterans of the Global War on Terrorism experienced unique moral dilem-
mas after their involvement. For starters, they all volunteered. This historic difference caused a wider division between the military and civilian society. "These

wars demanded the intense and prolonged participation of a tiny fraction of the nation's youth," David Wood points out.[57] Moral injury is an insightful concept for analyzing the narratives of Iraq and Afghanistan war veterans to understand the roots of their advocacy for justice. At its most fundamental level, moral injury is an act of injustice. It is a violation of right and wrong.[58] David Wood describes moral injury as "a jagged disconnect from our understanding of who we are and what we and others ought to do." It can result from "inflicting purposeful violence, witnessing the sudden violent maiming of a loved one, the suffering of civilians." These experiences "often shatter our understanding of the world." As the wars dragged on, post-9/11 service members felt like the rest of the public "turned its back" on them.[59] In turn, the nature of America's forever wars produced a vast military-civilian divide, and Afghanistan became known among some veterans as the "forgotten war."

After September 11, Patrick Dugan volunteered to serve the nation at war. As the Army mobilized for Iraq, he reenlisted at forty-three years old. "I had already been a cancer survivor. I had to drop a few pounds. I had some medical issues," though. Dugan says, "but I was able to get all these medical waivers because, at the time, they wanted bodies." He deployed almost immediately. On a Friday in 2003, he entered an MEPS (military entrance processing station) at Fort Dix, New Jersey. By Monday, he reported to a civil affairs unit in Norristown, Pennsylvania. By the next week, "we were on our way to Camp Shelby, Mississippi en route to Iraq." The process happened quickly. "On Friday, I had been out fifteen years. On Monday, I was handed a M-16. I was a squad leader in the Civil Affairs unit. It was crazy."[60] These missions were intended to win the "hearts and minds" of people living under US military occupation.[61]

Judge Dugan's advocacy for justice stems from traumatic experiences in Iraq and Afghanistan. "I had one hell of a tour while I was in Mosul," Dugan explains. "I was in civilian clothes. Sometimes I was riding a machine gun." His experiences on the ground contradicted his expectations of serving in civil affairs. Instinctively, he realized that "hearts and minds" campaigns during a military occupation did not achieve the goals of pacifying Iraqi civilians. "When I came home, I was still in the Civil Affairs. But I applied for direct commission, became an officer, and . . . went to the JAG Corps," believing he would serve for justice. After being commissioned as a JAG officer, he volunteered to deploy to Afghanistan in 2006.

Suicide attacks were a shocking feature of the "forgotten war" in

Afghanistan.[62] Dugan lived and worked as a JAG officer on Bagram Air Base. "When any local Afghan had a claim against our government," he investigated the claims and determined their merits. On February 27, 2007, Vice President Dick Cheney visited the base at Bagram. Twenty-three people were killed by a suicide bomber.[63] "The people would line up outside the front gates to make complaints or bring a legitimate issue; workers who came to work on base to clean our toilets, to clean the streets, etc., would be waiting in line," he recounts, "and a suicide bomber came up and just incinerated" the crowd. "Blew them to ka-bits, including an American soldier from Chicago, an American female, who was a contractor, and a Korean soldier," says Dugan. The terrorist attack had targeted the vice president. Later, at a White House correspondents' dinner, President George W. Bush joked that "it was safer for Dick Cheney to go to Afghanistan than to go on a hunting trip because, you know, he shot his friend on a hunting trip," Dugan recalls. "It still hurts me to the core that our leadership would make a joke about that because 2[3] people's bodies were just obliterated." This memory illustrates the fundamental difference between military and civilian society during the Afghanistan War and the disconnection between the two increasingly separated worlds.

A major difference between the Global War on Terrorism and the Vietnam War is most Americans did not see or have direct knowledge of war violence, which in turn widens the military-civilian divide and enables "forever war." During the First Gulf War, under then president George H. W. Bush, the Department of Defense first banned photographs of US casualties. Marilyn B. Young writes, "The result was a televised war relatively innocent of dead bodies."[64] By the time George W. Bush waged a war of his own in Iraq, the control of the media and the historical narrative necessary to wage preemptive, unilateral, and possibly permanent war without setting off massive public backlash had been nearly perfected.[65] It was not until 2009 that President Barack Obama lifted the ban.[66] The censorship of casualties, wounded bodies, and returning caskets takes root in memory of the Vietnam War, this idea that media sabotaged the war efforts and fomented the war's unpopularity.[67] This ban effectively sanitized the wars in Iraq and Afghanistan for public consumption.[68] As a result, the casualties of the newest, longest war were unseen in the United States. The only Americans to feel the wars personally were a small number of service members and their families. Patrick Dugan remembers, "Anytime a soldier or service member was killed in Afghanistan, they brought them through two places: Kandahar or Bagram. Almost every day, we would call time out. The horn would go off, and . . . you would walk down to the main road, and you would stand there at attention." They would line up and watch the funeral processions pass by with the "fallen, fellow American in a casket, going down Disney Road," named after a soldier who was killed, Jason Disney.[69] They would "put the body on a plane to take them home to Dover, then on to every little hometown or every big city in the United States."[70]

Casualties trickled back into the United States in a way that escaped sustained national attention and did not generate any type of mass movement against the wars. The war felt like a "slow drip," describes Dugan. In Afghanistan, "That's what I remember. That's what sticks with me was going out there on a continuous basis" despite the ubiquitous threat. "It wasn't the volume where there was fifty a day. No. It was one or two a day, which was too many." Dugan witnessed this slow procession of Americans casualties on a daily basis. He briefed every service member upon arrival at Bagram, watched them leave on missions, and "then drip, by drip, by drip, by drip—they would come back in these boxes," draped with the American flag.

Veterans of the forever wars feel a distinctive sense of abandonment from the public—but not exactly like the Vietnam generation. The war in Afghanistan took a disproportionate toll on a tiny fraction of the population. The American public turned its attention away from war "even as military families braced for second and third deployments."[71] To soldiers on multiple deployments, it seemed like life in the States went on without them. Transitioning between the United States and Afghanistan became a culture shock and the cause of readjustment difficulties. "Then to see the disconnect of leaders back home," caused some disillusionment. "I feel we've been a military at war—not a nation at war," Dugan laments. The war in Afghanistan is now the longest American war in history. "The mission still continued," says Dugan. "The wounded are medevac'd. The dead are sent home. . . . But the rest of the people in the unit, go right back out to a mission." He asks rhetorically, "How do you do that? You just go. You get up. You get back in a different Humvee. You get back up to ride that machine gun, going down the same damn roads that your friend was killed in or . . . out in this little village, you're in the same vicinity, in the same area where it occurred. And you just continue with your missions. How do you do that?" Dugan asks again. "I don't know why it doesn't paralyze every single human being from going back outside that gate. It's just something that gets inside you, and you just move forward as a unit with your friends. You do it. This is where you get that shock."[72]

In 2009, the US Senate Committee on Foreign Relations, chaired by Senator John Kerry (D-MA), convened a hearing on the war in Afghanistan, inviting veterans and experts to share their perspectives on the war. The views varied widely, but the overarching lesson was that the US military occupation of Afghanistan was radicalizing the civilian populations and creating more terrorists. For some, like Andrew Bacevich, the "protracted and indeterminate" war in Afghanistan paralleled Vietnam and contradicted the formerly longest war's most immediate lessons, characterized by the Powell Doctrine. "Once again, as in Vietnam, the enemy calls the tune, obliging us to fight on his terms. . . . [A]s fighting drags on, its purpose becomes increasingly difficult to discern. American soldiers are now said to face the prospect of perpetual conflict. We find ourselves in the midst of what the Pentagon calls 'The Long War,' a conflict global in scope."[73] Of course, not all the panelists shared Bacevich's conclusion.

Christopher McGurk, retired US Army staff sergeant, unequivocally believed the US should renew its efforts in full force. Marilyn Young argues that counterinsurgencies have "no time limit, no clear goals, no exit strategy." If counterinsurgency doesn't work in Afghanistan, she accurately foresaw, "it will be said to have not been pursued long or hard enough."[74] McGurk alluded to John Kerry's own 1971 testimony before the very same committee. "You spoke of men who have returned with a sense of anger and a sense of betrayal which no one has yet grasped," he reminded the former member of the Vietnam Veterans Against the War. "My own anger and sense of betrayal comes from the possibility that we may not come to a resolution in Afghanistan and that the blood that has been shed . . . would be forgotten."[75] More than a decade later, when the US military finally withdrew from Afghanistan in August 2021, a generation of US veterans mourned—not for the abandoned equipment or the billions of dollars wasted but because it represented the climactic failure of an otherwise forgotten twenty-year war.

INEQUALITY IN THE AGE OF JUSTICE REFORM

In 2010, the Tulsa Veterans Treatment Court became one of the founding models for replicating vet courts across the United States and trained members of the carceral state to identify veterans in jail and provide mental health treatment. That following year, an African American veteran of the Iraq War named Elliott Earl Williams died a brutal and humiliating death in the David L. Moss Detention Center in Tulsa, Oklahoma. Under custody, Williams sustained blunt-force trauma and starvation. His neck was broken. This veteran had a documented history of mental illness. But the nurse and jail psychiatrist accused him of faking the injuries. No one provided medical attention for six days. Guards taunted him as he lay dying. Surveillance cameras captured it all on video.[76]

Since 2010, twenty other prisoners were killed in the jail under grim circumstances, and there have been numerous allegations of prisoner abuse, medical neglect, and inadequately trained officers. One woman sued after being denied her medication. While having seizures, she had a cardiac arrest because a breathing tube was incorrectly inserted into her throat. More than a dozen lawsuits showed recurring issues within the institution involving poor training, lack of staff and proper care, and maltreatment resulting in deaths or near-fatal incidents. As Melanie Newport points out, "As with many sites of state violence, the jail archive is riddled with silences. Lies about jail conditions and the erasure of information . . . have been and remain central to jail governance."[77] Administrators and officials of the Tulsa jail have a documented pattern of attempting to cover up or dismiss the incidents.[78]

Despite the abundance of evidence against the jail, no one ever faced consequences for the death of Elliott Williams. According to the court records, Williams had been arrested and detained for a misdemeanor "obstruction of justice." According to his family, Williams and his wife were going through divorce. He was detained by Tulsa police but was never even officially charged with a crime until after his death.[79] The police report stated that it was "readily apparent" that Williams was having a "mental breakdown." Officers slammed his body on the concrete floor. Even though Williams reported suicidal ideations, officers failed to place him under suicide watch; he was confined to a holding cell where he allegedly rammed his head into the wall.

After Williams claimed that his neck was broken, officers still denied medical attention for ten hours. The next day, he was paralyzed, but the jail's head nurse cursed at him and accused him of faking the injuries. Officers then dumped him from a gurney into a shower, smacking his head on the floor. Unable to move his body, Williams was left there for three hours. Guards tried to force-feed him, but then moved him into a surveillance cell where

Williams starved for the next three days. At one point, officers threw food onto the cell floor. During that time, no one called 911, and he received no medical care. Three days after the injuries, Dr. Stephen Harnish, a psychiatrist employed by the jail's medical service provider, finally visited for only twelve minutes. He performed no neurological tests or any medical examination to rule out paralysis. Naked, shaking, and unable to move, Williams was left to die unattended on the cold, hard floor of a jail cell. On October 27, more than five days after the arrest, he had died of a broken neck and dehydration. In the years after Williams's death, in a series of legal defenses, those responsible claimed "qualified immunity," legal jargon meant to shield police and prison officials from prosecution. Any lawsuits would have to prove that the jailers were "'deliberately indifferent' to a 'substantial risk of harm.'"[80] In other words, the system protected itself from accountability, "obstructing" equal justice and denying protection under the law.

This horrific incident happened in 2011, three years after the Tulsa Veterans Treatment Court was founded.[81] The carceral system did not see Elliott Williams as a human being, much less a military veteran with mental health disorders.

CONCLUSION

Cultural change in mental health happens from the bottom up, but institutional change in the justice system requires coordinated, multilateral efforts to enact real, lasting progress.[82] Not only were the courts alarmed by the signature wounds of war, but their members proactively responded to a concurrent mental health crisis and opioid epidemic by advocating for treatment and wider reforms from within the criminal justice system. Veterans Treatment Courts aimed to provide robust rehabilitation services and actual care to veterans in the legal system. Again, and most important, it works. In doing so, over time specialty courts are slowly changing attitudes on mental health and substance use in the criminal justice system. As Matt Steiner earnestly admits, "I wouldn't have paid attention to the criminal justice system if it had not been for Veterans Treatment Courts."

The Obama presidency signified a *titanic* course correction in national drug policies away from carceral punishment. In May 2010, the Obama administration's National Drug Control Strategy called for "prevention, treatment, recovery, innovative criminal justice strategies" to address the problem of drugs as a public safety and health epidemic.[83] The following fiscal year, the Obama administration granted $101 million for the expansion of drug treatment and Veterans Treatment Courts.[84] In a letter addressed to Christopher Deutsch and the NADCP, President Obama stated, "My administration strongly supports alternatives to incarceration for non-violent offenders with substance use disorders. Drug courts are essential to our efforts to break the cycle of drug abuse, crime, incarceration, and rearrest."[85] In 2011, bipartisan congressional legislation allocated federal funding to state governments to establish Veterans Treatment Courts in their local communities.[86] With broad, popular support from both the Obama administration and Congress, Veterans Treatment Courts proliferated across the United States, totaling more than six hundred as of 2021.[87] But these top-down efforts alone might have only sunk more money into the criminal justice system were it not for the movement of volunteer veterans, saving countless lives and effecting a sea change.

In January 2017, at the end of his administration, President Barack Obama published an article in the *Harvard Law Review* titled "The President's Role in Advancing Criminal Justice Reform."[88] The crux of his argument rested with the role of executive power in influencing the nation's policies on criminal justice reform at the federal, state, and local levels. His administration was the first in decades to lower the number of people in federal prison by using clemency power and working with Congress and the US Sentencing Commission. Countering the "tough on crime" rhetoric, Obama promoted a "smart on crime" approach, and the Department of Justice revised policies on mandatory minimum sentencing for nonviolent drug offenses.[89] The Fair Sentencing Act redressed the disparity between crack and powder cocaine. (Of course, this legislation was three decades too late.) Calling on future administrations to carry forward the work left unfinished, Obama described opioids as a crisis of "public health" and called for treatment over carceral punishment. The shift in language under the Obama administration marks an important transition in the politics of drug intervention.

Despite modest reforms to the criminal justice system during the Obama administration, the military-carceral state continued to expand through the 1033 program, blurring the lines between war and policing in the United States. In the wake of the police killing of Michael Brown in 2014 and protests in Ferguson, Missouri, the President's Task Force on 21st Century Policing sought to investigate and propose reforms to policing.[90] It recommended more transparency, community policing and de-escalation training, and account-ability and oversight.[91] At the end of his presidency, Obama reflected on the legacy of his approach to criminal justice, outlining a cogent blueprint for future reforms. Much of Obama's commentary involved working with the Department of Justice (while maintaining its necessary separation from the White House), but his arguments failed to address the blurred lines between the Department of Defense and local, state, and federal law enforcement.[92] Since the 1996 Defense Authorization Act, Program 1033 authorized the Pentagon to funnel weapons of war and excess military equipment into civilian law enforcement.[93] As a consequence, armored vehicles, assault rifles, tactical gear, and militarized tactics have been deployed disproportionately against Black and Brown communities and peaceful protests.[94] In 2015, President Obama issued an executive order to curb the flow of specific types of military equip-ment into law enforcement, such as grenade launchers and tanks. But in 2021, the American Civil Liberties Union reported that reforms under the Obama administration did not significantly reduce the amount of military equipment in domestic law enforcement and that these types of weapons and aggressive tactics were deployed against Black Lives Matter protesters in 2020.[95] "There is so much work to be done," acknowledges President Obama. "Yet I remain hopeful that together we are moving in the right direction."[96]

The successes of Veterans Treatment Courts offer lessons for mass move-ments against carceral punishment and mass incarceration, giving a glimpse of hope for the future of criminal justice. But from the ground level, community members must actively push for cultural change, treatment, and equal justice for all—especially for the most marginalized groups in America. Until police, prison officials, veterans, and civilians alike are held to the same standards of justice, fairness, and accountability, then the people must continue to organize, speak out, rise up, protest, and hold officials accountable to enact meaningful criminal justice reforms.

CHAPTER 8

. . . And Justice for All

Women and Families of Veterans Treatment Court

Content warning: The first half of this chapter includes traumatic memories from survivors of sexual assault and may be particularly distressing for some readers.

In the spring of 2020, as the first wave of COVID-19 spread across the United States, news of the disappearance and brutal murder of PFC Vanessa Guillen went viral in veteran communities. Not once but twice, Guillen had reported sexual harassment by a fellow soldier at Fort Hood, Texas, but both times, the Army had failed to investigate the incidents. On April 22, SPC Aaron David Robinson bludgeoned Guillen to death with a hammer inside an armory building on base. Cecily Aguilar, Robinson's girlfriend, helped him dismember and dispose of the body, burying Guillen underneath concrete. Her body was uncovered more than two months later. On July 1, Robinson reportedly killed himself before police could apprehend him.[1] The gruesome deaths of Vanessa Guillen and Sgt. Elder Fernandes—whose body was found hanging from a tree after he reported sexual assault—caused a public outcry for justice and accountability.[2] On social media, under the hashtag #IAmVanessaGuillen, hundreds of women veterans shared similar stories of sexual trauma publicly. And a movement to reform the military justice system was reborn.

Under the national spotlight, the Army investigated the exceptionally high number of fatalities, missing persons, and assaults at Fort Hood. Thirty-nine service members there had died or gone missing that year alone, including five homicides and thirteen deaths by suicide, while eleven deaths remain unsolved.[3] In the aftermath of Guillen's death, an independent Fort Hood investigation concluded that the "command climate" rendered SHARP (the Army's Sexual Harassment/Assault Response and Prevention program) ineffective, and the leadership enabled a "permissive environment for sexual assault."[4] In consequence, fourteen Army leaders were fired or suspended.[5] But individual investigations such as these often occur in isolation, failing to produce effective systemic reforms needed to curb sexual violence on a national level.

The case of Vanessa Guillen illustrates a crisis of sexual violence in the military and systemic inequality in the military justice system. Even though Guillen reported the harassment, the chain of command failed to intervene, investigate, or protect her from the abuser. But she was not alone. Victims of military sexual trauma are twelve times more likely to experience retaliation than their rapists are to be convicted.[6] From 2004 to 2012, annual reports of sexual assault in the military doubled, increasing each single year from 1,700 reported in 2004 to 3,344 reported in 2012. But these numbers alone do not fully account for the depth of the military rape crisis or for the systemic problems that enable it to continue. Most survivors of sexual assault do not report it for fear of stigmas, ostracism, and retribution. Even when they do report, the perpetrators are rarely prosecuted. In 2012 alone, the *Annual Report on Sexual Assault in the Military* estimated 26,000 sexual assaults. That year, only 238 offenders were convicted. Sixty-four of the accused were acquitted.[7]

Since the Vietnam War era, as the number of women in the military increased, the nature of military sexual violence pivoted from war rape of civilians to "intra-military" assault within the ranks.[8] Infamous events like the Tailhook scandal in 1991 and Aberdeen in 1996 spotlighted high-profile cases of sexual violence against women in the US military.[9] Since then, the Department of Defense has initiated more training and resources to combat the pervasiveness of sexual violence, but, as historian Elizabeth Hillman notes, the US armed forces' "responses have largely failed, in part because of resistance within military institutions to cultural change."[10] The end of the draft and demographic shifts in the military created conditions for new problems among the 9/11 generation. In absence of the draft, the US military relies on women to fill the ranks of the all-volunteer force and carry out the Global War on Terrorism. Since 2001, a larger percentage of women also served in combat zones. Despite their indispensable roles, women in the military face discrimination and civil rights violations. The Uniform Code of Military Justice (UCMJ) persistently fails to uphold legal rights and due process. The everyday occurrences of harassment, abuse, and sexual assault of women add up to endemic and systemic gender inequality.

In 2013, for the first time in half a century, the US Commission on Civil Rights investigated human rights violations in the military. It found that women in the military were five times more likely to be sexually assaulted than civilian women. The Department of Defense has initiated policies designed to protect victims against retaliation, but "60 percent of women who reported unwanted sexual contact, believed they experienced negative social, professional, or administrative consequences."[11] In many cases, survivors of sexual assault were discharged for behavioral incidents and misdiagnosed with personality disorders and adjustment disorders—conditions that the military claims were preexisting. Instead of holding their assailants accountable, the military often punishes the victims of rape for deviant behavior and misconduct that can be attributed to comorbid MST and PTSD. Between 20 and 40 percent of women in the military report military sexual trauma that often results in PTSD, depression, or other major mental health disorders.[12] All too often, the military justice system then discharges the survivors of sexual trauma with bad paper for "preexisting" mental health problems—essentially pathologizing rape victimhood—and then denying them VA services and treatment.

On average, one in four women in the military are assaulted by a fellow service member, leading to military sexual trauma and post-traumatic stress disorder.[13] From 2006 to 2011, the number of sex crimes in the military increased each year.[14] In 2011, sex crimes accounted for 47 percent of all violent crimes in the Army.[15] Scholars of carceral feminism would caution against thinking of the military-carceral state as a "social remedy" or the solution to military sexual violence.[16] After all, the military has a long history of wielding false accusations of rape to disproportionately punish Black service members, as well as policing the bodies of women and LGBTQ members.[17] Even accounting for cases in which evidence was unfounded or inconclusive, the number of documented sex crimes in the post-9/11 Army constitutes a social crisis.[18]

Because the chain of command retains sole decision-making authority in cases of sexual assault in the military, few perpetrators are held accountable for their crimes, and most survivors never report it for fear of retribution. Spurred on by this grassroots veterans' movement to reform the UCMJ, Kirsten Gillibrand (D-NY) introduced the Military Justice Improvement Act in 2013. If passed, this legislation would remove the chain of command from cases of sexual assault, offering civilian oversight to ensure equal justice to victims. Amid these reform efforts, the Pentagon misled Congress by reporting inaccurate information on military sexual assault.[19] Consequentially, the bill failed to overcome a Republican filibuster, led by the late Senator John McCain (R-AZ), a former Vietnam War POW. It has failed every year since then. In 2016, it did not even go to the Senate floor for a vote.[20] Despite more sexual assault training, it remains difficult for survivors to report rape for the fear of retaliation. In practice, the UCMJ practically protects perpetrators and silences victims. A cultural deference to authority has enabled institutional injustices to escalate in the military justice system virtually unchecked. Since the failure of Congress to act, these problems have only worsened. In the aftermath of Guillen's murder, the aptly named "I Am Vanessa Guillen Act" similarly seeks to reform the military justice system by circumventing the chain of command in cases of sexual assault, establishing a process for compensation for military negligence, and reforming the SHARP program to provide civilian oversight.

Perpetrators of rape in the military are rarely held accountable by the justice system, and many male veterans continue to commit acts of sexual violence beyond the military. Shockingly, in 2012, 35 percent of male veterans in prison were violent sex offenders, a percentage which is consistent with Department of Justice studies since 1978.[21] In 2016, veterans were twice as likely as nonveterans to commit rape.[22] The vast majority of incarcerated veterans are male, with only 2 percent being women. One study indicated that survivors of military sexual trauma have a high probability of legal trouble.[23] In absence of justice reform for survivors of intra-military rape, Veterans Treatment Courts across the country are intercepting women veterans in the criminal justice system and providing treatment for military sexual trauma.

Women veterans too often experience distinctive co-occurring disorders—PTSD, MST, substance use, and depression—while also facing reintegration barriers, such as child care needs, unemployment, homelessness, and incarceration.[24] Research on women veterans in prison is relatively scant, but in practice, Veterans Treatment Courts are diverting women veterans from jails and providing appropriate treatment for military sexual trauma and other comorbid mental health disorders. Unknowingly, Jack O'Connor, mentor coordinator at the Buffalo Veterans Treatment Court, mentored a woman veteran for almost a year who had been the victim of assault. After she finally reported the incident to another woman, the Buffalo court began immediately recruiting women veteran mentors. In response, Veterans Treatment Courts started screening for MST and ensured that survivors have access to treatment and appropriate mentorship. Since then, Justice for Vets implements training to address military sexual trauma on a nationwide scale, dealing with the aftermath of the military rape crisis in civilian courts.

FIGURE 9: Vanessa Guillen Memorial Mural. Mark Felix, AFP-Getty Images, taken on August 14, 2020, in Houston, Texas.

SEXUAL ASSAULT SURVIVORS AND VOLUNTEER VETERAN MENTORS

A veteran mentor in the Buffalo Veterans Treatment Court, Alyssa Vasquez is an expert markswoman, a former drill sergeant for the US Army, and a survivor of military sexual violence.[25] On the surface, Vasquez is an accomplished woman and career soldier, having trained hundreds of soldiers, completing three combat tours, and serving honorably for thirteen and a half years. It took her fifteen years, however, to "speak the word *rape*." During the first weekend in Baghdad, she was assaulted by three fellow American soldiers.

From an early age, her life plan had been to serve in the military, go to college, get married, and then have kids. "I pretty much did it completely backwards," she explains. Vasquez grew up in an abusive home. At thirteen years old, she ran away. At fourteen years old, she got pregnant. The father went to prison for fifteen years. A month before graduating high school, she married a soldier. Her then husband was at basic training when the World Trade Towers were attacked. After 9/11, "I think we all felt a little more vulnerable," she says. "I was really happy that my ex-husband had joined the military—until that day, and then I became fearful." The possibilities of war loomed ominously over their marriage and family. She realized, "This isn't just a for-fun gig, and you don't actually just get to call yourself a soldier—now you might actually have to do something." At twenty years old, Vasquez decided "now is the time for me to step up for my family" and "become the bread-winner." She turned twenty-one in basic training at Fort Jackson. Her children were five and two years old when she first deployed to Iraq in 2004.

The first tour in Iraq forever changed Vasquez's outlook on humanity. Jonathan Shay writes that Americans in Vietnam "felt unsafe in the rear as out in the field."[26] Similarly, in Iraq, the external threats included incoming mortar attacks, rockets, and bombings. "A month and a half after I got in theater," Vasquez recalls, "one hit two trailers down from me, killing Staff Sergeant Darren J. Cunningham on September 30, 2004." The aftermath of his death caused a moral injury. "That deployment severed my ties to people," Vasquez states. Before recounting the memory, she reassured me: "I might get emotional, but it's not overwhelming." As Cunningham's trailer burned, an adjacent trailer caught fire while a soldier was trapped inside. "I jumped over a barrier to get that soldier out so that he wouldn't burn alive." She and a medic frantically worked to save his life. She presumed, "You're surrounded by soldiers, and everybody's in that mode where they're helping, and they're protecting." To her utter shock and disbelief, she "looked down and saw a line of soldiers, and they had their cameras, and everybody was taking pictures of the trailer that was on fire. And at that moment, I realized that *I fucking hate people*."

Moral injury is a betrayal of what's right in a high-stakes situation.[27] Vasquez understood, "In that moment, his family's lives were forever being changed, and they were getting ready to receive the worst information that they could ever imagine. And people were taking pictures," she laments. "I can't rationalize that, and I can't excuse that behavior, and I don't understand it." The betrayal set her apart, in her mind, from the rest of humanity, rendering her an aberration. "Ever since that moment, I have always felt like I am living on the other side of a painted glass, and I'm just watching these people around me." Vasquez reflects, "That deployment changed me big time."

Military sexual trauma is also a deep moral injury, the ultimate betrayal of trust and violation of the kinship between soldiers.[28] Living on base, Vasquez faced threats from both inside the compound as well as outside. "My first weekend that I was in Iraq, I experienced military sexual trauma by my first leaders," admits Vasquez. Three noncommissioned officers assaulted her. Afterward, she feared the consequences of speaking out. "I didn't [report them] but one of the non-commissioned officers in our unit, she suspected something. She raised the flag on it." Vasquez refused to cooperate with the investigation. All three NCOs "lost rank." She explains, "After they got back to the States, they got out of the military." One of the attackers eventually assaulted another soldier and "lost rank again."

The trauma of sexual violence often becomes compounded by an all too common institutional betrayal that happens when authorities fail to protect, defend, or ensure justice to survivors of sexual assault.[29] When word got out, Vasquez experienced retaliation and stigmatization. "I felt like the black sheep of the unit. Nobody liked me. I was the new person. Here I was getting their favorite NCOs in trouble."[30] Nancy Sherman describes the effect of this betrayal on survivors: "The attachment bond has been snapped, and with it the belief that fidelity ought to be reciprocated by support, and care, and empathetic leadership."[31] For the rest of her deployment in Iraq, Vasquez felt completely isolated and sank into depression. "I shrunk in on myself," Vasquez describes. "Just put my head down" and buried herself in work. Her mother sent care packages. "That would brighten up my day, and I had my kids' pictures up on my wall." She looked forward to coming home and leaving the Army. "I was supposed to get out of the military shortly after I got back from Iraq because I had a short enlistment, but the first sergeant intentionally sent me . . . to another unit specifically to redeploy to Iraq. 100% that was retribution."

In 2006, Vasquez redeployed to Baghdad. This time, the proximal leadership promoted a safer and mutually respectful culture for women in the Army. She believes, "The majority of people are followers, so it all boils down to who is the leader in the group, and . . . what kind of culture they create." In her professional opinion, weak leaders permit poor discipline, allowing problems like sexual assault to endanger not only women but the mission too. On the second tour, says Vasquez, the ranking officers promoted "good morals, good values. They lived by those seven core Army values"—loyalty, duty, respect, selfless service, honor, integrity, and personal courage. Nonetheless, the damage had been done. She lost faith in the narratives she once unquestionably believed about the US military, its leadership, and its role in the world. "I started to feel more of that internal conflict." She could not hate someone just because "they were born on the other side." Today, she cannot yet reconcile her previous beliefs about the United States and her actual experiences in the Iraq War.

In the military, Vasquez felt discouraged from seeking mental health treatment. "It's almost like you're encouraged to *not tell the truth*," she believes. "Because if you tell the truth, then more doors open. It's like when you walk into a doctor's office, 'have you had thoughts of harming yourself?' They don't really want you to say yes, or at least that's the feeling that you get." If you check the wrong boxes, then it leads to more delays, more questionnaires, more doctors, and more problems. Vasquez says, "Because if you say yes, then it leads to this other" question. "'How much do you drink?' You don't. You just have to tell them none," because then your behavior gets called into question. Vasquez feared, if she had reported any mental health problems, it would ruin her career. "I very much had a fear of any kind of mental weakness. That was stigmatized highly. I wouldn't be able to advance and get opportunities. I wouldn't have been able to be a drill sergeant." A failure of leadership pushed Vasquez to become a drill sergeant and lead by a better example. But untreated mental health and the demands of her career eventually strained family relationships, and she eventually divorced her husband.

The forever wars have a distinctive impact on military motherhood and children. The demands of her career required Vasquez to be absent from the lives of her children for months at a time. She focused on her career first and advanced through the ranks, seeking to provide a better life for her children. Over the years, however, Vasquez would become more comfortable in a military setting than the civilian world. After returning from Iraq in 2008, Vasquez was a "drill sergeant with the Delta 31st, a combat engineer unit at Fort Leonard Wood." She remained in Missouri for two years. Then, in late 2012, she redeployed to Afghanistan. "I was there for about a month and a half," she explains. "It was fluke thing that came up." Vasquez had a severe allergic reaction. Fortunately for her, doctors discovered an underlying heart condition. Vasquez flew to Walter Reed.

Suddenly taken out of the field in Afghanistan, Vasquez experienced survivor's guilt for leaving soldiers behind. "I felt guilty that I wasn't over there. I also wasn't with my kids, so 'what good am I doing?'" It planted seeds. "I had spent so much time away from family that it started to become all I knew," she realized. "I felt more comfortable in uniform." But still she took the next opportunity to advance her military career. "Out of nowhere, I got an offer to work at the survival school [SERE] and that's where I spent the last three years in my military" career. From SERE, she applied to special forces but was rejected because of her medical history. "The rest of the Army started to look less appealing to me. I only wanted to go one direction and medically I was disqualified."

In 2017, Vasquez decided to retire from the Army. "Something just kicked in me. I was getting ready to say goodbye to my kids," she recalls. "There was just something about the way my youngest son hugged me. It just broke me." Vasquez decided, "I've given enough time that I can walk away with pride." Her chain of command supported her decision. The Army discharged her honorably after more than thirteen years of service.

But Vasquez left the military completely unprepared for the realities of life after the Army. "I had a hard time adjusting to civilian life because I never had to" confront the traumatic memories. "I had responsibilities where I could throw myself into my work and not worry about any of that stuff." But outside the structure of military life, Vasquez felt completely lost in the civilian workplace. "I've got to walk into this job with these people that I do not vibe with. I don't understand them. They don't understand me. I was putting on a happy face, but I was freaking out at every turn." In retrospect, "I was super idealistic and overconfident in my ability to reintegrate." After a successful career in the military, Vasquez had also grown accustomed to financial stability. "I took a *huge* pay cut," she explains. "My bills started going unpaid. I'm feeling like I'm suffocating."

Despite those terrible experiences in Iraq, she had a remarkable career on paper. In effect, she had buried the PTSD and MST. After coming home, Vasquez isolated herself within the civilian world. The cultural rules of the military don't apply to the civilian sector. On the one hand, she enjoyed less responsibility at work. No one would die based on her decisions, but on the other hand, she felt purposeless. "The military, it really is a 24-hour job," she explains, "so you never have that ability to turn off or have to confront silence. That's when it started to creep up." Six months after discharge, she reached the nadir of her postmilitary life and a crisis of readjustment difficulties.

Many service members repress mental health problems while in the military, but once they return to the United States, the underlying issues eventually resurface, sometimes all at once. Many self-medicate with alcohol instead of seeking treatment. Drinking alcohol also intensifies the symptoms of underlying mental health disorders. "I made it worse by coupling alcohol with that. I was dealing with the financial stress." She explains, "That's when I really hit the wall. That's when the intrusive images" returned. She had mostly repressed the traumatic memories, but suddenly, "boom! It's in your face all the time." She experienced anger, rage, flashbacks, and stresses associated with PTSD. "You immediately shoot to that worst part of humanity, and you're immediately reminded of all the worst things that ever happened to you."

That's when Vasquez finally reported the assault to the VA. One night, she "got crappy drunk" and started an online disability claim. "I wrote everything that happened," she says. "I named everybody." She had been too drunk to remember filing the claim. Afterward, the Buffalo VA hospital contacted her for an appointment to be evaluated for PTSD. "That's when it all came back," she recalls. "It led to a lot of healing that wouldn't have taken place if I would have kept trying to" hammer it down. She sought appropriate counseling and rehabilitation and discovered a fulfilling career advocating for veterans. Informed by her own readjustment difficulties, she specialized in providing employment, social services, and community resources for veterans in Buffalo, New York.

More than any other legal system, Veterans Treatment Courts fulfill the needs of the most vulnerable people in the community, providing a type of socialized criminal justice, direct access to healthcare, disability benefits, housing services, and treatment. With the support of the Veterans Administration, the courtroom serves as a centralized location, connecting federal and local entities, to meet the needs of its members. Alyssa Vasquez currently works for one of the community partners of the Veterans Treatment Court in Buffalo, an organization called "Veterans' One Stop." In this role, she supports veterans by helping them locate housing and gainful employment opportunities. These social services are vital to veterans in the criminal justice system and their families.

Currently, Vasquez volunteers as a veteran mentor at the Buffalo Veterans Treatment Court. "It's absolutely necessary for women and other survivors of military sexual trauma to be present in Veterans Treatment Court communities because they understand." Women veterans often disclose sexual trauma to her without prompting. "I know that [MST] is one of the main factors that has led them to [legal troubles] because they unknowingly unveil that in the first interview." She describes, "It just pours out of them." As a survivor herself, she provides a type of solidarity that most male mentors cannot. "They don't ever have to know it, but they are looking at somebody who has worked through it, so there's hope. If I can convey that message of hope, that's an added bonus to our interaction." The bonds among survivors are "like a quantum entanglement,"

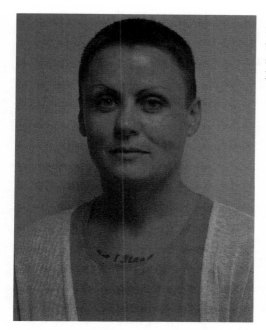

FIGURE 10. Photo provided by
the author and taken on July 10,
2019, at the Veterans' One Stop in
Buffalo, New York.

linking them together through the shared experience of sexual violence. Stories
like hers are tragically familiar for thousands of women in the military and the
hundreds of veterans who eventually speak out, advocate, and testify against
the crisis of sexual assault in the military.

As a combat medic, Kimberly Bailey experienced the wars in Iraq and
Afghanistan from a medical center in Germany, at a crucial juncture for wounded
American troops on their way to the United States. From 2004 to 2010, she served
active duty in the Army. "I didn't actually have combat experience," discloses
Bailey, expressing the type of remorse that comes from survivor's guilt.[32] "I wasn't
out there being shot at." As a member of a combat support unit, she took "care
of wounded soldiers that were directly from the battlefield. They literally flew
in, and we transported them . . . to Walter Reed or to any of the medical units."
She served in this role near the beginning of the Global War on Terrorism, "so
we saw the worst of the worst at that time." The injuries included "IED wounds,
and we saw the traumatic of traumatic; we saw people that didn't live," she says
somberly. Her job was "really chaotic." Critically wounded soldiers were transported through her workspace. Bailey remembers, "A lot of them came in really
scared," so "we would speak to them and talk to them and hold their hands and

transport them . . . from the medevac, straight to surgery or sometimes they were stabilized and put into certain clinics."

As she faced residual mental health effects, the secondary nature of the war trauma made her feel even more guilty. Bailey experienced "survivor's guilt because I was not there with them," she says, "and I didn't experience the things they experienced." She felt ashamed for being affected by the stress and weak for needing help. Bailey realizes, "That contributed a lot to repression and not talking about it," believing that "it wasn't my experience to talk about." Bailey quietly repressed the daily stress of her occupation, blocking out the haunting images of wounded bodies that passed through her life on stretchers and gurneys.

In 2006, Bailey was sexually assaulted by a noncommissioned officer in charge. "I was very low ranking" at the time, "just coming into the unit, probably E-3." This assailant was "probably an E-5 or an E-6." After the attack, "I felt very ashamed, very guilty, because . . . he was an NCO," She thought, "I don't want to tell anybody." At the encouragement of another soldier, however, Bailey reluctantly reported the attack. And the news spread like wildfire among the unit. "Within the next two days," she recounts, "everybody knew about what had happened—exactly the reason why I didn't want to tell." She wanted to avoid becoming a social pariah. "I know other women who . . . have similar stories." But when "everybody found out, I was blackballed. Nobody would talk to me. Nobody would sit next to me. I couldn't sit in the cafeteria to eat. I couldn't eat" without feeling ashamed. They all lived in the same barracks, but "everybody avoided me, wouldn't talk to me," she recalls. "It was a disaster. It was very traumatic." To give a sense of the wider issue, in 2011, 54 percent of rapes and sexual assaults in the military took place in "high density housing," like barracks.[33]

A combination of betrayal, retaliation, and abandonment caused moral injury. Kim Bailey explains, "For a lot of us in the military that have experienced military sexual trauma, I think it's a betrayal of the system that we trust." As a foster child, Bailey grew up in the liminal space between belonging and abandonment, always longing for kinship and community. Enlisting in the military, she thought, finally, "I found a family. I found a support system. I found other people who really understood where I was coming from, and who I could trust to have my back." Nancy Sherman writes, "To be betrayed by the new family is devastating, especially for those who sought it out because of earlier betrayals or traumas within their families of origin."[34] But after the assault, "nobody had my back," laments Bailey. "Nobody believed me. Nobody wanted to talk to me about it." This betrayal inflicted a double wound, the psychological scabs of military sexual trauma and the social stigmata that came with it.

Over the following year, Bailey met the man who became her husband and children's father. After giving birth, she dealt with postpartum depression, multiplied by the lingering guilt of aborting the fetus of her attacker and the comorbid symptoms of PTSD and MST. "I attempted suicide," she admits. "I was hospitalized for about two months in active duty" in "a military mental health ward," where she was threatened with a personality disorder.

During the hospitalization, Bailey sought counseling from an Army psychologist. During an exam, he accused her of seeking attention through self-harm. "He said that I probably had a personality disorder and that was probably pre-existing." With a diagnosis of a preexisting condition, the Army could separate her administratively and deny veterans' benefits. These practices revictimize survivors of rape and then disqualify them from treatment. Instinctively, Bailey realized, "I need to be silent. I need to be okay. I need to be mentally tough." She learned to mask mental illness. "I needed to be culturally competent. I needed to understand the culture of the military. I need to understand my place in the military, and I needed to be quiet about the trauma I had experienced." She thought, "because if I didn't, my career would be over," and she would be disqualified from the rights and entitlements of veteranhood. In effect, this Army doctor silenced Bailey by threatening her with administrative punishment, not only violating the Hippocratic oath but also breaking her trust again and failing to protect her rights. This act of institutional betrayal became the pivotal moment of her life. She would eventually become a social worker, dedicated to helping other survivors of abuse and trauma with an ethics of care.

In 2016, Human Rights Watch investigated the impact of "bad paper" discharges on victims of sexual assault in the military. The investigation uncovered systemic injustices and widespread punishment of survivors of military sexual trauma, based on 270 interviews and evidence provided under the Freedom of Information Act. Personality disorders were the "'the fastest and easiest way to get rid of someone'" in the military. In 2010, the military reformed its policies on personality disorder discharges in cases of military-related trauma; however, veterans with other-than-honorable discharges continue to be punished, often without "recourse to correct their record."[35]

Administrative discharges often deny survivors of sexual assault access to treatment, health care coverage, employment opportunities, education, and other financial benefits. Even more damaging, since only 15 percent of veterans are discharged with "bad paper," a less-than-honorable discharge is "deeply stigmatizing and may result in discrimination." Other-than-honorable discharges have also been "correlated with high suicide rates, homelessness, and imprisonment." Moreover, appealing a discharge is next to impossible without extensive legal resources and years of perseverance. US military veterans cannot sue the military for injuries or harm incurred during service, according to a Supreme Court precedent.[36] To circumvent these restrictions, Veterans Treatment Courts typically pair up with the VA and legal services to petition for discharge upgrades, while the Vet Center treats those with bad papers.

When Kimberly Bailey got out of the military, she coped with her traumas by drinking alcohol and using drugs. She recalls, "At the time, I was experiencing a lot of nightmares and a lot of flashbacks and a lot of hypervigilance." At that time, she did not understand "how the residual trauma was affecting" her mental health. Eventually, she started using cocaine and methamphetamines, sending her down this familiar path of mental health crisis and incarceration, nearly destroying her family along the way.

First, Bailey was arrested for driving under the influence. While still on probation, she got arrested again. "The judge was not happy with me because I literally just got arrested maybe a few months prior to that," she says. "It didn't come up that I was a veteran. Nobody ever asked me." Although in recent years the VA encourages jails to document veterans' status, the efforts are inconsistent across the United States. For some veterans, these crimes would have qualified for treatment court, but not every state or county has a Veterans Treatment Court or a specialty docket for veterans.

While sitting in a Virginia jail for a year, Bailey first made plans to change the trajectory of her life. After her release from jail, she flew home to California, reunited with her children, and enrolled in college. In 2016, Bailey earned a bachelor's degree, and now she has a master's in social work. As an advocate, she raises awareness on issues that women face in and beyond the military, including sexual trauma, mental health treatment, and incarceration. In January 2020, Bailey messaged me on social media, asking to share her story publicly for the first time.

After our interview, Bailey became inspired to advocate for other women veterans in the criminal justice system. It seemed like a type of social "uncertainty principle," an idea from the field of physics that basically suggests that studying something can influence the outcome. In a follow-up interview, Bailey revealed,

"After we had spoken, I wanted to learn more about what we had here [in Fresno, California] as far as resources for our female veterans" in the criminal justice system. She started searching for information but "couldn't find anything."[37] She finally got in touch with the mentor coordinator at the Fresno County Veterans Treatment Court. "He told me that they have no female veterans that are mentors." The court had been trying to recruit women to the mentor program but had not yet found any volunteers. Bailey responded enthusiastically, "'Well, I'll totally be a mentor,'" even though "I haven't actually been through the Veterans Treatment Court." Upon graduation from veterans court, the judge may dismiss the fines and expunge criminal records. She adds, "I wish that was afforded to me." Bailey represents one of the countless veterans who fell between the cracks of justice.

Through trial and error, the founders of the Buffalo Veterans Treatment Court discovered that some women in the program were victims of military sexual trauma and required specialized treatment, resources, and mentorship. Now, Veterans Treatment Courts actively recruit women mentors, and based on those early realizations, Justice for Vets implements appropriate training curriculum to meet women's needs on a nationwide basis. At the ground level, veterans and advocates are slowly healing the wounds inflicted during this crisis of sexual assault in the military and the total institutional failure to stop it.

For victims to receive equal justice, perpetrators must be held accountable for their crimes. The Department of Defense estimated that 25 percent of women in the military experience sexual assault. The failure of the military justice system becomes the inherent problem of the civilian criminal justice system. According to the newest national survey of veterans in prison, more than a quarter of male incarcerated veterans in prison committed acts of sexual violence (an actual decline in percentage from past reports).[38] But the rape crisis in the military is both systemic and cultural, which cannot be ended by implementing more training alone, nor by treating victims as an afterthought.

MILITARY FAMILIES, COMMUNITY JUSTICE, AND VETERANS TREATMENT COURTS

Military families felt the backdraft from the wars in Iraq and Afghanistan. Before the caskets are draped in flags and carried by honor guards, the service members who live and work near hospitals and morgues handle the wounded bodies of America's global wars. The slow drip of casualties from the wars in Iraq and Afghanistan produces psychiatric trauma, including PTSD.[39] Historically, women have borne this burden as nurses, widows, and caretakers of the disabled, the dying, and the dead. At the end of the Vietnam War, women in the military made up slightly more than 1 percent of total US armed forces. The end of the draft led to a major demographic shift since the 1970s.[40] Recruiters, then, relied on economic incentives to fill the ranks of the all-volunteer force.[41] In the civilian world, from 1967 to 2009, the US Census indicated that women in the workplace increased from fewer than 15 million to more than 43 million. The military paralleled this rise, with women accounting for 16–18 percent of the US armed services today.

Donna Sickels was the first in her family to serve. Her father would say, "'I had five sons, and my only daughter went into the military.'" She grew up in Philadelphia, where cocaine was popular in the late 1970s, until it was turned into crack in the 1980s. Her parents were both drug users. Growing up, she always wanted to go to college, but her family could not afford it. Military recruiters set up in shopping malls across America, selling a brighter future in the military.[42] One day, she stopped by the recruiters' office at the Roosevelt Mall. "I really wanted to go into the Marines," she says. "I really liked their uniforms." While the Marine recruiter was gone for lunch, "the Air Force recruiter just grabbed me, and I liked what he had to say." Recruiters promised money for college, a world of opportunity, and an exciting adventure. "That was a lot of the reason I went into the military."

In 1999, Sickels joined the US Air Force Reserves mostly to escape the vacuum of her neighborhood and family life. She completed training at Lackland Air Force Base. In the Air Force Reserves, she worked in the service industry, learning hotel management skills but normally working in the dining facility. "We were trained to be cooks," but she explains, "we handle[d] the mortuary affairs, working in the morgue." Sickels says, "I don't know how all that went together but it did." Still living in Philadelphia, she was stationed at McGuire Air Force Base until September 11, 2001. Sickels received a voice mail, giving her forty-eight hours to prepare for deployment to Dover, Delaware. In 2002, she was activated, in preparation for the casualties from the war in Afghanistan. That's "when I actually seen what the morgue was all about," she says. "That's when we'd seen a lot of fatalities."

At the dawn of the Global War on Terrorism, SSG Donna Sickels encountered the trauma of war vicariously from an air base in the United States, handling human remains and interacting with grieving families. "You feel like you're doing an honorable service. You're getting these people dressed, redressing them, putting them in their caskets to send them home to their families." Although handling remains was emotionally difficult, Sickels took comfort in the knowledge that her service was honorable and useful. "There were very young kids, and their families would come—I can't believe I'm getting upset," she paused. "Their families would come and get them, and that was the hard part. Seeing the families and how upset they are," she recalls. "At the time, I cried when I was working it, but I thought I was okay," she says. "I didn't realize that it was going to affect me in the way that it did."

When her enlistment ended in 2005, Sickels was seven months pregnant with her daughter, so she did not reenlist. "Then I started having issues sleeping," remembers Sickels. "I had a newborn baby. I should've been dead tired. But I couldn't sleep at night." She recalls, "I was restless and irritable. I didn't even realize it—Now I know." It took her years of "working programs" to realize that her mental health conditions stemmed from military service. Her anxiety got worse when her mother developed cancer. "When she was sick, I used to go over and sit with her," comforting her and never leaving her deathbed. In 2009, Donna's mother died of breast cancer. "She didn't want to die in a hospital. I let her be on hospice care at my home." That week was one of the longest of her life. "She found out April 1 that she only had a week to live. She passed on the fifth. For four days, I barely slept. That's because I was taking Percocet." Sickels developed a dependency to opioids, and "it just went on from there."

Sickels's family has a history of substance use disorder. Her parents both used cocaine. Her father died of liver damage from alcohol. Then, just a year after her mother's death, Donna's oldest brother also died, in 2010. "He was also an addict," she explains. "He passed away in prison from untreated HIV." After losing her job, Sickels started using heroin. "From 2012–16, I was putting down, picking up, putting down, picking up." She would be sober for a couple months and would decide, "I could drink, as long as I'm not doing heroin. Then I can just do coc[aine] because I'm not doing heroin." Her husband eventually moved out and took their daughter with him. "I dragged him into a drug addict's life that he didn't choose to live," she said with profound regret in her voice.

Several times, Sickels attempted to stop using drugs, but without mental health treatment, she would always relapse. In 2016, she was arrested for driving under the influence and went to Philadelphia Veterans Treatment Court. Resistant at first, she turned a twelve-month treatment program into two years. "I was brought into the back of the courtroom and told that, 'If you don't deal with your underlying issues, you're never going to be able to deal with your addiction.' At the time, it meant nothing to me. I was like 'whatever. There's nothing wrong with me.'" Sickels had been raised in a culture that believed mental health automatically means "crazy," something to hide or deny altogether. "Judge [Dugan] put me in jail because I wouldn't go see a psychiatrist. At the time, I thought, 'You're saying I'm crazy. You act like I'm going to go out and start shooting up people.'" But after time in rehab, it "started to make sense."

Drug Treatment Courts operate using "therapeutic surveillance, merging forms of care and control."[43] Kevin Revier argues that "participants are *storied*" into the treatment program as addicts, objects of criminal "control (associated with Black criminality)" and addicts in recovery and "objects of care (associated with White middle class citizenship)." This is a useful framework to understand the coercive nature of mandatory counseling and urinalysis of the courts. Veterans Treatment Court advocates repeat an expression that the members "save lives" (care) and "save tax dollars" (criminality). Judges in treatment courts often tell defendants that if they do not complete treatment, they will "end up in prison or dead."[44] Given the alarming rates of fentanyl overdoses amid the opioid epidemic, their warnings are not unfounded, and many speak from experiences with other participants. Still, I will never forget the day I heard one judge berate an elderly Black Vietnam veteran for failing a drug test over marijuana. "Even if it's legal in other states, it's not legal here, and when you buy weed, you enable the illegal drug trade, violence, and death in your community." The saviorism and condescension in the judge's tone unnerved me, and I imagined the stories of violence the veteran could tell from the Vietnam War.

The day Donna Sickels graduated from the Philadelphia Veterans Treatment Court, she relapsed immediately. Judge Dugan "completed me, I walked out, and didn't even make it home. I went the other way." She recounts, "I was supposed to make a right, and I made a left. I got high and I thought, 'okay, this is it. Just this one time.'" She wanted to celebrate the achievement but fell right back into the same old habits. "It lasted about six months. It was a terrible, terrible, terrible six months." She admits, "My marriage was about to

come to an end. My daughter was ashamed of me. It got really bad, really fast."
Judge Dugan refused to mail her completion certificate, suspecting something
had happened. "He made me come pick it up, and when I did, he knew. He
knew something was going on with me."

During the summer of 2018, Donna Sickels hit rock bottom. "My husband
Matt and I were separated," she disclosed. "I was still running. There was a
tunnel around my neighborhood, where they were all living in tents." Living
under that tunnel, she sank into a pit of despair and disgust. She thought,
"'I can't keep doing this. . . . I had so many reasons to stop getting high. My
daughter needed me. I lost my mom at 29." She dropped to below one hundred
pounds, just barely surviving in the streets of Philadelphia. "I was on the verge
of death," Sickels realizes. "The drugs were slowly killing me. I was killing myself.
I couldn't. I felt lost. I couldn't go on like that." She felt like a hopeless failure
as a wife and a mother, fearing that she might pass the intergenerational legacy
of trauma and substance use onto her daughter.

Finally, Sickels reached out to Judge Dugan and the veterans court coordinator, who put her in touch with the Vet Center. Sickels checked herself into
an in-patient rehab program. Doctors diagnosed her with service-connected
PTSD, anxiety, and depression. She continues to see a psychologist at the VA
today. "Just being aware really helped me," reflects Sickels. "I just thought if I
just put drugs and alcohol down, I'll be okay, and that never worked for me."
But now, "I have a support system," which carries her onward. She started
attending a "rap" group at the Vet Center and joined Narcotics Anonymous,
finding a community of people who could relate.

Through the process of recovery and counseling, Sickels discovered a new
purpose in advocacy for other similarly damaged people. "Helping other people gives me a sense of joy," she remarks. "Offering hope for other people, and
seeing how people's lives change, and seeing them light up with hope for their
future, it made me feel good." She applied and got her certification in mental
health aid. "I even got certified in Narcan," a prescription drug administered
during emergency opioid overdoses. Personal experience motivated her to
help the most vulnerable people in her community, like those still living under
tunnels. She volunteers at a safe injection site. "Prevention Point offers a lot
of different resources," she explains. "It's not just a needle exchange. They have
doctors on site for people dealing with HIV." In this way, her advocacy honors
the memory of her late brother, who died of substance use and untreated HIV.

Peer advocacy helps heal the intergenerational trauma in her family. Her husband patiently accompanied her during our interview in 2019. From time to time, she would glance in his direction, showing immense regret for their marital difficulties. But with kindness and understanding, he would nod, ensuring her that he and their daughter were still at her side. Since the oral history interview, Donna Sickels has been working full-time as a certified peer specialist and a recovery coach. Presently, she works for an organization that participates in Philadelphia Veterans Treatment Court, where she serves as a veteran mentor. "I really wanted this. It was something that I really worked hard for. I just felt like it would be good for me to help other people," she realizes. "Who else do you know that can make all those mistakes in their lives and turn it around to be something good that helps someone else?" She answered her own question: "Addicts and alcoholics." She concludes, "Maybe I can't change my past, but I can only move forward from it" and provide a better future for her family.

As the burdens of fighting forever wars fall on fewer people, the families of veterans today inherit a cycle of intergenerational trauma. When we first met, Joani Higgins smiled at the coincidence that her late husband and I share a last name. At that point, in the summer of 2019, I had completed nearly one hundred oral histories with veterans, but Joani was the first Gold Star spouse, and I was slightly nervous. After stumbling through the introductions, I sat my questions aside and asked her to tell me their story.

For a total of nineteen years, MSgt. Chuck Higgins served actively in the US Army and the National Guard. Higgins was admired by his troops, respected in the Buffalo community, and wore a size 13½ combat boot. He died by suicide June 19, 2017.[45] His sudden death sent shock waves into the Buffalo community and across the state, leaving a gaping hole in their family. In 2018, on average, more than seventeen American veterans died by suicide daily.[46] Her family's history is interwoven into the fabric of collective trauma in US military families, especially in the post-9/11 era.[47]

Joani Higgins never served in the military herself, but the women in her family apparently "are suckers for the uniform or punishment," she laughed, easing the tension of the interview. "All of my brothers-in-laws" are in the US Army. "My grandparents met in a bomb shelter in England. It trickled down through" the family. Joani's grandfather was an American soldier stationed in England during the Second World War, and afterward, her English grand-mother immigrated to the United States, starting a family and new life as Americans. Military service is family tradition. Between World War II and Vietnam, ten of Joani's uncles served in the military, and her nephews were serving at the time of the interview.

Beneath the appearance of a successful military career, MSgt. Higgins had a troubled past, and it eventually damaged his home life. He had suffered from depression and anger. In turn, these underlying mental health problems led to marital difficulties. Joani had been Chuck's second wife. "There was a lot of self-medicating and drinking," she reveals. "A lot of things were surfacing that . . . were never a part of our life but more issues from the past." They separated even-tually. "His behavior was becoming toxic for my children," she realized. They split amicably when he moved out. "We were civil, even being separated." She thought the family would move forward, even if they lived in separate homes.

Higgins had just been promoted to master sergeant before he died. It was "the biggest shock." To her knowledge, "there had never been prior suicide ideations. No thoughts of it. Never. If anything, he was completely against it." In fact, his unit had recently experienced a string of deaths by suicide within the same year. "That took a huge toll." At the time of Higgins's unexpected death, his twin brother was deployed to Afghanistan. For the funeral, he stayed for only five days and shipped back to Afghanistan. People from across New York attended the funeral. Chuck Higgins had trained countless soldiers over his long career. Now, "I had to be that much better at my job." Joani felt a duty to serve "our local troops as much as he did."

As a counselor, Joani Higgins specializes in working with veterans, and at the Veterans' One Stop in Buffalo, she provides a network of resources to help soldiers transition into the civilian world. "My job definitely helped because . . . it made me that much more motivated to get out of bed every day. My kids needed me." Her work with veterans helped her process grief. At the Buffalo Veterans Treatment Court, she typically works with veterans going through the five stages. She thinks, "My educational background has helped me," but "you don't really understand grief until you *really feel it.*"

As of 2019, Joani Higgins had become one of the first civilians to become a veteran mentor at the Buffalo Veterans Treatment Court. "I'm a Gold Star spouse. I'm not allowed to mentor a veteran on my own. Not in that setting," she explains. Even with a background in psychology, "we can't take our professional roles into the courtroom. It's completely different. That's one of the things they emphasize. 'You're not counseling here.'" Her interactions with veterans in court are informed by her painful personal experiences. "I can relate more to their pain," she explains. "That was not their spouse, but that's their battle buddy. That's their routine. To have to go on and do your job when that person is no longer there. I can empathize with that—not in a battlefield but in real life. This is my civilian battle. It's me and my kids now." The Vet Center provides mental health treatment to military families and children, such as Joani's. "If you have a support system, you can overcome anything."

Before her involvement with the Veterans Treatment Court, Joani struggled to empathize with people with substance use disorders. Although she had a graduate degree in psychology, she felt ambivalent toward people who used drugs. "I always felt initially it was choice to start," admits Joani. "However, now working with veterans and seeing them struggle and self-medicate. A lot of them are using heroin because they can't get their pain killers," but "there's always a story behind somebody." Now, she understands substance use disorder as "an illness" that affects the whole family. "To visibly see it in veterans court and to watch the strongman crumble in front of the judge at the podium is a really powerful experience. And then to watch women . . . lose their children because they can't beat their addiction. It's heart-breaking. Do they really want to relapse? Absolutely not." Members of the Veterans Treatment Court anticipate relapses because they recognize that substance use and mental health disorders are often lifelong.

Veteran Treatment Courts work partly because members of the court are willing to treat defendants not as criminals but as people. The police, lawyers, social workers, and volunteers all seem to care more because they see veterans as the "best that society has to offer."[48] Imagine if that benefit of doubt were extended to all people. When society understands how veterans—who are idealized as the embodiment of strength—are vulnerable to mass incarceration, we start to see the full impact of our wars in the United States.

A hybrid mental health and drug court, the Veterans Treatment Courts provide lessons that could potentially revolutionize the criminal justice system. Joani concludes, "Depending on what the offence is, maybe everyone should be given . . . a chance to rehabilitate, instead of being sent away to prison. Let's put them in work training programs . . . instead of sitting in a cell, just wasting taxpayers' money." Amid this cycle of trauma, substance use, and crime, people eventually become institutionalized rather than rehabilitated, making recidivism all but inevitable.

On the contrary, Veterans Treatment Courts provide critical resources to people transitioning into society—employment, job training, self-management skills, counseling, health services, and community partnerships. Since 1973, for "10 million Americans" and "tens of millions" of family members, "the military provided an elaborate social and economic safety net: medical and dental programs; housing assistance; subsistence payments" as well as "tax advantages; education and training; dozens of family welfare programs; childcare; and social services ranging from financial counseling to legal aid," writes historian Jennifer Mittelstadt.[49] During the era of the all-volunteer force, military personnel and their families rely on an expansive "military welfare state." For many veterans, the sudden loss of this support network makes the transition to civilian life even more challenging and troublesome.

Linking the courts with federal institutions, Judge Robert Russell first bypassed the competing interests of local, state, and federal entities and effectively recreated a new social safety net. The Veterans Administration, the Vet Center, and the Veterans Treatment Courts provide the infrastructure necessary to enable readjustment from the military, jail, or prison. Taken to the next logical step, the needs of veterans readjusting from the military are similar to many people leaving prison and on parole in the United States. But it would take a full force of federal resources, bipartisan congressional commitment, an army of mental health practitioners, an arsenal of social programs, and, most important, a groundswell of volunteers and communities willing to give people another chance.

CONCLUSION: A MODEL FOR REPARATIVE JUSTICE

Melissa Fitzgerald, former director of Justice for Vets, warns that the military-civilian divide has never been greater. "Civilians have an obligation to support veterans through our actions and by supporting policies that provide real support. Thanking veterans for their service" is not nearly enough. "Those words need to be backed up by actions."[50] In 2013, this former actress from *The West Wing* uprooted her life and moved across the continent, from Los Angeles to Washington, DC, to become the next director of Justice for Vets. With a large public platform, Fitzgerald helps raise awareness, funding, and recognition for Veterans Treatment Courts from Capitol Hill to Hollywood and beyond. Under her leadership, the Veterans Treatment Courts grew from one hundred in 2013 to more than four hundred by the end of her tenure.

In the beginning, Fitzgerald worked late into the midnight hours at her office in Alexandria, Virginia. From time to time, the phone would ring, and a distraught parent, loved one, or spouse would be in desperate need of help. "Oftentimes, it was from family members of veterans that wouldn't qualify for the Veterans Treatment Court program." She told the story of one such veteran, who came home from war with PTSD and accidently shot and killed his wife's grandmother. "Those kinds of calls, although incredibly sad and depressing, were also very motivating." Despite the harder parts of the job, "it has been the greatest honor of my life," says Fitzgerald. Attending graduation ceremonies at Veterans Treatment Courts made all the difficulties worthwhile. That's how she happened to meet and eventually became close friends with Timothy Wynn, who was graduating from the Philadelphia Veterans Treatment Court.

Graduation day has become a special rite of passage in Veterans Treatment Courts across the United States. The entire community turns out in support of the graduates—the judge, coordinators, clerks, attorneys, police, probation officers, the Veterans Justice Outreach officer, veterans' service providers, advocates, guests, local news, and families. A procession of community members enters the chambers. The graduates march down the aisle single file and stand at attention. Their arms are braced at their sides. Their chins are held high, chests stuck out, shoulders rolled back. Their veteran mentors stand faithfully at their side. The courtroom fills with energy. It's a communal celebration. Triumphantly, the men and women line up, front and center, before the flags of their branch of service and salute.

The Baltimore Veterans Treatment Court has a special graduation tradition, honoring recovered veterans by embroidering their names and completion dates into long, ornamental ribbons that drape from the top of their respective service flags. The honorable Judge Halee F. Weinstein is one of the very few women veterans presiding over a Veterans Treatment Court. She is the proud daughter of Lt. Gen. Sidney T. Weinstein, a decorated Army intelligence officer. All her life she planned to follow in her father's footsteps and serve her nation. After ROTC, she commissioned into the US Army in the 1980s and completed officer training school. She was assigned to military intelligence at Fort Bragg. But then the Army threatened to kick her out with a "blue discharge," forcing her to resign because of her sexual orientation.[51] Being rendered "unfit to serve" must have been earth-shattering.[52] After all these years, she still avoids talking about it. But, like so many other veterans in this book, Weinstein transformed a deeply painful, and intimately personal, institutional betrayal into advocacy for justice. She attended law school and graduated from Maryland School of Law in Baltimore in 1989. In 2015, she started a docket for veterans in the Baltimore city court. At the time of my visit in 2019, more than sixty veterans had graduated—and none had recidivated. Weinstein's life mission is interlaced within a complex pattern of military injustice and service to others.

The judge shakes each of their hands and gives them a coin. The mentor coordinator tells a quick story about challenge coins, tracing the tradition back to the First World War. Each Veterans Treatment Court has its own uniquely designed coin. Taking creative liberty, Judge Halee Weinstein insisted on its quintessential Baltimore vibe. The smooth, polished clear coat makes it shine brightly. The coin is adorned in the black and gold colors of the Ravens and checkered like the state flag of Maryland. On the heads side, in the center stands the iconic Battle Monument, commemorating the battle of Baltimore when the Royal Navy bombarded Fort McHenry, as Francis Scott Key composed "The Star-Spangled Banner." On the flip side, the coin serves to remind its recipients of the core values of American veterans. Arranged in a circular pattern are the seals of each US military branch: Army, Marines, Navy, Air Force, and Coast Guard. Below, an inscription reads, "Leave No Veteran Behind."

Veterans Treatment Courts can help break the pattern of trauma and incarceration among families. On graduation day, the audience feels the revolutionary potential of Veterans Treatment Court. Jack O'Connor remarks, "I'll tell you when I really woke up to what the program was about." Two years into launching the veteran mentor program, he witnessed transformations in the Buffalo community. "A guy came in the court. He was homeless. He had three or four felonies going, an order of protection against him. Lost his job. Unemployed. Lost his car. He had a chip on his shoulder." In the beginning, "Nobody was with him—nobody, except the mentor." Jack says, "Fast forward a year and a half, and the mentor is still with him, but now his parents are in the audience, his neighbors are in the audience, his son and daughter. He's no longer homeless. He's working. The order of protection has been lifted," and "he can see the kids." In retrospect, O'Connor realizes that "we did two things—it took the court to do that, meaning Judge Russell, the VA, and the mentors—we didn't just save a veteran. We saved the family. That was a revelation."[53]

Forever wars demand an unequal sacrifice from American military families. "We've been a military at war, not a nation at war," reflects Judge Patrick Dugan. "The families [have] felt it, but I don't believe that the rest of the nation has felt it the way that we should feel it." Military families are fractured by the vicarious trauma of American wars, damaging the interconnected lives of partners, parents, and children of veterans. But the treatment courts enable families the chance to reconnect, heal, and grow together as members of a tight-knit community. Wars and mass incarceration generate the rippling effects of intergenerational trauma, but treatment begins the long process of repairing wounded families.

Greater than the sum of its parts, Veterans Treatment Court is more than just another specialty court for veterans; it's a precedent for wider justice reform. They reinvest federal funding and social welfare programs (which were diverted toward prisons during the Nixon administration) and funnel those resources back into local communities. Veterans Treatment Courts provide alternatives to incarceration and help convicted people reconnect with their families, contribute to society, and advocate for others. Graduates of Veterans Treatment Courts—like Manny Welch, Greg Nini, Don Adkins, Donna Sickels, William Delaney, Tim Wynn, and countless more—then become volunteer mentors and reinvest in the recovery of others, becoming "force multipliers for" greater change.[54] Thus, the Veterans Treatment Courts are a new grassroots, self-sustaining movement for reparative community justice.[55]

CONCLUSION

No Peace, No Justice

Readers should not get the false impression of a happy ending. The central subjects of this history—American wars and mass incarceration—destroyed countless lives around the globe and in the United States. *Prisoners after War* shows how many formerly incarcerated veterans organized, spoke out, sought treatment, or became advocates, but (to state the obvious) countless more people never had that opportunity. Thousands of Vietnam veterans spent much of their lives behind bars—like Henry D. Burton. Many of these personal histories may be forever lost, as opportunities to document them are fading fast, between the health effects of Agent Orange, old age, and the recent pandemic. Despite the silences in archival records, the lingering effects of this history are still visible in the most recent Department of Justice report on veterans in prison. Fifty years since the end of the war, Vietnam vets are *still* the single largest population of war veterans in prison, illustrating the profound and enduring impact of the war on crime on their generation.[1]

The punishment and disproportionate exclusion of Black veterans from disability benefits continued throughout the Global War on Terrorism. In 2017, Protect Our Defenders, with data obtained through a Freedom of Information Act request, reported on racial disparities in the military justice system.[2] Available data show that for every year, between 2006 to 2015, Black service members were substantially more likely to be punished in the military or face disciplinary actions. This was true across all branches. In the Army, Black soldiers were, on average, 61 percent more likely than whites to face general or court-martial. Black marines were 160 percent more likely to be given a guilty verdict during a court-martial hearing or nonjudicial punishment that could deny veterans' benefits.

In 2022, Conley Monk Jr., a Black Vietnam veteran, sued the VA over historic and continuing racial disparities in veterans' benefits.[3] The Veterans Legal Services Clinic at Yale Law School provides representation to Monk and other groups of marginalized veterans, including women, LGBTQ, and veterans without US citizenship.[4] As the director of the National Veterans Council for Legal Redress, Monk partnered with the Black Veterans Project, a nonprofit advocacy organization that raises educational awareness on the history of Black veterans in the United States through storytelling and data-driven research.[5] Together, they sued the VA for its history of racial discrimination, seeking redress and laying a legal foundation for Black veterans to seek reparations. Cofounder of the Black Veterans Project Richard Brookshire filed a Freedom of Information Act request to obtain data from the VA on racial disparities in disability compensation and then sued the VA until it fully complied.[6] The findings were damning—even if unsurprising. Since the war in Iraq, Black veterans were denied disability claims at much higher rates than whites each year, and the VA took longer to determine claims for service-connected disability.[7]

As the second half of this book argues, Veterans Treatment Courts provide federal, state, and local resources to people in the justice system, helping them recover and avoid recidivism, and setting a precedent for systemic reform. But reforms in both military mental health and criminal justice have serious and noteworthy limitations. Today, there are more than six hundred Veterans Treatment Courts across the country, according to a 2021 VA report.[8] But they're not equally accessible to all veterans. For starters, not every state has them yet, nor do most counties.[9] This inequity exacerbates the ongoing social, economic, and racial inequality among military veterans in the United States. Although Justice for Vets provides a standardized curriculum, Veterans Treatment Courts still vary considerably. This book shows why veterans' advocacy and mentorship are the key elements of their success, but, as of 2016, less than two-thirds of Veterans Treatment Courts actually had veteran mentor programs.[10]

Most incarcerated veterans do not qualify for treatment court. Nearly three-quarters of the courts consider admitting felonies on a case-by-case basis and exclude 95 percent of violent felonies.[11] This means the vast majority of veterans in the criminal justice system are disqualified from this type of restorative treatment.[12] More than 60 percent of veterans in prison committed violent felonies and would be ineligible for treatment court.[13] This fact points to more endemic social and behavioral problems among veterans and raises unanswered questions. Why do so many veterans commit violent felonies? Furthermore, treatment courts vary widely due to differences between state laws. In courts, judges also wield considerable discretion in cases, potentially widening racial and social inequality in criminal punishment and perpetuating injustices.

Justice reform can benefit certain groups at the expense of the most marginalized. Nowhere is this inequity clearer than in state drug policies. Obama-era reforms on mandatory sentencing for crack cocaine were overturned in 2021 by the US Supreme Court.[14] Although recreational marijuana is now legal in nearly a third of states today, a disproportionate number of Black men are in prison for petty drug crimes. Military service does not exempt African Americans from this reality, as recent history reminds us. In 2012, an African American Gulf War veteran named Derek Harris was sentenced to life in the Louisiana State Penitentiary at Angola (a former slave plantation) for only thirty dollars' worth of marijuana.[15] Harris spent ten years behind bars until the state supreme court overruled the life sentence. Southern states like Louisiana, Mississippi, and Alabama severely criminalize simple possession of controlled substances and prohibit even medical marijuana.

Veteran status does not make Black men immune to systemic racism. During the summer of 2020, the *Washington Post* broke the story of Sean Worsley, a Black Iraq War veteran who was arrested for possession of prescribed medical marijuana. Worsley had a documented history of traumatic brain injury and post-traumatic stress disorder. In 2016, he was traveling home to Arizona after visiting family in Mississippi. When he stopped for fuel, police searched his vehicle, claiming it smelled like marijuana. The arresting officers charged Worsley with a felony and alleged that the medical marijuana was "other than personal use" and accused him of drug trafficking.[16] Six days later, an Alabama judge released him on bail. Worsley hoped the worst was over, but little did he know, the Pickens County, Alabama, court would treat him like a fugitive. Within the year, the judge revoked his bond and ordered him to return to Alabama and reappear before court. Without legal representation, Worsley signed a plea bargain for sixty months of probation, drug treatment (although he had a prescription), and thousands of dollars in fines. After Worsley missed a later court date, the Alabama judge issued a fugitive arrest warrant, extradited him from Arizona, and sentenced him to five years in prison. Once in the system, this veteran got trapped in the vortex of mass incarceration, the total combined effects of decades—if not centuries—of racial, economic, and legal inequality.

In a sense, the story of Sean Worsley seems from another era in history, yet it represents historic and ongoing inequality under law in the United States. A quick digression into the deeper history of unfreedom in Pickens County puts the experiences of Sean Worsley into perspective. Land once occupied by the Muscogee Creek, this county was settled in 1820 and named after Andrew Pickens, a Revolutionary War general from South Carolina.[17] In the antebellum period, enslaved Black people labored on cotton plantations. At the end of the Civil War, in 1865, American forces burned the first Pickens County Courthouse to the ground; the second courthouse was burned again in 1876 at the end of Reconstruction. As the political and constitutional rights of freed people were overturned, racial violence resumed in full force against Black people living in the area and across the country. In this single county, there were fourteen documented lynchings between the end of Reconstruction and the First World War.[18] In 1893, six Black people were murdered by a lynch mob at the jail. During and after World War II, much of the Black population migrated to other parts of the country, fleeing racial terror, segregation, and poverty. Then, in 2014, the population grew faster than any other county in Alabama, only because of the Federal Correctional Institution at Aliceville, a federal women's prison. But this type of forever Jim Crow is not limited to Louisiana, Mississippi, or Alabama.

The national story of incarcerated veterans is not exclusively about mental health and drugs; it's part of an ongoing history of racial inequality, punishment, and state violence. In 2012, Sgt. James Brown, a Black soldier serving in the Army, was arrested in West Texas for driving under the influence. He had survived two combat tours in Iraq. But he was killed in a jail cell, while experiencing PTSD. Five guards, wearing full riot gear, pinned this man to the hard concrete floor. Like Eric Garner, James Brown's last words were "Help me! I can't breathe." For most Americans, his crime would have been punishable by a ticket, fine, probation, or not at all. Did the military service of James Brown matter? As Henry Burton reminds us, "In prison, you don't have *veterans*— only convicts and inmates."

EPILOGUE

During the summer of 2019, as a PhD candidate, I drove my car hundreds of miles from New England to Buffalo and New York City and down the East Coast to Philadelphia, Baltimore, and Washington, DC, completing the last stretch of interviews for the Incarcerated Veterans Oral History Project. I visited and interviewed leaders of the Veterans Treatment Courts and founders of Justice for Vets. At the end of that summer, I was convinced that Veterans

Treatment Courts held the answer to the triplet crises of mental health, drugs, and mass incarceration in the United States.

Over the following year, the world experienced a new pandemic. By the summer of 2020, I was writing my dissertation under quarantine, while also witnessing massive social unrest and police violence in those very same cities. As COVID-19 swept the globe, the United States erupted in conflict. We saw waves of protests, sparked by the murders of George Floyd and Breonna Taylor. For a fleeting moment, it felt like a new multiracial reckoning with police violence against Black people.

As activists toppled monuments to white supremacy across the country, the military also grappled with enduring racism within its ranks. For more than three years under the Trump administration, the Department of Defense refused to release its most recent survey on racism and discrimination in the military.[19] Only weeks into the new Biden administration, the Department of Defense reported that right-wing extremism and white supremacy posed a threat to national security.[20]

The pandemic exposed long-buried skeletons in American institutions: racial inequality and white supremacy. In June 2020, retired four-star general David Petraeus—a cultural icon among Iraq and Afghanistan war veterans—called for the Army to rename US military bases named after Confederates. "The irony of training at bases named for those who took up arms against the United States, and for the right to enslave others," writes Petraeus, "is inescapable." Finally, it seemed like most Americans were ready to grapple with white supremacy throughout the sectors of our society. Then came the reactionaries in full force, digging deeper into their outdated beliefs and entrenching themselves as a type of minority ruling class.[21] Calls for justice and accountability were met with state-sanctioned violence.

Police rioted in the streets of America. The New York City police intentionally drove their vehicles into civilian crowds; Philadelphia police entrapped and teargassed peaceful demonstrators against a highway overpass.[22] Buffalo police shoved Martin Gugino, a seventy-five-year-old peace activist, to the ground, causing a severe brain injury.[23] Video shows how one officer tried to help him back up, but the other officers quickly pulled him away, leaving the old man in a puddle of blood. When police were reprimanded, fifty-seven Buffalo police officers resigned their positions in protest.[24] These exact cities had the most progressive models of criminal justice in the nation.

In June 2020, the president of the New York Police Union, Mike O'Meara, admonished the public on national TV, crying out, "Stop treating us like animals, and thugs!"[25] Police union representatives repeated a litany of dog whistles and exaggerated claims, turning cops into the primary victims of racial unrest. O'Meara invoked the memory of Vietnam veterans, saying police were being disrespected and "embarrassed" simply for doing their jobs. "All legislators have abandoned us!" he cried. "The press is villainizing us." Police pulled the victim-hero card. "Nobody talks about the police that were killed in the last week," he claimed without giving specifics. O'Meara described the killing of George Floyd as an isolated incident. "Our legislators demonize police officers as if we're the problem." Police invoked the image of fighting with one hand tied behind the back. "We will not prosecute criminals who looted," he said, "but you know what's on the *hearts* and *minds* of everybody that has a shield on their hip pocket today?" He said, "The DA prosecuted a police officer whose boss sent him out there to do a job, was put in a bad situation during a chaotic time." The police could have easily been describing Lt. William Calley. "The brass threw them under a bus," he accused. "Everybody walked away from them." Tropes of Vietnam veterans as victims shield authorities from criticism and accountability. After all, this is nothing new—think of how athlete protesters are called un-American, unpatriotic, or unsupportive of the troops—but this type of censorship is alarming, as the military-civilian divide deepens and the lines between policing and the military blur.

Despite this abandonment rhetoric, Congress has expanded prison budgets and militarized police forces ever since the war on drugs. In fact, New York City and Philadelphia were on the top-ten list of cities with the largest police budgets in the nation.[26] The Department of Defense's 1033 Program provides billions of dollars' worth of military-grade equipment to law enforcement agencies.[27] In the wake of George Floyd's murder, armored vehicles patrolled streets across America, and police departments deployed military-grade equipment against protesters.[28] In July 2020, the Senate rejected a measure to limit militarized equipment in civilian police forces. This modest reform would have regulated the amount of surplus military equipment—leftovers from the war in Afghanistan—that law enforcement could acquire from the Pentagon.

The economies of "defense" and "justice" dominate the national budget. The United States spends about $115 billion each year on policing. Prisons cost taxpayers $80 billion annually.[29] It costs over $41,000 each year to incarcerate one person. The US constitutes 5 percent of the world's population but holds 25 percent of the world's prisoners. The total yearly cost of mass incarceration in the United States amounts to more than $180 billion.[30]

The Department of Justice is outmatched only by the Department of Defense. Multiplying over the past sixty years, from $47 billion in 1960 to more than $800 billion per year in 2023, the financial and social costs of maintaining the largest military in the world go unquestioned in national media and largely undebated in politics. Paying for the forever wars seems to be the last area of bipartisan consensus in Congress. In 2020, the United States spent more on "national defense" than the next ten countries combined.[31] The Biden administration's FY2022 budget increased 1.6 percent, totaling more than $715 billion on defense.[32]

The expansion of the American military-carceral state eventually threatens democracy. Events we witnessed during the 2020 presidential election should serve as a warning to all Americans. More than seventeen thousand National Guard troops deployed to Washington, DC, and twenty-three states, marching against American citizens after the murder of George Floyd.[33] Inflaming the situation, republican senator of Arkansas Tom Cotton urged then-president Trump to invoke the Insurrection Act and mobilize the 82nd Airborne against mostly Black protesters in Lafayette Square.[34] Walls went up around the White House. Army National Guard and police used military tactics to disperse peaceful protesters, including aggressively low-flying helicopters and teargas.[35] Yet the National Guard was not deployed as mobs overran police at the US Capitol building during the January 6 insurrection.[36] It felt like watching an overthrow of the government in slow motion and in plain view.[37]

On January 6, 2020, veterans on both sides of the criminal justice system clashed on the steps of the US Capitol, battling for the future of America with flag poles, teargas, and firearms.[38] One Air Force veteran named Ashli Babbitt, a radicalized MAGA (Make America Great Again) and QAnon follower, was shot and killed by police as she breached the Capitol. Once the mob overran the building, a lone police officer, an Iraq War veteran named Eugene Goodman, lured a violent white mob away from the Senate chambers, possibly saving the lives of members of the presidential line of succession, including the vice president.[39] Goodman had served in the US Army and deployed to Iraq with the 101st Airborne. On that historic day, near the brink of its destruction, a single Black veteran narrowly saved American democracy.[40]

NOTES

PREFACE AND NOTE ON METHODOLOGY

1. James E. Westheider, *The African American Experience in Vietnam: Brothers in Arms* (New York: Rowman & Littlefield, 2008), 120.

2. Mimi Cantwell, *Veterans in Prison* (Washington, DC: Bureau of Justice Statistics, 1981).

3. Jennifer Bronson, E. Ann Carson, Margaret Noonan, and Marcus Berzofsky, *Veterans in Prison and Jail, 2011–12*, Veterans in State and Federal Prisons (Washington, DC: Bureau of Justice Statistics, 2015), 4, https://www.bjs.gov/content/pub/pdf/vpj1112.pdf.

4. Christian G. Appy, *Working-Class War: American Combat Soldiers and Vietnam* (Chapel Hill: University of North Carolina Press, 1993), 6.

5. *Channeling* is a term employed by Lawrence M. Baskir and William A. Strauss, in their still important analysis of the draft, in *Chance and Circumstance: The Draft, the War, and the Vietnam Generation* (New York: Alfred A. Knopf, 1978). For more on military manpower policy, militarization, and the Selective Service system, see Amy J. Rutenberg, *Rough Draft: Cold War Military Manpower Policy and the Origins of Vietnam-era Draft Resistance* (Ithaca, NY: Cornell University Press, 2019). For more on socioeconomic and racial inequality in the military during the Vietnam War, see Appy, *Working-Class War*.

6. Laura M. Maruschak, Jennifer Bronson, and Mariel Alper, *Veterans in Prison: Survey of Prison Inmates, 2016*, Veterans in State and Federal Prisons (Washington, DC: Bureau of Justice Statistics, 2021), https://bjs.ojp.gov/content/pub/pdf/vpspi16st.pdf.

7. Cantwell, *Veterans in Prison*.

8. See Patrick Hagopian, *The Vietnam War in American Memory* (Amherst: University of Massachusetts Press, 2009).

9. The most recent report in this series is Maruschak, Bronson, and Alper, *Veterans in Prison*.

10. See also Mika'il De Veaux, "The Trauma of the Incarceration Experience," *Harvard Civil Rights-Civil Liberties Law Review* 48 (2013): 257–77.

11. For more on PTSD as a socially constructed category, see Jerry Lembcke, *PTSD: Diagnosis and Identity in Post-empire America* (Lanham, MD: Lexington, 2013), xi.

12. For more on the evolution of post-traumatic stress disorder, see Carol S. North et al., "The Evolution of PTSD Criteria across Editions of the *DSM*," *Annals of Clinical Psychiatry* 28, no. 3 (2016): 197–208.

13. My analysis of trauma is most informed by the following key texts: Cathy Caruth, *Unclaimed Experience: Trauma, Narrative, and History*, 20th anniversary ed. (1996; Baltimore: Johns Hopkins University Press, 2016); Cathy Caruth, ed., *Listening to Trauma: Conversations with Leaders in the Theory & Practice of Catastrophic Experience* (Baltimore: Johns Hopkins University Press, 2014); Shoshana Felman and Dori Laub, MD, *Testimony: Crisis of Witnessing in Literature, Psychoanalysis, and History* (New York: Routledge, 1992); Arthur Frank, *The Wounded Story-Teller: Body, Illness, and Ethics* (Chicago: University of Chicago Press, 1995); Judith Lewis Herman, *Trauma and Recovery: The Aftermath of Violence—from Domestic Abuse to Political Terror* (New York: Basic Books, 1992); Bessel van der Kolk, *The Body Keeps the Score: Brain, Mind,*

and Body in the Healing of Trauma (New York: Penguin, 2014); Robert J. Lifton, *Home from War* (New York: Simon and Schuster, 1973) and *Home from War: Learning from Vietnam Veterans* (New York: Simon and Schuster, 2015); Elaine Scarry, *The Body in Pain: The Making and Unmaking of the World* (New York: Oxford University Press, 1985); Christina Sharp, *In the Wake: On Blackness and Being* (Durham, NC: Duke University Press, 2016).

14   Lembcke, *PTSD*, xi.

15   Influential texts on moral injury include the following: Rita Nakashima Brock and Gabriella Lettini, *Soul Repair: Recovering from Moral Injury after War* (Boston: Beacon Press, 2013); Alice Lynd and Staughton Lynd, *Moral Injury and Nonviolent Resistance: Breaking the Cycle of Violence in the Military and behind Bars* (Oakland, CA: PM Press, 2017); Robert Meagher, *Killing from the Inside Out: Moral Injury and Just War* (Eugene, OR: Cascade, 2014); Robert Emmet Meagher and Douglas Pryor, eds., *War and Moral Injury* (Eugene, OR: Cascade, 2018); Jonathan Shay, *Achilles in Vietnam: Combat Trauma and the Undoing of Character* (New York: Scribner, 1994) and *Odysseus in America: Combat Trauma and the Trials of Homecoming* (New York: Scribner, 2002); Nancy Sherman, *Afterwar: Healing the Moral Wounds of Our Soldiers* (New York: Oxford University Press, 2015); and David Wood, *What Have We Done: The Moral Injury of Our Longest Wars* (New York: Little, Brown, 2016).

16   See Jonathan Shay, "Moral Injury," *Intertexts* 16, no. 1 (2012): 57, https://search.ebsco host.com/login.aspx?direct=true&db=edsglr&AN=edsglr.A321058561&site=eds -live&scope=site.

17   Brett T. Litz et al., "Moral Injury and Moral Repair in War Veterans: A Preliminary Model and Intervention Strategy," *Clinical Psychology Review* 29, no. 8 (2009): 695–706, https://doi.org/10.1016/j.cpr.2009.07.003.

18   Lynd and Lynd, *Moral Injury and Nonviolent Resistance*.

19   My analysis of disability is influenced by a rich historiography of disability studies and veterans studies, including some of the following key texts: Liat Ben-Moshe, Chris Chapman, and Allison C. Carey, eds., *Disability Incarcerated: Imprisonment and Disability in the United States and Canada* (New York: Palgrave Macmillan, 2014); Deborah Cohen, *The War Come Home: Disabled Veterans in Great Britain and Germany, 1914–1939* (Berkeley: University of California Press, 2001); Joanna Bourke, *Dismembering the Male: Men's Bodies, Britain, and the Great War* (Chicago: University of Chicago Press, 1996); Beth Linker, *War's Waste: Rehabilitation in World War I America* (Chicago: University of Chicago Press, 2011); Paul Longmore and Lauri Unmasky, eds., *The New Disability History: American Perspectives* (New York: New York University Press, 2001); Stephen R. Ortiz, ed., *Veteran Policies, Veteran Politics: New Perspectives in the Modern United States* (Gainesville: University Press of Florida, 2012); David R. B. Ross, *Preparing for Ulysses: Politics and Veterans during World War II* (New York: Columbia University Press, 1969); David Gerber, *Disabled Veterans in History* (Ann Arbor: University of Michigan Press, 2000); Aaron Glantz, *The War Comes Home: Washington's Battles against America's Veterans* (Berkeley: University of California Press, 2009); Ann Jones, *They Were Soldiers: How the Wounded Returned from America's Wars—the Untold Story* (Chicago: Haymarket Books, 2013); David Kieran and Edward A. Martini, eds., *At War: The Military and American Culture in the Twentieth Century and Beyond* (New Brunswick, NJ: Rutgers University Press, 2018); John M. Kinder, *Paying with Their Bodies: American War and the Problem of the Disabled Veteran* (Chicago: University of Chicago Press, 2015); John M. Kinder, "The Embodiment of War: Bodies for, in, and after War," in Kieran and Martini, *At War*; and Wilbur J. Scott, *Vietnam Veterans since*

the War: The Politics of PTSD, Agent Orange, and the National Memorial (Norman: University of Oklahoma Press, 2004).

20   Kinder, *Paying with Their Bodies*, 11.

21   All the narrators in this project have access to help if they require it, they assure me. Recalling and communicating trauma can potentially resurface and destabilize the survivor's recovery. See Caruth, *Trauma and Experience*.

22   See also Stephen M. Sloan and Mark Cave, eds., *Listening on the Edge: Oral History in the Aftermath of Crisis* (New York: Oxford University Press, 2014).

23   Laub, quoted in Caruth, *Listening to Trauma*, 48.

24   Caruth, *Trauma and Experience*, 10.

25   Cathy Caruth, ed., *Trauma: Explorations in Memory* (Baltimore: Johns Hopkins University Press, 1995).

26   Caruth, *Listening to Trauma*, 142.

27   For a deeper exploration of these questions, see Anna Sheftel and Stacey Zembrzycki, "Slowing Down to Listen in the Digital Age: How New Technology Is Changing Oral History Practice," *Oral History Review*, 44, no. 1 (2017): 106.

28   For more on shared authority, see Michael Frisch, *A Shared Authority: Essays on the Craft and Meaning of Oral and Public History* (Albany: State University of New York Press, 1990).

29   On ethical concerns of naming participants, see Mia Martin Hobbs, "(Un)Naming: Ethics, Agency, and Anonymity in Oral Histories with Veteran-Narrators," *Oral History Review* 48, no. 1 (2021), https://doi.org/10.1080/00940798.2021.1885982.

30   For a brief overview of memory and oral history, see Alistair Thomson, "Memory and Remembering in Oral History," in *The Oxford Handbook of Oral History*, ed. Donald A. Ritchie (New York: Oxford University Press, 2011), 77–95.

31   See Christopher R. Browning, "Remembering Survival: Inside a Nazi Slave-Labor Camp," in *The Oral History Reader*, ed. Robert Perks and Alistair Thomson, 3rd ed. (New York: Routledge, 2016), 311–19; and Mark Roseman, "'Surviving Memory': Truth and Inaccuracy in Holocaust Testimony," in Perks and Thomson, *The Oral History Reader*, 320–33; Herman, *Trauma and Recovery*; and Caruth, *Listening to Trauma*.

32   Alessandro Portelli, "What Makes Oral History Different?," in *The Oral History Reader*, 3rd ed., ed. Robert Perks and Alistair Thomson (New York: Routledge, 2016), 52.

33   See also Alistair Thomson, "*Anzac Memories* Revisited: Trauma, Memory, and Oral History," *Oral History Review* 42, no. 1 (2019): 1–29, https://doi.org/10.1093/ohr/ohv010.

INTRODUCTION: LOCATING INCARCERATED VETERANS IN AMERICAN HISTORY

1   The "wake" alludes to the work of Christina Sharpe on intergenerational racial trauma. See Christina Sharpe, *In the Wake: On Blackness and Being* (Durham, NC: Duke University Press, 2016). For an analysis of trauma transmitted from Vietnam War veterans to their children, see Christian D. Weber, *Social Memory and War Narratives: Transmitted Trauma among Children of War Veterans* (New York: Palgrave, 2015).

2   Unless otherwise noted, all quotations from Carlson come from the following interview. David Carlson, Incarcerated Veterans Oral History Project, telephone interview by the author, January 23, 2017, Amherst, MA.

3   A study conducted beginning in 1985 found that more than half of those who served under Project 100,000 came from the South and 46 percent were minorities. They had

an average reading level of sixth grade. Subcommittee on Oversight and Investigations of the House Veterans' Affairs Committee, *Readjustment of Project 100,000 Veterans: Hearing before the Subcommittee on Oversight and Investigations of the Committee on Veterans' Affairs*, 101st Cong., 1st sess., February 28, 1990 (Washington, DC: US Government Printing Office, 1990), 3.

4   Christian G. Appy, *Working-Class War: American Combat Soldiers and Vietnam* (Chapel Hill: University of North Carolina Press, 1993), 32.

5   For more on the effects of incarceration on children, see Christopher Wildeman et al., "Implications for Mass Imprisonment for Inequality among American Children," in *The Punitive Turn: New Approaches to Race and Incarceration*, ed. Deborah E. McDowell, Claudrena N. Harold, and Juan Battle (Charlottesville: University of Virginia Press, 2013), 178–91.

6   Other scholars have written about how foreign policies since the Vietnam War influenced the state's response to domestic issues, showing how counterinsurgency and police training abroad influenced the development of militarized policing in the United States. See Stuart Schrader, *Badges without Borders: How Global Counterinsurgency Transformed American Policing* (Berkeley: University of California Press, 2019). For more on the militarization of law enforcement, SWAT, and the LAPD from the urban rebellions in California in the 1960s through the 1990s, see Max Felker-Kantor, *Policing Los Angeles: Race, Resistance, and the Rise of the LAPD* (Chapel Hill: University of North Carolina Press, 2018). For more on how the United States has engaged in national building, police training, and security forces from the Cold War through the Global War on Terrorism, see Jeremy Kuzmarov, *Modernizing Repression: Police Training and Nation Building in the American Century* (Amherst: University of Massachusetts Press, 2012). Kristina Shull argues that the detention of immigrants reflects American war making, US foreign policy, and carceral punishment. Her work focuses on the 1980s when the Reagan administration enforced punitive immigration policies against Central American migrants. Kristina Shull, *Detention Empire: Reagan's War on Immigrants and the Seeds of Resistance* (Chapel Hill: University of North Carolina Press, 2022).

7   Historians of policing tend to focus on the local level; see Simon Balto, *Occupied Territory: Policing Black Chicago from Red Summer to Black Power* (Chapel Hill: University of North Carolina Press, 2019). Focusing on policing in Chicago from the end of the First World War to the Black Power movement of the 1960s and '70s, Balto argues that the shifting nature of policing at local levels in the decades before the rising rates of mass incarceration of the late twentieth-century forms the backdrop of the racialized war on drugs. Scholarship by Ruth Wilson Gilmore, Kelly Lytle Hernandez, and Max Felker-Kantor focuses on the city of Los Angeles. Ruth Wilson Gilmore, *Golden Gulag: Prisons, Surplus, Crisis, and Opposition in Globalizing California* (Berkeley: University of California Press, 2007); Kelly Lytle Hernandez, *City of Inmates: Conquest, Rebellion, and the Rise of Human Caging in Los Angeles, 1771–1965* (Chapel Hill: University of North Carolina Press, 2017); Felker-Kantor, *Policing Los Angeles*. More recently, Melanie D. Newport has written an incisive local history of jails, focusing on Chicago. Newport cogently argues, "All politics are local, and the politics of mass incarceration depend on local jails." Melanie D. Newport, *This Is My Jail: Local Politics and the Rise of Mass Incarceration* (Philadelphia: University of Pennsylvania Press, 2023), 1. For more on the role of the state, see Julilly Kohler-Hausmann, *Getting Tough: Welfare and Imprisonment in 1970s America* (Princeton, NJ: Princeton University Press, 2017); and Robert T. Chase, *We Are Not Slaves: State Violence, Coerced Labor, and Prisoners' Rights in Postwar America* (Chapel Hill: University of North Carolina Press, 2019).

For more on the role of the federal government and the rise of mass incarceration, see Elizabeth Hinton, *From the War on Poverty to the War on Crime: The Making of Mass Incarceration in America* (Cambridge, MA: Harvard University Press, 2016).

Very few scholars of mass incarceration have ventured into the twenty-first century as I attempt.

8   Mary L. Dudziak, *Cold War Civil Rights: Race and the Image of American Democracy* (Princeton, NJ: Princeton University Press, 2001); Kimberley L. Phillips, "'Did the Battlefield Kill Jim Crow?': The Cold War Military, Civil Rights, and Black Freedom Struggles," in *Fog of War: The Second World War and the Civil Rights Movement*, ed. Kevin Kruse and Stephen Tuck (New York: Oxford University Press, 2012), 209–18. See also Appy, *Working-Class War*; Lawrence Baskir and William Strauss, *Chance and Circumstance: The Draft, the War, and the Vietnam Generation* (New York: Alfred A. Knopf, 1978); Amy Rutenberg, *Rough Draft: Cold War Military Manpower Policy and the Origins of the Vietnam War-Era Draft Resistance* (Ithaca, NY: Cornell University Press, 2019); James E. Westheider, *Fighting on Two Fronts: African Americans and the Vietnam War* (New York: New York University Press, 1997); and James E. Westheider, *The African American Experience in Vietnam: Brothers in Arms* (New York: Rowman, 2008).

9   Phillips, "'Did the Battlefield Kill Jim Crow?'," 213.

10   Christopher S. Parker, *Black Veterans and the Struggle against White Supremacy in the Postwar South* (Princeton, NJ: Princeton University Press, 2009), 54.

11   Daniel S. Lucks, *Selma to Saigon: The Civil Rights Movement and the Vietnam War* (Lexington: University of Kentucky Press, 2014), 112

12   Richard Rothstein, *The Color of Law: A Forgotten History of How Our Government Segregated America* (New York: Liveright, 2017), xi–xiv. For more on the roots of redlining, see LaDale C. Winling and Todd M. Michney, "The Roots of Redlining: Academic, Governmental, and Professional Networks in the Making of the New Deal Lending Machine," *Journal of American History* 123, no. 4 (2021): https://doi.org/10.1093/jahist/jaab066.

13   Thomas J. Sugrue, *The Origins of the Urban Crisis: Race and Inequality in Postwar Detroit* (1996; Princeton, NJ: Princeton University Press, 2005), 5.

14   Keeanga-Yamahtta Taylor, *Race for Profit: How Banks and the Real Estate Industry Undermined Black Homeownership* (Chapel Hill: University of North Carolina Press, 2019), 31.

15   See Elizabeth Hinton, *America on Fire: The Untold History of Police Violence and Black Rebellion since the 1960s* (New York: Liveright, 2021), 2–3.

16   Sylvie Laurent, *King and the Other America: The Poor People's Campaign and the Quest for Economic Equality* (Oakland: University of California Press, 2018), 112.

17   See Michael W. Flamm, "The War on Crime," chap. 12 in *In the Heat of the Summer: The New York Riots and the War on Crime* (Philadelphia: University of Pennsylvania Press, 2016).

18   Steve Estes, *I Am a Man! Race, Manhood, and the Civil Rights Movement* (Chapel Hill: University of North Carolina Press, 2006), 108–23.

19   Appy, *Working-Class War*, 6.

20   "Sub-terranean poor" comes directly from Robert McNamara. John Worsencroft, "Salvaging Marginalized Men: How the Department of Defense Waged the War on Poverty," *Journal of Policy History* 33, no. 4 (2021): 374, https://doi.org/10.1017/S0898030621000178.

21   See also Beth Bailey, *America's Army: Making the All-Volunteer Force* (Cambridge, MA: Harvard University Press, 2009).

22   Appy, *Working-Class War*, 31. See also Kimberley L. Phillips, *War! What Is It Good For?*
      Black Freedom Struggles and the U.S. Military from World War II to Iraq (Chapel Hill:
      University of North Carolina Press, 2012), 205. Phillips argued that Project 100,000
      could be used to punish civil rights activists, dissidents, and rioters.

23   Subcommittee on Oversight and Investigations of the House Veterans' Affairs Com-
      mittee, *Readjustment of Project 100,000 Veterans*, 4.

24   Appy, *Working-Class War*, 32.

25   In 1968, African Americans made up 8 percent of military personnel in Vietnam; 16.3
      percent were assigned to combat roles. Westheider, *Fighting on Two Fronts*, 38–40.

26   Martin Luther King Jr., "Beyond Vietnam—a Time to Break Silence," speech deliv-
      ered at Riverside Church, New York, April 4, 1967, in the American Rhetoric Online
      Speech Bank, accessed November 1, 2019, http://www.americanrhetoric.com/speeches
      /mlkatimetobreaksilence.htm.

27   Westheider, *Fighting on Two Fronts*.

28   Ron Carver, David Cortright, and Barbara Doherty, eds., *Waging Peace in Vietnam*
      (New York: New Village Press, 2019), 107.

29   Robert D. Heinl, "Collapse in the Armed Forces," *Armed Forces Journal*, June 7, 1971. The
      full report is available at https://msuweb.montclair.edu/~furrg/Vietnam/heinl.html.

30   Beth Bailey's new book, *An Army Afire: How the US Army Confronted Its Racial Crisis
      in the Vietnam Era* (Chapel Hill: University of North Carolina Press, 2023) argues
      that the Army saw race as a problem that disrupted the function of the Army. Bailey
      explores how the Army addressed racial tensions, discrimination, and inequality, relying
      on tools of hierarchy and authority.

31   Westheider, *Fighting on Two Fronts*, 59.

32   Jessica Adler argues, "While the advent of a veterans' indicated a massive expansion
      of the reach of the state, it also illustrated the wider tendency of the government to
      award health entitlements selectively—to individuals based on their social standing
      and membership in a clearly definable group." I would add that less-than-honorable
      discharges function to both reinforce this social inequality and further limit the group
      entitled to benefits. Jessica L. Adler, *Burdens of Care: Creating the United States Veterans
      Health System* (Baltimore: Johns Hopkins University Press, 2017), 6.

33   Herman Graham III, *The Brothers' Vietnam War: Black Power, Manhood, and the
      Military Experience* (Gainesville: University Press of Florida, 2003).

34   Westheider, *Fighting on Two Fronts*, 63.

35   See also Jeremy Kuzmarov, *The Myth of the Addicted Army: Vietnam and the Modern
      War on Drugs* (Amherst: University of Massachusetts Press, 2009).

36   Richard M. Nixon, "Remarks about an Intensified Program for Drug Abuse Prevention and
      Control," Office of the Under Secretary of Defense for Personnel & Readiness, June 17, 1971,
      https://prhome.defense.gov/Portals/52/Documents/RFM/Readiness/DDRP/docs
      /41%20Nixon%20Remarks%20Intensified%20Program%20for%20Drug%20Abuse
      .pdf.

37   See Kathleen Frydl, *The Drug Wars in America, 1940–1973* (New York: Cambridge
      University Press, 2013).

38   Donna Murch, "Crack in Los Angeles: Crisis, Militarization, and Black Response to
      the Late Twentieth-Century War on Drugs," *Journal of American History* 102, no. 1
      (2015): 164.

39   See also Susan Stuart, "All Roads Lead from Vietnam to Your Home Town: How Vet-
      erans Have Become Casualties of the War on Drugs," *Albany Government Law Review*
      6, no. 2 (2013): 490.

40   Elizabeth Hinton, *From the War on Poverty to the War on Crime: The Making of Mass Incarceration in America* (Cambridge, MA: Harvard University Press, 2016), 4, 3, 138.

41   See Peter K. Enns, *Incarceration Nation: How the United States Became the Most Punitive Democracy in the World* (New York: Cambridge University Press, 2016).

42   See Kohler-Hausmann, *Getting Tough*, 2.

43   Anne E. Parsons, *From Asylum to Prison: Deinstitutionalization and the Rise of Mass Incarceration after 1945* (Chapel Hill: University of North Carolina Press, 2018), 3–5.

44   Seth J. Prins, "Does Transinstitutionalization Explain the Overrepresentation of People with Serious Mental Illnesses in the Criminal Justice System?," *Community Mental Health Journal* 47 (2011): 719.

45   Mimi Cantwell, *Veterans in Prison* (Washington, DC: Bureau of Justice Statistics, 1981).

46   Ari Merretazon, Incarcerated Veterans Oral History Project, interviewed remotely from Wyncote Pennsylvania by the author, January 12, 2023, Blacksburg, VA. Formerly known as Haywood "the Kid" Kirkland, Merretazon's oral history is included in Wallace Terry, *Bloods: Black Veterans of the Vietnam War: An Oral History* (1984; New York: Presido Press, 2006), 106. A relatively underexplored topic at the intersection of military and carceral history, incarcerated soldiers and veterans in the Vietnam War era engaged in hunger strikes, sit-ins, and protests of prison conditions, brutal mistreatment of incarcerated people, negligible deaths under guards, and racial injustices. For example, the Presidio 27, a group of incarcerated antiwar GIs at Presidio stockade in San Francisco organized a protest after a guard shot Richard Bunch in the back and killed him on October 11, 1968. Bunch had been experiencing psychological problems and was denied his medication. See Carver, Cortright, and Doherty, *Waging Peace in Vietnam*, 112. For more on prison organizing, see Dan Berger, *Captive Nation: Black Prison Organizing in the Civil Rights Era* (Chapel Hill: University of North Carolina Press, 2014).

47   *Oversight on Issues Relating to Incarcerated Veterans: Hearing before the Committee on Veterans' Affairs*, 96th Cong., 1st sess., July 11, 1979 (Washington, DC: Government Printing Office, 1979), 178–81.

48   Cantwell, *Veterans in Prison*.

49   See also Edwin Martini, *Agent Orange: History, Science, and the Politics of Uncertainty* (Amherst: University of Massachusetts Press, 2012); Wilbur Scott, *The Politics of Readjustment: Vietnam Veterans since the War* (New York: Aldine De Gruyer, 1993); and John A. Wood, *Veteran Narratives and the Collective Memory of the Vietnam War* (Athens: Ohio University Press, 2016).

50   For more scholarship on national memory of the Vietnam War, see Patrick Hagopian, *The Vietnam War in American Memory* (Amherst: University of Massachusetts Press, 2009); H. Bruce Franklin, *M.I.A. or Mythmaking in America* (Brooklyn: Lawrence Hill Books, 1992); David Kieran, *Forever Vietnam: How a Divisive War Changed American Public Memory* (Amherst: University of Massachusetts Press, 2014); Jerry Lembcke, *The Spitting Image: Myth, Memory, and the Legacy of Vietnam* (New York: New York University Press, 1998); and Ed Martini, *Invisible Enemies: The American War on Vietnam, 1975–2000* (Amherst: University of Massachusetts Press, 2007). For more on veterans organizing and politics, see Scott, *Politics of Readjustment*; and Stephen R. Ortiz, ed., *Veterans' Policies, Veterans Politics: New Perspectives in the Modern United States* (Gainesville: University Press of Florida, 2012).

51   Christopher J. Mumola, *Veterans in Prison or Jail* (Washington, DC: Bureau of Justice Statistics, 2000), 1, https://bjs.ojp.gov/content/pub/pdf/vpj.pdf.

52   Hagopian, *Vietnam War in American Memory*, 11.

53   *Drug Abuse in the Military: Hearing before the Subcommittee on Children, Family, Drugs,*

and Alcoholism of the Committee on Labor and Human Resources, United States Senate, 99th Cong., 1st sess., June 27, 1985 (Washington, DC: US Government Printing Office, 1985), 2.

54   See David Farber, *Crack: Rock Cocaine, Street Capitalism, and the Decade of Greed* (New York: Cambridge University Press: 2019); and Alfred McCoy, *In the Shadows of the American Century: The Rise and Decline of U.S. Global Power* (Quezon City: Ateneo de Manila University Press, 2017), 86. See also Bruce Western, *Punishment and Inequality in America* (New York: Russell Sage, 2006).

55   Economic Recovery Act of 1981, H.R. 4242, 97th Congress (1981–82), https://www .congress.gov/bill/97th-congress/house-bill/4242/text.

56   Kohler-Hausmann, *Getting Tough*, 164.

57   Anti-Drug Abuse Act of 1986, H.R. 5484, 99th Cong. (1985–86), https://www.congress .gov/bill/99th-congress/house-bill/5484/text.

58   Murch, "Crack in Los Angeles," 165–67.

59   Felker-Kantor, *Policing Los Angeles*, 191.

60   Alexia Cooper and Erica L. Smith, *Homicide Trends in the United States, 1980–2008* (Washington, DC: Bureau of Justice Statistics, 2011), https://bjs.ojp.gov/content/pub /pdf/htus8008.pdf.

61   Allen J. Beck and Paige M. Harrison, *Prisoners in 2000,* (Washington, DC: Bureau of Justice Statistics, 2001), 11, https://bjs.ojp.gov/content/pub/pdf/p00.pdf.

62   Michelle Alexander, *The New Jim Crow: Mass Incarceration in the Age of Color Blindness* (New York: The New Press, 2010), 6.

63   This includes 1,518,104 people in prison, 748,723 in jail, and 4,887,900 on probation and parole. Lauren E. Glaze, *Correctional Populations in the United States, 2010* (Washington, DC: Bureau of Justice Statistics, 2011), 3, https://bjs.ojp.gov/content/pub/pdf/cpus10 .pdf.

64   E. Ann Carson, *Prisoners in 2021: Statistical Tables* (Washington, DC: Bureau of Justice Statistics, 2022), https://bjs.ojp.gov/sites/g/files/xyckuh236/files/media/documen /p21st.pdf; Zhen Zeng, *Jail Inmates in 2021—Statistical Tables* (Washington, DC: Bureau of Justice Statistics, 2022), https://bjs.ojp.gov/sites/g/files/xyckuh236/files /media/document/ji21st.pdf; Danielle Kaeble, *Probation and Parole in the United States, 2020* (Washington, DC: Bureau of Justice Statistics, 2021), https://bjs.ojp.gov /content/pub/pdf/ppus20.pdf. See Reuben Jonathan Miller, *Halfway Home: Race, Punishment, and the Afterlife of Mass Incarceration* (New York: Bay Back Books, 2021). Beyond the millions in prisons, jails, and paroles and under supervision, urinalysis, and surveillance, and the social and economic consequences of criminal records. There is a "hidden social world and alternate legal reality." Incarceration affects the families and descendants of those entrapped within the system (8).

65   Heather Ann Thompson. "Why Mass Incarceration Matters: Rethinking Crisis, Decline, and Transformation in Postwar American History," *Journal of American History* 97, no. 3 (2010): 703.

66   Heidi Carlson, telephone interview with the author, August 19, 2022.

67   To meet its recruitment goals, the Army lowered its entrance requirements by enlist-ing those without high school diplomas and with lower scores on aptitude tests and criminal records. Documents obtained by NPR showed that waivers for serious misde-meanors from 3,002 in 2005 to 8,259 in 2007, including charges of burglary, narcotics, assault, larceny, and breaking and entering. Steve Inskeep and Tom Bowman, "Army Doc-uments Show Lower Recruiting Standards," NPR, special series, "The Impact of War," April 17, 2008, https://www.npr.org/templates/story/story.php?storyId=89702118.

See also Eric Schmitt, "Its Recruitment Goals Pressing, the Army Will Ease Some Standards," *New York Times*, October 1, 2004, https://www.nytimes.com/2004/10/01/politics/its -recruitment-goals-pressing-the-army-will-ease-some-standards.html.

68   Jim Tankersley, "Biden Awards Medals of Honor for Bravery in Iraq and Afghanistan," *New York Times*, December 16, 2021, https://www.nytimes.com/2021/12/16/us/politics /medals-of-honor-biden.html.

69   White House, "President Joseph R. Biden Jr. to Award Medal of Honor," Statements and Releases, December 10, 2021, https://www.whitehouse.gov/briefing-room/statements -releases/2021/12/10/president-joseph-r-biden-jr-to-award-medal-of-honor/. Melvin Morris, a Black Vietnam veteran who was denied the Medal of Honor at the time due to racial discrimination, was awarded the medal by president Barack Obama in 2014. See Oklahoma Oral History Research Program, "Oral History with Melvin Morris Sr.," interview by the author, August 5, 2014, Oklahoma State University, https://cdm17279 .contentdm.oclc.org/digital/collection/Spot/id/919/rec/1.

CHAPTER 1: "LESS THAN" VETERANS

1   Henry D. Burton, Incarcerated Veterans Oral History Project, interview by the author, July 25, 2018, Amherst, MA.

2   This is a story that Henry Burton requested a follow-up interview in order to tell. It's a memory that is still difficult to process and talk about today.

3   See the following works: Mark Baker, *Nam: The Vietnam War in the Words of the Men and Women Who Fought There* (New York: Morrow, 1981); Harry Maurer, *Strange Ground: Americans in Vietnam, 1945–1975, An Oral History* (New York: Henry Holt, 1989); Al Santoli, *Everything We Had: An Oral History of the Vietnam War by Thirty-Three American Soldiers Who Fought It* (New York: Random, 1981); and Al Santoli, *To Bear Any Burden: The Vietnam War and Its Aftermath in the Words of Americans and Southeast Asians* (Bloomington: Indiana University Press, 1999).

4   "Appendix C: Character of Discharge," March 24, 1978, in *Oversight on Issues Relating to Incarcerated Veterans: Hearing before the Committee on Veterans' Affairs*, 96th Cong., 1st sess., July 11, 1979 (Washington, DC: Government Printing Office, 1979), 85.

       See also Major Bryant A. Boohar, "Combat Stress Claims: Veterans' Benefits and Post-Separation Character of Service Upgrades for 'Bad Paper' Veterans After the Fairness for Veterans Act," *Military Law Review* 227, no. 2 (2019): 95–118. This article provides legal information for commanders to understand the punitive consequences of "bad paper" discharges and lists the various types forms of "misconduct" that can disqualify a former service member of "veterans status" and VA benefits, including health care and education.

5   *Oversight on Issues Relating to Incarcerated Veterans*, 85.

6   Lieutenant Colonel Donald W. Hansen, "Discharge for the Good of the Service: Historical, Administrative, and Judicial Potpourri," *Military Law Review* 74 (1976): 100.

7   Boohar, "Combat Stress Claims," 108.

8   Secretary of Defense, "Memorandum from Secretary of Defense to Secretaries of the Military Departments, Subject: Supplemental Guidance to Military Boards for Correction of Military/Naval Records Considering Discharge Upgrade Requests by Veterans Claiming Post Traumatic Stress Disorder," September 3, 2014. Also known as the "Hagel Memo."

9   Scholars of the "Carceral State" are still debating and constructing a widely acceptable definition of the term. Scholars owe much to Michael Foucault's *Discipline and Punish* (1975). I will not venture to offer my own original definition here, but Dan Berger has written on the evolving usage of the term by sociologists, historians, and other interdisciplinary scholars who have studied institutions of punishment and confinement, prison systems, police forces, immigration, and asylums. To my knowledge, no scholar has directly connected the carceral state to the military, the military justice system, and the VA, in a way that I am seeking in this project. See Dan Berger, "Finding and Defining the Carceral State," *Reviews in American History* 47, no. 2 (2019): 279–85, https://doi.org/10.1353/rah.2019.0040.

10 Jonathan Simon, "The 'Hard Back' of Mass Incarceration: Fear, Structural Racism, and the Overpunishment of Violent Crime," in *The Punitive Turn: New Approaches to Race and Incarceration*, ed. Deborah E. McDowell, Claudrena N. Harold, and Juan Battle (Charlottesville: University of Virginia Press, 2013), 192–209.

11 Mimi Cantwell, *Veterans in Prison* (Washington, DC: Bureau of Justice Statistics, 1981).

12 Keeanga-Yamahtta Taylor, *Race for Profit: How Banks and the Real Estate Industry Undermined Black Homeownership* (Chapel Hill: University of North Carolina Press, 2019), 35.

13 Kathleen Frydl, *The GI Bill* (New York: Cambridge University Press, 2009), 223.

14 Richard Rothstein, *The Color of Law: A Forgotten History of How Our Government Segregated America* (New York: Liveright Publishing, 2017), xi–xiv.

15 Donna Jean Murch, *Living for the City: Migration, Education, and the Rise of the Black Panther Party in Oakland, California* (Chapel Hill: University of North Carolina Press, 2010), 16. See also Elizabeth Hinton, *America on Fire: The Untold History of Police Violence and Black Rebellion since the 1960s* (New York: Liveright, 2021).

16 John Clegg and Adaner Usmani, "The Economic Origins of Mass Incarceration," *Catalyst* 3, no. 3 (Fall 2019): 11–22. Focusing on the rise of violent crime in the 1960s, Clegg and Usmani argue that class disparity had a significant impact on the rise of mass incarceration. By 1960, 25 percent of African American men between ages eighteen and fifty were unemployed and not in school (23). Between 1960 and 1980, homicide rates doubled. By 1970, African Americans constituted the majority of both victims and perpetrators of violent crime.

17 Christian G. Appy, *Working-Class War: American Combat Soldiers and Vietnam* (Chapel Hill: University of North Carolina Press, 1993), 31.

18 Khalil Gibran Muhammad, *Condemnation of Blackness: Race, Crime, and the Making of Modern Urban America* (Cambridge, MA: Harvard University Press, 2010), 4.

19 Gilbran Muhammad, *Condemnation of Blackness*, 4.

20 Appy, *Working-Class War*, 32–33.

21 For further reading see Appy, *Working-Class War*; Steve Estes, *I Am A Man! Race, Manhood, and the Civil Rights Movement* (Chapel Hill: University of North Carolina Press, 2005); Daniel S. Lucks, *Selma to Saigon: The Civil Rights Movement and the Vietnam War* (Lexington: University of Kentucky Press, 2014); Kimberly L. Phillips, *War! What Is It Good For? Black Freedom Struggles and the U.S. Military from World War II to Iraq* (Chapel Hill: University of North Carolina Press, 2012); James E. Westheider, *Fighting on Two Fronts: African Americans and the Vietnam War* (New York: New York University Press, 1997).

22 Westheider, *Fighting on Two Fronts*, 39.

23 Phillips, *War! What Is It Good For?*, 188–89.

24 Lucks, *Selma to Saigon*, 112–13.

25   Martin Luther King Jr., "Beyond Vietnam—A Time to Break Silence," speech delivered
      at Riverside Church, New York City, April 4, 1967, in the American Rhetoric Online
      Speech Bank, accessed November 1, 2019, http://www.americanrhetoric.com/speeches
      /mlkatimetobreaksilence.htm.

26   Sylvie Laurent, *King and the Other America: The Poor People's Campaign and the Quest
      for Economic Equality* (Oakland: University of California Press, 2018), 132–35.

27   Herman Graham III, *The Brothers' Vietnam War: Black Power, Manhood, and the
      Military Experience* (Gainesville: University Press of Florida, 2003), 91.

28   In 1970, only 2.1 percent of all officers were African Americans, although more than
      10 percent of enlisted men were Black. Graham, *The Brothers' Vietnam War*, 93.

29   Graham, *The Brothers' Vietnam War*, 95.

30   Clarence Fitch, "That Year in Vietnam Was Like Twenty Years," in *Waging Peace in
      Vietnam*, ed. Ron Carver, David Cortright, and Barbara Doherty (New York: New
      Village Press: 2019), 106.

31   Westheider, *Fighting on Two Fronts*, 56–7.

32   Greg Payton, "There Was a Lot of Rage; It Just Began to Build and Build," in Carver,
      Cortright, and Doherty, *Waging Peace in Vietnam*, 103, 105.

33   Payton, "There Was a Lot of Rage," 105.

34   Appy, *Working-Class War*, 246.

35   Carver, Cortright, and Doherty, *Waging Peace in Vietnam*, 120–21.

36   Beth Bailey, *America's Army, Making the All-Volunteer Force* (Cambridge, MA: Harvard
      University Press, 2009), 32–33.

37   Bailey, *America's Army*, 95.

38   Westheider, *Fighting on Two Fronts*, 58.

39   Subcommittee on Oversight and Investigations of the House Veterans' Affairs Com-
      mittee, *Readjustment of Project 100,000 Veterans: Hearing before the Subcommittee on
      Oversight and Investigations of the Committee on Veterans' Affairs*, 101st Cong., 1st sess.,
      February 28, 1990 (Washington, DC: US Government Printing Office, 1990), 12.

40   Westheider, *Fighting on Two Fronts*, 59.

41   Quoted in Westheider, *Fighting on Two Fronts*, 60.

42   Subcommittee on Oversight and Investigations of the House Veterans' Affairs Com-
      mittee, *Readjustment of Project 100,000 Veterans*, 12.

43   Subcommittee on Oversight and Investigations of the House Veterans' Affairs Com-
      mittee, *Readjustment of Project 100,000 Veterans*, 15.

44   John Keegan, *The Face of Battle* (New York: Barnes and Noble, 1993), 270.

45   Wilbur J. Scott, *The Politics of Readjustment: Vietnam Veterans since the War* (New York:
      Aldine De Gruyter, 1993), 9. See also Kyle Longley, *Grunts: The American Combat
      Soldier in Vietnam* (Armonk, NY: M. E. Sharpe, 2008). Longley observes that casualty
      rates between Korea and Vietnam were decreased by nearly half. In Korea, 22 percent
      of all wounded soldiers died; in Vietnam, only 13 percent died (166).

46   *Veterans' Unemployment Problems: Hearing before the Subcommittee on Readjustment,
      Education, and Employment of the Committee on Veterans' Affairs, United States Senate*,
      94th Cong., 1st sess., Session on S. 760 and Related Bills, October 22, 1975 (Washington,
      DC: Government Printing Office, 1976), 880.

47   *Veterans' Unemployment Problems*, 879.

48   Westheider, *Fighting on Two Fronts*, 63.

49   Louis Charles McNair Collection (AFC/2001/001/92683), Veterans History Project,
      American Folklife Center, Library of Congress. All quotations from McNair are from
      this collection.

50   Rita Nakashima Brock and Gabriella Lettini, *Soul Repair: Recovering from Moral Injury after War* (Boston: Beacon, 2012). Although each symptom of war trauma often contributes to other psychological consequences of war, they are exclusive, but often difficult to distinguish. Brock and Lettini note, "Recently Veteran's Affairs clinicians have begun to conceptualize moral injury as separate from PTSD and as a hidden wound of war" (xv).

51   Jonathan Shay, *Achilles in Vietnam: Combat Trauma and the Undoing of Character* (New York: Scribner, 1994), 9.

52   Brock and Lettini, *Soul Repair*, xiv.

53   Chaim F. Shatan," The Grief of Soldiers: Vietnam Veterans' Self-Help Movement," *American Journal of Orthopsychiatry* 43, no. 4 (1973): 651.

54   Brock and Lettini, *Soul Repair*, xiv–xv.

55   Brock and Lettini, *Soul Repair*, xii.

56   Jonathan Shay, *Odysseus in America: Combat Trauma and the Trials of Homecoming* (New York: Scribner, 2002), 76.

57   The same year that *Bloods* was published, historian Myra MacPherson pointed out a lack of data on incarcerated veterans, identifying a number of scattered surveys, but the total number of incarcerated veterans varies because veteran status depends on self-identifying. Myra MacPherson, *Long Time Passing: Vietnam and the Haunted Generation* (New York: Doubleday, 1984), 583.

58   See also Kim Masters, "Dead Presidents' Precedent," *Washington Post*, October 15, 1995, https://www.washingtonpost.com/archive/lifestyle/style/1995/10/15/dead-presidents -precedent/aab9754e-310e-4e3c-a762-2969c0eca92e/.

59   Wallace Terry, *Bloods: An Oral History of the Vietnam War by Black Veterans* (New York: Random, 1984), 93–94.

60   Ari Sesu Merretazon, Incarcerated Veterans Oral History Project, interview by the author, January 12, 2023, remote interview in Blacksburg, VA, and Wyncotte, PA.

61   Terry, *Bloods*, 105.

62   Ari Sesu Merretazon, Incarcerated Veterans Oral History Project, interview by the author, January 10, 2023, remote interview in Blacksburg, VA, and Wyncotte, PA.

63   Wallace, *Bloods*, 104.

64   Merretazon interview, January 10, 2023.

65   Merretazon interview, January 12, 2023.

66   *Oversight on Issues Relating to Incarcerated Veterans*, 150.

67   *Veterans' Unemployment Problems*, 879.

68   Wallace, *Bloods*, 109.

69   Merretazon interview, January 12, 2023.

70   See also Kim Masters, "The Heist Is Only Half of the Story, Says the Man Who Pulled It Off," *Washington Post*, October 15, 1995, https://www.washingtonpost.com /archive/lifestyle/style/1995/10/15/dead-presidents-precedent/aab9754e-310e-4e3c -a762-2969c0eca92e/.

71   Phil McCombs, "Prison Less Crowded, Still Human Warehouse," *Washington Post*, November 28, 1981, https://www.washingtonpost.com/archive/politics/1981/11/28/prison -less-crowded-still-human-warehouse/7796b28a-7e4b-44c3-a36b-c43a66f2aee3/.

72   Merretazon interview, January 10, 2023.

73   Wallace, *Bloods*, 110.

74   *Oversight on Issues Relating to Incarcerated Veterans*, 12.

75   Merretazon interview, January 10, 2023. See also Wallace, *Bloods*, 110.

76   Merretazon interview, January 12, 2023.

77   Paul W. Valentine, "War Veterans at Lorton Organize," *Washington Post*, March 14, 1975, http://login.ezproxy.lib.vt.edu/login?url=https://www.proquest.com/historical -newspapers/war-veterans-at-lorton-organize/docview/146343388/se-2.

78   Cantwell, *Veterans in Prison*.

79   See also the Honorable Ronald V. Dellums, "U.S. Representative of California Inter-view," recorded June 19, 2012, History, Art & Archives, U.S. House of Representatives, https://history.house.gov/Oral-History/People/Ronald-V-Dellums/.

80   Merretazon interview, January 12, 2023.

81   Merretazon interview, January 12, 2023.

82   *Oversight on Issues Relating to Incarcerated Veterans*, 179.

83   *Oversight on Issues Relating to Incarcerated Veterans*, 5.

84   *Oversight on Issues Relating to Incarcerated Veterans*, 2.

85   Ronald F. Lauve, "Prepared statement as Associate Director, Human Resources Division," in *Oversight on Issues Relating to Incarcerated Veterans*, 17.

86   Wallace, *Bloods*, 106.

87   *Oversight on Issues Relating to Incarcerated Veterans*, 150.

88   *Oversight on Issues Relating to Incarcerated Veterans*, 1.

89   *Oversight on Issues Relating to Incarcerated Veterans*, 180.

90   "Veterans in Prison Not Told Their Rights, GAO Report Says," *New York Times*, January 27, 1975, http://www.nytimes.com/1975/01/27/archives/veterans-in-prison-not-told-of -rights-gao-report-says.html.

91   Cantwell, *Veterans in Prison*; Christopher J. Mumola, *Veterans in Prison or Jail* (Wash-ington, DC: Bureau of Justice Statistics, 2000), 1, https://bjs.ojp.gov/content/pub/pdf /vpj.pdf; Margaret E. Noonan and Christopher J. Mumola, *Veterans in State and Federal Prison, 2004* (Washington, DC: Bureau of Justice Statistics, 2007), 6, https://bjs.ojp .gov/content/pub/pdf/vsfp04.pdf; Jennifer Bronson, E. Ann Carson, Margaret Noonan, and Marcus Berzofsky, *Veterans in Prison and Jail, 2011–12*, Veterans in State and Federal Prisons (Washington, DC: Bureau of Justice Statistics, 2015).

92   Department of Veterans' Benefits, "Veterans Benefits: Inside . . . Out," included in the appendix of *Oversight on Issues Relating to Incarcerated Veterans*, 141–47.

93   "Veterans in Prison Not Told Their Rights, GAO Report Says."

94   Some policies, however, worsened the situations of incarcerated veterans altogether. As Bruce Pentland and Gene Rotham note, President Carter signed a law in 1980, which "suspended the subsistence portion of educational benefits awarded to eligible incarcerated veterans" (10). After the law, enrollment rates declined among Vietnam veterans. Many believe that myths and stereotypes involving Vietnam veterans led to the cuts in educational funding, i.e., incarcerated veterans were taking advantage of the financial incentives of the program. Advocates of the law suggested veterans were more concerned with "'dollar-ship' than scholarship" (10). Pentland and Bruce demonstrate that the funding cuts and educational benefits further "stigmatized and discriminated" against Vietnam era veterans, who experienced the collective rejection of their nonveteran peers after the war. Bruce Pentland and Gene Rotham, "The Incar-cerated Vietnam-Service Veteran: Stereotypes and Realities," *Journal of Correctional Education* 33 (March 1981): 10–14.

95   *Oversight on Issues Relating to Incarcerated Veterans*, 126.

96   Wesley G. Pippert, "Reagan Cuts Social Programs," UPI Archives, March 10, 1981, https:// www.upi.com/Archives/1981/03/10/Reagan-cuts-social-programs/6509353048400/.

97   Christopher J. Mumola, *Veterans in Prison or Jail* (Washington, DC: Bureau of Justice Statistics, 2000), https://bjs.ojp.gov/content/pub/pdf/vpj.pdf.

98   Merretazon interview, January 12, 2023.

99   Ari Sesu Merretazon, Incarcerated Veterans Oral History Project, interview by the
      author, January 18, 2023, remote interview in Blacksburg, VA, and Wyncotte, PA.

100   *JET* 66, no. 8 (April 30, 1984): 30.

101   Cantwell, *Veterans in Prison.*

102   Cantwell, *Veterans in Prison*; Mumola, *Veterans in Prison or Jail,* 1.

103   Noonan and Mumola, *Veterans in State and Federal Prison, 2004,* 6

104   Richard A. Kulka et al., *Contractual Report of Findings from the National Vietnam
      Veterans Readjustment Study,* vol. 1 (Research Triangle Park, NC: Research Triangle
      Institute, 1988), 2. Some critics of the NVVRS have argued that the study over-estimated
      the number of Vietnam veterans with PTSD because many had not served in combat
      operations. I did not intend to refute or prove the accuracy of the study, but it's worth
      pointing out that PTSD is not exclusively caused by combat trauma. It can result from
      repeated or extreme exposure to the details of the traumatic event, for example han-
      dling human remains, and it can result from learning about violent traumatic events
      that happened to a close personal friend or family member. It does not always require
      directly experiencing or witnessing combat.

105   Over 34 percent had been to jail multiple times and 11.5 percent were convicted of a
      felony. Kulka et al., *Contractual Report of Findings from the National Vietnam Veterans
      Readjustment Study,* 13–14.

106   American Psychiatric Association, *Diagnostic and Statistical Manual of Mental Dis-
      orders,* 3rd ed. (Washington, DC: American Psychiatric Association, 1980). See also
      Matthew J. Friedman, "PTSD History and Overview," PTSD: National Center for
      PTSD, U.S. Department of Affairs, last updated October 6, 2022, http://www.ptsd
      .va.gov/professional/PTSD-overview/ptsd-overview.asp.

107   "USA: The Execution of Mentally Ill Offenders," Amnesty International, January 31,
      2006, 156, https://www.amnesty.org/en/documents/AMR51/003/2006/en/.

108   Aaron Glantz, *The War Comes Home: Washington's Battle against America's Veterans*
      (Berkeley: University of California Press, 2009), 143–44.

109   Aaron Glantz, "Remembering Manny Babbit," *Truthdig,* July 18, 2007, https://www
      .truthdig.com/articles/remembering-manny-babbitt/.

110   "USA: The Execution of Mentally Ill Offenders," 154–56.

111   "USA: The Execution of Mentally Ill Offenders," 154–56.

112   "Florida Murderer Becomes First Vietnam Veteran to Be Executed," *Los Angeles Times,*
      April 23, 1986, https://www.latimes.com/archives/la-xpm-1986-04-23-mn-1002-story
      .html.

113   Philip Caputo, "The Unrelenting Army," *Playboy,* January 1982.

114   "USA: The Execution of Mentally Ill Offenders," 171.

115   Clint Smith, *How the Word Is Passed: A Reckoning with the History of Slavery across
      America* (New York: Little, Brown, 2021), 111.

116   For more documents detailing the life and death of Wayne Felde, see Murderpedia.org,
      https://murderpedia.org/male.F/f1/felde-wayne-robert.htm.

117   E. A. Brett, R. L. Spitzer, and J. B. Williams, "DSM-III-R Criteria for Posttraumatic
      Stress Disorder," *American Journal of Psychiatry* 145, no. 10 (1988): 1232–36, https://
      doi.org/10.1176/ajp.145.10.1232.

118   Equal Justice Initiative, "Herbert Richardson," https://eji.org/cases/herbert-richardson/.

119   Equal Justice Initiative, "Herbert Richardson."

120   Joan Thompson, "Pipe Bomb Killer Dies Without Seeing the Execution Chamber," *AP
      News,* August 19, 1989, https://apnews.com/article/71230e1ceac42fb054e41822fb30820b.

121   "Alabama Man, 43, Is Executed for Killing Girl with Pipebomb," *New York Times*, August 19, 1989, https://www.nytimes.com/1989/08/19/us/alabama-man-43-is-executed-for-killing-girl-with-pipe-bomb.html.

122   Christian G. Appy, *American Reckoning: The Vietnam War and Our National Identity* (New York: Penguin, 2015), 244–45.

123   "Incarcerated Veterans in the Criminal Justice System," *VVA Veteran*, September 1984, 8.

124   Cantwell, *Veterans in Prison*.

125   See also Steve Estes, *I Am a Man! Race, Manhood, and the Civil Rights Movement* (Chapel Hill: University of North Carolina Press, 2006).

CHAPTER 2: WAR, DRUGS, AND THE WAR ON DRUGS

1   Haywood Fennell, Incarcerated Veterans Project, interviewed by the author, in Boston, MA, on July 7, 2017.

2   David Vine argues that military bases around the globe have destabilized the economies of nations and created a string of sex industries. In Okinawa the drug and sex trade fueled violence. During the Korean War era, the US military helped develop red-light districts in Okinawa to "'protect' Okinawan women because so many were being raped." The Okinawan Women Act Against Military Violence has reported over 350 rapes and sexual assaults against women in Okinawa from 1945–2011. David Vine, "Chapter 9: Sex For Sale," in *Base Nation: How U.S. Military Bases Abroad Harm American and the World* (New York: Metropolitan, 2015), 184.

3   For a deeper history of racial inequality in the military and the history of lynching of Black veterans, the myth of the Black rapists, the impunity of white male rapists, see the following works: Adrian Lentz-Smith, *Freedom Struggles: African Americans and World War I* (Cambridge, MA: Harvard University Press, 2009); Chad L. Williams, *Torchbearers of Democracy: African American Soldiers in the World War I Era* (Chapel Hill: University of North Carolina Press, 2010); and Crystal Nicole Fiemster, *Southern Horrors: Women and the Politics of Rape and Lynching* (Cambridge, MA: Harvard University Press, 2009).

4   See Elizabeth Hillman, *Defending America: Military Culture and the Cold War Court-Martial* (Princeton, NJ: Princeton University Press, 2005). See also Susan Brownmiller, *Against Our Will: Men, Women, and Rape* (New York: Simon and Schuster, 1975).

5   David Wood writes about institutional betrayal as a "violation of trust" and "a most basic violation of our sense of right and wrong and can carve a jagged moral wound deep in the soul" (174–76). Wood, *What Have We Done: The Moral Injury of Our Longest Wars* (New York: Little, Brown, 2016). For Black veterans, moral injury may be a useful concept to explore in a carceral context. Sociologist Noah De Lissovoy, who conceptualized the carceral turn and the "logic of violation," argues that "the principle of violation aims at once to plunder and to injure, to produce and to lay low; it is a characteristic of a form of capitalism linked at its birth to slavery, and experimenting in the present with new forms of racial caste and racialized repression." Noah De Lissovoy, "Conceptualizing the Carceral Turn: Neoliberalism, Racism, and Violation," *Critical Sociology* 39 no. 5 (2012): 744. Thus, the consequences of trauma on a lifetime are multiplied by poverty, race, and caste.

6   Eric C. Schneider, *Smack: Heroin and the American City*, Politics and Culture in Modern America (Philadelphia: University of Pennsylvania Press, 2008), 1.

7   Alfred W. McCoy, *The Politics of Heroin in Southeast Asia*, with Cathleen B. Read and Leonard P. Adams III (New York: Harper, 1973), 1.

8   Noah De Lissovoy, "Conceptualizing the Carceral Turn," 740.

9   Eric C. Schneider notes that in 1971 the VA only five hospitals that offered treatment to heroin uses. He argues that as Vietnam veterans returned with substance-use issues, the Nixon administration approved methadone treatment to veterans (*Smack*, 164).

10   See Haywood Fennell Sr., *Coota and the Magic Quilt* (Boston: Tri-Ad Veterans League, 2004).

11   Stanford University, "Beyond Vietnam," The Martin Luther King, Jr. Research and Education Institute, https://kinginstitute.stanford.edu/encyclopedia/beyond-vietnam.

12   Stanford University, "Beyond Vietnam."

13   Incarceration has a significant impact on not only on individuals incarcerated individual and their families (an extreme number of whom are disproportionately African American men, including lower income, higher unemployment, risk of substance use, and mental health issues. Charles E. Lewis Jr., "Economic and Relational Penalties of Incarceration," in *The Punitive Turn: New Approaches to Race and Incarceration*, ed. Deborah E. McDowell et al. (Charlottesville: University of Virginia Press, 2013). As Heather Ann Thompson notes, "the nation's turn to new levels of racialized mass incarceration after the 1960s devastated the black community. From orphaning more than a generation of black children to . . . eroding public health in neighborhoods of color, to disproportionately disenfranchising these same communities of color, the mass incarceration crisis of today is cataclysmic in its reach." "From Researching the Past to Reimagining the Future: Locating the Carceral Crisis and the Key to Its End," in *The Punitive Turn*, 59. See also Bruce Western, "Chapter 6: Incarceration, Marriage, and Family Life," in *Punishment and Inequality in America* (New York: Russell Sage, 2006), 131–67.

14   Margaret E. Noonan and Christopher J. Mumola, *Veterans in State and Federal Prison, 2004* (Washington, DC: Bureau of Justice Statistics, 2007), 6, https://bjs.ojp.gov/content/pub/pdf/vsfp04.pdf.

15   Steve Estes, *I Am a Man! Race, Manhood, and the Civil Rights Movement* (Chapel Hill: University of North Carolina Press, 2006), 123. See also Daniel S. Lucks, *Selma to Saigon: The Civil Rights Movement and the Vietnam War* (Lexington: University of Kentucky Press, 2014), 96.

16   Elizabeth Hinton, *From the War on Poverty to the War on Crime: The Making of Mass Incarceration in America* (Cambridge, MA: Harvard University Press, 2016).

17   Hinton, *From the War on Poverty to the War on Crime*, 3.

18   Dan Baum, "Legalize It All," *Harper's Magazine*, April 2016, https://harpers.org/archive/2016/04/legalize-it-all/.

19   Heather Ann Thompson, *Blood in the Water: The Attica Prison Uprising and Its Legacy* (New York: Pantheon, 2016), 10–14.

20   Thompson, *Blood in the Water*, 29.

21   For more on the influence of George Jackson's writings and his death, see Dan Berger, *Captive Nation: Black Prison Organizing in the Civil Rights Era* (Chapel Hill: University of North Carolina Press, 2014), 109–38.

22   Berger, *Captive Nation*, 148.

23   Thompson, *Blood in the Water*, 33.

24   Thompson, *Blood in the Water*, 57.

25   Thompson, *Blood in the Water*, 81–82.

26   Garrett Felber, *Those Who Don't Know Don't Say: The Nation of Islam, the Black Freedom

Movement, and the Carceral State (Chapel Hill: University of North Carolina Press, 2020), 155.

27   Sam Roberts, "Rockefeller on the Attica Raid, From Boastful to Subdued," *New York Times*, September 12, 2011, https://www.nytimes.com/2011/09/13/nyregion/rockefeller-initially-boasted-to-nixon-about-attica-raid.html.

28   Quoted in Thompson, *Blood in the Water*, 199.

29   See also Daniel S. Chard, *Nixon's War at Home: The FBI, Leftist Guerillas, and the Origins of Counterterrorism* (Chapel Hill: University of North Carolina Press, 2021).

30   "Hundreds of GI Prisoners Riot in Viet Stockade; One Killed," *Chicago Tribune*, August 31, 1968.

31   Gerald F. Goodwin, *Race in the Crucible of War: African American Servicemen and the War in Vietnam* (Amherst: University of Massachusetts Press, 2023), 90.

32   Goodwin, *Race in the Crucible of War*, 91–93.

33   African American newspapers reported the incident at Long Binh Jail and raised attention to the conditions that led to violence while white media often depicted the prisoners as violent criminals and militants. For examples of these differences in reporting, see "Study Sees More Bloodshed from GI Racial Troubles," *Afro-American*, January 30, 1971, 3; and George C. Wilson, "Vietnam Race Trouble Seen by Pentagon Aide," *Los Angeles Times*, November 20, 1968, A3.

34   Goodwin, *Race in the Crucible of War*, 100.

35   Goodwin, *Race in the Crucible of War*, 108–9.

36   Goodwin, *Race in the Crucible of War*, 115.

37   Chard, *Nixon's War at Home*, 7.

38   "Doubt on Vietnam Eported [*sic*] in Poll: Gallup Finds Public Lack of Confidence in President," *New York Times*, March 7, 1971, https://www.nytimes.com/1971/03/07/archives/doubt-on-vietnam-reported-in-poll-gallup-finds-public-lack-of.html.

39   George C. Herring, ed., "McNaughton Hints at Compromise," *The Pentagon Papers*, abridged edition, (New York: McGraw-Hill, 1993), 138–39.

40   "Winter Soldier Investigation: Testimony Given in Detroit, Michigan, on January 31, 1971, February 1 and 2, 1971," The Sixties Project, Vietnam Veterans Against the War, Inc., updated January 28,1999, http://www2.iath.virginia.edu/sixties/HTML_docs/Resources/Primary/Winter_Soldier/WS_entry.html.

41   VVAW, "Vets' History: Operation Dewey Canyon III," *Veteran* 7, no. 2 (1977), http://www.vvaw.org/veteran/article/?id=1656.

42   "Transcript: John Kerry Testifies before Senate Panel, 1971," NPR, April 25, 2006, https://www.npr.org/templates/story/story.php?storyId=3875422.

43   David Cortright, "Dissent and Resistance within the Military during the Vietnam War," in *Waging Peace in Vietnam*, ed. Ron Carver, David Cortright, and Barbara Doherty (New York: New Village Press, 2019), 4.

44   Christian Appy argues that Nixon was "obsessed" with leakers like Ellsberg. Christian G. Appy, "How Richard Nixon's Obsession with Daniel Ellsberg and the Pentagon Papers Sowed the Seeds for the President's Downfall," *Conversation*, April 23, 2021, https://theconversation.com/how-richard-nixons-obsession-with-daniel-ellsberg-and-the-pentagon-papers-sowed-the-seeds-for-the-presidents-downfall-159113. While the Pentagon Papers did not reveal any damning information on Nixon (as the study ended in 1967), Nixon nevertheless viewed the publication of classified information as an active attempt to delegitimize his presidency and, in his mind, overthrow his administration. See Jordan Moran, "Nixon and the Pentagon Papers: Why President Nixon was deeply concerned—perhaps even obsessed with leaks related to the

Johnson administration Policies," UVA Miller Center, https://millercenter.org/the
-presidency/educational-resources/first-domino-nixon-and-the-pentagon-papers.

45   For more on Nixon's responses to the events in the spring and summer of 1971 from the
     VVAW protests, Daniel Ellsberg and the Pentagon Papers, the May Day protests, and
     the administration's targeting of media and political opponents, see Jeffrey Kimball,
     Nixon's Vietnam War (Lawrence: University of Kansas Press, 1998), 249–58.

46   See also Thomas M. Grace, *Kent State: Death and Dissent in the Long Sixties*
     (Amherst: University of Massachusetts Press, 2016). A wounded survivor of the
     massacre, Grace argues that the massacre was a culmination of state repression
     and an increasingly radicalized youth. Richard Nixon stated this in a speech after
     the Kent State shootings and the killings of African American students at Jackson
     State, Mississippi in May of 1970. Scott Laderman, "How Richard Nixon Captured
     White Rage—and Laid the Groundwork for Donald Trump," *Washington Post*,
     November 3, 2019, https://www.washingtonpost.com/outlook/2019/11/03/how
     -richard-nixon-captured-white-rage-laid-groundwork-donald-trump/.

47   Christian G. Appy, *Working-Class War: American Combat Soldiers and Vietnam* (Chapel
     Hill: University of North Carolina Press, 1993), 246.

48   Appy, *Working-Class War*, 284.

49   Eric C. Schneider, *Smack: Heroin and the American City*, Politics and Culture in Modern
     America (Philadelphia: University of Pennsylvania Press, 2008), 161.

50   Robert D. Heinl, "Collapse in the Armed Forces," *Armed Forces Journal* (June 7, 1971):
     98.

51   Appy, *Working-Class War*, 247.

52   Jeremy Kuzmarov, *The Myth of the Addicted Army: Vietnam and the Modern War on
     Drugs* (Amherst: University of Massachusetts Press, 2009), 38.

53   Susan Stuart, "All Roads Lead from Vietnam to Your Home Town: How Veterans
     Have Become Casualties of the War on Drugs," *Albany Government Law Review* 6,
     no. 2 (2013): 490.

54   Department of Defense, *Drug Abuse Control Program Activities in Vietnam*, August 11,
     1972, 2, https://www.gao.gov/assets/b-164031%282%29-094040.pdf.

55   Department of Defense, *Drug Abuse Control Program Activities in Vietnam*.

56   Wayne Hall and Megan Weier, "Lee Robins' Studies of Heroin Use among US Vietnam
     Veterans," *Addiction* 112, no. 1 (January 2017): 176–80.

57   The focus on drug use was heroin, but marijuana and alcohol were also subjects of
     concern in the military. Administrative discharges were an extralegal process that
     could kick service members out of the military while avoiding legal action. *Drug Abuse
     in the Military: Hearing before the Subcommittee on Drug Abuse in the Military of the
     Committee on Armed Services, United States Senate*, 92nd Cong., 2nd sess. (Washington,
     DC: Government Printing Office, 1972), 6.

58   Hailed as a preventive and progressive measure by Nixon's defenders and recommended
     by Dr. Jerome Jaffe, head of the White House Drug Office, Operation Golden Stream
     produced a system to punish and discharge soldiers who tested positive for drugs. For
     more of a defense of the policy, see Chris Barber who describes Nixon "as not inter-
     ested in ideological battles" and says Nixon is "blamed, rather unfairly, for steering the
     national drug policy to the law enforcement" in his article "Public Enemy Number
     One: A Pragmatic Approach to America's Drug Problem," Richard Nixon Foundation,
     June 29, 2016, https://www.nixonfoundation.org/2016/06/26404/. However, the plan
     required soldiers who tested positive to stay in Vietnam and detox before returning
     to the United States, without being court-martialed. But the very soldiers booted out

of the Army with an other-than-honorable discharge were barred from VA care and rehabilitation services. In 1971, at the congressional hearing on drug abuse in the military, it was reported that of sixteen thousand soldiers administratively discharged for drug use, eleven thousand were discharged without access to benefits or VA treatment. *Drug Abuse in the Military*, 69.

59   *Drug Abuse in the Military*, 7.

60   See Schneider, "The War and the War at Home," in *Smack*, 160.

61   Kathleen J. Frydl, *The Drug Wars in America, 1940–1973* (New York: Cambridge University Press, 2013), 404.

62   Beth Bailey, *An Army Afire: How the US Army Confronted Its Racial Crisis in the Vietnam Era* (Chapel Hill: University of North Carolina Press, 2023), 210.

63   Beth Bailey, *America's Army, Making the All-Volunteer Force* (Cambridge, MA: Harvard University Press, 2009), 37, 89.

64   Bailey, *An Army Afire*, 213.

65   Hillman, *Defending America*, 97, 92.

66   James E. Westheider, *Fighting on Two Fronts: African Americans and the Vietnam War* (New York: New York University Press, 1997), 56–57.

67   Frydl, *The Drug Wars in America*, 414.

68   "Discharge Problem," *Baltimore Afro-American*, September 29, 1973.

69   Robert Rosenheck et al., "Homeless Mentally Ill Veterans: Race, Service Use, and Treatment Outcomes," *American Journal of Orthopsychiatry* 67, no. 4 (October 1997): 634. See also Families against Mandatory Minimums, an organization dedicated to raising social awareness of the growing numbers of imprisoned people in the United States, recently reached out to incarcerated veterans on Veterans Day 2015. FAMM compiled letters, photographs, and emails from men and women serving time in prison. FAMM created a virtual Wall including their experiences and memories. Here are a few: B. David, U.S. Army, 1966–1970, Vietnam War, Purple Heart Recipient, "Serving 30 years for drug conspiracy charge. I am working on my seventeenth year on these charges"; and M. Benton, U.S. Navy, 1968: "Serving life in prison for drug offense. The Vietnam wall in Washington DC. shows me how lucky I was." https://famm.org/.

70   Lee Slemmons Ewing Collection (AFC/2001/001/00400), Veterans History Project, American Folklife Center, Library of Congress, Washington, DC, http://memory.loc.gov/diglib/vhp/story/loc.natlib.afc2001001.00400/transcript?ID=sr0001.

71   Schneider, *Smack*, 160.

72   Lee Slemmons Ewing Collection.

73   Lewis B. Puller Jr., *Fortunate Son: The Healing of the Vietnam Vet* (New York: Grove Press, 1991), 166.

74   Lee Slemmons Ewing Collection; unless otherwise noted, quotations from Ewing come from this source.

75   Barbara Carlson, "New Anti-Drug Ideas Needed," *Hartford Courant*, July 7, 1971.

76   Jerry Taylor, "The Veterans behind Bars—A Vietnam Legacy," *Boston Globe*, July 18, 1976.

77   Leonard Colon Jr., "Jails Hold Veterans," *Hartford Courant*, June 25, 1979.

78   Mimi Cantwell, *Veterans in Prison* (Washington, DC: Bureau of Justice Statistics, 1981), 2.

79   M. J. Boivin, "Forgotten Warriors: An Evaluation of the Emotional Well-Being of Presently Incarcerated Vietnam Veterans," *Genetic, Social, and General Psychology Monographs* 113 (February 1987): 109–24, 112.

80   Christopher J. Mumola, *Veterans in Prison or Jail* (Washington, DC: Bureau of Justice Statistics, 2000), 1, https://bjs.ojp.gov/content/pub/pdf/vpj.pdf.

81   Mumola, *Veterans in Prison or Jail*, 1.

82   Andrew J. Saxon, MD, et al. "Trauma, Symptoms of Posttraumatic Stress Disorder, and Associated Problems Among Incarcerated Veterans," *Psychiatric Services* 52, no. 7 (July 1, 2001): 959.

83   Rumi Kato Price et al., "Post-traumatic Stress Disorder, Drug Dependence, and Suicidality among Male Vietnam Veterans with a History of Heavy Drug Use," *Drug and Alcohol Dependence* 76, no. Supplement (January 1, 2004): S31–S43, https://doi.org/10.1016/j.drugalcdep.2004.08.005.

84   Cantwell, *Veterans in Prison*, 2.

85   Kendell L. Coker and Robert Rosenheck, "Race and Incarceration in an Aging Cohort of Vietnam Veterans in Treatment for Post-traumatic Stress Disorder (PTSD)," *Psychiatric Quarterly* 85 (September 2014): 79, 86.

86   Benjamin Fleury-Steiner et al., "From the Battlefield to the War on Drugs: Lessons from the Lives of Marginalized African American Military Veterans," *Albany Government Law Review* 6, no. 2 (2013): 467.

87   Benjamin Fleury-Steiner, *Disposable Heroes: The Betrayal of African American Veterans* (New York: Rowman, 2012), 115.

88   Fleury-Steiner et al., "From the Battlefield to the War on Drugs," 475.

89   Warren Weaver Jr., "Nixon's Justice," *New York Times*, March 18, 1973, https://www.nytimes.com/1973/03/18/archives/strong-medicine-indeed-nixons-justice.html.

90   "Statistics," Federal Bureau of Prison, http://www.bop.gov/about/statistics/population_statistics.jsp.

91   *Report to the Congress: Mandatory Minimum Penalties in the Federal Criminal Justice System*, October 2011, 123, http://www.ussc.gov/sites/default/files/pdf/news/congressional-testimony-and-reports/mandatory-minimum-penalties/20111031-rtc-pdf/Chapter_07.pdf.

92   Bruce Western, *Punishment and Inequality in America* (New York: Russel Sage, 2006), 3; Michelle Alexander, *The New Jim Crow: Mass Incarceration in the Age of Color Blindness* (New York: The New Press, 2010), 6.

93   Heather Ann Thompson, "Why Mass Incarceration Matters: Rethinking Crisis, Decline, and Transformation in Postwar American History," *Journal of American History* 97, no. 3 (2010): 703.

94   Mumola, *Veterans in Prison or Jail*, (2000), 3.

95   Jennifer Bronson, E. Ann Carson, Margaret Noonan, and Marcus Berzofsky, *Veterans in Prison and Jail, 2011–12*, Veterans in State and Federal Prisons (Washington, DC: Bureau of Justice Statistics, 2015), 2, https://www.bjs.gov/content/pub/pdf/vpj1112.pdf.

CHAPTER 3: ANOTHER WAR, ANOTHER DRUG

1   Ronald Reagan, "V-Day Ceremony at the Vietnam Veterans Memorial," delivered in Washington, DC, 11 November 11, 1988, in the American Rhetoric Online Speech Bank, https://www.americanrhetoric.com/speeches/ronaldreaganvietnammemorial.html.

2   Reagan, "V-Day Ceremony at the Vietnam Veterans Memorial."

3   His interpretation is more popular today than factual. The Pentagon Papers documented the explicit reasons for escalating the war and its initial prospects for victory. The 1965 McNaughton memo stated that 70 percent of US goals were to avoid humiliating

defeat and preserve America's reputation. Only 10 percent of efforts were to promote freedom in South Vietnam. George C. Herring, ed., "McNaughton's 1965 Proposals," *The Pentagon Papers*, abridged edition, (New York: McGraw-Hill, 1993), 115. According to Secretary of Defense McNamara's 1965 assessment of the war, the United States expected one thousand American soldiers killed per month and that, within two years, the US forces would be mired in a prolonged stalemate. "McNamara's November 1965 Assessment of the War," in Herring, ed., *The Pentagon Papers*, 135–36. Despite these dire predictions, the US government escalated and sustained the war, sending 58,000 Americans to their deaths.

4   Patrick Hagopian, *The Vietnam War in American Memory* (Amherst: University of Massachusetts Press, 2009), 11.

5   A table of Gallup and Roper Organization Polls is provided in Hagopian, *The Vietnam War in American Memory*, 13.

6   Hagopian, *The Vietnam War in American Memory*, 17.

7   Jeremy Kuzmarov, *The Myth of the Addicted Army: Vietnam and the Modern War on Drugs* (Amherst: University of Massachusetts Press, 2009), 167, 176.

8   Alfred McCoy, *In the Shadows of the American Century: The Rise and Decline of U.S. Global Power* (Quezon City: Ateneo de Manila University Press, 2017), 86.

9   A list of declassified documents can be accessed at "The Contras, Cocaine, and Covert Operations," National Security Electronic Briefing Book No. 2, The National Security Archive, The George Washington University, accessed June 12, 2022, https://nsarchive2.gwu .edu/NSAEBB/NSAEBB2/index.html.

10 McCoy, *In the Shadows of the American Century*, 86.

11 Doris Marie Provine, *Unequal under Law: Race in the War on Drugs* (Chicago: University of Chicago Press, 2007), 103.

12 Kuzmarov, *The Myth of the Addicted Army*, 186.

13 Margaret E. Noonan and Christopher J. Mumola, *Veterans in State and Federal Prison, 2004* (Washington, DC: Bureau of Justice Statistics, 2007), 1, https://bjs.ojp.gov/ content/pub/pdf/vsfp04.pdf.

14 Small had recently graduated from the Baltimore Veterans Treatment Court, where he received treatment for mental health. He has a medical history with psychosis, which could possibly affect his memories.

15 Beth Bailey, *America's Army: Making the All-Volunteer Force* (Cambridge, MA: Harvard University Press, 2009), 193–97.

16 Hagopian, *The Vietnam War in American Memory*, 40.

17 Benjamin Fleury-Steiner et al., "From the Battlefield to the War on Drugs: Lessons from the Lives of Marginalized African American Military Veterans," *Albany Government Law Review* 6, no. 2 (2013): 482.

18 Bailey, *America's Army*, 88, 123. Between 1978 and 1980, the number of soldiers in Army prisons jumped 47 percent.

19 Bailey, *America's Army*, 174.

20 Drew Desilver, "Black Unemployment Rate Is Consistently Twice That of Whites," Pew Research Center, August 21, 2013, https://www.pewresearch.org/fact-tank/2013/08/21 /through-good-times-and-bad-black-unemployment-is-consistently-double-that-of-whites/.

21 "The Discharge Problem," *Baltimore Afro-American*, September 29, 1973.

22 Rumi Kato Price et. al, "Post-Traumatic Stress Disorder, Drug Dependence, and Suicidality among Male Vietnam Veterans with a History of Heavy Drug Use," *Drug and Alcohol Dependence* 76, no. supp. (January 1, 2004): S31–S43, https://doi.org/10.1016 /j.drugalcdep.2004.08.005.

23 Syrus Ware, Joan Ruzsa, and Giselle Dias, "It Can't Be Fixed Because It's Not Broken: Racism and Disability in the Prison Industrial Complex, in *Disability Incarcerated*, ed. Liat Ben-Moshe, Chris Chapman, and Allison C. Carey (New York: Palgrave-MacMillan, 2014), 164.

24 Ware, Ruzsa, and Dias, "It Can't Be Fixed Because It's Not Broken," 174.

25 *Drug Abuse in the Military: Hearing before the Subcommittee on Children, Family, Drugs, and Alcoholism of the Committee on Labor and Human Resources, United States Senate*, 99th Cong., 1st sess., June 27, 1985 (Washington, DC: US Government Printing Office, 1985), 6.

26 David Farber, *Crack: Rock Cocaine, Street Capitalism, and the Decade of Greed* (New York: Cambridge University Press, 2019), 129, 133.

27 "Anti-Drug Legislation Introduced," *PR Newswire*, April 25, 1989.

28 Kuzmarov, *The Myth of the Addicted Army*, 175.

29 Christian G. Appy, *American Reckoning: The Vietnam War and Our National Identity* (New York: Penguin, 2015), 255.

30 *Drug Abuse in the Military*, 1.

31 *Drug Abuse in the Military*, 19.

32 *Drug Abuse in the Military*, 2.

33 Ronald Reagan, "Address to the Nation on the Campaign against Drug Abuse," September 14, 1986, in the Ronald Reagan Presidential Library & Museum, https://www.reagan library.gov/archives/speech/address-nation-campaign-against-drug-abuse.

34 Quoted in Brenda Rodriguez, "HIV, Aids, and Rape in Texas Prisons," in *States of Confinement: Policing, Detention, and Prisons*, ed. Joy James (New York: St. Martin's, 2000), 170.

35 Provine, *Unequal under Law*, 1–2, 3.

36 Equal Justice Initiative, "Criminal Justice Reform," https://eji.org/criminal-justice -reform/.

37 Terry Ann Craigie et al., "Conviction, Imprisonment, and Lost Earnings: How Involvement with the Criminal Justice System Deepens Inequality," Brennan Center for Justice, September 15, 2020, https://www.brennancenter.org/our-work/research-reports/conviction -imprisonment-and-lost-earnings-how-involvement-criminal.

38 Peter K. Enns, *Incarceration Nation: How the United States Became the Most Punitive Democracy in the World* (New York: Cambridge University Press, 2016), 6.

39 Manning Marable, "Black Radicalism and the Economy of Incarceration," in James, *States of Confinement*, 57.

40 Enns, *Incarceration Nation*, 5.

CHAPTER 4: LEAVE NO VET BEHIND

1 For more on drug-treatment courts from the perspectives of participants, see Susan H. Witkin and Scott P. Hays, "Drug Court through the Eyes of Participants," *Criminal Justice Policy Review* 30, no. 7 (2019): 971–89, https://doi.org/10.1177/0887403417773180; and Alana Rosenberg et al., "Drug Treatment Accessed through the Criminal Justice System: Participants' Perspectives and Uses, *Journal of Urban Health* 96 (2019): 390–99, https://doi.org/10.1007/s11524-018-0308-9.

2 Judge Robert Russell, Incarcerated Veterans Project, interview by the author, July 9, 2019, Buffalo, NY.

3 Jack O'Connor, Incarcerated Veterans Project, interview by the author, July 9, 2019, Buffalo, NY.

4   Judge Russell interview, July 9, 2019.

5   Matthew Daneman, "N.Y. Court Gives Veterans Chance to Straighten Out," *USA Today*, June 2, 2008, 3A, http://www.usatoday.com/news/nation/2008-06-01-veterans -court_N.htm.

6   O'Connor interview, July 9, 2019.

7   "Remembering Hank Pirowski (Dec. 17, 1952–Feb. 12, 2012)," National Association of Drug Court Professionals, https://www.ca2c.org/remembering-hank-pirowski/.

8   O'Connor interview, July 9, 2019.

9   Judge Russell interview, July 9, 2019.

10   Manny Welch, Incarcerated Veterans Oral History Project, interview by the author, July 9, 2019, Buffalo, NY.

11   See "A Court For Veterans," *New York Times*, June 4, 2008, https://www.nytimes. com/2008/06/04/opinion/04wed4.html?smid=url-share; "Vets in Legal Trouble Find Help in Court," NPR, May 7, 2008, https://www.npr.org/templates/story/story .php?storyId=90254410; "Judge: Keep Vets Out of Jail," hosted by Cheryl Corley, NPR, June 18, 2008, https://www.npr.org/templates/story/story.php?storyId=91633166.

12   Daneman, "N.Y. Court Gives Veterans Chance to Straighten Out."

13   O'Connor interview, July 9, 2019. Unless otherwise noted, quotations from O'Conner come from this oral history interview.

14   For more on how the Vietnam War shapes remembrance and memorialization of other national disasters and historic events, from the Civil War to the Global War on Terror, see David Kieran, *Forever Vietnam: How a Divisive War Changed American Public Memory* (Amherst: University of Massachusetts Press, 2014).

15   See chapter 7, "Lost Fathers," in Fred Turner, *Echoes of Combat: The Vietnam War in American Memory* (New York: Anchor Books, 1996). For more on victory culture, see Tom Englehardt, *The End of Victory Culture: Cold War America and the Disillusioning of a Generation* (1995; Amherst: University of Massachusetts Press, 2007).

16   Sociologist and veteran Murray Polner, produced one of the early works on Vietnam veterans that showed a generational shift in wartime and reintegration experiences based on the accounts of nine Vietnam veterans. Murray Polner, *No Victory Parades: The Return of the Vietnam Veteran* (New York: Holt, 1971).

17   See also Turner, *Echoes of Combat.*

18   See also Wilbur Scott, "Veterans and Veterans' Issues," in *At War: The Military and American Culture in the Twentieth Century and Beyond*, ed. David Kieran and Edwin Martini (New Brunswick, NJ: Rutgers University Press, 2018), 138.

19   For more on the myth of POWs left in Vietnam, see Michael J. Allen, *Until the Last Man Comes Home: POWs, MIAs, and the Unending Vietnam War* (Chapel Hill: University of North Carolina Press).

20   "House Veterans' Affairs Committee Holds Roundtable," Government Press Releases (USA), September 18, 2009.

21   Patrick Welch, Incarcerated Veterans Oral History Project, interview by the author, July 9, 2019, Buffalo, NY. Unless otherwise noted, quotations from Patrick Welch come from this oral history interview.

22   Philip Caputo writes, "The old salts used to tell us that the most memorable experience in an officer's life is his first command. It is supposed to be like first love, a milestone on the road to manhood." Philip Caputo, *A Rumor of War* (New York: Ballantine, 1977), 23.

23   Caputo, *A Rumor of War*, xiv.

24   Lyndon B. Johnson, "August 4, 1964: Report on the Gulf of Tonkin Incident," UVA Miller

Center, accessed June 14, 2022, https://millercenter.org/the-presidency/presidential
-speeches/august-4-1964-report-gulf-tonkin-incident.

25   Christian G. Appy, *Patriots: The Vietnam War Remembered from All Sides* (New York:
      Viking, 2003), 116.

26   Robert Dallek, *Lyndon B. Johnson: Portrait of a President* (New York: Oxford University
      Press, 2004), 179.

27   Christian G. Appy, *American Reckoning: The Vietnam War and Our National Identity*
      (New York: Penguin, 2015), 48.

28   Caputo, *A Rumor of War*, xiv.

29   Christian G. Appy, "A War for Nothing," in *Working-Class War: American Combat
      Soldiers and Vietnam* (Chapel Hill: University of North Carolina Press, 1993), 207.

30   Võ Nguyên Giáp, *People's War, People's Army: the Viet Công Insurrection Manual for
      Underdeveloped Countries* (Praeger, 1962), iii. The Vietnamese often fought when the
      odds of success were high. The strategy proved effective in a protracted freedom struggle,
      even against a technologically superior enemy.

31   Appy, *Working-Class War*, 163.

32   Even by conservative estimates, US forces killed half a million enemy forces. The US
      suffered 58,000 casualties. See Appy, *Working-Class War*, 165.

33   See also Edwin Martini, *Agent Orange: History, Science, and the Politics of Uncertainty*
      (Amherst: University of Massachusetts Press, 2012).

34   Appy, *Working-Class War*, 205.

35   See Appy, *Working-Class War*, 234–49.

36   By 1971, veterans of the war in Vietnam gather to protest the war and demand imme-
      diate withdrawal, tossing their medals on the steps of the Capitol building. This act
      symbolized the apparent meaningless of the war and their sacrifice in it. See Appy,
      Working-Class War, 235.

37   Quoted in Turner, *Echoes of Combat*, 62. See also American Psychiatric Association,
      Diagnostic and Statistical Manual of Mental Disorders, 3rd ed. (Washington, DC:
      American Psychiatric Association, 1980).

38   Gerald Nicosia, *Home to War: A History of Vietnam Veterans' Movement* (New York:
      Three Rivers Press, 2001), 159.

39   Nicosia, *Home to War*, 159.

40   Turner, *Echoes of Combat*, 63, 62; Robert Jay Lifton, *Home from the War: Vietnam
      Veterans—Neither Victims Nor Executioners* (New York: Simon and Schuster, 1973).

41   Jonathan Shay, *Achilles in Vietnam: Combat Trauma and the Undoing of Character*
      (New York: Scribner, 1994), 9.

42   See also Richard Stacewitz, *Winter Soldiers: An Oral History of Vietnam Veterans against
      the War* (New York: Twayne, 1997), 192–93.

43   A study conducted in 1968 estimated that 15–20 percent of US casualties were friendly
      fire. Appy, *Working-Class War*, 185.

44   For more on moral injury and killing or releasing prisoners of war, see David Wood,
      What Have We Done: The Moral Injury of Our Longest Wars (New York: Little, Brown,
      2016), 196–204.

45   Lewis B. Puller Jr., *Fortunate Son: The Healing of the Vietnam Vet* (New York: Grove
      Press, 1991), 157.

46   John M. Kinder, "The Embodiment of War," in Kieran and Martini, *At War*, 218.

47   Ron Kovic, *Born on the Fourth of July, with a New Introduction by the Author* (1976;
      New York: Akashic, 2005), 48.

48   Nicosia, *Home to War*.

49   Quoted in Nicosia, *Home to War*, 298.

50   See also Wilbur Scott, *The Politics of Readjustment: Vietnam Veterans since the War* (New York: Aldine De Gruyer, 1993), 87–119.

51   *Vietnam Veterans of America, Inc.* (Washington, DC: Government Printing Office, 1986). https://search.ebscohost.com/login.aspx?direct=true&db=cat06087a&AN=umass.003491410&site=eds-live&scope=site.

52   Robert E. Jackson, "Incarcerated Veterans . . . from Behind the Walls," *VVA Veteran*, August 1984.

53   "Incarcerated Veterans . . . in the Criminal Justice System," *VVA Veteran*, September 1984.

54   One court case in Shreveport, Louisiana, in 1982 struck a chord with the local veterans, as numerous Vietnam veterans gave public testimonies about their war memories at the trial. Gean Heads, a Marine Corps combat veteran, pled not guilty to the charge of first-degree murder of his brother-in-law. "'The insanity defense never got off the ground because no one had heard of post-traumatic stress until February 1980,'" said his attorney. The second jury found him not guilty on reason of "temporary insanity." Reginald Stuart, "Jailed Veteran's Case Brings Post-Vietnam Problems into Focus," *New York Times* February 26, 1982, http://www.nytimes.com/1982/02/26/us/jailed-veteran-s-case-brings-post-vietnam-problem-into-focus.html.

55   O'Connor interview, July 9, 2019.

56   See also Appy, *Working-Class War*, 27.

57   Martini, *Agent Orange*, 85.

58   For more information on the litigation and legislative history of Agent Orange, see Sidath Viranga Panangala and Daniel T. Shedd, *Veterans Exposed to Agent Orange: Legislative History, Litigation, and Current Issues*, Congressional Research Service Report, November 18, 2014, https://sgp.fas.org/crs/misc/R43790.pdf.

59   Caputo, *A Rumor of War*, xvi.

60   Jerry Lembcke, *The Spitting Image: Myth, Memory, and Legacy in Vietnam* (New York: New York University Press, 1998).

61   Appy notes, "Few people thought to thank veterans for their service to their country, because most Americans did not believe their country had been well served in Vietnam" (*American Reckoning*, 237).

62   For more on the evacuation planning of Saigon, see Amanda Demmer, *After Saigon's Fall: Refugees and US-Vietnamese Relations, 1975–2000* (New York: Cambridge University Press, 2021), 27–34. Demmer argues that US policymakers feared that the fall of Saigon would damage US prestige and credibility among the international community and that it would be viewed as a betrayal to American allies (32).

63   O'Connor interview, July 9, 2019.

64   Appy, *American Reckoning*, 239.

65   Demmer, *After Saigon's Fall*, 9.

66   Appy, *American Reckoning*, 238.

67   Appy, *American Reckoning*, 237.

68   "History," Vietnam Veterans of America, https://vva.org/who-we-are/history/.

69   See also Patrick Hagopian, *The Vietnam War in American Memory: Veterans, Memorials, and the Politics of Healing* (Amherst: University of Massachusetts Press, 2009).

70   Robert T. Russell, "Veterans Treatment Court: A Proactive Approach," *New England Journal on Criminal and Civil Confinement* 35, no. 2 (Summer 2009): 357–72.

71   "New Veterans Drug Court Focuses on Rehabilitating Our Soldiers through Mental Health Treatment," *U.S. Newswire*, May 28, 2008, Gale Academic OneFile Select.

72   Russell, "Veterans Treatment Court," 372.

73   Hon. Robert T. Russell, "Veterans Treatment Courts Developing throughout the Nation,"
      National Center for State Courts, 2009, https://justiceforvets.org/wp-content/uploads/
      Veterans_Treatment_Courts_Developing_Throughout_the_Nation%20%281%29.pdf.

74   "Hon. Robert Russell Reflects on the Founding and Future of Veterans Treatment Courts,"
      Harvard Law Today, December 5, 2016, https://today.law.harvard.edu/hon-robert
      -russell-reflects-founding-future-veterans-treatment-courts/.

75   Robert T. Russell, "Veterans Treatment Courts," *Touro Law Review* 31, no. 3 (2015):
      385–402.

76   Russell, "Veterans Treatment Courts Developing throughout the Nation."

77   Russell, "Veterans Treatment Courts," 387.

78   "Veterans Treatment Courts and Other Veteran-Focused Courts Served by VA Veterans
      Justice Outreach Specialists," Office of Public Affairs Media Relations, U.S. Department of
      Veterans Affairs, January 2021, https://www.va.gov/HOMELESS/docs/VJO/Veterans
      -Treatment-Court-Inventory-Update-Fact-Sheet-Jan-2021.pdf.

79   See also John Dower, *The Violent American Century: War and Terror since World War
      II* (Chicago: Dispatch, 2017).

CHAPTER 5: GENERATION 9/11

1   "Get Started," Army National Guard, https://www.nationalguard.com/hometown?.

2   Institute of Medicine (US) Committee on the Initial Assessment of Readjustment
      Needs of Military Personnel, Veterans, and Their Families, *Returning Home from Iraq
      and Afghanistan: Preliminary Assessment of Readjustment Needs of Veterans, Service
      Members, and Their Families*, (Washington, DC: National Academies Press, 2010),
      28, https://www.ncbi.nlm.nih.gov/books/NBK220068/.

3   Institute of Medicine, *Returning Home from Iraq and Afghanistan*, 21. Demographic
      information on Iraq and Afghanistan veterans in this paragraph comes from this
      source.

4   Institute of Medicine, *Returning Home from Iraq and Afghanistan*, 25.

5   David Kieran, *Signature Wounds: The Untold Story of the Military's Mental Health
      Crisis* (New York: New York University Press, 2019).

6   Kieran, *Signature Wounds*, 16.

7   Kieran, *Signature Wounds*, 46–47.

8   See Debra A. Pinals, "Veterans and the Justice System: The Next Forensic Frontier,"
      Journal of the American Academy of Psychiatry and the Law 38, no. 1 (2010): 163–67.
      For rates on mental health disorders among incarcerated veterans see also Robert A.
      Rosenheck, Steven Banks, John Pandiani, and Rani Hoff, "Bed Closures and Incar-
      ceration Rates among Users of Veterans Affairs Mental Health Services," *Psychiatric
      Services* 51, no. 10 (2000): 1282–87, https://doi.org/10.1176/appi.ps.51.10.1282.

9   Jennifer Bronson, E. Ann Carson, Margaret Noonan, and Marcus Berzofsky, *Veterans
      in Prison and Jail, 2011–12*, Veterans in State and Federal Prisons (Washington, DC:
      Bureau of Justice Statistics, 2015), 2, https://www.bjs.gov/content/pub/pdf/vpj1112.
      pdf.

10   Katherine Schaeffer, "The Changing Face of America's Veteran Population," Pew
      Research Center, April 5, 2021, https://www.pewresearch.org/fact-tank/2021/04/05/the
      -changing-face-of-americas-veteran-population/.

11   Laura M. Maruschak, Jennifer Bronson, and Mariel Alper, *Veterans in Prison: Survey of*

Prison Inmates, 2016, Veterans in State and Federal Prisons (Washington, DC: Bureau of Justice Statistics, 2021), https://bjs.ojp.gov/content/pub/pdf/vpspi16st.pdf.

12   Mimi Cantwell, *Veterans in Prison* (Washington, DC: Bureau of Justice Statistics, 1981).

13   Bronson et al., *Veterans in Prison and Jail, 2011–12.*

14   Margaret E. Noonan and Christopher J. Mumola, *Veterans in State and Federal Prison, 2004* (Washington, DC: Bureau of Justice Statistics, 2007), https://bjs.ojp.gov/content pub/pdf/vsfp04.pdf.

15   Jack Tsai, Robert A. Rosenheck, Wesley J. Kasprow, and James F. McGuire, "Risks of Incarceration and Clinical Characteristics of Incarcerated Veterans by Race/Ethnicity," *Social Psychiatry and Psychiatric Epidemiology* 48, no. 11 (2013): 1777–86, https://doi.org /10.1007/s00127-013-0677-z.

16   Twenty-eight percent of incarcerated veterans served in Iraq and 16 percent served in Afghanistan; 41 percent served in Vietnam. Maruschak, Bronson, and Alper, *Veterans in Prison.*

17   For more on mental health diagnoses and VA treatment of OEF/OIF (Operation Enduring Freedom/Operation Iraqi Freedom) veterans, see Karen H. Seal et. al., "Trends and Risk Factors for Mental Health Diagnoses among Iraq and Afghanistan Veterans Using Department of Veterans Affairs Health Care, 2002–2008," *Research and Practice* 99, no. 9 (2009): 1651–58.

18   Kieran, *Signature Wounds,* 46–47.

19   Department of Defense Task Force on Mental Health, *An Achievable Vision: Report of the Department of Defense Task Force on Mental Health,* June 2007, https://apps.dtic.mil /sti/pdfs/ADA469411.pdf.

20   Kieran, *Signature Wounds,* 105, 32.

21   Dave Phillips and Tom Arango, "Who Signs Up to Fight? Makeup of U.S. Recruits Shows Glaring Disparity," *New York Times,* January 10, 2020, https://www.nytimes. com/2020/01/10/us/military-enlistment.html.

22   Department of Defense, "Military Accessions Vital to National Interest (MAVNI) Recruitment Pilot Program, Factsheet," Department of Defense, 2016, https://dod.defense .gov/news/mavni-fact-sheet.pdf.

23   Kevin Ogo, Incarcerated Veterans Oral History Project, telephone interview by the author, February 11, 2018, Amherst, MA.

24   Beth Bailey and Richard H. Immerman, eds., introduction to *Understanding the U.S. Wars in Iraq and Afghanistan* (New York: New York University Press, 2015), 2.

25   In the first years of the Iraq War, there was controversy on military recruiters on college campuses. Some universities sought to ban this practice on their campus. Congressed passed legislation to deny funds to universities that ban military recruitment. Alyson Klein, "House Panel Passes Bill to Ensure Military Recruiters' Access to Colleges," *Chronicle of Higher Education* 50, no. 30 (2004): Gale Academic OneFile.

26   "Army Staff Sergeant Eric J. Lindstrom: Died July 12, 2009 Serving during Operation Enduring Freedom," *Military Times,* https://thefallen.militarytimes.com/army-staff -sgt-eric-j-lindstrom/4190548.

27   Jonathan Shay, *Achilles in Vietnam: Combat Trauma and the Undoing of Character* (New York: Scribner, 1994), 39.

28   Nancy Sherman, *The Untold War: Inside the Hearts, Minds, and Souls of Our Soldiers* (New York: Norton, 2010), 100.

29   David Kieran tells the account of one Iraq War veteran who committed suicide. The soldier recounted memories of executing Iraqi prisoners. "The father said that the night

before his son's suicide, the vet sat in the lap of his father, "a story of regression that asserted that war had profoundly unmade a man, returning him to infancy" (Kieran, *Signature Wounds*, 84).

30 For details on the increased risk of suicide among incarcerated veterans, see Hal S. Worrtzel, Ingrid A. Binswanger, C. Alan Anderson, and Lawrence E. Adler, "Suicide among Incarcerated Veterans," *Journal of the American Academy of Psychiatry and the Law* 37, no. 1 (2009): 82–91.

31 Bernard Edelman and Deanne Benos, *Barracks behind Bars: In Veteran-Specific Housing Units, Veterans Help Veterans Help Themselves* (Washington, DC: U.S. Department of Justice, National Institute of Corrections, 2018), 1.

32 For example, in 2009, the Pentagon rejected the idea that PTSD might be eligible for a Purple Heart. Sherman, *The Untold War*, 174–75. Jonathan Shay maintained that the language of "disorder" is stigmatizing.

33 Kieran, *Signature Wounds*, 141.

34 Quoted in Kieran, *Signature Wounds*, 132.

35 See also Benjamin D. Dickstein, Dawne S. Vogt, Sonia Handa, and Brett T. Litz, "Targeting Self-Stigma in Returning Military Personnel and Veterans: A Review of Intervention Strategies," *Military Psychology* 22 (2010): 224–36, https://doi.org/10.1080/08995600903417399.

36 Kieran, *Signature Wounds*, 114.

37 Major Bryant A. Boohar, "Combat Stress Claims: Veterans' Benefits and Post-Separation Character of Service Upgrades for 'Bad Paper' Veterans After the Fairness for Veterans Act," *Military Law Review* 227, no. 2 (2019): 105.

38 Maria M. Steenkamp et al., "Predictors of PTSD 40 Years after Combat: Findings from the National Vietnam Veterans Longitudinal Study," *Depression and Anxiety* 34, no. 8 (2017): 711, https://doi.org/10.1002/da.22628.

39 Boohar, "Combat Stress Claims," 105.

40 Daniel Zwerdling and Michael De Yoanna, "Missed Treatment: Soldiers with Mental Health Issues Dismissed for 'Misconduct,'" NPR/Colorado Public Radio, October 28, 2015, https://www.npr.org/2015/10/28/451146230/missed-treatment-soldiers-with-mental-health-issues-dismissed-for-misconduct.

41 Zwerdling and Yoanna, "Missed Treatment."

42 Report to Congressional Committees, "Actions Needed to Ensure Post-Traumatic Stress Disorder and Traumatic Brain Injury Are Considered in Misconduct Separations," United States Government Accountability Office, May 2017, https://www.gao.gov/products/gao-17-260.

43 Andrew Kubacki, Incarcerated Veterans Oral History Project, telephone interview by the author, May 8, 2018, Amherst, MA.

44 Kieran, *Signature Wounds*, 112–13.

45 David Wood, *What Have We Done: The Moral Injury of Our Longest Wars* (New York: Little, Brown, 2016), 9.

46 Neal Mays, Incarcerated Veterans Oral History Project, telephone interview by the author, April 23, 2019, Amherst, MA.

47 See part two of the interview, May 3, 2019.

48 *Army 2020: Generating Health and Discipline in the Force Ahead of the Strategic Reset* (Washington, DC: Headquarters, US Army, 2012), 33.

49 *Army 2020*, 27.

50 John Rowan, "A Less than Honorable Policy," *New York Times*, December 30, 2016, https://www.nytimes.com/2016/12/30/opinion/a-less-than-honorable-policy.html.

51 Rowan, "A Less than Honorable Policy."

52 Fairness For Veterans Act of 2016, H.R. 4683, 114th Congress (2015–16).

53 "VVA Celebrates Passage of Fairness for Veterans Act; Calls for Investigation into 'Bad Paper' Discharges," Vietnam Veterans of America, December 13, 2016, https://vva.org/wp-content /uploads/2016/12/VVA-Press-Release-16-35.pdf.

CHAPTER 6: ANOTHER SIGNATURE WOUND

1   Less than half of 1 percent of the US population serves in the armed forces. "Demographics of the U.S. Military," Council on Foreign Relations, July 13, 2020, https://www.cfr.org /backgrounder/demographics-us-military#:~:text=At%20that%20time%2C%20 the%20active,percent%20of%20the%20U.S.%20population.

The US Army engages in a variety of recruitment strategies, including social media campaigns designed to attract Generation Z. Leila Fadel and Amanda Morris, "After Falling Short, U.S. Army Gets Creative with New Recruiting Strategy," NPR, January 6, 2019, https://www.npr.org/2019/01/06/682608011/after-falling -short-u-s-army-gets-creative-with-new-recruiting-strategy.

The US Army focuses on recruiting from high schools, appealing to parents, emphasizing education and career opportunities, and being familiar with/living in the communities where they seek to recruit. Kyle Jahner, "Secret Tactics of Successful Army Recruiters," *Army Times*, March 2, 2015, https://www.armytimes.com/education-transition/jobs/2015 /03/02/secret-tactics-of-successful-army-recruiters/.

2   "Benefit Explorer," Marines.com, https://www.marines.com/become-a-marine/benefit-explorer/enlisted.html.

3   Robyn M. Highfill-McRoy, Gerald E. Larson, Stephanie Booth-Kewley, and Cedric F. Garland, "Psychiatric Diagnoses and Punishment for Misconduct: The Effects of PTSD in Combat-Deployed Marines," BMC Psychiatry, 10 (2010): http://www.biomedcentral.com /1471-244X/10/88; Margaret E. Noonan and Christopher J. Mumola, *Veterans in State and Federal Prison, 2004* (Washington, DC: Bureau of Justice Statistics, 2007), https:// bjs.ojp.gov/content/pub/pdf/vsfp04.pdf.

4   James Torrey, Incarcerated Veterans Oral History Project, interview by the author, July 18, 2017, Leeds, MA.

5   For more on the basic training process, see Michael Volkin, *The Ultimate Basic Training Guidebook: Tips, Tricks, and Tactics for Surviving Boot Camp*, 4th ed. (New York: Savas Beatie, 2009), EBSCO.

6   E. M. Olivia, "Opioid Overdose Education and Naloxone Distribution (OEND): Preventing and Responding to an Opioid Overdose," VA Program Evaluation and Resources Center, Palo Alto, CA, 2014.

7   Department of Veterans Affairs, *Healthcare Inspection—VA Patterns of Dispensing Take-Home Opioids and Monitoring Patients on Opioid Therapy* (Washington DC: Office of Inspector General, 2014).

8   Alex S. Bennett et al., "Opioid-Involved Overdose among Male Afghanistan/Iraq-Era U.S. Military Veterans: A Multi-Dimensional Perspective," *Substance Use & Misuse* 52, no. 13 (2017): 1702, https://doi.org/10.1080/10826084.2017.1306563.

9   Bennett et al., "Opioid-Involved Overdose," 1702.

10 Amy Bohnert et al., "Accidental Poisoning Mortality among Patients in the Department of Veterans Affairs Health System," *Medical Care* 49, no. 4 (2011): 393–96.

11 Institute of Medicine, *Substance Use Disorder in the Armed Forces*, September 2012, 2.

12   See Aaron Belkin on military masculinity in *Bring Me Men: Military Masculinity and the Benign Façade of American Empire, 1898–2001* (New York: Columbia University Press, 2012).

13   Matt Nicholas, Incarcerated Veterans Oral History Project, interviewed by the author, June 18, 2019, Philadelphia, PA.

14   Andrew J. MacGregor, Peggy P. Han, Amber L. Dougherty, and Michael R. Galarneau, "Effect of Dwell Time on the Mental Health of US Military Personnel with Multiple Combat Tours," *American Journal of Public Health* 102 (2012): 55–59, https://doi.org /10.2105/AJPH.2011.300341; Christina M. Marini, Christina L. Collins, and Shelley M. MacDermid Wadsworth, "Examining Multiple Rhythms of Military and Veteran Family Life," *Journal of Family Theory and Review* 10, no. 3 (2018): 516–34, https:// doi.org/10.1111/jftr.12275.

15   Alana Rosenberg et al., "Drug Treatment Accessed through the Criminal Justice System: Participants' Perspectives and Uses," *Journal of Urban Health* 96 (2019): 390–99, https://doi.org/10.1007/s11524-018-0308-9.

16   The term *battle space* transforms the idea of a battlefield beyond the traditional concept, extending military operations into civilian domains, argue Ross Caputi, Richard Hil, and Donna Mulhearn in *The Sacking of Fallujah: A People's History* (Amherst: University of Massachusetts Press, 2019), 6.

17   Craig Whitlock, *The Afghanistan Papers: A Secret History of the War* (New York: Simon and Schuster, 2021), 135.

18   Whitlock, *The Afghanistan Papers*, 134. For more on the opium trade before the US invasion, see "Afghanistan: How Did Afghanistan Become a Major Supplier of Illicit Opium?" in *Global Illicit Drug Trends 2001* (New York: United Nations Office for Drug Control and Crime Prevention, 2001), 30–42.

19   Whitlock, *The Afghanistan Papers*, 130, 137.

20   See also Christopher J. Coyne et al., "The War on Drugs in Afghanistan: Another Failed Experiment in Drug Interdiction," *Independent Review* 21, no. 1 (2016): 95–119.

21   Whitlock, *The Afghanistan Papers*, 132, 138.

22   See United Nations Office on Drugs and Crime, *Opium Cultivation in Afghanistan: Latest Findings and Emerging Threats*, November 2022.

23   Whitlock, *The Afghanistan Papers*, 259.

24   *The Afghanistan Papers: Costs and Benefits of America's Longest War: Hearing before the Committee on Homeland Security and Governmental Affairs, United States Senate*, 116th Cong., 2nd sess., February 11, 2020 (Washington, DC: US Government Printing Office, 2020), 14, https://www.congress.gov/event/116th-congress/senate-event/LC65119/ text?s=1&r=6.

25   Whitlock, *The Afghanistan Papers*, 259.

26   *Voices of Veterans from the Afghan War: Hearing before the Committee on Foreign Relations, United States Senate*, 111th Cong., 1st sess., April 23, 2009 (Washington, DC: Government Printing Office, 2010), 8.

27   Whitlock, *The Afghanistan Papers*, 253.

28   Justin Rowlatt, "How the US Military's Opium War in Afghanistan Was Lost," *BBC News*, April 25, 2019, https://www.bbc.com/news/world-us-canada-47861444. See also W. J. Hennigan, "The U.S. Sent Its Most Advanced Fighter Jets to Blow Up Cheap Opium Labs. Now It's Canceling the Program," *Time*, February 12, 2019, https://time.com /5534783/iron-tempest-afghanistan-opium/.

29   Whitlock, *The Afghanistan Papers*, 254.

30   Victoria A. Greenfield, Bryce Pardo, and Jirka Taylor, "Afghanistan in the Era of Fentanyl," Rand Corporation, July 2021.

31   Col. Zygmunt F. Dembek, Tesema Chekol, and Aiguo Wu, "The Opioid Epidemic: Challenge to Military Medicine and National Security," *Military Medicine* 185 (2020): e662–e667.

32   James Marciano, Incarcerated Veterans Oral History Project, interview by the author, July 1, 2019, Deerfield, MA.

33   Lisa Mundey, "The Combatants' Experiences," in *Understanding the U.S. Wars in Iraq and Afghanistan*, ed. Beth Bailey and Richard H. Immerman (New York: New York University Press, 2015), 177, http://www.jstor.org/stable/j.ctt13x0q17.11.

34   Mundey, "The Combatants' Experiences," 176.

35   Mark A. Reger, Gregory A. Gahm, Robert S. Swanson, and Susan J. Duma, "Association between Number of Deployments to Iraq and Mental Health Screening Outcomes in US Army Soldiers," *Journal of Clinical Psychiatry* 70, no. 9 (2009): 1266–72, https://doi.org /10.4088/JCP.08m04361. See also Alejandro Interian et al., "Multiple Deployments and Combat Trauma: Do Homefront Stressors Increase the Risk for Posttraumatic Stress Symptoms," *Journal of Traumatic Stress* 27 (2014): 90–97.

36   Attacks in Afghanistan increased substantially in 2008. U.S. Department of Justice, "Armed Conflicts Report," updated January 2009, https://www.justice.gov/sites/default /files/eoir/legacy/2014/02/25/Afghanistan.pdf.

37   Marciano interview, July 1, 2019.

38   Anlys Olivera et al., "Peripheral Total Tau in Military Personnel Who Sustain Traumatic Brain Injuries during Deployment," *JAMA Neurology* 72, no. 10 (October 2015): 1109–16, https://doi.org/10.1001/jamaneurol.2015.1383.

39   David Kieran, *Signature Wounds: The Untold Story of the Military's Mental Health Crisis* (New York: New York University Press, 2019), 179–80.

40   Terri Tanielian et al., *Invisible Wounds of War: Summary and Recommendation for Addressing Psychological and Cognitive Injuries* (Pittsburgh: Rand Center for Military Health Policy Research, 2008), 1.

41   Jack Tsai, Robert A. Rosenheck, Wesley J. Kasprow, and James F. McGuire, "Risk of Incarceration and Other Characteristics of Iraq and Afghanistan Era Veterans in State and Federal Prisons," *Psychiatric Services* 64, no. 1 (2013): 36–43, https://doi.org/10.1176/appi .ps.201200188.

42   Dave Phillips and Tom Arango, "Who Signs Up to Fight? Makeup of U.S. Recruits Shows Glaring Disparity," *New York Times*, January 10, 2020, https://www.nytimes .com/2020/01/10/us/military-enlistment.html. See also Jim Garamore, "DOD Official Cites Widening Military-Civilian Gap," U.S. Department of Defense, May 16, 2019, https://www.defense.gov/Explore/News/Article/Article/1850344/dod-official -cites-widening-military-civilian-gap/.

43   The average soldier in Vietnam was twenty years old; the average soldier today is twenty-eight. Mundey, "The Combatants' Experiences," 177.

44   Mary Jo Larson, Nikki R. Wooten, Rachel Sayko Adams, and Elizabeth L. Merrick, "Military Combat Deployments and Substance Use: Review and Future Directions," *Journal of Social Work Practice in the Addictions* 12, no. 1 (2012): 6–27, https://doi.org /10.1080/1533256X.2012.647586.

45   Greg H. Jones, Eduardo Bruera, Salahadin Abdi, and Hagop M. Kantarjian, "The Opioid Epidemic in the United States: Overview, Origins, and Potential Solutions," *Cancer* 124, no. 22 (2018): 4279, https://doi.org/10.1002/cncr.31713.

46   Claire Felter, "The U.S. Opioid Epidemic," *Council on Foreign Relations*, last updated May 12, 2022, https://www.cfr.org/backgrounder/us-opioid-epidemic.

47   Jones et al., "The Opioid Epidemic in the United States."

48   Karen H. Seal et al., "Association of Mental Health Disorders with Prescription Opioids and High-Risk Opioid Use in US Veterans of Iraq and Afghanistan," *JAMA* 307 no. 9 (2012): https://jamanetwork.com/journals/jama/fullarticle/1105046.

49   Walid F. Gellad, Chester B. Good, and David J. Shulkin "Addressing the Opioid Epidemic in the United States: Lessons from the Departments of Veterans Affairs," *JAMA Internal Medicine* 177, no. 5 (2017).

CHAPTER 7: "JUSTICE FOR VETS"

1   Paul A. Lucas and Kathleen Hanrahan, "No Soldier Left Behind: The Veterans Court Solution," *International Journal of Law and Psychiatry* 45 (2016): 52. See also Debra A. Pinals, "Veterans and the Justice System: The Next Forensic Frontier," *Journal of the American Academy of Psychiatry and the Law* 38, no. 1 (2010): 163–67.

2   "New Veterans Drug Court Focuses on Rehabilitating Our Soldiers through Mental Health Treatment," *US Newswire*, May 28, 2008, Gale Academic OneFile Select.

3   Judge David Youll, "Tulsa County Veterans Treatment Court," *Oklahoma Bar Journal* 82, no. 31 (2011): 2746.

4   In 2018, Oklahoma had the highest incarceration rate in the nation. Peter Wanger and Wendy Sawyer, "States of Incarceration: The Global Context of 2018," *Prison Policy Initiative*, June 2018, https://www.prisonpolicy.org/global/2018.html?gclid=Cjw KCAjwqcKFBhAhEiwAfEr7zcqYaFSv5h958vVLmBiFfiWSt8DrgJ6NuFEoPCYev GPDfbsLPjMwpBoCnUUQAvD_BwE.

5   Youll, "Tulsa County Veterans Treatment Court," 2746.

6   See J. M. Baldwin, "Investigating the Programmatic Attack: A National Survey of Veterans Treatment Courts," *Journal of Criminal Law and Criminology* 105 (2016): 101–8; Richard D. Hartley and Julie Marie Baldwin, "Waging War on Recidivism among Justice-Involved Veterans: An Impact Evaluation of a Large Urban Veterans Treatment Court," *Criminal Justice Policy Review* 30, no. 1 (2019).

7   U.S. Department of Justice, "FY 2020 Budget Request at a Glance," https://www .justice.gov/jmd/page/file/1142306/download.

8   See also Hartley and Baldwin, "Waging War on Recidivism among Justice-Involved Veterans," 53.

9   See also Claudia Arno, "Proportional Response: The Need for More—And More Standardized—Veterans' Courts," *University of Michigan Journal of Law Reform* 48 (2015): 1044.

10   See Paul A. Lucas and Kathleen Hanrahan, "No Soldier Left Behind: The Veterans Court Solution," *International Journal of Law and Psychiatry* 45 (2016): 52.

11   Robert T. Russell, "Veterans Treatment Court: A Proactive Approach," *New England Journal on Criminal and Civil Confinement* 35, no. 2 (Summer 2009): 357–72.

12   Barack Obama, "Transcript: Speech on Race," NPR, March 18, 2008, https://www .npr.org/templates/story/story.php?storyId=88478467.

13   See also "Statement of Benjamin B. Tucker, Office of National Drug Control Policy, Executive Office of the President," *Drug and Veterans Treatment Courts: Seeking Cost-Effective Solutions for protecting Public Safety and Reducing Recidivism*, July 19, 2011 (Washington, DC: US Senate Judiciary Committee, Subcommittee on Crime and Terrorism, 2011).

14   "Sen. Kerry, Rep. Kennedy Introduce Legislation to—," *US Fed News (USA)*, November

16, 2009. See also Services, Education, and Rehabilitation for Veterans Act, S.3379, 110th Congress (2007–2008), https://www.congress.gov/bill/110th-congress/senate -bill/3379/text.

15   U.S. Department of Veterans Affairs, "Justice Outreach Coordinator," https://www.va .gov/homeless/vjo.asp.

16   Jim McGuire, Ph.D., National Program Director and Sean Clark, Office of Mental Health Service, "Veteran Justice Outreach Initiative," https://justiceforvets.org /wp-content/uploads/VJO%20White%20Paper.pdf\.

17   "Community and Military Task Force Relations," C-SPAN, January 20, 2012, https:// www.c-span.org/video/?303798-5/community-military-task-force-relations.

18   Chris Deutsch, Incarcerated Veterans Oral History Project, interview by the author, August 30, 2019, Alexandria, VA.

19   The Veterans Treatment Court Planning Initiative developed the curriculum in collaboration with Veterans Treatment Court experts, the National Drug Court Institute, the Department of Justice, and the Department of Veterans Affairs. See "Statement of Benjamin B. Tucker."

20   Ginnie Graham, "Court Serves with Honor," *Tulsa World,* May 18, 2010, A9, NewsBank: Access World News.

21   Baldwin, "Investigating the Programmatic Attack," 727–28.

22   Judge Robert T. Russell pointed to a study that showed diverting 18,000 people saved $254 million in costs of incarceration. "Veterans Treatment Court: A Proactive Approach," 370. See also Ronald D. Castile, "A Special Court for Veterans," *New York Times,* November 10, 2010, https://www.nytimes.com/2010/11/11/opinion/11castille.html ?smid=url-share.

23   "Drug and Veterans Treatment Courts: Witnesses Testified on the Cost-Effectiveness of Drug and Veterans Treatment Courts," C-SPAN, July 19, 2011, https://www.c-span .org/video/?300592-1/drug-veterans-treatment-courts.

24   Deutsch interview, August 30, 2019.

25   Deutsch interview, August 30, 2019.

26   For more on military masculinity, see Aaron Belkin, *Bring Me Men: Military Masculinity and the Benign Façade of American Empire, 1898–2001* (New York: Columbia University Press, 2012).

27   Timothy J. Wynn, "On Male Myths," Incarcerated Veterans Oral History Project, interview by the author, May 29, 2019, Center for Criminal Justice, Philadelphia, https:// www.youtube.com/watch?v=XK7GkNe860Q.

28   Nancy Sherman, *The Untold War: Inside the Hearts, Minds, and Souls of Our Soldiers* (New York: Norton, 2010), 173.

29   Lizette Alvarez, "After the Battle, Fighting the Bottle at Home," *New York Times,* July 8, 2008, https://www.nytimes.com/2008/07/08/world/americas/08iht-08vets.14317624.html ?searchResultPosition=5.

30   Research suggests that between 25 and 40 percent of veterans of the Global War on Terrorism experience PTSD, TBI and as many as 40 percent binge drink. Patrick S. Calhoun et al., "Hazardous Alcohol Use and Receipt of Risk-Reduction Counseling among U.S. Veterans of the Wars in Iraq and Afghanistan" *Clinical Psychiatry* 69 (2008): 1686; and Baldwin, "Investigating the Programmatic Attack," 708.

31   See also Center for Mental Health Services, *Responding to the Needs of Justice Involved Combat Veterans with Service-Related Trauma and Mental Health Conditions,* 2008, 6.

32   For more on the role of peer support and trauma-informed approaches to treatment

court, see Laura Tach et al., "Trauma-Informed Care in a Family Drug Court," *Social Service Review* 96, no. 3 (2022): 470, https://www.journals.uchicago.edu/doi /10.1086/721234.

33   For more on therapeutic surveillance in drug treatment courts, see Kevin Revier, "'Without Drug Court, You'll End Up in Prison or Dead': Therapeutic Surveillance and Addiction Narratives in Treatment Court," *Critical Criminology* 29 (2021): 915–30, https://doi.org/10.1007/s10612-021-09592-y.

34   "Fighting Back: Iraq War Vet Battles Substance Abuse, Personal Demons and Reality on His Road to Redemption," *Metro Philadelphia*, October 21, 2013, https://metrophil adelphia.com/fighting-back-an-iraq-war-vet-battles-substance-abuse-personal-demons -andreality-on-his-road-to-redemption/.

35   Global War on Terrorism Memorial Foundation, https://www.gwotmemorialfoun dation.org/.

36   David Kieran, *Signature Wounds: The Untold Story of the Military's Mental Health Crisis* (New York: New York University Press, 2019), 142–43.

37   "One in Five Iraq and Afghanistan Veterans Suffer from PTSD or Major Depression," RAND Corporation. April 17, 2008, https://www.rand.org/news/press/2008/04/17.

38   See Kieran's chapter, "The Culture of the Army Wasn't Ready," in *Signature Wounds*, 111.

39   Jeremy Redmon, "The Inside Story of the Deadliest Attack on a U.S. Military Base during the Iraq War," *Task & Purpose,* December 2, 2020, https://taskandpurpose. com/history/iraq-war-fob-marez-bombing/.

40   Nancy Montgomery, "A General Battles Post-Combat Stress," *Stars & Stripe*s, January 11, 2009, https://www.stripes.com/news/a-general-battles-post-combat-stress-1.87036.

41   Judge Patrick Dugan, Incarcerated Veterans Oral History Project, interview by the author, June 17, 2019, Philadelphia, PA.

42   Montgomery, "A General Battles Post-Combat Stress."

43   Kieran, *Signature Wounds,* 13, 126.

44   Dugan interview, June 17, 2019.

45   Dugan interview, June 17, 2019.

46   "Winter Soldier," Iraq Veterans Against the War, https://ivaw.org/wintersoldier; see also Iraq Veterans Against the War and Aaron Glantz, *Winter Soldier Iraq and Afghanistan: Eyewitness Accounts of the Occupations* (New York: Haymarket, 2008).

47   Ron Carver, David Cortright, and Barbara Doherty, eds., *Waging Peace in Vietnam* (New York: New Village Press, 2019), 159.

48   Andrew J. Bacevich, *The New American Militarism: How Americans Are Seduced by War* (2005; New York: Oxford University Press, 2013), 1, https://ebookcentral.proquest. com/lib/vt/detail.action?docID=1154805.

49   See "Statement of Laura A. Belmonte," *Article 1: Constitutional Perspectives on the Responsibility and Authority of the Legislative Branch: Meeting of the Committee on Rules, House of Representatives,* One 116th Cong., 2nd sess., March 3, 2020 (Washington, DC: Government Printing Office, 2020), 5–6, https://www.govinfo.gov/content /pkg/CHRG-116hhrg40628/pdf/CHRG-116hhrg40628.pdf. For more on US propaganda since the Cold War, see Laura A. Belmonte, *Selling the American Way: U.S. Propaganda and the Cold War* (Philadelphia: University of Pennsylvania Press, 2008).

50   See Michael S. Sherry, *In the Shadow of War: The United States since the 1930s* (New Haven, CT: Yale University Press, 1995), xi.

51   Ron Suskind, "Faith, Certainty, and the Presidency of George W. Bush," *New York*

Times, October 17, 2004, https://www.nytimes.com/2004/10/17/magazine/faith
-certainty-and-the-presidency-of-george-w-bush.html.

52   Mark Philip Bradley and Mary L. Dudziak, eds., *Making the Forever War: Marilyn B. Young on the Culture and Politics of American Militarism* (Amherst: University of Massachusetts Press, 2021), 187.

53   Bradley and Dudziak, introduction to *Making the Forever War,* 6.

54   Christian G. Appy, *American Reckoning: The Vietnam War and Our National Identity* (New York: Penguin, 2015), 289–90.

55   "Full Text of Colin Powell's Speech," *The Guardian,* February 5, 2003, https://www.the guardian.com/world/2003/feb/05/iraq.usa.

56   Jonathan Shay, "Moral Injury," *Psychoanalytic Psychology* 31, no. 2 (2014): 183.

57   David Wood, *What Have We Done: The Moral Injury of Our Longest Wars* (New York: Little, Brown, 2016), 9.

58   Jonathan Shay, *Achilles in Vietnam: Combat and the Undoing of Character* (New York: Scriber, 1994), 3.

59   Wood, *What Have We Done,* 8, 9.

60   Dugan interview, June 17, 2019.

61   See Lt. Comm. Jamie Lynn De Coster, "Building and Undermining Legitimacy: Recon-
struction and Development in Afghanistan," in *Our Latest Longest War: Losing Hearts and Minds in Afghanistan,* ed. Lt. Col. Aaron B. O'Connell (Chicago: University of Chicago Press, 2017), 157–88.

62   Brian Glyn Williams, *Counter Jihad: America's Military Experience in Afghanistan, Iraq, and Syria* (Philadelphia: University of Pennsylvania Press, 2017), 224.

63   Media interpreted the attack as evidence of the Taliban's resurgence as justification for an increase in US military force. David E. Sanger, "Afghan Bombing Sends a Danger Signal to U.S.," *New York Times,* February 27, 2007, https://www.nytimes.com/2007/02/28 /washington/28security.html.

64   Bradley and Dudziak, *Making the Forever War,* 168.

65   Marilyn B. Young outlined a top ten list of lessons that the Bush administrations had learned from the Vietnam War, including control of the media, craft the historical narrative, show support for the troops, avoid a draft, body counts, blame bad apples for atrocities, and heroize the architects. See "U.S. in Asia, U.S. in Iraq: Lessons Not Learned," in *Making Forever War,* 182–83. For more on US efforts to control the historical narrative in Fallujah, see Ross Caputi, Richard Hil, and Donna Mulhearn, *The Sacking of Fallujah: A People's History* (Amherst: University of Massachusetts Press, 2019), 5.

66   Sarah Sentilles, "When We See Photographs of Some Dead Bodies and Not Others," *New York Times,* At War, August 14, 2018, https://www.nytimes.com/2018/08/14 /magazine/media-bodies-censorship.html. See also Susan L. Carruthers, "Communications Media, the U.S. Military, and the War Brought Home," in *At War: The Military and American Culture in the Twentieth Century and Beyond,* ed. David Kieran and Edwin Martini (New Brunswick, NJ: Rutgers University Press, 2018), 258.

67   William M. Hammond challenges this claim that media were responsible for the United States' inability to win the war. See *Reporting Vietnam: Media and the Military at War* (Lawrence: University of Kansas Press, 1998).

68   See also John M. Kinder, "The Embodiment of War," in Kieran and Martini, *At War,* 221.

69   Army SPC Jason A. Disney, 21, of Fallon, NV died February 13, 2002, serving during Operation Enduring Freedom; assigned to the 7th Transportation Battalion, based at

Fort Bragg, NC; killed in a heavy equipment accident, on February 13, 2002, at Bagram Air Base, Afghanistan.

70 Dugan interview, June 17, 2019.

71 Wood, *What Have We Done,* 176.

72 Dugan interview, June 17, 2019.

73 *Voices of Veterans from the Afghan War: Hearing before the Committee on Foreign Relations, United States Senate,* 111th Cong., 1st sess., April 23, 2009 (Washington, DC: Government Printing Office, 2010), 20–21.

74 Bradley and Dudziak, *Making the Forever War,* 198.

75 *Voices of Veterans from the Afghan War,* 15.

76 Ziva Branstetter, "Judge's Order: Elliot Williams's Jail Cell became a Burial Crypt," *The Frontier,* July 21, 2016, https://www.readfrontier.org/stories/judges-order-elliott -williams-jail-cell-became-burial-crypt/.

77 Melanie D. Newport, *This Is My Jail: Local Politics and the Rise of Mass Incarceration* (Philadelphia: University of Pennsylvania Press, 2023), 14.

78 Andrew Cohen, "An Oklahoma Horror Story," The Marshall Project, January 23, 2017, https://www.themarshallproject.org/2017/01/23/an-oklahoma-horror-story.

79 Branstetter, "Judge's Order."

80 Cohen, "An Oklahoma Horror Story."

81 Youll, "Tulsa County Veterans Treatment Court," 2746.

82 Kieran, *Signature Wounds,* 13.

83 "Statement of Benjamin B. Tucker."

84 "Drug Courts: A Smart Approach to Criminal Justice," Office of Drug Control Policy, May 2011, https://obamawhitehouse.archives.gov/ondcp/ondcp-fact-sheets/drug-courts -smart-approach-to-criminal-justice.

85 Barack Obama, "National Drug Court Month," The White House, Washington, DC, May 23, 2012, https://obamawhitehouse.archives.gov/sites/default/files/email-files/national _drug_court_month.pdf.

86 "Bipartisan legislation helps establish Veterans Treatment Courts across the country— Rep. Pat Meehan (R-PA) News Release," Government Press Releases (USA), December 20, 2011, NewsBank: America's News Magazines.

87 "Veterans Treatment Courts and Other Veteran-Focused Courts Served by VA Veterans Justice Outreach Specialists," Office of Public Affairs Media Relations, U.S. Department of Veterans Affairs, January 2021, https://www.va.gov/HOMELESS/docs/VJO/Veterans -Treatment-Court-Inventory-Update-Fact-Sheet-Jan-2021.pdf.

88 Barack Obama, "The President's Role in Advancing Criminal Justice Reform," *Harvard Law Review* 130, no. 3 (2017): 811–66.

89 Obama, "The President's Role in Advancing Criminal Justice Reform," 825.

90 Obama, "The President's Role in Advancing Criminal Justice Reform," 864.

91 Office of Community Oriented Policing Services, *The President's Task Force on 21st Century Policing Implementation Guide: Moving from Recommendations to Action* (Washington, DC: Office of Community Oriented Policing Services, 2015).

92 Obama, "The President's Role in Advancing Criminal Justice Reform," 823.

93 National Defense Authorization Act for Fiscal Year 1997, Public Law 104–201, 110 Stat. 2423 (1996), https://www.congress.gov/104/plaws/publ201/PLAW-104publ201.pdf.

94 American Civil Liberties Union, *War Comes Home: The Excessive Militarization of American Policing* (New York: ACLU, 2014), https://www.aclu.org/report/war-comes -home-excessive-militarization-american-police.

95 American Civil Liberties Union, "ACLU Analysis Reveals Reforms to Controversial

1033 Program that Gives Police Weapons of War Had No Impact," press release, May 12, 2021, https://www.aclu.org/press-releases/aclu-analysis-reveals-reforms-controversial -1033-program-gives-police-weapons-war-had.

96　　Obama, "The President's Role in Advancing Criminal Justice Reform," 866.

CHAPTER 8: . . . AND JUSTICE FOR ALL

1　　Johnny Diaz, Maria Cramer, and Christina Morales, "What to Know about the Death of Vanessa Guillen," *New York Times*, April 30, 2021, https://www.nytimes.com/article /vanessa-guillen-fort-hood.html.

2　　Ryan Morgan, "Missing Fort Hood Soldier Found Dead Hanging from a Tree," *American Military News*, August 26, 2020, https://americanmilitarynews.com/2020/08/missing -fort-hood-soldier-found-dead-hanging-from-tree/.

3　　May Jeong, "The Only Thing I Knew Was How to Kill People: Inside the Rash of Unexplained Deaths at Ft. Hood," *Vanity Fair*, July 6, 2021, https://www.vanityfair.com /news/2021/06/inside-the-rash-of-unexplained-deaths-at-fort-hood/amp.

4　　US Army, *Report of the Ft. Hood Independent Review Committee*," November 6, 2020, https://www.army.mil/e2/downloads/rv7/forthoodreview/2020-12-03_FHIRC_re port_redacted.pdf.

5　　Tom Vanden Brook, "Panel Blasts Army Leaders, Army after Disappearance, Death of Spc. Vanessa Guillen; 14 Fired or Suspended," *USA Today*, December 8, 2020, https://www.usatoday.com/story/news/politics/2020/12/08/fort-hood-panel-faults -army-ignoring-sexual-assaults-some-fired/6481836002/.

6　　Human Rights Watch, *Embattled: Retaliation Against Sexual Assault Survivors in the U.S. Military*, May 18, 2015, https://www.hrw.org/report/2015/05/18/embattled/retaliation -against-sexual-assault-survivors-us-military.

7　　Rosemarie Skaine, *Sexual Assault in the Military* (Santa Barbara, CA: Praeger, 2016).

8　　Elizabeth L. Hillman and Kate Walsham, "Sexual Violence in the Military," in *The Routledge History of Gender, War, and the U.S. Military*, ed. Kara Dixon Vuic (New York: Routledge, 2018), 288.

9　　For a brief but substantial analysis of the deeper history of sexual violence in the US military since the American Revolution, see Kellie Wilson-Buford, "Problematic Policies and Far-Reaching Consequences: Historicizing Sexual Violence in the U.S. Military," in *Managing Sex in the Military: Gender, Identity, and Behavior*, ed. Beth Bailey, Alesha E. Doan, Shannon Portillo, and Kara Dixon Vuic (Lincoln: University of Nebraska Press, 2022), 197–218.

10　　Elizabeth Hillman, "Front and Center: Sexual Violence in U.S. Military Law," *Politics & Society* 37, no. 1 (2009): 119.

11　　Shawn Woodham, *Sexual Assault in the Military: Analysis, Response, and Resources*, (New York: Nova Publishers, 2014), 14.

12　　*Army 2020: Generating Health and Discipline in the Force Ahead of the Strategic Reset* (Washington, DC: Headquarters, US Army, 2012), 121.

13　　"Facts on United States Military Sexual Violence," Protect Our Defenders, May 2017, http://www.protectourdefenders.com/wp-content/uploads/2013/05/1.-MSA-Fact- Sheet-170629.pdf.

14　　*Army 2020: Generating Health and Discipline in the Force Ahead of the Strategic Reset* (Washington, DC: Headquarters, US Army, 2012), 22.

15　　*Army 2020*, 93.

16 See Elizabeth Bernstein, "The Sexual Politics of the 'New Abolitionism'," *Differences: A Journal of Feminist Cultural Studies* 18, no. 5 (2007): 138, https://doi.org/10.1215/10407391-2007-013; Beth E. Richie argues that the (largely white) feminist movement against violence has benefited from and allied with the rise of the carceral state, which ultimately endangers the lives of marginalized women, especially Black women and women of color. Richie, *Arrested Justice: Black Women, Violence, and America's Prison Nation* (New York: New York University Press, 2012).

17 See Elizabeth Hillman, *Defending America: Military Culture and the Cold War Court-Martial* (Princeton: Princeton University Press, 2005), https://doi.org/10.2307/j.ctv18zhf3r.

18 CID found that 63 percent of cases were founded, 27 percent were unfounded, and 10 percent were inconclusive. *Army 2020*, 129.

19 Richard Lardner, "Pentagon Misled Lawmakers on Military Sexual Assault Cases," Associated Press, April 18, 2016, https://apnews.com/23aed8a571f64a9d9c81271f0c6ae2fa/pentagon-misled-lawmakers-military-sexual-assault-cases.

20 Brian Tumulty, "Senate Vote Blocked on Gillibrand's Military Sex Assault Proposal," *lohud*, June 14, 2016, http://www.lohud.com/story/news/2016/06/14/senate-vote-blocked-gillibrands-military-sex-assault-proposal/85869282/.

21 Jennifer Bronson, E. Ann Carson, Margaret Noonan, and Marcus Berzofsky, *Veterans in Prison and Jail, 2011–12*, Veterans in State and Federal Prisons (Washington, DC: Bureau of Justice Statistics, 2015), https://www.bjs.gov/content/pub/pdf/vpji1112.pdf.

22 Laura M. Maruschak, Jennifer Bronson, and Mariel Alper, *Veterans in Prison: Survey of Prison Inmates, 2016*, Veterans in State and Federal Prisons (Washington, DC: Bureau of Justice Statistics, 2021), https://bjs.ojp.gov/content/pub/pdf/vpspi16st.pdf.

23 Autumn Backhaus et al., "The Many Wounds of War: The Association of Service-Related and Clinical Characteristics with Problems with the Law in Iraq and Afghanistan Veterans," *International Journal of Law and Psychiatry* 49 (2016): 205–13, https://doi.org/10.1016/j.ijlp.2016.10.007.

24 "Responding to the Needs of Women Veterans Involved in the Criminal Justice System," National Resource Center for Justice-Involved Women, Bureau of Justice Assistance, 2013, https://cjinvolvedwomen.org/wp-content/uploads/2015/09/WomenVeterans-REV1-21-14.pdf.

25 Alyssa Vasquez, Incarcerated Veterans Oral History Project, interview by the author, July 10, 2019, Buffalo, NY.

26 Jonathan Shay, *Achilles in Vietnam: Combat Trauma and the Undoing of Character* (New York: Scribner, 1994), 60.

27 Jonathan Shay, "Moral Injury," *Psychoanalytic Psychology* 31, no. 2 (2014): 183.

28 David Wood, *What Have We Done: The Moral Injury of Our Longest Wars* (New York: Little, Brown, 2016), 174.

29 See also Sheila B. Frankfurt et al., "Mechanisms of Moral Injury Following Military Sexual Trauma and Combat in Post-9/11 U.S. War Veterans," *Frontiers in Psychiatry* 9 (November 2018): https://doi.org/10.3389/fpsyt.2018.00520.

30 Vasquez interview, July 10, 2019.

31 Nancy Sherman, *The Untold War: Inside the Minds, Hearts, and Souls of Our Soldiers* (New York: Norton, 2010), 57.

32 Kimberly Bailey, Incarcerated Veterans Oral History Interview, interview by the author, January 10, 2020, recorded via Zoom.

33 *Army 2020*, 124.

34 Sherman, *The Untold War*, 56.

35 Human Rights Watch, *Booted: A Lack of Recourse for Wrongfully Discharged U.S. Military*

Rape Survivors, May 19, 2016, 3, https://www.hrw.org/report/2016/05/19/booted /lack-recourse-wrongfully-discharged-us-military-rape-survivors.

36   Human Rights Watch, *Booted*, 5.

37   Bailey interview, January 19, 2020.

38   Laura M. Maruschak, Jennifer Bronson, and Mariel Alper, *Veterans in Prison: Survey of Prison Inmates, 2016*, Veterans in State and Federal Prisons (Washington, DC: Bureau of Justice Statistics, 2021), https://bjs.ojp.gov/content/pub/pdf/vpspi16st.pdf.

39   See also Shay, *Achilles in Vietnam*, 58–59.

40   For more on the underlying causes of demographic shifts since the all-volunteer force, see Beth Bailey, *America's Army: Making the All-Volunteer Force* (Cambridge, MA: Belknap Press, 2009), 108.

41   Melissa T. Brown, "Transitioning to an All-Volunteer Force," in Vuic, *The Routledge History of Gender, War, and the U.S. Military.* During the 1980s when the nation was attempting to heal the so-called Vietnam syndrome, the military attempted to recruit a more masculine military, but the Gulf War necessitated more women serving in supporting roles (137–42). The "forever wars" in the twenty-first century have all but insured a more racially and sexually diverse military, in which women fill combat roles. Nonetheless, more equal participation has not always meant legal or social equality.

42   In the 1970s and 1980s, the Army perfected it recruiting techniques based on economic incentives. Bailey, *America's Army*, 175.

43   Kevin Revier, "'Without Drug Court, You'll End Up in Prison or Dead': Therapeutic Surveillance and Addiction Narratives in Treatment Court," *Critical Criminology* 29 (2021): 915–30, https://doi.org/10.1007/s10612-021-09592-y.

44   Revier, "'Without Drug Court, You'll End Up in Prison or Dead,'" 922.

45   "Charles L. Higgins," *Buffalo News*, June 25, 2017, https://buffalonews.com/obituaries /higgins-charles-l-msg/article_5a6b23b9-0be9-54cf-9487-a41573e70070.html.

46   Office of Mental Health and Suicide Prevention, *2020 National Prevention Annual Report*, U.S. Department of Veterans Affairs, November 2020, https://www.mental health.va.gov/docs/data-sheets/2020/2020-National-Veteran-Suicide-Prevention -Annual-Report-11-2020-508.pdf.

47   See also David Kieran, "'Leaders Can Once Again Determine the Kind of Culture the Army Is Building,'" in *Signature Wounds*, 214–47.

48   Judge Patrick Dugan, Incarcerated Veterans Oral History Project, interview by the author, June 17, 2019, Philadelphia, PA.

49   Jennifer Mittelstadt, *The Rise of the Military Welfare State* (Cambridge, MA: Harvard University Press, 2015), 3.

50   Melissa Fitzgerald, Incarcerated Veterans Project, interview by the author, August 30, 2019, Alexandria, VA.

51   For more on Blue Discharges, see Heather M. Stur, "Red, White, Lavender, and Blue: LGBT Soldiers and Veterans and the Fight for Military Recognition," in *Service Denied: Marginalized Veterans in Modern American History*, ed. John M. Kinder and Jason A. Higgins (Amherst: University of Massachusetts Press, 2022), 107.

52   Susan Ingram, "Courting Compassion," *Baltimore Jewish Times*, January 23, 2019, https://www.jewishtimes.com/courting-compassion/.

53   Jack O'Connor, Incarcerated Veterans Project, interview by the author, July 9, 2019, Buffalo, NY.

54   Dugan interview, June 17, 2019; Don Adkins, Incarcerated Veterans Oral History Project, interview by the author, June 18, 2019, Philadelphia, PA.

55   See also Julie Marie Baldwin and Joseph Rukus, "Healing the Wounds: An Examination

of Veterans Treatment Courts in the Context of Restorative Justice," *Criminal Justice Policy Review* 26, no. 2 (2015): 183–207.

CONCLUSION: NO PEACE, NO JUSTICE

1   Laura M. Maruschak, Jennifer Bronson, and Mariel Alper, *Veterans in Prison: Survey of Prison Inmates, 2016*, Veterans in State and Federal Prisons (Washington, DC: Bureau of Justice Statistics, 2021), https://bjs.ojp.gov/content/pub/pdf/vpspi16st.pdf. Together, Iraq and Afghanistan veterans now outnumber Vietnam veterans.

2   Don Christensen et al., *Racial Disparities in Military Justice: Findings of Substantial and Persistent Racial Disparities within the United States Military Justice System*, Protect Our Defenders, May 5, 2017, https://www.protectourdefenders.com/racial -disparities-reports/.

3   "Black Veteran Sues over Racial Disparities in VA Benefits Administration," Yale Law School News, November 28, 2022, https://law.yale.edu/yls-today/news/black-veteran -sues-over-racial-disparities-va-benefits-administration.

4   "Veterans Legal Services Clinic," Yale Law School, https://law.yale.edu/clinics/vlsc.

5   Black Veterans Project, https://www.blackveteransproject.org/veteran-advocacy.

6   Richard Brookshire, "BVP Sues the Department of Veterans Affairs," Black Veterans Project News, July 8, 2021, https://www.blackveteransproject.org/post/bvp-sues -the-department-of-veterans-affairs.

7   The data in the following thirteen charts measures denial of disability benefits by race and gender, compared to the national average, and show the rates for each year from 2002 to 2020. Romeo Arahan, "Black Veterans Project," Flourish, April 25, 2022, https:// public.flourish.studio/story/1263826/.

8   "Veterans Treatment Courts and Other Veteran-Focused Courts Served by VA Veterans Justice Outreach Specialists," Office of Public Affairs Media Relations, U.S. Department of Veterans Affairs, January 2021, https://www.va.gov/HOMELESS/docs/VJO /Veterans-Treatment-Court-Inventory-Update-Fact-Sheet-Jan-2021.pdf.

9   Tina B. Craddock, "Veteran's Treatment Courts: Will More Be Necessary Now that the 20-Year War on Terror Has Concluded for US Soldiers?" *Journal of Veterans Studies* 8, no. 2 (2022): 1–13, https://doi.org/10.21061/jvs.v8i2.359.

10 Christine Timko et al., "A Longitudinal Examination of Veterans Treatment Courts' Characteristics and Eligibility Requirements," *Justice Research and Policy* 17, no. 2 (2016), 130.

11 Timko et al., "Longitudinal Examination," 130.

12 For more on treatment courts as restorative justice, see Andrew Fulkerson, "The Drug Treatment Court as a Form of Restorative Justice," *Contemporary Justice Review* 12, no. 3 (2009): 253–67, https://doi.org/10.1080/10282580903105772.

13 See also Samantha Luna and Allison D. Redlich, "A National Survey of Veterans Treatment Court Actors," *Criminal Justice Policy Review* 32 no. 2 (2021): 132–61.

14 The US Supreme Court recently ruled against granting reduced charges to low-level crack cocaine offenders. The First Step Act, signed during the Trump Administration, built on the Obama-era Fair Sentencing Act, which aimed to reduce the sentences of drug users incarcerated during previous wars on drugs. Pete Williams, "Supreme Court Won't Extend Reduced Charges to Low-Level Crack Cocaine Offenders," *NBC News*, June 14, 2021, https://www.nbcnews.com/politics/supreme-court/supreme -court-won-t-extend-reduced-charges-low-level-drug-n1270675.

15 Tim Balk, "Black Veteran Serving Life in Louisiana Prison over $30 Drug Sale Is Set

to be Freed," *New York Daily News*, August 7, 2020, https://www.nydailynews.com
/news/national/ny-black-veteran-30-pot-life-sentence-20200808-x65xsjq5ivf5zp6r63e-
5rh7ddi-story.html.

16   Teo Armus, "A Disabled Black Veteran Drove through Alabama with Medical Marijuana. Now He Faces Five Years in Prison," *Washington Post*, July 14, 2020, https://
www.washingtonpost.com/nation/2020/07/14/alabama-veteran-marijuana-prison/?
outputType=amp.

17   Wikipedia, s.v., "Pickens County, Alabama," https://en.wikipedia.org/wiki/Pickens
_County,_Alabama#Notes.

18   Equal Justice Initiative, "Lynchings by County," in *Lynching in America: Confronting
the Legacy of Racial Terror*, 3rd ed. (Montgomery, AL: Equal Justice Initiative, 2015),
https://eji.org/sites/default/files/lynching-in-america-third-edition-summary.pdf.

19   It refused to release a survey conducted every four years on racial discrimination in
the military. Phil Stewart, "For Years, the Pentagon Sits on Racial Discrimination
Survey Data," *Reuters*, December 18, 2020. https://www.reuters.com/article/us-us
a-military-civilrights-exclusive-idUSKBN28S0YF.

20   Dan De Luce, "Pentagon Report Warns of Threat from White Supremacists inside the
Military," *NBC News*, February 25, 2021, https://www.nbcnews.com/news/military
/pentagon-report-warns-threat-white-supremacists-inside-military-n1258871.

21   Former Senate majority leader McConnell forced through the confirmation of Amy
Coney Barrett, a Trump nominee to the Supreme Court, just one week before the
2020 presidential election. Millions had already voted for the next president of the
United States. With a 6–3 supermajority in the Supreme Court, the Trump administration guaranteed the influence of MAGA in our government for at least another
generation.

22   Christoph Koetll et al, "How the Philadelphia Police Tear-Gassed a Group of Protesters,"
New York Times, June 25, 2020, https://www.nytimes.com/video/us/10000000717494
1/philadelphia-tear-gas-george-floyd-protests.html.

23   Sarah Taddeo, "75-Year-Old Buffalo Man Shoved by Police Speaks out on Incident
after Month in Hospital," *USA Today*, August 31, 2020, https://www.usatoday.com
/story/news/nation/2020/08/31/buffalo-man-martin-gugino-talks-recovery-after
-police-shoved-him/3445610001/.

24   Neil Vigdor, Daniel Victor, and Christine Hauser, "Buffalo Police Officers Suspended after
Shoving 75-Year-Old Protester," *New York Times*, June 5, 2020, https://www.nytimes.com
/2020/06/05/us/buffalo-police-shove-protester-unrest.html. The officers kept their jobs,
however, and eventually charges were dropped. Jordan Williams, "Charges Dropped
against Buffalo Officers Who Pushed 75-Year-Old Protester," *The Hill*, February 11,
2021, https://thehill.com/homenews/state-watch/538544-charges-dropped-against-2
-buffalo-police-officers-who-pushed-75-year-old.

25   "NY Police Union Chief Mike O'Meara Speech Transcript: 'Stop Treating Us Like
Animals,'" *Rev*, June 9, 2020, https://www.rev.com/blog/transcripts/ny-police-union
-chief-speech-transcript-stop-treating-us-like-animals.

26   Deidre McPhillips, "How Much America's 10 Largest Cities Spend on Police," *U.S. News*,
June 11, 2020, https://www.usnews.com/news/cities/articles/2020-06-11/how-much
-the-10-largest-us-cities-spend-on-police.

27   Rosa Brooks, "Stop Training Police Like They're the Military," *The Atlantic*, June 10,
2020. See also Rosa Brooks, *Tangled Up in Blue: Policing the American City* (New York:
Penguin, 2021).

28   Andrew W. Lehren, Did Martinez, Emmanuelle Saliba, and Robert Windrem,

"Floyd Protests Renew Debate about Police Use of Armored Vehicles and Other Military Gear," *NBC News*, June 20, 2020, https://www.nbcnews.com/news/us-news/floyd-protests-renew-debate-about-police-use-armored-vehicles-other-n1231288.

29 Nicole Lewis and Beatrix Lockwood, "The Hidden Cost of Incarceration," The Marshall Project, December 17, 2019, https://www.themarshallproject.org/2019/12/17/the-hidden-cost-of-incarceration.

30 Peter Wagner and Bernadette Rabuy, *Following the Money of Mass Incarceration*, Prison Policy Initiative, January 25, 2017, https://www.prisonpolicy.org/reports/money.html.

31 "Data for All Countries from 1988–2019," Stockholm International Peace Research Institute (SIPRI), 2019, https://sipri.org/sites/default/files/Data%20for%20all%20countries%20from%201988%E2%80%932020%20in%20constant%20%282019%29%20USD%20%28pdf%29.pdf.

32 "The Department of Defense Releases the President's Fiscal Year 2022 Defense Budget," U.S. Department of Defense, May 28. 2021, https://www.defense.gov/Newsroom/Releases/Release/Article/2638711/the-department-of-defense-releases-the-presidents-fiscal-year-2022-defense-budg/.

33 For an oral history of a protester from the events in Washington, DC, on June 1, 2020, see Alan Siegal, "One Night in D.C.: The Oral History of June 1, 2020," *The Ringer*, July 13, 2020, https://www.theringer.com/2020/7/13/21322010/washington-dc-protests-june-1-trump-lafayette-square.

Howard Altman, "National Guard Civil Unrest Update: More than 17,000 Troops in 23 States and DC Activated," *Military Times*, June 1, 2020, https://www.militarytimes.com/news/your-military/2020/06/01/national-guard-civil-unrest-update-more-than-17000-troops-in-23-states-and-dc-activated/.

34 Tom Cotton, "Send in the Troops," *New York Times*, June 3, 2020, https://www.nytimes.com/2020/06/03/opinion/tom-cotton-protests-military.html; Tom Cotton (@TomCottonAR), "And, if necessary, the 10th Mountain, 82nd Airborne, 1st Cav, 3rd Infantry—whatever it takes to restore order. No quarter for insurrectionists, anarchists, rioters, and looters," Twitter, June 1, 2020, 10:14 a.m., https://twitter.com/tomcottonar/status/1267459561675468800?lang=en.

35 Tom Gjelten, "Peaceful Protesters Tear-Gassed to Clear Way For Trump Church Photo-Op," NPR, June 1, 2020, https://www.npr.org/2020/06/01/867532070/trumps-unannounced-church-visit-angers-church-officials; Thomas Gibbons-Neff and Eric Schmitt, "Pentagon Ordered National Guards Helicopters' Aggressive Response in D.C.," *New York Times*, June 6, 2020, https://www.nytimes.com/2020/06/06/us/politics/protests-trump-helicopters-national-guard.html.

36 Tom Dreisbach, "New Videos Show Alleged Assault on Officer Brian Sicknick during Capitol Riot," NPR, April 28, 2021, https://www.npr.org/2021/04/28/991654947/new-videos-show-alleged-assault-on-officer-brian-sicknick-during-capitol-riot.

37 Tactics we witnessed in 2020 presidential elections were first deployed by the CIA in Iran in 1953 and Guatemala in 1954—mass media misinformation campaigns, rightwing extremism, covert operation during a moment of transition, civil unrest, and amid the confusion of mobs. See Stephen Kinzer, *Overthrow: America's Century of Regime Change from Hawaii to Iraq* (New York: Times Books, 2006).

38 Tom Dreisbach and Meg Anderson, "Nearly 1 in 5 Defendants in Capital Riot Cases Served in the Military," NPR, January 21, 2021, https://www.npr.org/2021/01/21/958915267/nearly-one-in-five-defendants-in-capitol-riot-cases-served-in-the-military. See also Jennifer Steinhauer, "In the Battle for the Capitol Veterans Fought on Opposite Sides," *New*

York Times, February 8, 2021, https://www.nytimes.com/2021/02/08/us/politics/capitol-riot-trump-veterans-cops.html?referringSource=articleShare.

39   Scott Stump, "How a Capitol Police Officer's Split-Second Decision Saved Lives during Riot," *Today*, January 11, 2021, https://www.today.com/news/how-capitol-officer-s-split-second-decision-may-have-saved-t205464.

40   Rebecca Tan, "A Black Officer Faced Down a Mostly White Mob at the Capitol. Meet Eugene Goodman," *Washington Post*, January 14, 2021, https://www.washingtonpost.com/local/public-safety/goodman-capitol-police-video/2021/01/13/08ab3eb6-546b-11eb-a93-5b162d0d033d_story.html.

INDEX

Page numbers in *italics* indicate figures.

1996 Defense Authorization Act Program
1033, 182

9/11 (September 11, 2001, terrorist attacks),
xi, 13, 83, 133, 137, 138, 149, 155, 160,
168, 174–75, 187, 198; post-9/11 era,
185, 202; post-9/11 veterans, xi, xx,
104, 115, 117–18, 124, 126, 130, 137,
146, 160, 164, 169, 184
absence without official leave (AWOL), 7,
29, 31, 33, 67, 73, 74, 78
addiction. *See* substance use disorder
administrative discharge, xi, 7, 20, 23–24,
30, 53, 56, 57, 129, 133–34, 144, 185,
195
administrative separation. *See* administrative discharge
Afghanistan Papers, 146–49
Afghanistan veterans. *See* Afghanistan
War veterans
Afghanistan War, 146, 176
Afghanistan War veterans, xii, 16, 113, 115–
17, 141, 158, 168, 170
African Americans in the military, 1–4, 6,
13, 18, 25, 26, 33, 44, 45, 73; discrimination of Black veterans and, xi–xii,
xv, 4–5, 7, 9, 25, 27–30, 35, 45, 49, 57,
58, 65; African American veterans,
xi, xii, xx, 4, 8, 9, 18, 22, 24, 33–34,
42–44, 57, 63–65, 85–86, 116, 178,
209–11, 215
Agent Orange, 10, 102, 106–7, 109, 147,
209
alcohol abuse, xiv, xx, 2, 31, 41, 61, 64, 75,
79–80, 99, 122, 129–30, 132–33, 142,
144, 150, 153, 161, 163, 165, 191, 196,
199, 201

all-volunteer army. *See* all-volunteer force
all-volunteer force, 7, 29, 53, 72, 74, 80,
114, 118, 169, 173, 184, 198,
205
all-volunteer military. *See* all-volunteer
force
American Civil Liberties Union (ACLU),
182
Angola state prison, 43, 211
*Annual Report on Sexual Assault in the
Military* (2012), 184
Appy, Christian G., xvi, xxi, 7, 96, 109
Army of the Republic of Vietnam (South
Vietnam) (ARVN), 106
Article 15–6 of the Uniform Code of
Military Justice, 15, 74
Attica prison, 50–52

Babbitt, Manuel "Manny," 41
Bad paper. *See* less-than-honorable
discharge
Bailey, Kimberly, 193–97
basic training, 93, 105, 119, 187–88
Biden, Joseph, 213, 215
Biden administration. *See* Biden, Joseph
Black Lives Matter, xxiv, 182
Black veterans. *See* African Americans in
the military
Black Veterans Project, 210
body count, 95
boot camp, 18, 57–58, 92–93, 138
brig, 28, 60, 140
Brookshire, Richard, 210
Broujos, John, 79
Brown, Michael, 181
Burton, Henry D., 18–22, 35, 209
Bush, George, H.W., 176

Bush, George, W., 147, 173–74, 176
Bush administration. *See* Bush, George, W.

Camp Lejeune, 58, 93, 143
Caputo, Philip, 42, 93–94, 108
Carceral state, xi, 2–3, 8, 11, 13, 39
Carlson, David, 1, 12–*16*
Carter, James (Jimmy) Earl, Jr., xiii, 9, 24,
        36–37, 68, 134, 161
Carter administration. *See* Carter, James
        (Jimmy) Earl, Jr.
Cashe, Alwyn, 13
Cheney, Richard (Dick), 176
Civil Rights Act of 1964, 6, 27
Civil Rights Movement, 4
Clinton, William (Bill) J., 11
Clinton administration. *See* Clinton,
        William (Bill) J.
Cocaine, 10, 11, 64, 70, 80–82, 84, 181, 196,
        198–99, 211
Cold War, xii, 4, 72–74, 80
collective memory of the Vietnam War.
        See Vietnam War memory
counseling, xvi, 15–16, 37, 39, 77–78, 86–
        87, 98, 110–11, 121, 128–29, 133, 144,
        159, 166, 192, 195, 200–201, 204–5;
        group counseling, *see* rap sessions
court martial, 5, 23, 29–30, 56, 58, 74, 81,
        121, 209
COVID-19 pandemic, xxiv, 21, 183, 213
criminal justice reform, 10, 15–16, 38, 87,
        89–91, 112, 157, 159–61, 167–69, 171,
        178, 181, 186, 208, 211

Dellums, Ronald V., 37
Deutsch, Christopher, 162–63, 181
*Diagnostic and Statistical Manual of
        Mental Diseases (DSM) III*, xiv, 35,
        41, 97
DSM-5, 131–32
disability, xii, xv, 9, 12; benefits, 16, 18, 20,
        21, 33, 38, 47, 83, 101–2, 107, 111, 123–
        24, 156, 159, 192; claims, filing, 9, 38,
        110, 208, 215–16; denial of, xi, xiii, xv,
        8–9, 31, 36, 38, 117, 209–10; service-
        connected, 22–24, 33, 75, 153, 210
discharge: administrative, 22–23, 30, 36,
        53, 56–57, 129, 134, 195; bad conduct,
        23, 57–58, 129, 140; blue, 206;

Chapter 9, 133; Chapter 14, 133;
        dishonorable, 106–7; general under
        honorable conditions, 129, 133; less-
        than-honorable, xiii, xv, 7, 8, 22–24,
        29–30, 38–39, 44, 57, 63, 74–75, 80,
        82, 102, 111, 124–25, 129, 134, 156,
        185, 195–96; other-than-honorable,
        see less-than-honorable discharge
discharge upgrade, 75, 78, 135
draft, xii, 1–2, 4, 6, 25–26, 29, 31, 34, 44,
        50, 57, 105; resistance to, 53, 134; end
        of, 54, 114, 116, 155, 184, 198
Dugan, Patrick, 168–72, 174–77

Ellsberg, Daniel, 53–54
Equal Justice Initiative, 43
Ewing, Lee Slemmons, 57–62
explosive ordinance disposal, 131, 145

Felde, Robert, 41–42
Fennell, Haywood, Sr., 45–*49*
Fentanyl, 141, 155, 200
Fitzgerald, Melissa, 205–6
Floyd, George, murder of, 213–15
forever war, 3, 90, 113, 150, 155, 172, 174–77,
        190, 202, 208, 215
Fort Benning, Georgia, 127
Fort Bragg, North Carolina, (Fort Lib-
        erty), 118
Fort Carson, Colorado, 125–26
Fort Dix, New Jersey, 105, 175
Fort Hood, Texas, 183
Fort Jackson, South Carolina, 188
Fort Leonard Wood, Missouri, 190
Fort McCoy, Wisconsin, 132
Fort Polk, Louisiana, 31
free-fire zone, 95–96
Funchess, David Livingston, 41–42

gender: Black manhood, 28, 44; manhood
        and denial of trauma, 13, 61, 121,
        142, 164; military masculinity, 59,
        125, 126, 167; military service and
        manhood, 4, 18, 93, 99, 142
General Accounting Office (GAO), 35, 37
GI Bill, xi, 5, 25, 157
Gillibrand, Kirsten, 185
Global War on Terrorism (GWOT), xxiv,
        3, 10, 12–13, 48, 114–15, 117, 125, 128,

133, 146, 149, 151, 155, 160, 166, 168–
     69, 172–74, 176, 184, 193, 199, 209
Goldsmith, Kristofer, 134–35
Goodman, Eugene, 215
Great Society, 6, 8, 26–27, 50
Guillen, Vanessa, 183–84, *187*
Gulf of Tonkin incident, 93–94

Hallman, Matt, 167
Ham, Carter, 170
Hawkins, Paula, 79–80
Hayes, Abra, 1, 6, 15
Heroin, 8, 42, 45–47, 50, 55–56, 62–64,
     66, 71, 80, 141, 146, 149, 153, 156,
     199, 204
Higgins, Joani, 202–4
HIV (human immunodeficiency syn-
     drome) 49, 65, 81–83, 199, 201

I Am Vanessa Guillen Act of 2020, 186
Incarcerated veterans: advocacy, 102–3,
     109, 124–25, 134, 157, 209; data and
     demographics of, xii–xiii, 9–10, 17,
     31, 36, 38–41, 48, 62–64, 66, 115–17,
     123, 125, 140, 151, 186, 197, 210, 211;
     identification of, xiii, 4, 9, 17, 36–38,
     43–44, 47, 101, 112, 161
Incarcerated Veterans Assistance Organi-
     zation, 9, 35–37
Incarcerated Veterans Oral History
     Project, xiii, xviii, xx, xxiii, 12,
     212
Incarceration, xi–xiv, xvii, 1, 3–4, 12, 15–17,
     25, 33, 45–47, 49, 65, 77, 83–84, 113,
     115–16, 124, 149, 158, 162, 164, 170,
     196; alternatives to, 83, 162, 164, 172,
     181, 186, 208
Iraq and Afghanistan Veterans of America
     (IAVA), 161
Iraq Veterans Against the War, 173
Iraq War, 12–13, 127, 166–68, 170, 173–76,
     188–91, 193, 197–98, 210
Iraq War veterans, xii, 1, 16, 157, 170,
     174–75, 178, 210, 211, 215

Johnson, Lyndon B., 5–6, 25, 27, 50, 53,
     93–94, 106
Johnson administration. *See* Johnson,
     Lyndon B.

Justice for Vets, 112–13, 159–63, 167–68,
     171, 186, 197, 205, 210, 212

Kennedy, John F., 94, 106
Kennedy administration. *See* Kennedy,
     John F.
Kennedy-Crosby, Pearson, 167
Kerry, John, 54, 70, 78, 161, 178
King, Martin Luther, Jr., 6, 7, 27, 28, 34,
     46, 48
Kirkland, Haywood. *See* Merretazon, Ari
     Sesu
Korean War, 5, 31, 91, 101
Kovic, Ron, 100
Kubacki, Andrew, 127–30

Laplante, Andy, 80
Lawson, William Edward, 36
less- than-honorable discharge, 56
Lewis, John, 27
LGBTQ (lesbian, gay, bisexual, transgen-
     der, queer) people in the military,
     185, 209
LGBTQ veterans. *See* LGBTQ (lesbian,
     gay, bisexual, transgender, queer)
     people in the military
Lifton, Robert Jay, 96–97, 101
Long Binh Jail, 29, 52

mandatory minimum sentences, 9–10, 50,
     66, 70, 82, 84, 181
Marciano, James, 149–55
marijuana, 17, 33, 50, 52, 58, 60, 62, 79, 132,
     145, 200, 211
Marshall, Thurgood, 5
masculinity. *See* gender
mass incarceration, xii, xx, 2–3, 6, 8–12, 17,
     24, 26, 44, 49, 66, 84, 182, 204, 208,
     209, 211, 213, 215
Mays, Neal, 130–33
McNair, Louis Charles, 31–33
McNamara, Robert S., 6, 26
mental health, xiii, xiv, xv, xvii, 14, 17, 77,
     87, 119, 123, 140–41, 150, 152; access
     to services, 73, 77; advocacy for
     treatment, 15, 47, 89, 92, 101, 103, 111,
     130, 141, 159, 164, 166–67, 171–72,
     196, 201; as a crisis, 115, 146, 155–56,
     166, 172–73, 180, 196, 213; coping or

self-medicating, xiv, xx, 153, 165, 191, 200, 204; punishment for, 3, 12, 13, 24, 54, 116, 124–26, 128–29, 133–35, 137, 144, 150, 178, 185, 195, 212; reforms, xx–xxi, 15, 16, 86–87, 110, 115, 117, 125, 133, 137, 156, 160–61, 163, 170, 178, 180, 204, 210; reporting, xx, 117, 120–21, 125, 128, 131, 143, 164, 190; stigmas, 117, 121, 125, 126, 128, 130, 132, 141–42, 150, 164, 170, 178, 200; treatment, 16, 87, 101, 117, 163, 170–71, 178, 190, 196, 200, 204

mental health disorder, 3, 17, 43, 70, 88, 101, 124–27, 133, 151, 160, 163, 168, 180, 185

Merretazon, Ari Sesu., 9, 33–40

militarism, 3, 48, 85, 173

military-carceral state, 3, 50, 55, 56, 67, 68, 181, 185, 215

military-civilian divide, 117, 120, 154, 164, 166, 168, 173–76, 205, 214

military justice system, xvi, 3, 7, 23, 24, 25, 28, 30, 45, 48, 63, 117, 124, 129, 183–86, 197, 209

military sexual trauma (MST), xvi, 3, 159–60, 184–86, 188, 192, 194, 195, 197

misconduct, 13, 22, 28, 117, 122, 125–29, 133–35, 137, 144

Monk, Conley, Jr., 209–10

moral injury, xv, 3, 15, 32, 46, 77, 113, 119, 174–75, 188, 194

Moynihan, Daniel Patrick, 5–6, 25–26

multiple deployments, 73, 115, 117, 120, 137, 142, 149–50, 152, 155, 160, 170, 177

Murkowski, Lisa, 161

Musgrave, John, 100–101

National Association for the Advancement of Colored People (NAACP), 5, 8–9, 27, 39

National Association of Drug Court Professionals (NADCP), 112–13, 161–63, 181

Naval Criminal Investigative Service (NCIS), 140

Nicholas, Matt, 142–46

Nieves, Ricardo "Rico," Jr., 80–84

Nixon, Richard M., 8–9, 29–30, 50–56, 62, 65–66, 69, 208

Nixon administration. See Nixon, Richard M.

North, Oliver, 70

Obama, Barack, 134–35, 147–48, 157, 159–60, 168, 176, 180–82, 211

Obama administration. See Obama, Barack

O'Connor, Jack, 86–90, 104–12, 111

Ogo, Kevin, 117–24

Operation Enduring Freedom. See Global War on Terrorism

Operation Golden Flow, 56

Operation Iraqi Freedom. See Iraq War

Operation Iron Tempest, 148

Operation River Dance, 147

opioids, 36, 137, 141, 146, 155; as epidemic, 137, 142, 146, 149, 155, 167, 173, 180, 200; as public health crisis, 155–56

opioid use disorder, 141, 149, 156

Oral History Association, xvi–xvii

oral history methods, xiii, xiv–xx, 3

other-than-honorable discharge. See less-than-honorable discharge

peer-counseling, 100–101, 166

Pentagon Papers, 53, 107, 146

People's Army of Vietnam (NVA), 95–96

People's Liberation Armed Forces ("Vietcong"), 34, 89, 95–96

Pirowski, Hank, 86–87, 90, 112–13, 157, 168

post-9/11 veterans, See 9/11

post-traumatic stress disorder (PTSD), xi, xiv–xv, xx, 10, 13, 18, 21, 24, 32–34, 40–44, 63–65, 76–77, 89, 91–92, 97–98, 100–103, 113, 115, 117, 121, 123–29, 131–35, 137, 142–45, 149–51, 153, 155, 160, 164–65, 170–71, 185–86, 191–92, 195, 198, 201, 206, 212

post-Vietnam stress syndrome, 32, 35, 63, 96–97, 101

Powell, Colin, 174

Powell Doctrine, 174, 178

prisoners of war (POW), 43–44, 74, 90, 109, 185

Project 100,000, 1–2, 6, 13, 26, 30

Puller, Lewis B., Jr., 60, 99

punishment, xix, 3, 7; carceral, xiii, 11; of African American service members and veterans, 7, 24, 31, 37, 41, 52, 56–57, 75, 79–80, 209–10, 212; of service members with mental health issues, 12, 57, 117, 126–27, 129, 134, 137, 151, 195

racism. *See* African Americans in the military
racial segregation, 5–6, 25, 212
racial violence, 1, 38, 52, 212
Rangel, Charles, 38
rap sessions, 100–101, 109, 201
rape. *See* sexual assault
readjustment. *See* reintegration
Reagan, Ronald W., 10–11, 39, 68–70, 72–74, 79–81
Reagan administration. *See* Reagan, Ronald W.
reintegration, xv, 3; difficulties, 8, 10, 31, 34, 41, 61, 64, 90, 109, 115–16, 126, 164, 167, 169, 170, 177, 186, 191–92, 205; experiences of, 46, 130, 164
resistance, 7: Black resistance, 4, 7, 23, 28, 52–53; to draft, *see* draft; GI resistance, 7, 29–30, 52, 55–56, 67
Richardson, Herbert, 43
robbery, 21, 34–35, 37, 42
Rowan, John, 134–35
Russell, Robert T., 86–89, 110, 112–13, 158, 162, 205, 207

Saigon, 29, 52, 55, 96, 105–6; fall of, 108
search-and-destroy, 32–34, 58
selective service system. *See* draft
September 11, 2001, terrorist attacks. *See* 9/11
sexual assault (rape), xiv, xv, 34, 173, 183–87, 189, 193–95, 197
Sexual Harassment/Assault Response and Prevention (SHARP) program, 183, 186
Sheen, Martin, 162
Shinseki, Eric, 159, 161
Sickels, Donna, 198–202, 208
signature wounds, 115, 117, 125, 151, 155, 160, 180
Small, Shawn, 70–78

Steiner, Matt, 157–59, 161–64, 180
Stevenson, Bryan, 43
Student Non-Violent Coordinating Committee (SNCC), 5, 27
substance use disorder, 2, 46, 55–56, 62, 65, 81–82, 88, 100, 115, 122, 127, 133, 137, 141, 144, 149, 155, 158, 163, 167, 199–200, 204
suicide, 3, 14, 61, 77, 85, 113, 115, 120, 123, 126, 131, 134–35, 143, 157, 167, 170, 179, 183, 196, 195, 202–3
suicide bomber, 175–76

Taylor, Breonna, 213
Terry, Wallace, 33
Tet Offensive, 19
Torrey, James, 137–42
trauma, xiv–xvii, xix, 15, 21; as intergenerational, 1, 15, 46–47, 84, 202, 208; incarceration as, xv, 15, 21, 76–77, 124, 208; talking about traumatic memories, xvi–xvii, xx, 20, 130, 145, 168, 194, 207
Traumatic Brain Injury (TBI), xv, xvi, 3, 113, 115, 117, 120, 126, 135, 140, 151, 155, 158, 160, 170, 211
Trump, Donald, 148, 213, 215
Trump administration. *See* Trump, Donald

unemployment, 6, 8, 18, 25, 27, 35, 57, 65, 74–75, 84, 113, 160, 186
Uniform Code of Military Justice. *See* military justice system
urban rebellion, 5–6, 25, 28–29, 51–52
urinalysis, 7, 14, 17, 56, 78–81, 129, 132, 143–45, 167, 200
US Air Force, 45, 98, 119, 198, 207, 215
US Army: culture of, 13–14, 117, 121, 125–26, 128, 132, 164, 167, 169–71; family legacies, 1, 45, 71, 91, 104–105, 118, 168; image of, 29, 55–57, 69, 74, 79; in Afghanistan, 119–22, 176–77; in Iraq, 127–28, 130–31, 164, 168–70, 175; in Vietnam, 6–7, 23, 26, 29, 31, 45–46, 52–56, 70–71, 73, 77; mental health care in, 13–14, 115, 121, 125–27, 130–35, 164–65, 169–71; policies of, 30, 53, 56, 72, 75, 78, 117, 121, 125–27, 128–29, 131, 133, 134; reforms, 29,

125–27, 133; veteran of, 38, 62, 76, 89, 123
US Army National Guard: during Global War on Terrorism, 114; in Iraq, 13–14; image of, 114
US Department of Defense, 23, 106, 182, 215; investigations by, 30, 53, 55–56, 126, 141, 197, 213; policies, 115, 127, 141, 176, 184
US Department of Justice, 162, 181–82, 215; studies and reports on veterans in prison and jail, xii, xiii, 9, 24, 39–40, 49, 63–64, 66, 116, 186, 209
US Department of Veterans Affairs: See Veterans Administration (VA)
US Marine Corps (marines): culture of, 140, 142–43, 164, 167; experiences in Iraq, 138–40, 142–44, 149–50; experiences in Afghanistan, 150–52; image of, 136–37; mental health care, 140, 142–44, 150–52, 164, 167; policies, 137, 140, 143–44, 150
US Navy, in Vietnam, 93; policies, 80–82

Vasquez, Alyssa, 187–93
Veterans Administration (VA), xi, xv, xvii, 5, 15, 18, 20, 22, 25, 39, 44, 47, 75, 77, 83, 91, 100, 141, 155–56, 161, 207, 209–10; benefits, see veterans' benefits; care, 23–24, 47, 56, 73, 102, 111–12, 127, 144, 165; hospitals, 31, 61, 75, 88, 99–100, 109, 170, 192; outreach programs, 37–38, 56, 124, 141, 144, 161, 196; services, 35, 44, 89, 101, 117, 161, 164, 185, 201, 210
veterans' advocacy, 10, 12, 15, 35, 37, 40, 47, 89–91, 100, 102, 104, 111–12, 125, 134, 159, 162, 167, 169, 172, 193, 196–97, 200, 208, 209, 210
veterans' benefits, xiii, 23–25, 30, 44, 67, 80, 91, 104, 134, 137, 195, 209
Veterans Center, xvii, 39, 100–101, 196, 201
Veterans Justice Outreach (VJO), 161
Veterans Treatment Court, 15–17, 88, 100, 104, 110–13, 123, 129, 156, 161, 165, 171, 180–82, 186, 192, 196, 200, 204–8, 210, 212; as a veterans movement, 89–91, 103–4, 112–13, 160–63, 210;

Baltimore Veterans Treatment Court, 77–78, 206–7; Buffalo Veterans Treatment Court, 38, 87–91, 107, 112–13, 157–58, 186–87, 192, 197, 203, 207; Eau Claire County Veterans Treatment Court (WI), 15; Fresno County Veterans Treatment Court (CA), 197; Holyoke Veterans Treatment Court (MA), 141, 153; Philadelphia Veterans Treatment Court, 144–45, 164, 166–69, 200, 202, 206; Tulsa Veterans Treatment Court, 158–59, 162, 178, 180
Vietcong. See People's Liberation Armed Forces
Vietnam veterans. See Vietnam War veterans
Vietnam Veterans Against the War (VVAW), 54, 78, 100, 173, 178
Vietnam Veterans of America (VVA), 10, 44, 101–2, 109, 133
Vietnam Veterans Memorial, 68–69, 109–10
Vietnam War, 1–3, 6–7, 12; collective memory of, xii–xiv, 9–10, 16, 33, 39, 43, 63, 68–69, 87, 90, 95, 100–104, 107–110, 112, 134, 176, 214; experiences of, 12, 18–21, 91, 96, 104, 110; opposition to, 5, 7, 27, 28, 36, 48, 53–54; policies during, xi, 2, 23–24, 26, 28, 37, 39, 44, 50, 63–64, 106, 147, 152
Vietnam War era, xiv, xx, 2–3, 5, 9–10, 12, 22, 24–25, 31, 35, 40, 48–49, 63–65, 89, 100, 109, 115–117, 174, 184, 198
Vietnam War memory, 69, 90, 109
Vietnam War syndrome, 10, 68
Vietnam War veterans, xv, xx, 16, 36, 57, 60, 63, 69, 86, 89, 90, 93, 104, 134; advocacy and organizing of, 9–10, 16, 35, 39–40, 44, 54, 78, 86–87, 89, 91, 96–97, 100–104, 107, 109–11, 113, 134–35, 156–57, 165, 173; capital punishment of, 41–43; generational divides between veterans, 90, 101, 108, 112–13; incarceration of, 24, 35, 37, 38, 40–44, 49, 51, 62, 64, 66, 86, 102, 109, 116, 209; reintegration of, xiv, xx, 8, 10, 19–20, 31, 33, 41, 55,

62, 64–65, 94, 96, 102, 104, 108–9,
126, 160
Voting Rights Act of 1965, 6, 27

war on crime, xiii, 5
war on drugs, 7–8, 10–11, 47, 49, 53, 55, 62,
65–66, 69–70, 79, 84, 116, 146–47,
214
war on poverty, 6, 8–9, 27, 50, 62
war on terror. *See* Global War on
Terrorism
Watergate, 50, 54
Weinstein, Halee F., 206–7

Welch, Patrick, 87, 90–104, *103*, 109
Westmoreland, William, 19, 15
Williams, Elliott Earl, 178–80
William, Robert F., 27
women in the military, xiii, 159, 183, 184–
185, 186, 192 193, 196, 197–198, 206
women veterans. *See* women in the
military
Wynn, Timothy J., 164–*69*, 206, 208

X, Malcolm, 27

Younge, Sammy, Jr., 5, 27